Beckford of Fonthill

BRIAN FOTHERGILL

BECKFORD
of
FONTHILL

FABER AND FABER
LONDON & BOSTON

First published in 1979
by Faber & Faber Limited
3 Queen Square, London WC1
Printed in Great Britain by
Latimer Trend & Company Ltd Plymouth
All rights reserved

British Library Cataloguing in Publication Data

Fothergill, Brian
Beckford of Fonthill.
1. Beckford, William – Biography   2. Authors,
English – Biography
1. Title
828'.6'09   PR4092
ISBN 0-571-10794-X

To Dacre Punt

So, oft it chances in particular men
That, for some vicious mole of nature in them,
As, in their birth,—wherein they are not guilty,
Since nature cannot choose his origin,—
By their o'ergrowth of some complexion,
Oft breaking down the pales and forts of reason,
Or by some habit that too much o'er-leavens
The form of plausive manners, that these men,—
Carrying, I say, the stamp of one defect,
Being nature's livery, or fortune's star,—
Their virtues else—be they as pure as grace,
As infinite as man may undergo—
Shall in the general censure take corruption
From that particular fault.

SHAKESPEARE, *Hamlet*, I. iv

What will be my Life? What misfortunes lurk in wait for me?
What Glory?

Beckford to Alexander Cozens,
3 October 1777

Contents

CONTENTS

Illustrations

Preface

THE FIRST LIFE of William Beckford of Fonthill to be written since Lewis Melville's biography, published in 1910, was Dr. J. W. Oliver's *Life of William Beckford* which appeared in 1932. This was followed by Professor Guy Chapman's *Beckford* in 1937 (reissued in 1952); but since these works came out the publication of Beckford's letters and journals by Mr. Boyd Alexander in 1954 and 1957 and his important study published in 1962 have shown the need for a new assessment of the whole of Beckford's life and work. In venturing to attempt this task I am conscious of my great debt to these pioneer works, and am especially grateful to Mr. Alexander for his kindness and patience in answering various queries I have addressed to him, and for permitting me to quote from his *England's Wealthiest Son* (published by the Centaur Press) and from *Life at Fonthill* (published by Rupert Hart-Davis).

I must gratefully thank his Grace the Duke of Hamilton and Brandon for allowing me access to the Beckford Papers, and also acknowledge the helpful assistance of the staff at the West Register House, Edinburgh, of the National Register of Archives (Scotland). I am grateful to Sir Sacheverell Sitwell for kindly allowing me to quote two short passages from his works. I must also thank Mr. James Lees-Milne for help in relation to Beckford's years in Bath and to Mr. and Mrs. Leonard Schuster for allowing me to see over 20 Lansdown Crescent. Dr. and Mrs. L. T. Hilliard kindly showed me over the Lansdown Tower and Mr. Sidney Blackmore gave me much generous assistance, not least in motoring me many miles to visit Beckfordian sites. I am also grateful for help from Mr. Terence Davis, Professor Fatma Moussa Mahmoud, Mr. Michael W. F. Cottrill and Mr. Douglas Sellick.

I

Inheritance

WHEN A MAN who could boast openly of 'my thirty children', and had certainly fathered seven or more, was attending the baptism of his only child to be born in lawful wedlock, it was clearly an event of some importance. All the more so when the proud father was an Alderman and Sheriff of the City of London, would twice hold the office of Lord Mayor, was the City's representative in the House of Commons and reputedly the richest subject in the Kingdom. Such was the case when Alderman William Beckford stood by the font in the parish church of Fonthill Gifford in Wiltshire on 29 September 1760 to see his sole legitimate offspring made a Christian. So singular an occasion required august sponsorship, and the godfather who renounced the devil and all his works on behalf of the inarticulate infant was William Pitt, soon to be created Earl of Chatham.[1]

The Alderman, at fifty-one, had already reached the meridian of life when his heir (if not his first-born) came into the world. He had married somewhat late in life. Born in 1709 it was not until the year 1756 that he had abandoned a career of gallantry and settled down to respectable domesticity. Like any sensible middle-aged man he had selected a widow; and as many a successful merchant might wish to do he had improved his social standing by marrying into the aristocracy. His wife, born Maria Hamilton, was a grand-daughter of the sixth Earl of Abercorn. By a previous marriage to a certain Francis March she had a daughter named Elizabeth who was by this time a girl of some ten or eleven years old.

The nobility and ancient lineage of the house of Hamilton was later to be a source of great consolation to the infant who was now receiving the names of William Thomas at the hands of the vicar of the parish. Pride of ancestry, if it be a sin, was not washed away in the water of baptism. The name of Beckford, on the other hand, could offer no such dazzling a descent. Here was no heritage of coronets or feudal lands, of romantic titles or royal blood, but a crude accumulation of hard-won wealth built up against a garish background of sun-bleached plantations, sweating slaves and cargoes of sugar. If the child derived from his mother's family those leisured, cultivated tastes and the romantic imagination that characterised his maturity, his father's near-buccaneer forebears bequeathed him a legacy of toughness and shrewd close-fistedness which was to be no less a part of his personality as a grown man.

The combination of city wealth with the aristocratic landed interest was one which, in eighteenth-century England, was the obvious basis for political power. To those gathered in the little church on that September day, as the parson performed his sacred rite, it would seem that they were witnessing the first appearance on the world's stage of a future proconsul, a secretary of state, possibly even a First Lord of the Treasury. That certainly was what the proud parents hoped and intended for their son. It would have surprised them both, and pleased neither of them, had they known that they had produced an artist.

As the guests dispersed or made their way back to Fonthill House the Alderman had every reason to be pleased with himself. The birth of an heir to so much wealth and distinction crowned a career of advancement and assiduous social climbing both for himself and his family. To contemplate a future of power and influence in the exclusive world of Whig politics, which must have seemed the almost inevitable lot of his son, cast into ever deeper shadow the obscure origins from which the Beckford family had emerged a bare three generations before. Not that the Alderman was ashamed of the humble great-grandfather whose dim avocation in the purlieus of Clerkenwell appeared to have been connected with the shoddy-clothing business, a slop-seller or clothworker; indeed he would later on taunt his son with this unsavoury connection when that proud boy became too vaunting of his aristocratic maternal descent. Alderman Beckford was altogether too robust a character to conceal the common clay from which he sprang. He could be proud of it, and was—especially when he could remind himself that the intervening generations had heaped up one of the largest fortunes of the century.

The break in the fortunes of the Beckford family came when a son of this clothworker, born in 1643, sailed for Jamaica some time shortly after the restoration of the monarchy in 1660. His name was Peter Beckford and he soon established himself there as a planter as well as in the administration of the island, becoming President of the Council of Jamaica under Charles II and later, during the reign of William III, being appointed Lieutenant-Governor and Commander-in-Chief. His rapid rise to a position of wealth and importance was helped by the fact that other Beckfords, probably distant cousins (the exact connection has not been made clear), were also settled there or else were living prosperously in England on revenues drawn from the island.

In this Jamaican planter we see already manifest certain of the less attractive characteristics which were to be passed on to his descendants. He was a man of violent temper, ruthless and not over-scrupulous in the conduct of his affairs, and given to exaggerations of a very misleading sort on the question of the exact extent of his worldly possessions. Certainly, when he died in 1710, he was a very rich man; but not quite so rich as would appear from the claim later made that when his strong-box was opened it was discovered to contain the best part of a million pounds in cash.[2] It was the sort of boast that his grandson the Alderman would delight to indulge in, and which, if not strictly true, did no great harm to his credit as a man of business.

The violence of Governor Beckford's temper showed itself in the irascibility of his life and was ultimately to be the cause of his death. He was accustomed to carry a large stick about with him and was not above using it to belabour recalcitrant members of the Jamaican Assembly when they had the temerity to question his edicts. His son, also called Peter, was of an equally excitable temperament and had at least one death laid to his charge, though he managed to escape the penalties of his crime and even to end up as Speaker of the Assembly whose members smarted under the blows of his father's cane.

The Governor's end came during a session of this Assembly. A debate was in progress on some topic that caused tempers to flare up and the house showed signs of dissolving in an uproar. When matters began to get out of hand the Speaker attempted to leave his chair and so bring the session to a close. The members, however, were determined to have their say and perhaps avenge the insults some of them had received from the Speaker's father. Swords were drawn and directed at the younger Beckford to prevent him from rising. In the midst of this clamour the Governor, in his room in the same building, heard his son's cry for help and rushed to his assistance. In the general *mêlée* that followed the Governor, surrounded by fighting members and jostled by the sentinels who had been summoned to quell the fray, missed his footing at the head of the staircase and fell down the flight to his death.

The younger Peter Beckford had made a prudent marriage to the daughter and heiress of Colonel Julines Hering, a member of one of the leading families in the colony, connected with the Vassal family, also of Jamaica, from whom the author of *Vathek*'s contemporary Elizabeth Lady Holland was descended. It was an alliance that further consolidated the position of the Beckfords with regard both to social standing and to wealth. His wife Bathshua duly presented him with twelve children, eight sons and four daughters. Alderman Beckford was the second son of this marriage, but two years after his father's death in 1735 his elder brother, another Peter, died prematurely and the future Alderman inherited the place and portion of an eldest son.

The portion which fell to him was considerable, but just how considerable, we shall probably never know. The Beckford family had developed a certain artistry in presenting to an eager but gullible public a picture of their wealth which was designed to astonish the credulous and at the same time bolster up their credit with the more worldly-wise. They were among the first to exploit the simple idea that if someone is known to be rich then almost everyone is ready to believe that he is even richer still. The story of the Governor's strong-box was an early example of this technique at work. Of his son the Speaker the great Beckford myth was first circulated that he lived the richest subject in Europe (a tradition that would continue for two generations until his grandson's extravagances ultimately rendered it untenable) and died a multi-millionaire. These opulent rumours cast a golden haze over the exact state of the family finances; it can, however, be said that the elder William Beckford fell heir to one of the greatest fortunes to come out of Jamaica in an age when to have a vast commercial fortune one must be either a Nabob from India or a sugar king from the West Indies.

The first fourteen years of his life were spent in the island of his birth and he never lost his Jamaican accent or the somewhat uncouth manner which this colonial background had bred in him. In 1723 he became a pupil at Westminster School, where he excelled in the classics, and in due course proceeded to Balliol College, Oxford. This was not to presage a career at the bar or in some other learned profession; from the first Beckford was destined for the City to preside over the family business, and he soon became the acknowledged leader of the West Indian merchant interest there.

We must take a close look at this man who was to have so strong an influence on his son's life, for all that the younger William was not yet ten years old when his father died; for the memory of this parent was to stay with him, and in many ways dominate his personality, until the end of his life.

The Alderman had been a prominent figure on the political stage since 1738 when he had exhibited the earless Captain Jenkins at the bar of the House of Commons, precipitating the war with Spain. A portrait of him painted in his robes as Lord Mayor of London shows us a figure of formidable strength of character. The grim mouth, the great beak of a nose and the staring eyes beneath a strongly marked brow all indicate the violent temper he had inherited from his father and grandfather as well as the habit of authority which his own position in the world had made second nature to him. Stern and forbidding he certainly was; but he was also a man of strong political principles, devoted to the Whig interest and bitterly opposed to any encroachment on the liberties that had been wrested from the monarchy at the time of the Revolution of 1688, the glorious and *necessary* Revolution as he was himself to describe it on a notable occasion in the presence of his own sovereign. Lest there should be any doubt on this score the Lord Mayor had himself represented by the artist with one hand resting on a copy of Magna Carta while in the other he held a copy of the Bill of Rights.

Beckford did not achieve the office of Lord Mayor for the first time until two years after the birth of his son, but he had been elected an Alderman in 1752 and since 1754 had represented the City in parliament where his close ties with the elder Pitt caused Horace Walpole to refer to him somewhat contemptuously as the latter's zany. 'Beckford is a patriot,' declared Walpole at the close of the Seven Years' War, 'because he will clamour if Guadaloupe or Martinico is given up, and the price of sugar falls.'[3] His performance in the House of Commons was not brilliant; his speeches were wild and rambling; nor were they helped by the strong colonial accent in which they were delivered. His chief usefulness to his radical colleagues lay in his skill at party management and in his readiness to undertake some of the less spectacular tasks that fall to any political leader's trusted lieutenant. In this sense, and in this sense only, was he anyone's zany or underling.

But even if the more sophisticated members ridiculed his uncouth delivery or mocked at his undisguised interest in the price of sugar, the Alderman was not an inconsiderable figure in political circles as was discovered when his voice was no longer heard in the debates. 'Instead of Wilkes having been so,' Walpole then wrote, 'it looks as if Beckford had been the firebrand of politics, for the flame has gone out since his death.'[4]

In private life he liked to surround himself with luxury, whether in his house in Soho Square or at the country estate of Fonthill which he had bought in 1736. He collected pictures and works of art, but more as an attribute of ostentatious wealth than from any enlightened connoisseurship. He had a predilection for crimson velvet hangings, a taste that would be inherited by his son. For some years he shared his life with a certain Hannah Thwaites and had seven illegitimate children living at the time of his marriage, some possibly by other women. In a period when infant mortality was high he no doubt brought others into the world who did not survive. In this, as in other matters, the Alderman was prone to exaggeration. When Lord Holland told him that he was sending his delicate youngest son to Richmond for the air he was startled to hear Beckford reply: 'Oh, Richmond is the worst air in the world; I lost twelve natural children there last year!'[5]

He was a man of abundant energy, an eccentric, a figure larger than life, though this would be less noticeable in the mid-eighteenth century than today for it was a period when the human personality blossomed rather than shrank. He needed constant outlets for his vigour and industry. An unexpected opportunity came to him in February 1755 when the news was brought to him that his house at Fonthill, with all its furniture and pictures, had been destroyed by fire. This was a Jacobean house, once the seat of the Lords Cottington, which stood on the estate when he purchased it with the four or five thousand acres that surrounded it. The Alderman received the news of the disaster with stoic indifference, calmly declaring that he had an odd fifty thousand pounds somewhere in a drawer which he imagined would be enough to build it up again. The sum would not, he added, make more than a thousand pounds apiece difference to his thirty

children.[6] It was a boast in his grandest manner and he fulfilled it
with equal grandeur, at least in so far as the house was concerned,
which was to earn for itself the name of Fonthill Splendens.

As a Whig magnate, or as one who hoped to be considered as
such, Alderman Beckford chose the Palladian style for his new
mansion, that style which Lord Burlington, the great arbiter of
taste, had a generation before considered to be *de rigueur* for a
nobleman's country seat. The plan, in fact, bore a strong resemblance to Holkham in Norfolk which had been built by William
Kent under Burlington's supervision. The central block of three
storeys, with its pillared portico, had a rusticated ground-floor
and Venetian windows at each end of the main storey. The house
was flanked by two pavilions, each a storey lower than the main
building, to which they were connected by gracefully curving
colonnades.

Built on the site of the previous house beside an elegant stretch
of ornamental lake and backed by a wooded slope, there was
nothing exceptional in either design or position. It was the
interior, rather than the formal elevation of the exterior, that
earned for the Alderman's house the distinctive name of 'Splendens'. It was here that he had indulged himself fully in his love
of the luxurious and the exotic. 'Its apartments', the antiquary
John Britton later noted, 'were numerous and splendidly furnished. They displayed the riches and luxury of the east; and on
particular occasions were superbly brilliant and dazzling.'[7]

We must take a walk through the rooms of this great house for
it was here that young William Beckford was born and where he
formed his first impressions of life and art. Already the eastern
note has been mentioned, that influence which showed itself so
early in his precocious mind. Wherever the eye turned it fell on
gold cornices, painted ceilings, coloured marbles and sumptuous
fabrics. The grand entrance hall with its organ and porphyry
busts of Roman emperors had its walls frescoed by Duhamil and
Andrea Casali with historical and allegorical scenes. The library
was hung with lilac silk and had busts of Virgil and Homer; the
dining-room and state bedchamber were both hung with the
Alderman's favourite crimson, one silk-damask, the other velvet,
while the same colour predominated in the Great Saloon with its
bronze figures of Apollo and Daphne and the rape of Proserpine.
There was a picture gallery lighted by the great Venetian windows, a tapestry room with Gobelins depicting the marriage of

Esther, and a state dressing-room adjacent to the bedchamber whose vast bed was reputed to be the finest in England. But most important of all to an impressionable and lonely child was the Turkish room (sometimes also referred to as the Egyptian Hall) with its ceiling painted with oriental scenes and its two mysterious tripods *à la Turque*. Grandeur, opulence and, it must be admitted, a touch of vulgarity were the prevailing notes struck in this palace of a merchant prince.[8]

Fonthill House, like its successor the Abbey, was to have a strangely brief existence. Begun in 1755 it was still unfinished fourteen years later when young Beckford's tutor, Robelrt Drysdale, described it as 'exceedingly grand'. It was finally demolished in 1807 on the orders of its builder's son when he moved from its stately proportioned rooms to take up permanent residence in his gothic creation on the neighbouring hill. It has also, curiously enough for so well publicised a building, never been attributed with certainty to any particular architect.[9]

It was to this great house that the Alderman took his wife after their marriage in 1756, having previously found suitable accommodation in the neighbourhood for his son Richard, the eldest and favourite of his illegitimate brood, who until then had shared with his father the splendours of the family seat. Beckford was then forty-seven years old, his bride thirty-two.

Mrs. Beckford's character differed so radically from her husband's that one is left wondering what first brought them together beyond the wealth which he was able to lay at her feet and the valuable aristocratic connections (with all the political significance which this would then imply) which she was able to offer him in return; for there could certainly be no doubt that the new Mrs. Beckford was well-born. Indeed one of her most marked characteristics, and perhaps the least endearing, was her complacent consciousness of her own social superiority and the corresponding awareness that she had married somewhat below her station in life.

By birth Maria Hamilton, she was the daughter of George Hamilton, Member of Parliament for Wells, himself a son of the sixth Earl of Abercorn. Through her father's family she could trace descent from James II, King of Scotland, and Edward III, King of England. Neither she nor her son ever allowed themselves to forget this interesting fact. It was to counterbalance this snobbish tendency that the Alderman and his city cronies would remind the young Beckford of his no less authentic ancestors of less exalted extraction, such as a certain Maddox whose profession was that of shoemaker, and they would laugh at the 'little storm of infantile petulance' which this information would produce.[10]

The chief difference between husband and wife lay in their attitude to religion. The Alderman was a free-thinker, an avowed sceptic in such matters. Mrs. Beckford, on the other hand, was of a profoundly evangelical turn of mind, and strictly puritanical into the bargain. Her God was the God of Calvin; her gospel was a gloomy one in which predestination, damnation and hell took precedence over the gentler virtues of compassion and forgiveness. The spirit of Divine Wrath, of the vengeance of God, hovered over the head of her son from his earliest years leaving an indelible impression on his soul.

In one way only did Maria Beckford resemble her husband: in her strength of will and in her ability to get her own way in life. This probably produced less friction than might be expected, for the Alderman's duties kept him often away from home. Though he would descend occasionally with all the force of a whirlwind, laughing loudly when in a good humour and terrifying everyone in sight with one of his ferocious glances when in a fury, for the most part the management of the home and the nursery came under the autocratic sway of his wife, and her rule there was absolute.

This ill-assorted couple did not produce a child until they had been married for four years. It would seem that the young William was born at Fonthill House; certainly his baptism was duly recorded in the local parish register of Fonthill Gifford, and a letter from the Alderman to Lord Chatham announcing the event was dated from his country seat and declared that the ceremony had taken place the evening before.[11] The boy, so long and ardently expected, was said to be delicate and every care and attention was lavished on his health and physical welfare. Thus from his very earliest years the young William Beckford felt himself to be a person of importance, the idol of adoring parents without rivalry from competing brothers and sisters. Like many delicate infants he was destined to live to a great age: born a month before the death of George II he was to survive into the seventh year of the reign of Queen Victoria.

He was well aware, from the first dawn of reason, that his parents were people of consequence in the great world. The genealogical ramifications of his mother's family and her grand connections fascinated him as much as her stern religious principles frightened and repressed him, while his father's awe-inspiring figure, especially the tremendous rages inherited from his rapacious forebears that so dilated his hawk-like eyes, made a mark on the boy's mind that was never effaced.

The consciousness that he was the sole object of the parental affection as well as of the vaunting ambition of this formidable couple (for the Alderman's illegitimate children were by this time launched on the world) gave him a sense of pride and isolation. From an early age he began to take stock of his place in the world. 'He is of a very agreeable disposition,' his tutor wrote of him when he was only eight years old, 'but begins already to think of being master of a great fortune. I am apprehensive that both his father and mother contrary to their own desire and inclination may hurt him by indulgence.'[12] The tutor's fears were well grounded.

2
Solitary Childhood

IN HIS OLD AGE Beckford confessed to a Bath journalist when speaking of George II: 'I was not a year old when he died, but the King saw me when I was an infant in arms in my Aunt Effingham's apartment in St. James's Palace. She was a great favourite with the young King George III and with his mother. I well remember both of them petting me.'¹ The remark was highly characteristic. It displayed the narrator's aristocratic connections by reference to his father's sister who had married the Earl of Effingham and also showed the easy terms upon which they had stood with the royal family, a point of great importance to the aged Beckford who had by then experienced the bitterness of more than half a lifetime's social ostracism. It also had just a little of the boast of an *arriviste* about it; the remark of someone who for all his wealth and grandeur, for all his distinguished ancestry, never entirely succeeded in achieving the manner of a *grand seigneur*.

The seeds of this curious, almost indefinable malaise, this core of insecurity hidden so deeply beneath layers of pride, assertiveness and ostentation, were sown early in life in a solitary and introspective childhood.

A child considered to be delicate was not to be exposed to the rank and sulphurous air of London. Fonthill, the wooded and hilly Wiltshire acres of his father's country estate, was destined to be the setting for young William's years of childhood and early adolescence. All through life he responded ardently to the influence of his natural surroundings, a response that was heightened by an acute observation and an intense love of nature whether in the broader sense of landscape or in the more intimate and immediate appeal of flowers, birds and animals of every variety. This was the legacy bequeathed to him by the woods and lakes of Fonthill, and it became fundamental to his personality, finding expression in the many written descriptions of natural scenery or romantic prospects that fell from his pen from his very earliest jottings, and perhaps also in his life-long habit of referring to his fellow human beings, usually ironically or contemptuously, as 'animals'.

What then was it like, this Eden from the protection of whose shade the still-innocent child gazed on a hostile and indifferent world outside? The thickly wooded and contrivedly wild scene we see today in its full maturity is largely the creation of Beckford's own planting and design; at the period of his childhood the outlook would have been more pastoral, more ordered, more in keeping with the earlier eighteenth-century notion of nature tamed and trimmed to the requirements of a civilised humanity. All the same it must have been an idyllically beautiful spot and tranquil beyond the conception of modern man.

The Fonthill estate lies to the south of the small town or village of Hindon, then a Parliamentary borough controlled by Beckford's father. The mansion itself stood between the villages of Fonthill Bishop and Fonthill Gifford facing a lake just over a mile in length and backed by rising woodlands. The approach to the house from Fonthill Bishop took the visitor through a splendid arched gateway which an unreliable tradition attributed to Inigo Jones. The drive, which was also a public right of way, continued on, leaving the house on the right and the romantic stretch of water on the left, until it reached the south gate which stood opposite an inn appropriately called the Beckford Arms and close to the church where the young heir to all these acres had been christened. This was a small building with a classical pediment supported by four Doric columns and topped by a neat cupola which had been built for the Alderman in 1748. Like so many other buildings on this estate the church has vanished, pulled down in the late nineteenth century and replaced by an erection in elaborate and rather heavy-handed gothic.

The territory surrounding Fonthill Splendens was laid out in parkland with lawns and neatly grouped clumps of trees. Here the deer grazed and the scene was one of ordered rusticity. To the west and south of this pleasance, behind the straggling village of Fonthill Gifford, the land became more hilly and wild, a mixture of woods and undulating downs, reaching its highest point at Stop's Beacon on the southern extremity of the estate, which rose to a height of seven hundred feet above sea level. Here Alderman Beckford had planned to raise a tower but the scheme was never completed, indeed scarcely begun at the time of his death, and only the foundations remain as a witness to one of the few excursions of this hard-headed merchant into the realms of folly.

Such was the world inhabited by this child, pampered and precocious, heir to a vast fortune yet denied what might well be considered the right of every boy or girl, the uninhibited contact in work and play with companions of his own age. Beckford's childhood seems to have been unnecessarily isolated and solitary. True, he had the society of his half-sister, but she was too much his senior in years to become an intimate and they were never at any time particularly close to each other. There is no record of his having any intimate friend of his own age at this period of his life; he had no companions at his lessons; and he never in later times spoke of any friendship that could be traced back to his nursery or schoolroom years. There were occasional visits to friends and relations, but that was all.

A child must, however, have companions of some sort, and Beckford fell back upon the resources of his imagination, filling the glades of Fonthill with the creatures of his fancy: knights in armour, mysterious travellers from distant lands, gods, heroes and the fugitive woodland creatures that only the mind of a child can conjure up. Thus stimulated, his imagination quickly took wings and created a whole realm of fantasy almost as real as the solid world of everyday life, but a world in which he was sovereign master and which was always there to welcome him when he wished to escape from the sharp exigencies of mundane existence or the stern opposition of wills stronger than his own.

If friendship among his contemporaries was wittingly or unwittingly (we cannot tell which) denied the boy, the best masters and instructors were not. It was a matter of principle no less than prestige with his parents that he should receive a thorough grounding in the classics and in French as well as in the appreciation of the arts. Before the age of seven he had embarked on Latin, and French was probably started even earlier; certainly he became the complete master of the language which came to him as easily as his own and which he used until the end of his life for much of his intimate writing and family correspondence.

Drawing, music, and even the principles of architecture were included in the curriculum. The latter, according to Beckford's own account, was placed in the hands of Sir William Chambers, a founder member of the Royal Academy and architect, among other buildings, of Somerset House. If this was true Sir William can have had little time to give more than superficial instruction to his pupil, for in the year after Beckford's birth he was made Architect of the Works and was promoted to Comptroller eight years later, both official appointments; and at the same time he was fulfilling important commissions in Dublin and Edinburgh, at Kew and Blenheim palaces as well as many other public and private works in various parts of the kingdom. However, such an appointment, even if little more than nominal, would have been in character with the Alderman's grandiose ideas, for Chambers had once been architectural tutor to George III when Prince of Wales, and there can be no doubt that Beckford himself was familiar with the basic principles of the art and could even produce competent, if not professional, architectural drawings.[2]

The question of his musical instruction raises more complex problems. It was always Beckford's boast that he had received lessons from no less a genius than Mozart. 'He passed some time at Fonthill, having been engaged, though quite a child, to give me—his junior by four or five years—lessons of composition', Beckford later wrote, adding, 'We renewed our acquaintance in Vienna, where I found him as strange, as melancholy, but more wonderful than ever.'[3] This would make master and pupil respectively roughly nine and six years old. It is pleasant to imagine the two children sitting at the harpsichord busy with the problems of counterpoint; it is a scene calculated to satisfy the most ambitious amateur of music. Beckford, however, felt the need to add a further touch.

In his late seventies he entertained a young artist, Howard Venn Lansdown, at his house in Bath. In the course of discussions upon many subjects connected with the arts, which Lansdown later recorded, the old man turned the conversation to the subject of music, declaring how much 'poor dear Mozart' would have been frightened by some modern music. He then went on: 'My father was very fond of music, and invited Mozart to Fonthill . . . It was rather ludicrous one child being the pupil of another. He went to Vienna where he obtained vast celebrity, and wrote to me saying, "Do you remember that march you composed which I kept so long? Well, I have just composed a new opera and I have introduced your air." ' When Lansdown enquired what the air might be Beckford sat down at the piano and 'with energy and force' struck off the famous aria 'Non piu andrai' from *The Marriage of Figaro*.[4]

Lansdown was not the first to have been regaled with this story; it was a theme upon which Beckford played different variations, sometimes claiming that Mozart had himself introduced the air into their lessons as a subject for exercises in improvisation. In either case it was a splendid claim to make and had all the extravagance and enormity of those boastful assertions his Beckford ancestors had made in the matter of hidden hoards of gold and uncalculated wealth—and must be taken at the same valuation.

In fact it is unlikely that Beckford had any lessons in music from Mozart at all. The young prodigy's progress during his visit to England was carefully recorded by his father Leopold, his concerts and appearances all noted in his travel diary. In letters sent home to Salzburg the names of the great and famous whom they had met or visited were discussed, and surely a Lord Mayor of London would have ranked among these, yet nowhere does the name of Beckford or of Fonthill occur. There is one tenuous link; a reference to a visit to Lady Effingham at St. James's Palace. It was perhaps here, at his aunt's, that Beckford and Mozart met. There is much independent testimony to Beckford's brilliance at the keyboard and it is possible that the younger boy was prevailed upon to show off his talents, and perhaps the elder gave him a kindly hint or two. But there is no evidence that Mozart ever visited Fonthill. There is no letter from Beckford in the Mozart archives nor did Beckford himself, a great hoarder, preserve a single letter from Mozart among his papers.[5]

This curious episode is yet another example of the underlying insecurity, the basic immaturity that Beckford never completely outgrew. It sprang not so much from a desire to deceive as from a need to impress. There was always a grain of truth, or probable truth, behind these flights of fancy; quite possibly the two did meet as children at Lady Effingham's; they could have met again in Vienna years later. But the rest is fantasy.

What makes it all the more extraordinary is the fact that Beckford had no need to apologise for his musical talents, which were considerable. He played the harpsichord and later on the piano with great skill. He was much admired for his ability at improvisation and his compositions, though slight, were not of the sort for which any amateur need feel ashamed, including a published overture, anthems, settings for Italian songs, a march scored for clarinets, oboes, horns and bassoons as well as the score for an opera by Lady Craven which will be considered in its place. Whoever was responsible for Beckford's musical education obviously did a creditable job, but there is no evidence in existence, beyond Beckford's own boast, to suggest that it was Mozart.

For the more routine subjects a resident tutor was employed. In a period when the English universities had not fully recovered from the torpor induced by those 'dull and deep potations' that Edward Gibbon had stigmatized, Alderman Beckford and his wife wisely chose a young man from one of the Scottish universities. Robert Drysdale, a native of Fife, had received his education at St. Andrews and was about twenty-seven years of age when he took up his duties at Fonthill in June 1768.

Not the least of Drysdale's qualifications in Mrs. Beckford's eyes was the strict Presbyterian religion in which he had been nurtured; and his inexperience of the great world, of which he was himself a little self-conscious, seemed to her a guarantee that his influence upon her son would be wholesome and elevating. Already her Calvinistic soul trembled at the thought of the temptations that lay to ensnare her tender offspring, and she told the edified Drysdale that she preferred virtue and religion to every other accomplishment. 'May Almighty God succeed her pious devises and intentions in the Religious Education of her son,' he confided in a letter to a friend, assuring his correspondent a shade priggishly that Mr. and Mrs. Beckford were of a true philosophic taste and 'look more to essentials and less to ornament than perhaps any others of their station in great Britain'.[6]

Whether the Alderman shared his wife's enthusiasm for the young Scot is difficult to say. He kept his religious views, or his lack of them, to himself, but was no doubt satisfied with the tutor's abilities in so far as merely secular instruction was concerned. 'I cannot say how Mr. Beckford is pleased with me,' was Drysdale's own comment, 'for he speaks very little to me, he has numberless things to attend to.' These did not, at least at this early stage, much include the education of his son. For the present he was content to leave that problem in the capable hands of his wife.

Drysdale was a little overawed by the splendours of Fonthill, 'this house or palace', as he called it; and the Alderman, always ready to impress, was not above telling the tutor that 'the article of painting' alone had cost him above ten thousand pounds. But if the young man felt himself in something of an alien world in so far as his surroundings were concerned he was on surer ground in dealing with his pupil, whom he found 'exceedingly sprightly' in spite of those airs of being the master of a great fortune which we have already noted.

Two portraits of William Beckford as a boy exist. One, at the age of about six, painted by Andrea Casali (who worked for the Alderman at Fonthill), shows us an engaging child, sensitive and rather delicate-looking, holding a bird's nest in one hand while the bird itself perches on the finger of the other. A later portrait, attributed variously to William Hoare or Nathaniel Dance, shows Beckford at the age of eight or nine, about the time he began his lessons with Drysdale. The scene is again rustic, and the boy, wearing a Van Dyke suit, nurses a spaniel in his arms while another dog jumps up as though to distract his attention from the artist. In this picture the features are more robust, the nervousness evident in the earlier painting has disappeared and has been replaced by a look of self-confidence and bright intelligence. This is the child about whom the tutor would comment, some year or so after taking up his duties, of 'the hopes he gives of his extraordinary Abilities at present to everyone that knows him'.[7]

These hopes were fed and encouraged by a rigorous routine of study. When in London, at his father's house in Soho Square, he would be visited each week by a French tutor from whom he would have instruction in reading and conversation. Already, at eight years of age, he 'understood French pretty well' in Drysdale's opinion, from which we may assume that he spoke it better than Drysdale himself, for the Scotsman showed evident relief at the visits of his French-speaking colleague. In the matter of the classics, that basic ingredient of eighteenth-century education, Drysdale felt more confident to guide his pupil among authors noted for the purity of their sentiments no less than their style. In December 1769 he could record that Beckford had 'been reading by turns since April last Cornelius Nepos and Phaedrus, and makes very good progress'.

Thus, between Fonthill and London, but chiefly at the former place, their pleasant life continued. A happy relationship must

have been established between master and pupil for though
Drysdale left after three or four years he was to return briefly into
Beckford's life some years later at a moment of crisis, which
suggests that some sort of contact remained between them after
the period of his duties at Fonthill came to an end.

Beckford was a quick and apt pupil, aided by the curiosity
and thirst for knowledge and information that characterised
him through life. If he had a fault it was a corresponding one, an
impatience to master a subject or to acquire some knowledge
that tended sometimes to a rather rapid and superficial approach.
This could be checked when parents or tutors were at hand to
keep an eye on him; in later life it developed into a serious defect
of which Beckford himself was only too well aware.

More serious, and more unpleasant, was a violent and often
uncontrollable temper. This was in the main an inheritance from
his Beckford blood and was paralleled by the sudden outbursts of
his father's that periodically brought panic and terror to the
household. The boy would sometimes work himself up into a
frenzy of rage which quite frightened those who witnessed it. The
storms would pass, penitence would follow, but the fault remained. Beckford's inability to control these fits of passion sprang
to some extent from his secluded and sheltered life. If his mother
had indulged him less and managed to stifle her fears of moral
contamination by allowing him some youthful companionship he
might have learnt to govern his temper in the give-and-take
which contact with contemporaries would have forced upon him.
As it was, sometimes the pampered object of parental pride and
indulgence, sometimes threatened with the dire penalties of hell
fire, he lived in a world of extremes where moderation was rarely
encountered. The escape from this was into the surrounding
woodlands which he had peopled with his childish fantasies.
Neither world, that of the crimson-hung drawing-rooms of
Splendens or of the shadowy woods that surrounded it, had
much connection with ordinary everyday reality.

In his immediate family his half-sister Elizabeth Marsh was, as
has been noted, just a little too old to be a real companion to
him, though she shared with him a colourful imagination and a
tendency to scribble down her impressions in hectic and romantic
prose, a habit perhaps to be expected in the future authoress of
Louisa, or the Reward of an Affectionate Daughter and other sentimental novels. When Drysdale arrived to take charge of her

brother she was already eighteen or nineteen years old. To the susceptible tutor she appeared a prodigy of a young lady who played charmingly upon various musical instruments, drew surprisingly well and (in his opinion) 'writes more than some of our fellow students sometimes used to read'.[8] We know from a later letter of Beckford's that he and his sister read Ariosto together, but apart from this she does not seem to have had much of an influence upon his childhood except as one of the accustomed circle of admiring relatives.

The saving influence in Beckford's childhood was his father's, but it was an influence all too rarely present and all too suddenly removed. There was no nonsense about the Alderman while, undeniably, there was a good deal of it about both his wife and his step-daughter. It was a misfortune that his common sense, his ability to deflate pride and to laugh at precocious posturings was so seldom felt in the sequestered and slightly self-satisfied atmosphere that surrounded Mrs. Beckford and her friends. His sudden flashes of anger might terrify but they managed to clear the air of much that was false or pretentious.

When Robert Drysdale remarked with a certain ingenuousness that the elder Beckford rarely spoke to him because he had numberless things to attend to he was saying little more than the truth. It was the period of the turmoil over the Middlesex election and the House of Commons' rejection of John Wilkes's claim to the seat despite his repeated victories at the polls. The cry of 'Wilkes and Liberty' was again alarming the supporters of the Court party and providing effective artillery for the Alderman and his Whig friends in parliament.

In November 1769 Beckford had been elected for the second time as Lord Mayor of London. At first he had demurred on grounds of age, though he was only just over sixty, but once the office was accepted he made his political position admirably clear in a series of toasts given at a private party at the Mansion House. These included the patriotic sentiment that the fundamental liberties of England be revered and defended, that the violation of the rights of election and petition against grievances be confounded, and (more dynamite to his opponents and in particular to the Court) that wicked advisers be taken away from before the king and his throne be established in righteousness. This private demonstration was shortly afterwards followed by a public protest delivered to the king in the name of the City of London against the corruption of parliament. The terms of this address, which was presented at the royal levee, were so intemperate that the king received it in cold silence and then pointedly snubbed the Lord Mayor by immediately turning away from him to speak with the Danish ambassador. Not surprisingly a second petition, delivered in March 1770, was rejected outright.

Here matters might have ended had not the whole country been in a state of tumult with petitions against the arbitrary action of the government being organised in all parts. The City decided to present a third protest to the king. On 17 May, accompanied by the City Livery and supported by a noisy and unruly crowd, the Lord Mayor made his way to St. James's Palace. His reception was frosty. The king rejected the petition in a few formal phrases and was about to leave the apartment when to his amazement he found the Lord Mayor arguing the point with him in what was afterwards worked-up and published as a speech requesting his Majesty to banish from his councils those whose advice was a violation of peace and a betrayal of the Constitution as it was established at the glorious and necessary revolution of 1688. The king was too astounded to reply and the Lord Mayor withdrew from the royal presence to find himself the hero of the mob.

Whether Beckford actually addressed George III in the words afterwards published is open to doubt. The speech was impromptu and his own effort; he did not, as malicious enemies suggested, repeat words already prepared for him by Lord Chatham. To the Court party, and to the king himself, his conduct was unpardonable not only on political grounds but also as a startling breach of proper etiquette; it is difficult to say which shocked them most.

The Lord Mayor's own reaction, upon later reflection, was a mixture of bravado and self-justification. This was evident from a letter written a week after the event to Lord Chatham; a letter which not only gives us a hint of Beckford's feelings on the matter but shows conclusively that Chatham himself had nothing to do with the planning or composition of the words spoken to the king. 'What I spoke in the King's presence was uttered in the language of truth,' the Lord Mayor wrote, 'and with that humility and submission which becomes a subject speaking to his lawful King: at least I endeavoured to behave properly and decently; but I am inclined to believe I was mistaken, for the language of Court is, that my deportment was imprudent, insolent, and unprecedented. God forgive them all! Their wickedness and folly will ruin this country.'[9] Whatever feelings Alderman Beckford may have entertained neither regret nor repentance was included among them.

The impression caused by these dramatic events upon the mind of the Lord Mayor's small son can well be imagined. In what form they were communicated to him we cannot tell except that his father must have emerged from the telling all the more of a hero than he had appeared before. The drama and excitement of the occasion was intensified by the tragic events that were to follow, for the Lord Mayor did not survive his celebrated encounter with his sovereign by more than a few weeks. Early in June he caught a chill while travelling between Fonthill and London, and by the fifteenth of the month it was announced that he was in a critical state. His condition deteriorated rapidly and by June 21 'the only man of his time who durst tell a king upon his throne, surrounded by his flatterers, the plain and honest truth'[10] lay dead.

Historians have not been kind to the memory of Alderman Beckford. To Horace Walpole he had 'boldness, promptness, spirit, a heap of confused knowledge, displayed with the usual ostentation of his temper, and so uncorrected by judgement, that his absurdities were made but more conspicuous by his vanity', and he summed up his career with the phrase: 'Vainglory seemed to be the real motive of all his actions.'[11] Macaulay dismissed him as a person who 'neither had, nor deserved to have, the ear of the House, a noisy, purseproud, illiterate demagogue, whose Cockney English and scraps of mispronounced Latin were the jest of the newspapers'.[12] Neither opinion quite catches the truth. A slave-owner, a man whose political principles were dominated by the price of sugar, he does not appear to us in a particularly attractive light. But he had a profound dedication to the cause of liberty as far as his own countrymen were concerned, and was prepared to take great risks in its defence.

Perhaps the kindest tribute to his memory was written on the very day of his death. 'Alas! poor Beckford,' Lord Lyttelton wrote to the celebrated blue-stocking Mrs. Montague on 21 June 1770, 'I am sorry for his death ... His Spirit was too good-humoured to make a Devil, and too Turbulent for an Angel; but will be a proper companion for the Ghosts that Ossian sings of, who ride in the Whirlwinds and direct storms.'[13] A fitting obituary for the father of the future author of *Vathek*.

B

3
Education of an Heir

THE DEATH of Beckford's father when he was only nine years old was the first tragedy in his life, and perhaps the greatest. Whatever this strange, vital, vulgar, overbearing man had meant to others he had been both loved and venerated by his son. To his father alone did the young Beckford stand in a relationship of awe; no one else was to usurp this place in his affections; the void caused by his death was to remain always unfilled. To a child already solitary and introspective the loss was traumatic.

It has often been stressed how the Alderman's death left Beckford the heir to one of the greatest fortunes in Europe. As a minor he had, of course, no control over his inheritance. The elder Beckford's will was complicated by his attempts to do justice to the claims of his illegitimate children and led to much confusion; indeed, it might be claimed that the decline in the great Beckford fortune began at the moment of the Alderman's death. As executors he appointed Lord Bruce (soon to be created Earl of Aylesbury) and his neighbour Henry Hoare of Stourhead of the famous banking family, but these two honourable men soon resigned their trust, finding the will too complicated to administer and alarmed at the not over-scrupulous attitude of some of their fellow executors who included the clergyman husband of one of old Beckford's illegitimate daughters and two West Indian cronies of the Alderman's, Sir John Gibbons and a former Governor Burt of the Leeward Islands. Of these remaining trustees the two former considered that their duty lay in safeguarding the interests of the bastards and only Burt can be said to have had young William Beckford's interests at heart.[1]

The alarmed widow, seeing only one friend among the three remaining executors of her husband's will, took what steps she could to protect the interests of her son. One point in particular

aroused her worst suspicions and fears; the executors not only had
power over the property and revenues of the estate, they were
also appointed the guardians of the young heir during his
minority.

That the child who had been so carefully secluded from
wordly influences should now be at the mercy of these guardians
seemed to her an appalling consequence of her husband's testi-
mentary settlement, and she found herself quite unable to abide
by it. No doubt the Alderman had been determined, in drawing
up his will, to protect that other unofficial family for whose
members he felt strong ties of affection, for they, rather than their
legitimate cousins, were to become the outright owners of the
Fonthill estate should the delicate son born in lawful wedlock
fail to achieve his majority.

This arrangement must have been a great blow to Mrs. Beckford's pride, for while she might have conceded the need for help
in administering the estate, in the matter of her son's education
she hardly supposed that she required assistance from others. In
particular she saw as her enemy Richard Beckford, the Alderman's
eldest and favourite illegitimate son who had lived with him at
Fonthill until her own advent there had made it necessary for him
to find other quarters. Very soon it became clear that in collusion
with two of the executors, his clerical brother-in-law Wade and
the Barbadan absentee landlord Gibbons, he would be interpret-
ing some of the financial clauses in his father's will very much in
his own interest, a process which neither Burt nor Mrs. Beckford
found it in their power to prevent.

In October 1770 they lodged an official complaint in Chancery
in young Beckford's name, a tedious and protracted business, but
with little practical result beyond compelling the executors to
render proper accounts. Mrs. Beckford's one triumph was to have
her son declared a Ward in Chancery, so that in the matter of
guardianship at least she got the control of affairs back into her
own hands, for the Court appears to have offered little or no
opposition to her subsequent plans for her son's education.

One unfortunate consequence of the squabbles over Alderman
Beckford's will, and one which he could hardly have foreseen
when he drew it up, was that a complete rift developed between
his wife and son at Fonthill and those people, more or less the
associates of Richard and the other bastard relations, who were
managing the business interests, and thus controlling the revenues,

of the family. Beckford never took very much interest in the source of his fortune, leaving it to others to look after his affairs, and more often than not being exploited by them in consequence. But this lazy tendency, this boredom with the minutiae of business affairs (he was always very concerned with the results) might have been prevented had his trustees been capable of interesting him in these matters, of taking him into their confidence and evoking in him some response to the responsibilities of vast wealth. As it was he became very indifferent as to how matters were managed so long as the profits were there to be enjoyed—though he cried out loud enough when these showed signs of diminishing.

With the question of the guardianship settled to her satisfaction Mrs. Beckford was able to give her mind to the problem of her son's continued education. It was clear that he had reached a point where the gentle Robert Drysdale's services were no longer adequate, for all the moral worthiness of that young man, and a more serious and adventurous course of studies undertaken. For advice she turned to her son's godfather Lord Chatham, who showed a benevolent interest in young William and his problems, and also to the poet-peer Lord Lyttelton of whose poetic work Dr. Johnson had declared that it contained 'nothing to be despised and little to be admired' and who had invoked the name of Ossian upon hearing news of the Alderman's death. As the author, moreover, of a prose work on the conversion of St. Paul he was just the sort of man in whom Maria Beckford felt that she could repose the utmost confidence. To these two, for extra weight, was added the name of Charles Pratt, Lord Camden, a formidable lawyer who had only just vacated the Woolsack.

It was determined that young Beckford should not go to a public school but should continue his education under private tutors. This decision was undoubtedly Mrs. Beckford's, who still feared the moral contamination she felt would result from association with boisterous contemporaries more given to worldly desires than to religious aspirations, and she could bolster up her decision by appealing to her son's delicate health, for the strong constitution that was to see him through eighty-four years of life had not yet made itself manifest.

Would Alderman Beckford, had he lived, have acquiesced in this decision? It is possible to think that he would not, and a battle of wills would have ensued, but at least we may be sure that Mrs. Beckford had the support of Lord Chatham, for, having

himself endured the rigorous régime of Eton, and not greatly enjoyed the experience, he had had his own sons privately educated
at home.[2]

All the same the decision was a wrong one in so far as the
particular case of William Beckford was concerned. It is true that
one would hesitate to have committed anyone to the brutal and
philistine environment of an eighteenth-century public school,
but some schools were better than others (or at least all were not
equally bad), and Westminster, where the Alderman had himself
been educated and for which he might well have intended his son,
had a comparatively liberal tradition and had produced both
Edward Gibbon and Sir William Hamilton, Mrs. Beckford's ur-
bane and cultivated cousin. Furthermore young William was in
need of a change from the rather cloying atmosphere of Fonthill
House—all the more so now that his father could no longer descend upon it to laugh him out of his more precious attitudes. He
needed to be shown that he was not the only or indeed the most
important being in his little world, and he needed influences that
would not crush, but would direct, a wayward, capricious, and
already at times morbid imagination. In short, he lacked intellectual discipline, just as he lacked a proper control over his
temper, and a public school might have provided both these
wants. But most important of all, as has already been emphasised,
he lacked companions of his own age.

Beckford himself later acknowledged that he might have bene-
fited from attending school. In a conversation with the artist
Benjamin West in 1807 he admitted that at a public school he
would have had to make his own way with others 'taking the consequence of things as they might happen'. Instead of this, 'incense
was offered to him and flowers strewed in his way, wherever he
went; that being brought up in private he had not experienced
those checks which are useful.'[3]

As things were he was now destined to spend his time in a
household almost entirely dominated by women who watched his
progress with over-anxious care and who, impregnated as they
were by the strict evangelical teachings of the Methodist revival,
were constantly on the lookout for indications of moral collapse.
As though to match the more liberal, worldly but benevolent influence of Chatham, Lyttelton and Camden, was this other triumvirate consisting of Maria Beckford, Aunt Effingham (in the
moments she could spare from her duties as Lady of the Bed-

chamber to the Queen), and Mrs. Beckford's great friend and con-
fidante Lady Euphemia Stewart. This lady, the spinster daughter
of the sixth Earl of Galloway, was of a type not uncommon
among people of narrow religious views: she was possessed of an
irritating tendency always to believe the worst of others and to
warn them upon every possible occasion that they were failing to
live up to the high ideals demanded by their Creator. It was an
attitude likely to be counter-productive at the best of times, and
all the more so when confronted by a temperament already inclined to mock at what it failed to sympathise with or to comprehend. Before very long all three ladies would be described by
Beckford under the uncomplimentary heading of 'Methodistical
dowagers'.

Their influence, none the less, was not to be ignored. However
much young Beckford might mock at their piety and rebel against
the inhibitions of their narrow creed he was never quite able to
throw off the haunting spectre of predestination which for him
implied not the hope of heaven but the inevitable certainty of hell.
These ideas perhaps hardly touched his childhood but their dark
origins lay in that otherwise idyllic period and were mysteriously
associated with the death of his father and the loss of childish
innocence.

Another no less compelling influence added to the sense of
doom-laden destiny. Alderman Beckford had allowed his son free
access to the library at Fonthill House, and there on the shelves
the boy had discovered the *Arabian Nights* and had devoured their
contents 'when other children are seldom of an age to do more
than comprehend their letters'.[4] The sense of *kismet*, of the inexorable will of heaven inherent in oriental fatalism found an immediate echo in the mind of this child already conditioned by the
Calvinistic teaching he had received from his mother and her
pious friends.

Beckford's mind was, therefore, to some extent already formed
(at least in certain basic characteristics) when the tutor chosen for
him by Lord Lyttelton arrived to take up his duties in 1771.
Lyttelton had applied to Dr. William Cleaver, fellow of Brasenose
College and later Bishop of St. Asaph, and this ecclesiastic with
complacent nepotism immediately suggested his own cousin as
being suitable to fulfil the task and also to enjoy the salary offered
of three hundred pounds a year, a comfortable stipend by the
values of the period, especially when it included the enjoyable

prospect of living in one of the most luxurious houses in England.

John Lettice, the chosen candidate, was thirty-four years of age, and had been educated at Sidney Sussex College, Cambridge. At the time of his appointment he was acting as secretary to the British Minister at the Danish Court, at the same time supervising the education of the envoy's daughter. He was in holy orders and had one link with Lord Lyttelton in being the author of a now wholly forgotten poem which had won him the Seatonian prize in 1764. He was a good, scholarly man with literary tastes, kind and painstaking, but essentially mild in disposition. In no sense whatever was he to be a substitute for the father William Beckford had just lost. While capable of providing his pupil with the conventional education expected of an eighteenth-century gentleman, and indeed in making him a respectable scholar, he had no positive influence upon him at all. Fanny Burney, who had met him upon one occasion at her father's house in London, described him as a 'good sort of half-stupid man', and this rather unkind description just about sums him up. He was to be no counter-balance to Mrs. Beckford and the Methodistical dowagers.

Such influence as there was to temper the religious sensibility of the Fonthill ladies came from the direction of Burton Pynsent in Somerset, the country retreat of Lord Chatham. Having supervised the education of his own children, he now began to take a fatherly interest in the affairs of the bright young son of his old friend the Alderman.

Like all his generation Chatham was a firm believer in a sound classical education. Religious 'enthusiasm' would have shocked him. He based his severe code rather upon the lessons to be derived from Homer and Virgil, 'lessons of honour, courage, disinterestedness, love of truth, command of temper, gentleness of behaviour, humanity, and in one word virtue in its true signification',[5] and he had earlier urged his own nephew to drink as deep as he could from 'these divine springs'. The same virtues he now hoped to see planted firmly in the mind of his young godson through the interventions of Lettice, who was encouraged to report on his pupil's progress to the retired statesman.

Chatham quickly took a liking to the boy. In the autumn of 1772 Beckford went to stay at Burton Pynsent and so endeared himself to the Pitt family that when the time came for him to return to Fonthill the entire family drew up and signed a mock petition to Mrs. Beckford asking that he might be allowed to pro-

long his stay and join in their amateur theatricals. When Beckford
had recited a speech from Thucydides which he had translated
himself the old parliamentary orator was so impressed that he
turned to his son William, a year Beckford's senior, and expressed the hope that that young man might himself one day
make as brilliant a speaker.

What the younger Pitt made of this comparison we do not
know, but at this period there seems to have been a warm feeling
between the two boys. A year later (October 1773) when Beckford
arrived at Burton Pynsent to find that his friend had just left,
Chatham wrote to his son: 'Little Beckford was really disappointed
at not being in time to see you—a good mark for my young vivid
friend. He is just as much compounded of the elements of air and
fire as he was. A due proportion of terrestrial solidity will, I trust,
come and make him perfect.'[6]

The problem of reconciling these disparate elements in Beckford's character was a subject of earnest discussion between
Chatham and the tutor. In particular they were alarmed at the
fascination he already showed for all things oriental that came his
way, not only the enthralling tales from the *Arabian Nights* but
the oriental pictures and drawings that he loved to collect. Their
objection seems unreasonable; but in a highly-strung and sensitive
boy they clearly considered this interest in the exotic to be
dangerous. A long letter from Lettice to Lord Chatham, written
in December 1773 after their return to Fonthill, shows the fruits
(some of which were unnecessarily bitter) of their talks on the
education of a boy just turned thirteen years of age.

'Mr. Beckford has read one third part of the Essay on Human
Understanding' the tutor wrote, 'and I believe not unprofitably; as
I call upon him for an account of every paragraph as soon as he
has read it; which he generally gives me with much facility. The
habit of frequently tracing the footsteps of so regular and clear a
reader as Mr. Locke through the course of an argument may, it is
hoped, be no ineffective method of learning to set his own
thoughts in the best order, and to express them with perspicuity;
and perhaps this would be a point gained, much to be wished;
that of making a gentleman think and speak with precision without the pedantry of art.

'Your Lordship's advice on the article of arithmetic was too
pressing to suffer me to defer a trial of Mr. Beckford's talent for
numbers; and I may say, that the little time which he has been

able to dedicate to them has been well employed, and I do not despair of his becoming proficient. The cultivation of our own language and studies of the politer kind are by no means neglected; though they are not to be preferred to the others; inasmuch as we must look upon taste and sentiment as acquisitions of less importance than the right use of reason. Mr. Beckford may, however, name Homer, Livy, Cicero, and Horace among his present classical acquaintance, and he is every day becoming more intimate with them.'

In seeing his task as that of establishing the ascendancy of reason over the lesser claims of taste and sentiment Lettice was carrying out the wishes of Mrs. Beckford no less than those of Lord Chatham, for though they started from very different viewpoints their objective was one and the same: to make William Beckford a model of those virtues expected of an eighteenth-century magnate who would in due course take his seat in parliament and his place in the affairs of his country as a man of influence and wealth. The predilection he already showed for taste and sentiment they saw as a tendency to be discouraged, if needs be eradicated altogether. Just how they set about this task was made clear in the next paragraph of the letter.

'I assure myself', Lettice continued, 'that it will give your Lordship pleasure to be informed that, about a month ago, that splendid heap of oriental drawings, &c., which filled a large table at Burton, has been sacrificed at the shrine of good taste. Mr. Beckford had firmness enough to burn them with his own hand. I hope that, as his judgement grows maturer, it will give me an opportunity of acquainting your Lordship with other sacrifices to the same power . . .'[7]

The complacent insensitivity of Lettice's words bring out all the more clearly the plight of the unfortunate lad who was forced to make this bonfire of vanities and throw on to it his most treasured possessions. The tutor's professed satisfaction at the pleasure this news would bring to Lord Chatham emphasises his inability to conceive of the pain it was causing his pupil or the deepness of the wound it inflicted.

Beckford had already learnt to wear a mask, and was actor enough to conceal his real feelings behind a pose of stoic indifference. What the action really cost him we know from an episode he introduced into an unfinished fictional fragment, autobiographical like all his writings, written in his later adolescence. The scene is appropriately Islamic, and a Mahometan youth, the hero of the tale, is discovered by his father to have made drawings of the human form, a thing prohibited by his religion. The forbidden drawings are torn up and thrown to the winds. At this, 'the youth sobbed, not daring to reply or to make any attempt to save the children of his fancy. But the loss affected him more than can be imagined; he turned angrily from his father and, hiding his face with his hands, gave way to violent indignation. What can my father mean, what crime have I committed.'[8] It never occurred to the tutor or his advisers that the boy's perfectly natural interest in the heap of drawings (which Lettice himself acknowledged as being 'splendid') could be encouraged and directed into paths which even they might have considered as safe. Instead their action gave to Beckford's oriental interests all the additional glamour of forbidden fruit.

The forced repression of this absorbing interest might have had even more serious psychological results but for the appearance upon the scene, some time between Beckford's thirteenth and fifteenth year, of the one really sympathetic figure to come into his life since the death of his father. This was the man appointed to teach him drawing, the strange and rather mysterious Alexander Cozens.[9]

Cozens had been born in Russia, and there the mystery began, for rumour declared that he had entered the world in St. Petersburg, the illegitimate son of Peter the Great by the daughter of a Deptford inn-keeper with whom the emperor had lodged while in England. In fact he seems to have been born in Archangel (which, with 'the Persian', was one of the nicknames Beckford later gave him) and was the son of one Richard Cozens, shipwright to the Russian emperor, by his lawful wife Mary, the daughter of a certain Robert Davenport. He settled in England in 1746, travelling from his native Russia by way of Italy, and since the late 1760s had been drawing master at Eton. He was a small man—Beckford later described him as 'creeping about like a domestic Animal; t'would be no bad scheme to cut a little cat's door for him in the great Portals of the Saloon'—and had a lively enquiring mind, 'almost as full of Systems as the Universe'.[10]

It is a curious coincidence that both of Beckford's instructors in the arts should have had contacts with the East. Chambers, if indeed he did teach Beckford the rudiments of architecture, had travelled widely and had been as far east as Bengal and China;

while Cozens, during his years in Russia, had met Persian travellers, Tartar princes and other exotic personages. Beckford, in an undated fragment addressed to Cozens, recalled how his art master had told him of 'your audience of the Georgian princess, surrounded by a melancholy Court in long black robes of mourning, who received you with such benignity' and the Tartar prince 'who presented you with curious drawings, entertained you with strange tales of his native country, and girded on your side a dagger curiously purpled after the mode of Damascus'.[11] It was the sort of stuff nicely calculated to capture and hold an adolescent mind.

What made Cozens unique amidst the adults who surrounded the young Beckford was the fact that, alone among them, he was able to enter into the boy's imaginary world, and not only to enter into it but to extend its frontiers. This was the gift he brought his pupil, and the boy in return confided in him with an intimacy no one else at that period of his life was able to share. 'Could I have imagined any person so penetrated with the same rays as you are with those that transfix me?' Beckford was to write to him at the age of seventeen when he was on his first trip abroad. 'Strange, very strange, that such a perfect conformity should subsist.' And he assured his friend that all the letters he had received from him were deposited in a drawer 'lined with blue, the colour of the Aether'.[12]

A slightly sinister atmosphere has always surrounded the relationship between Beckford and Cozens. It has been suggested that he was interested in magic and instilled similar occult ideas into Beckford's mind. It has even been hinted that the elder man initiated the younger into ways of sexual deviation. For the latter charge, at least, there is no shred of evidence; but one of the problems that confronts anyone trying to assess the character of Alexander Cozens is the fact that practically nothing is known about his life at all. We have many of Beckford's letters to him all written in adolescence or early manhood but these, with their effusive phrases and extravagant flights of fancy, tell us more about the sender than the recipient. The replies by Cozens himself, for all that they were treasured in a blue-lined drawer, have disappeared.

A few biographical details survive, such as his marriage in 1752 and the birth in the same year of his son the brilliant but tragically unstable John Robert. It is known that he exhibited at the Royal

Academy, that he taught drawing to two of George III's sons as well as at Eton, and that he worked briefly for the College of Arms. For the rest history has virtually nothing to say about him and Beckford's brief account of him creeping about Fonthill House like a domestic animal is the only contemporary description of him to have survived.

It is plain, however, from the extent to which Beckford was able to open his heart to this man that a very strong bond was soon established between them. This is not, after all, very unusual between master and pupil or between an older and a younger man and there is no need to read sinister implications into it; and in Beckford's case, where other emotional outlets were practically non-existent, it is not surprising that once the ice was melted he made Cozens the recipient of all his previously secretly held notions and romantic dreams. Cozens for his part saw no necessity to crush or discourage this side of the boy's personality and was perhaps the first person to perceive and even encourage the artistic temperament which all the weight of conventional erudition and religious austerity as applied by Lettice and Mrs. Beckford had so far failed to extinguish.

Certainly Beckford was developing in a way that would have surprised them had their eyes rested on some of the pages which were being covered by his compulsive scribbling. From a very early age his thoughts and mental images were transmitted to paper, at first, no doubt, because he had no one to communicate them to but himself or some imaginary correspondent; later because the habit had become fixed and it was, for many years, the only outlet for a suppressed literary talent.

A glance at two compositions written in his late teens gives us a sufficient glimpse into the mind of this precocious young man to show how completely the combined efforts of the Methodistical dowagers and the well-meaning tutor had failed to make of him a conventional country squire.

The first extract comes from a reverie set in the grounds of Fonthill which he called 'The Fountain of Merlin'. It shows us how he was able to romanticise his surroundings and transport himself in his imagination to other places and times. Wandering among the groves and plantations of Fonthill, he writes: 'I almost fancy myself transported to that famous Forest [of Arden] so celebrated in romance for the feats of the highest Chivalry—and as I advance into its recesses expect at every step to reach the

memorable fountain of hatred which Merlin raised to free illustrious Knights and Damsels from the torments of rejected love . . .

'These shades and fountains were destined for the refreshment
of errant Knights after the horrors of perilous engagements.
T'was here frequently their lovely sovereigns rested in the heat of
the day, screened by impending woods and lulled by the babbling
of waters. The garlands which they wreathed around the brows of
their Defenders were gathered in the neighbouring Thickets. Such
flowers bloomed not in the fairest gardens; for Merlin planted
them, and his prophetic art told him they flourished for the
brave . . .

'Is it not pleasing to recollect the scenes recorded to have
passed in these solitudes: Damsels and palfreys continually arriving
escorted by their Knights and attendant Dwarfs who, struck with
the sylvan prospect intreat their Princes to halt and enjoy its
charms . . .' The knights hear the distant clash of arms and snatch
their lances from the surrounding trees where they have rested
them. Any boy but the young William Beckford would surely
have given us a fight at this point with the clash of sword upon
shield, but no: 'All hostile thoughts were soon dispelled for no
insulting foes invade the fountain but friends whom a long separation had endeared still more to each other meet unexpectedly at its
polished margin . . . Stretched carelessly beneath the boughs we
hear them relating to each other what tedious nights were wasted
in some gloomy cave or wilderness visible alone by the glare of
necromantic towers.'13

Thus early some of the characteristics of the later Beckford are
manifest; the feeling for the countryside and flowers, the love of
seclusion and mystery, the gothic imagery and even the dwarf
who was later to appear in reality in the grounds of Fonthill
Abbey. Finally that persistent symbol here makes one of its
earliest appearances—the Tower, already invested with magic
properties.

The second extract is perhaps a bit later (neither is dated) for it
exhibits a more erotic fancy. This time we are concerned not with
gothic chivalry but with the pagan world of gods and goddesses,
and are introduced, with a wealth of classical allusions, to the
secret grove of Pan. 'His happiness consists', Beckford wrote, 'in
slumbering at noon in some cool grotto, and when the twilight
prevails the soft notes of his pipe echo thro' out the Forests. 'Tis
then a crowd of nimble Fauns gambol around him as he sits

warbling upon his reeds in the centre of some secret glade, sheltered by impending woods: and often, inspired by his song, they frolic after the Naiads, who lifting their heads above the waves to hear the melody, discover their blue eyes and alluring tresses. The old Pan continues, breathing the most harmonious sounds, till the helpless Nymphs, rising from their streams, become the Victims of these perfidious warblings. Too soon they find themselves exposed to the glances of a wanton crew that starting from their concealments multiply every instant on the lawn. They shriek, fly thro all the mazes of the thickets, and plunge into the waters. But alas, the Satyrs are not so easily repulsed. With difficulty even Doris escapes, for Pan favours their revels. In vain therefore the unlucky Naiads implore his assistance; the Diety himself joins in the pursuit, and the Traveller wandering at the extremities of the forest hears the silence of the night interrupted by hectic cries and loud peals of tumultuous ferocity.'[14]

This scene, though possibly better expressed, illustrates no more than what passes in most adolescent minds; but it shows how little even Chatham's advice to drink deeply at the divine spring of classical learning had had quite the result he would have hoped for or expected. It also demonstrates how completely Beckford had failed to absorb the evangelical principles of his mother and her set. His love of beauty, physical, natural and artificial, drew much of its inspiration from the classical and pagan past. In this, as in the hedonism which persisted all through his life, he was more pagan than anything else, though a pagan with a Calvinistic conscience.

4
Switzerland

❧❦❧

BECKFORD, like any other young man, was not lacking in the high spirits of youth, but in the unnatural seclusion of his upbringing this tendency found expression in literary *jeux d'esprit* rather than in the practical jokes and rough horseplay more usual to his time of life.

One of his amusements was to eavesdrop on the housekeeper of Splendens when she was showing the treasures of art it contained to occasional visitors. This worthy lady was not well versed in the niceties of art history and her many mis-pronunciations and wrong or imaginary attributions were to Beckford a source of delight. In his sixteenth year[1] he amused himself by composing a parody of the art manuals of the period in which the housekeeper's malapropisms were combined with some of the more pretentious or credulous critical works of the day to produce the *Biographical Memoirs of Extraordinary Painters*.

There is even now plenty to amuse us in this youthful effort which tells the life stories of such improbable masters as Aldrovandus Magnus, Andrew Guelph, Og of Basan, Sucrewasser of Vienna, Blunderbussiana and Watersouchy and introduces us at the same time to their patrons and admirers who enjoy such names as Count Zigzaggi and Monsieur Baise-la-main, 'a banker of the first eminence and an encourager of the fine arts, who united the greatest wealth with the most exemplary politeness', or to lesser artists such as 'an Italian painter by name Insignificanti'.

An example of Beckford's youthful humour can be taken from his description of a visit to the studio of his first subject: 'Aldrovandus . . . began an altar-piece for the Cathedral, in which he may be said to have surpassed himself. The subject, Moses and the burning bush, was composed in the most masterly manner, and the flames represented with such truth and vivacity, that the young Princess Ferdinanda Joanna Maria being brought by the Duchess for a little recreation to see him work, cried out, "La! Mamma, I won't touch that bramble bush, for fear I should burn my fingers!" This circumstance, which I am well aware some readers will deem trifling, gained our painter great reputation amongst all the courtiers, and not a little applause to her Serene Highness, for her astonishing discernment and sagacity. All the nurses and some of the ladies in waiting declared, she was too clever to live long, and they were not mistaken, for this admirable Princess departed this life Jan. 23rd., 1493, and it was unanimously observed, that had she lived, she would have been indubitably the jewel of Bohemia.'

In another episode we learn of the artist Watersouchy and his admiration for the female painter Sibylla Merian: 'He adored the extreme nicety of her touch, and not a little admired that strict sense of propriety which had induced her to marriage; for it seems she had chosen Jean Graff of Nuremburg for her husband, merely to study the *Nud* in a modest way.'

Another figure, which like the symbol of the Tower was to be a main feature of Beckford's life, makes a first light-hearted appearance in these pages. We are given a description of Og of Basan at work on a picture of St. Antony of Padua preaching to the fishes: 'he placed St. Antony on a rock projecting over the sea, almost surrounded by shoals of every species of fish, whose countenances, all different, were highly expressive of the most profound attention and veneration. Many persons fancied they distinguished the likeness of most of the Conclave in these animals; but this is generally believed to be a false observation, as the painter had no pique against any of their Eminences.'² The reference to St. Antony is brief and amusing enough, but it shows that even at sixteen Beckford was already familiar with the legend of this saint whose influence he was later to find so curiously fascinating. Scattered among these essentially farcical stories are also sudden brief glimpses of a more sinister world; tempests and whirlwinds, strangely ominous dreams, terrifying precipices and divine vengeance.

The *Biographical Memoirs* sufficiently entertained John Lettice for him to produce the manuscript in the Senior Common Room of Sidney Sussex College when he was visiting Cambridge a couple of years after it was written. It was read to one or two Fellows and was generally declared to have 'many charming

strokes of humour in it'. Having submitted it to this test Lettice
agreed that he would see the book through the press (after first
making a few corrections) as he was sure that it would be extremely well received.[3] Thus it was that Beckford's first published
work made its appearance in the world early in 1780.

The author, who always liked to improve a story, as an elderly
man told Howard Venn Lansdown, the Bath artist and drawing
teacher we have already met, that he himself sent his manuscript
to a London publisher enquiring what the expense of printing it
would be. 'The publisher read it with delight', Lansdown was informed, 'and instantly offered the youthful author £50 for the
manuscript.'[4] Beckford was clearly still pleased with his early
effort; nor had he any need to feel ashamed, for the book came
out in more than one edition during his lifetime, the last appearing
when he was seventy-four years old.

As Beckford's seventeenth birthday approached his mother had
once again to consider his educational future. Was he to proceed
to a university? The arguments in favour of his doing so were
strong, stronger, in fact than those she had refused to countenance when the question of his going to a public school had been
discussed, for her son was now reaching an age when some sort of
independence could not much longer be denied him. But once
again all her old fears and prejudices came into play, and she
dreaded the dissipation into which she believed someone of his
temperament and wealth must inevitably be led, an opinion not
very flattering to her son or complimentary to those whose task
it had been to form his character. But perhaps this time reason was
on her side, for without the preparation of a public school the
sudden impact of university life on a person of Beckford's volatile
disposition might have had catastrophic results. Whatever the
possibilities, one way or the other, it was never put to the test.
The temptations no less than the opportunities of Oxford or
Cambridge were not to be risked, and it was determined that
Beckford should continue his studies abroad.

The choice fell upon Geneva. In many ways the choice was an
obvious one. Geneva at that time was a recognised intellectual
centre where many distinguished luminaries of art and science had
collected, attracted, perhaps, by the presence at Ferney of the
aged Voltaire; it was a place where Mrs. Beckford had distant
relatives, a Colonel Edward Hamilton and his family, with whom
her son could stay in wholesome domestic surroundings; and

finally, an important factor for her no doubt, Geneva was the
citadel of Protestantism. Here any attractions her impressionable
son might feel for the alluring mysteries of Roman Catholicism
would meet with a stern and forbidding check. For his mother the
city of Calvin promised safety from corruption and breathed an
atmosphere of moral rectitude which (at least in her estimation)
was wholly lacking at either of the English universities.

And so, shortly before his seventeenth birthday, Beckford set
off on his first trip abroad and his first prolonged absence from
Fonthill and from the immediate care and anxious protection of
his mother and her *camarilla* of pious middle-aged matrons. Only
John Lettice went with him, for Geneva had no lack of savants to
supervise his studies there. This meant a separation from Cozens.
That Beckford missed this sympathetic friend is plain from the
letters he addressed to him from Switzerland, letters which show
very clearly that however much his mind was expanded and his
experience enriched by impact with a strange environment, the
influence of Calvin at least was kept well in the background.

Indeed, many pitfalls unenvisaged by Mrs. Beckford when
making her careful plans awaited the young traveller upon his
arrival in the late summer of 1777. To begin with Colonel Hamilton himself had seen service in India, and what retired officer is
not garrulous about his campaigning experiences? The topic must
soon have come into the open and Beckford's obsession with
orientalism took on a new lease of life. India and Indians peopled
his imagination and it was probably at this time that he first
bestowed upon his mother the nick-name of 'the Begum' by
which she was to be known in future among his intimate friends.
Before many months had been passed on the shores of Lake
Léman rumours of this once forbidden subject being again
openly aired must have reached England, for Beckford felt
obliged to write a justification of his attitude to Eastern studies in
a letter to his sister.

'Don't fancy, my Dear Sister,' he wrote, 'I am enraptured with
the orientals themselves. It is the country they inhabit which
claims all the admiration I bestow on that quarter of the Globe. It
is their woods of Spice trees, their strange animals, their vast
rivers which I delight in. The East must be better known than it
is to be sufficiently liked or disliked. If you would form a tolerable
judgement upon it not a single relation, not one voyage or volume
of travels must be neglected, whether in Portuguese, Spanish or

any other language. With this intent I am learning Portuguese and find great treasures indeed, uncommon descriptions, marvellous Histories and perilous adventures ... And why read such un-meaning stuff? What matters it whether we are conversant with India or no? Is it not better to study the histories of Europe? I answer—these I look upon as occupations, the other as amuzements. Such is my taste; it may very easily be a lamentable one.'[5]

Another contact which his mother would certainly have con-sidered deplorable was with the Huber family, connections of her Hamilton cousins in Geneva. This talented and vivacious family consisted of Jean Huber, artist, naturalist, musician, man of the world, and his two artist sons François and Jean-Daniel. Not only was the father a friend of Voltaire's (his silhouette of the latter lounging at ease in a chair with a slipper precariously balanced on his toes is well-known), but he was a declared agnostic. Such dangerous contacts had formed no part of the Begum's plans for her son, but to Beckford the influence of the elder Huber, this entertaining and stimulating polymath, opened up vistas of know-ledge and experience which had not been included in John Lettice's cautious scheme of education.

Here, rather in the style of Alexander Cozens, was another 'father-figure' to capture the young man's enthusiastic admiration. Something of this can still be felt in the description of Jean Huber (who was at this time in his mid-fifties) which Beckford sent to his sister in the course of a long account of his activities at Geneva written in January 1778.

Among the things he liked there, he told her, were the original characters to be met with: 'In the first rank of these', the letter continues, 'shines my friend Huber whose particular excellence would be very hard to discover, as he is changeable as the wind and sometimes as boisterous. One day he wanders with his Faucons over Hill and Dale, marsh and river, wood and garden; the next, shut up in his Cabinet he will reflect on the nature of the Universe and the first principle of all things. The following week perhaps he is totally engaged in drawing caricatures and saying the queerest drollest things imaginable, and if he writes during this humour, probably it will be a dissertation upon the nature of Cats' whiskers. See him the day after this whim has left him and you will find a profound Musician, composing *Misereres* and de-claming Recitatives with all the taste and judgement of an eminent professor ...' A few of Huber's remarks are recorded: after feeding his birds of prey he comes in 'all over filthiness and garbage', but if one passes a comment on the state of his hands he merely answers, '*Ah, si vous voiez mes pieds!*' More alarming to the ears of the ladies of Fonthill was his comment upon the Almighty. When asked if he had ever heard of the Supreme Being 'with all the *sang froid* and gravity conceivable he will answer, *Oui j'ai entendu dise du bien de lui.*' The description leaves him in the evening 'serene, full of agreeable ideas; ideas that breathe the most delicate sensibility. It is then he will talk of the adventures of his Youth, recount his rambles thro' Italy and describe the various scenes that have just passed before his eyes. His descriptions are covered with vivacity and affect me in a degree superior to any I have ever heard ...'[6]

Together Huber and Beckford would 'exult in the glories of Ariosto and Shakespeare', quoting long passages from memory in a manner that made people 'stare again and say the Devil [had] left the Swine' to possess them. Huber was a man of suddenly changing moods, of periods of indolence as well as of feverish energy; not altogether the best influence on a young man of similar temperament, for he had in his personality a good deal of the Quixote-like character which he was later to see and regret in his young friend.[7] But he certainly had a liberating effect on the mind of the younger man, and through family and other connections was able to open doors to new worlds of experience.

It was probably Huber who introduced Beckford to Voltaire. Just how many visits he made to Ferney is difficult to say. In a letter to Cozens he would speak of going to see Voltaire 'sometimes', and in that to his sister just referred to he writes, with a degree of complacency unusual for so youthful a letter-writer, that Voltaire had asked him to spend two or three days at Ferney, adding, 'he adores, worships and glorifies Ariosto as well as myself so we shall agree very well I believe, and as soon as the snow takes itself away I shall set off.'

Did he indeed spend these few days at Ferney on intimate terms with its venerable inhabitant? There is no record of it other than Beckford's own. Voltaire at this time was in his eighty-fourth year and on the threshold of his final departure for Paris; it is unlikely that he would have had much time to spare for so young and so unknown a man. On the other hand he readily made himself available to visitors and pilgrims, always receiving them with unfailing courtesy, and there is no doubt that Beckford visited him at least once when Voltaire spoke in flattering terms of his father and, before dismissing his guests, placed his hand on Beckford's head with the words, 'There, young Englishman, I give you the blessing of a very old man.'[8] It would seem that this was just before Voltaire left Ferney for the last time (5 February 1778), for in a letter to Lord Thurlow Beckford wrote: 'I luckily caught the moment of seeing Voltaire before his setting on our Horizon. All we shall ever see of him more at Geneva is the light of his Genius reflected from his Works.'[9] This would suggest that the two only met upon a single occasion.

It was also through Huber that Beckford was able to secure an introduction to the Necker family, Madame Huber being a cousin of the celebrated financier's wife. At this time the Neckers were living in Paris, for it was the period of Jacques Necker's Ministry, but it is possible that Beckford might have met Madame Necker and the young Germaine (the future Madame de Staël was six years his junior and at this age known by the less romantic name of Louise) on a family visit to Geneva. He was certainly to know them later on in France.

Though study was the chief reason for Beckford's presence in Geneva it was also a time when he first began to move in society on the footing of an adult and became conscious of that gift of charming and amusing people with which nature had very generously endowed him. This social talent he was quickly to learn to develop and exploit. His charm was very considerable, both men and women felt its effect, and he himself was not slow to appreciate the power which this gift conferred upon him. But like many young men to whom such success comes easily he affected to despise the triumphs and conquests of the drawing-room and developed a pose of languid indifference. 'The people crowded round me, and asked me where I had been,' he wrote, describing his return home on a cold, windy night. 'I answered, to the Devil . . . Then they fell to teazing me to play at cards, complimenting of me and telling me there was Monsieur *This* and Madame *T'other* who were come in purpose to hear me say clever things *forsooth*. I told them I never said any such kind of things. They replied, *pardonnez-moi*. They hoped I would play on the pianoforte; not at all, I never touched such an Instrument; besides my fingers were frozen . . .'[10] It was the behaviour of a spoilt young man, but one who knew that he could get away with it. In another mood he could have everyone in fits of laughter, willingly conceding to him the centre of the stage.

For the entertainment of Cozens he drew a picture of himself as he appeared in Genevan society: 'Delivered up to a sword, Bag and pretty Cloathes, I am obliged to go dangling about to assemblies of sweet dear, prim tulipy variegated Creatures, oppressed with powder and pomatum, and tired with the lisping nonsense I hear all around me. Fifty times have I wished myself amongst all the Bears of the Pole. At home I am infested with a species which, like mathematical points, have neither *parts* nor magnitude. Alas, fat Bulls of Basan encompass me around. Tubs upon two legs, crammed with stupidity, amble about me. Some of them mere trivets and Footstools, supple, pliant and complaisant; others people of good sound sense and solid Acquirements. I love to bark a tough Understanding, it is much better than to be always peeling Willows. Nothing then gives me more pleasure than a good mouthing Dispute with such as these.'

Though Beckford certainly enjoyed the purely social success which his charm of manner (when he chose to exercise it) and his reputation for wealth brought him, it was during his year in Switzerland that he decided very definitely that the life of fashion, the existence of a mere social butterfly, was not at all what he wanted from life. 'To receive visits and to return them,' he wrote to Cozens in October 1777, 'to be mighty civil, well-bred, quiet, prettily-dressed and smart is to be what your old Ladies call in England a charming Gentleman and what those of the same stamp abroad know by the appellation of *un homme comme il faut*. Such an animal how often am I doomed to be! To pay and to receive fulsome Compliments from the Learned, to talk with modesty and precision, to sport an opinion gracefully, to adore Buffon and d'Alembert, to delight in Mathematicks, logic, Geometry and the rule of Right, the *mal moral* and the *mal physique*, to despise poetry and venerable Antiquity, murder Taste, abhor imagination, detest all the charms of Eloquence unless capable of mathematical Demonstration, and more than all to be vigorously incredulous, is to gain the reputation of good sound Sense. Such an animal I am sometimes doomed to be! To glory in Horses, to know how to knock up and how to cure them, to smell of the stable, swear, talk bawdy, eat roast beef, drink, speak bad French, go to Lyons, and come back with manly disorders, are qualifications not despicable in the Eyes of the English here. Such an animal I am determined not to be! Were I not to hear from you sometimes, to see a Genius or two sometimes, to go to Voltaire's sometimes and to the Mountains very often, I should die.'

This was a sort of negative creed from whose principles Beckford never departed. It was formed partly by an adolescent revolt from the ideals of his upbringing, partly from a genuine disgust at the grosser side of conventional life as it was generally accepted and lived by the bulk of his contemporaries.

As to the more positive side, the question of his future, here a vaguer note prevailed. Romantic rhetoric quickly replaced the earlier denunciations. He is writing about the mountain whose summit, he assures Cozens, is his chief comfort: 'Lifted high above the Multitudes that swarm in the Plain, in a situation as placid as the present tone of my mind, I am thinking of England, recollecting all that has happened to me and remembering a thousand little circumstances about those that are absent and those that are *no more*. Next I am filled with Futurity. That Aweful Idea is attended by mystery and sublimity—they make me tremble. What will be my Life? What misfortunes lurk in wait for me? What Glory?'[11]

For Beckford at any moment of crisis or indecision there was always ready at hand the retreat into the world of imagination which was to gain new properties from his present surroundings. His natural response to the beauties of landscape was stimulated by the great Alpine peaks that overshadowed him and a new feeling for the mystery of gothic was aroused by some of the castles he visited. Thus, from the château of Baron Prangin, an acquaintance of Colonel Hamilton's, he sent some lines to Cozens that presaged the galleries and cloisters he was later to create at Fonthill Abbey.

'Could you transport yourself here in a moment,' he wrote, 'you would find me writing in a Bedchamber 30 feet square, hung with old Hobgoblin Tapestry full of Savages and monsters slaughtering one another, which cruelty occasions innumerable streams of red silk to flow copiously from every quarter. If murder were catching we should take care not to lie in this room.

'This room opens into a gallery of immense length which receives a dim wan sort of light thro' a series of tall windows painted with every colour you can imagine. Here you would find the history of Saints and Dragons and the adventures of Heroes long since forgotten and whose prowess (once perhaps the subject of admiration) is now totally buried in Oblivion. In one corner of this antiquated hall or gallery or whatever you please to call it, I shortly expect to be summoned (by a large Kettle Drum) to Dinner under the protection of a five leaved Japanese Screen, so what with the monsters gilt and blazoned on this piece of furniture and the uncouth animals on the painted glass I shall fancy myself in the land of Chimaeras. As soon as the night approaches, eight enormous braziers are kindled in this stately apartment which light it in a very uncommon manner and I declare the Gallery with its brown polished pillars, gilded cornices and wide folding doors presents one of the strangest spectacles I ever beheld. Every evening we have musick at one end in a sort of latticed balcony over the great door and nothing can be more aweful than the sound ringing among columns and echoing through the Gothic Arches of the roof till by degrees it dies upon the ear.'[12]

Beckford was one of those people who find it necessary to express all their thoughts on paper whether in letters addressed to sympathetic friends (but not always dispatched) or in stories and reveries jotted down usually with a particular recipient or auditor in mind. Like the confessional to a Catholic or the psychiatrist's couch to a twentieth-century neurotic these literary effusions gave him release from tension and to some extent helped him sort out his problems or at least to present a justification of his conduct, his feelings of guilt, or his repressed desires, by projecting them onto fictitious characters or introducing them into imaginary situations.

During his winter in Switzerland he spent such time as he could spare from his other activities in composing a narrative, sometimes referred to as the 'Long Story' and sometimes more quaintly as his 'Centrical History', intended for the eye of Alexander Cozens. He was anxious to keep it from others, warning his friend to be very careful to whom he showed it 'for certain I am the greatest number of readers would despise, ridicule or make neither head nor Tail of it ... The subject is very grave and serious. When I reflect that you see and feel the Scenes and the actions I describe, their being concealed from eyes in general does not at all concern me. It is to you then that I deliver up my work, and it is in your Bosom that I deposit it.'[13]

The story is written in the first person and the narrator of the adventure is so clearly identified with the author that at one point he actually refers to him, in a rhetorical passage, as 'William'. It is briefly the story of a young man who, lost on a bleak mountain range, finds himself confronted by two mysterious strangers at the mouth of a cave. They conduct him into their secret subterranean territory having first given him the choice of returning home or of being initiated, through trials of fire and water, into their mysteries, which include the enjoyment of pure knowledge. For the ordeal of initiation (which is also a rite of purification) the young man is given into the care of two radiant creatures who conduct him through vast grottoes whose inhabitants, scenery, vegetation and abundant animal population are all meticulously described.

The ceremonies performed by those who boldly contemplate the terrors of the cavern and thus merit initiation draw their inspiration from the masonic cults that flourished among European intellectuals at the close of the eighteenth century (Mozart's librettist Schikaneder was to use a similar idea fourteen years later in *The Magic Flute*), but what makes the whole story characteristically Beckfordian is that the two main protagonists, the sage Moisasour and his beautiful female companion Nouronihar, a name Beckford was later to use in *Vathek*, are both orientals, the former a Brahmin, the latter an Indian princess, and the whole story is permeated with the atmosphere of the East in which 'Firenguis'—that is, Europeans—are not only strangers but rather unwelcome ones who must prove their worth in order to be accepted. Thus the narrator, having passed the initial test and been admitted into the presence of Moisasour as an initiate, feels that he must justify himself by an even greater trial. But his desire to be led into other worlds of danger and be purged by new terrors receives a chilling rebuke from the Brahmin: 'Repress so daring a curiosity. This last initiation is Death!'[14]

The manuscript of the 'Long Story' as it survives is incomplete, breaking off suddenly at a point where the narrator and Nouronihar have refreshed themselves with a banquet of 'the milk of cocoas and the juices of a thousand fruits' and the latter brings from the interior of a cave 'two large volumes covered with mystic writings' and begins to explain their contents. Here the text comes to a sudden end, either because it was never finished or because the concluding portion was lost or never transcribed.

Various aspects of Beckford's character are discovered in this story which shows, first and foremost, that by the age of seventeen he had already formed his literary style and had mastered the romantic idiom in which his exotic tale is expressed. The sense of guilt emerges at an early point. He imagines himself in a place where dwell 'haggard wretches abandoned by the mercy of Heaven' and seems to hear their cry: 'Hark! was not that their yell amongst the mountain peaks on high? No; it was but the wind thro' that time-worn crevice; but it was enough to chill my heart. And art thou so sunk, William! art thou reduced to the level of such as these? Is thy conscience troubled, is thy reason fled, fearest thou the harmless gust of air that makes mock melody amongst the cliffs?'[15]

We also find displayed the reluctance to grow up, to shoulder the responsibilities of manhood that increased as Beckford approached his majority and was coupled with a romantic idealisation of the innocence of childhood. Gazing at the moonlit scenery and musing that the one to whom his story is addressed may also be lost in contemplation of the same planet he writes: 'Yes, tho' so far distant, we may both regard this same object. With what pleasure then did I dwell upon its sight. Yet a little while and the cares of this vile earth will rob me of these serene enjoyments. A few years the projects of ambition, the sordid schemes of interest and all the occupations of the world must seclude from such meditations. No, I will resist them, I will repulse their influence if they rob me of meridian sunshine, if I must waste those hours in cabinets and councils, if the evenings must be sacrificed to debates and to watchful consultations, still they shall not rob me of the midnight moon. Then shall we walk and gather plants by her light and her soothing influence shall calm my soul.'[16]

Beckford's guilt feelings were allied to a sense of doom and self-destruction; feelings which had already started to haunt his thoughts, aided by the awareness of insecurity which this first prolonged separation from home influences had failed to banish. In his story this takes a familiar form: 'my eye fixed itself on something that bore the semblance of a pool, fed by the snow which melts from the mountains. Into this abyss will I plunge; I will extinguish the flame of Life, I will start into eternity; my curiosity shall be satisfied, I will know if . . . As I was moving to my destruction something held me back. I trembled; a cold chill froze my blood, my hair softened with a frigid sweat, my soul was shrivelled. I thought my good Angel interposed. I heard his instinct speak in me. "If Mercy has preserved thee from crimes must thou form them thyself, wilt thou work thy own ruin?" '[17]

The 'Long Story' is a curious document to come from a writer not yet eighteen years old. The morbid sensibility, the somewhat decadent air that pervades it, are all good reasons why its author was anxious that Alexander Cozens should not exhibit its pages to unsympathetic eyes. At the same time the flow of narrative, the flights of imagination, and the literary assurance with which it is composed are impressive. It is the work of a natural writer confident and at ease in his style.

Though the story as ultimately published is unfinished, there is the fragment of an oriental tale among Beckford's papers which might well be part of the concluding pages of the 'Long Story'.[18] In that story the Brahmin Moisasour can easily be traced back to Beckford's own father in his awe-inspiring presence and omniscient authority. In the fragment there is an episode which has a direct bearing on the Alderman's last months of life. It describes a scene where the representatives of a neighbouring power break in on the presence of King Kristna: 'After a solemn silence the eldest Sage arraigned the Monarch with his presumption and accused him of a guilty weakness in suffering himself to be adored. Kristna appalled by this sudden address, knew not how to carry himself, but his favourites immediately entering, delivered him from his perplexities. They rushed on the determined Old Men with the fury of Tygers and brutally deprived them of their existence.'

The parallel with Alderman Beckford and George III is obvious, but it throws an interesting light on the younger Beckford's thoughts about the whole episode. Did he blame the king indirectly for his father's death? It was common gossip at the time, as Horace Walpole recorded, that the Alderman's death was due to 'the agitation into which his violence had thrown his blood'. If Beckford himself held to this view it would account for the disrespectful manner in which he would sometimes refer to the king in later years. As Cyrus Redding was to remark: 'He had a very mean opinion of that monarch.' But if the episode tells us nothing else, it shows that his father's confrontation with the king and his death that followed so closely afterwards were still very much in his son's thoughts seven years later.

One of the most significant events for Beckford during the eighteen months he spent in Switzerland was the visit he paid with Lettice to the monastery of the Grande Chartreuse in June 1778. His mind prepared by reading Gray's ode, he approached the Carthusian retreat 'with as much awe as some novice or candidate newly arrived to solicit the holy retirement of the order'.[19]

On the ascent to the gateway he had as usual absorbed vivid impressions from the wild scenery and allowed his mind to play with the sombre and gloomy ideas suggested by thoughts of the stern life of silent renunciation endured by the monks whose cloister he was about to visit as a guest. 'In an hour's time we were drawing near', he recorded, 'and could discern the opening of a narrow valley overhung by shaggy precipices, above which rose lofty peaks, covered to their very summits with wood. We could now distinguish the roar of torrents, and a confusion of strange sounds, issuing from dark forests of pine. I confess at this moment I was somewhat startled. I experienced some disagreeable sensations, and it was not without a degree of unwillingness that I left the gay pastures and enlivening sunshine, to throw myself into this gloomy and disturbed region. How dreadful, thought I, must be the despair of those, who enter it, never to return!'

Beckford was received with the greatest courtesy by the acting superior of the community, all the more so because they had discovered that he was the present owner of Witham, in pre-reformation days one of the great houses of the Carthusian order in England. 'The secretary', Beckford noted, 'almost with tears in his eyes, beseeched me to revere those consecrated edifices, and to preserve their remains, for the sake of St. Hugo, their canonized prior. I replied greatly to his satisfaction, and then declaimed so much in favour of St. Bruno, and the holy prior of Witham, that the good fathers grew exceedingly delighted with the conversation, and made me promise to remain some days with them.'

Beckford's praise of St. Bruno, who had founded the Carthusian order in 1084, and for his English disciple, might at first sight seem insincere, as though no more than an attempt to impress his monastic hosts with his interest and erudition, but this would be a mistaken view. He was always able to absorb the special atmosphere of his surroundings and to react with complete (though perhaps not lasting) sincerity to the ethos of any place that struck a responding note of sympathy in his mind. The life of St. Bruno had much in it that appealed to his impressionable mind, not least the saint's dread of being condemned by the just judgement of God which had made him renounce the world and retire to the bleak solitude of Chartreuse. A considerable passage in Beckford's account of his visit to the monastery is taken up with a description of the life of its holy founder.[20]

He passed in all three days as the guest of the fathers, spending much of his time wandering through the surrounding woods and mountains, filling his mind with impressions of its austere grandeur. He was much struck by the architecture of the monastery itself which he described in some detail, noting especially the vistas of cloister and the effects of long ranges of windows. In particular he was fascinated by the glimmer of the altar lights in the monastic church as the gradually diminishing light of day threw the glowing altar into ever-brighter focus. 'The illumination of so many tapers', he wrote, 'striking on the shrines, censers, and pillars of polished jasper sustaining the canopy of the altar, produced a wonderful effect; and, as the rest of the chapel was visible only by the faint external light admitted from above, the splendour and dignity of the altar was enhanced by contrast. I retired a moment from it, and seating myself in one of the furthermost stalls of the choir, looked towards it, and fancied the whole structure had risen by "subtle magic" like an exhalation.' Many seeds were sown in his mind which would later bear fruit at Fonthill Abbey.

Beckford left the Grande Chartreuse with the blessing of the fathers who had clearly been won over, and perhaps a little led astray, by the vivid and congenial impression he had made, the Superior telling him that if he was ever disgusted with the world he could be assured of finding an asylum among them. A curious melancholy descended on his spirit as he started his journey home. 'We returned to Les Echelles,' he wrote, 'from thence to Chambery, and, instead of going through Aix, passed by Annecy; but nothing in all the route engaged my attention, nor had I any pleasing sensations till I beheld the glassy lake of Geneva, and its lovely environs.'

5

Wayward Passions

WHILE BECKFORD was indulging in the effects upon a refined
sensibility of exposure to the grandeur of the mountains or the
tranquillity of the lakes that surrounded his Genevan home, his
family in England, less tolerant of his moods and fancies, was
getting a bit worried about the direction his life was taking. His
sister, now Mrs. Hervey,[1] was the chief recipient of his confidences, but we may be sure that the contents of his letters to her
were soon passed on to the Begum who became perplexed and
anxious by some of the things she read. Her son's love of strange
by-paths of learning, of outlandish names and places, had not
been cured by the sharp air of Switzerland. What could she make
of a young man who instead of acquiring the manly attributes
suitable to a future member of Parliament could euologize to his
sister upon the perfections of Japanese art or, worse still, advise
her to cure a fit of melancholy by attending Mass for consolation?

But even worse was happening, did she but know it, in the city
where Calvin's shadow seemed to offer so little protection against
the temptations of the world and the flesh if not of the very Devil
himself; for by the shores of the lake of Geneva her son found
himself involved in a romantic entanglement with another youth.
That at the age of seventeen or eighteen Beckford should fall in
love was no more than might have been expected. That the object
of his affections should be another boy or youth was not so surprising as an alarmed parent might suppose, for the same thing
was surely happening in boarding schools and colleges all over the
country.

In Beckford's case the dangers, such as they were, in this little
affair sprang from the intensity of his response to any stimulation
of the senses, be it personal or artistic in origin. His conduct was
quite soon to show that his emotions were by no means anchored

solely to members of his own sex at this period of his life, but his propensity to extract the maximum emotional capital from any situation he found himself in tended to give an exaggerated importance to what was in reality no more than an adolescent infatuation.

For Beckford it was a fervid business of exchanged glances, meaningful looks and palpitating hearts; of one who seemed to hang on his words—'whose dark eyes drank eager draughts of pleasure from my sight, whose inmost soul was dissolved in tenderness when by chance he touched me, whose countenance was flushed with conscious blushes . . .' He noticed how the other lingered at parting from him, 'how he departed and returned, confused and not daring to confess for why . . .'[2] It was all very intense and probably equally innocent, but Beckford never troubled much to hide his feelings. Perhaps Colonel Hamilton intercepted some of those pregnant looks, some of those languishing glances, and the Begum was warned; or perhaps some maternal instinct urged her to come out to Geneva and bring her son back home. Whatever the reason, whether merely the evidence in the letters to his sister that those morbid interests the family so much deplored still prevailed, or whether from some hint of his emotional involvement we can but guess; something or someone sounded the alarm at Fonthill and his mother resolved to effect a rescue.

Beckford's own reason, given to his sister, for this rather sudden end to his sojourn in Switzerland was his health: 'My letter would scramble over ten more pages . . . but I have been indisposed lately and must not write any more. My Mother has taken the alarm. I expect her today bag and baggage.' In fact his health seems to have been rather good at this period, the illnesses of childhood were outgrown and left behind; and in any case Geneva was a better place to recoup one's health than Wiltshire. It was her son's spiritual health (that constant anxiety of hers) that had brought the Begum on her journey. She had been content for him to make the outward journey with no other companion but Lettice; now, in her apprehension over his welfare, she felt that she must come herself to see her wayward son safely home.

They set out in November 1778, not the best month for travel under the conditions prevailing at the time, but Mrs. Beckford was obviously impatient of delay. Beckford himself took his recall in good part and wrote to his sister in a jovial mood upon their arrival at Dover: 'Here we arrived last Night in a tottering condition after a most tedious passage of twelve hours during which you may reasonably conjecture our time was pretty well employed. I was fortunately able to own myself the idlest person on board and to lay dozing and gaping in the Cabbin whilst everybody else was contributing as much as lay in their power to the Sea. Your Mother bore the voyage admirably well. She is now as well as ever I saw her in my Life.'³

The eighteen months spent by Beckford in Switzerland had not been wasted in spite of his mother's abrupt decision to bring him home. From the purely educational point of view (and it had been to 'finish' his education that he had been sent out there) he had considerably widened the horizons of his knowledge. Apart from Jean Huber, Beckford had profited from other valuable contacts. As his biographer Dr. Oliver noted, 'the professors at the university included Mallet, the author of *Northern Antiquities*, and Horace Benedict de Saussure, physicist, geographer, and mountaineer, and author of *Voyages dans les Alpes*. With them Beckford soon came to be on friendly terms, while, outside the academic circle, he made the acquaintance of Charles de Connet, the naturalist and psychologist, of Jean Louis de Lolme, at that time regarded as the leading authority on the English Constitution,' and he had received instruction in experimental science from Monsieur D'Espinasse who had previously imparted similar knowledge to the young George III.⁴ He had also extended his natural gift for foreign languages. Already fluent in French he perfected his knowledge of Italian and added Portuguese and Spanish, while the use of certain words in the 'Long Story' suggest that he had also started to study some Arabic.

His love of nature and animal life (in the 'Long Story' all the animals are tame and free from the perils of the hunter) needed no development, but the grand scenery of the Alps with its lofty mountain peaks appealed strongly to his imagination. At least one of his letters to Cozens was written 'on the Summit of a lofty Mountain' from which he could 'gaze at an Assemblage of substantial Vapours' which hovered all around him.⁵ His desire to be placed in some high position, whether mountain top or tower, from where he could gaze serenely on the world below, detached and superior to its turmoil, which was to occur so often in his writings and musings, appears first in these letters. Isolated thus above the world and its problems he felt a security of spirit, a freedom from the calls of ambition or from the ordinary complexities of everyday existence.

Despite this desire for solitude and the need to feel himself lifted above the vulgar crowd, Beckford was by no means indifferent to the pleasures of company. It was here that he first found himself in a truly cosmopolitan world where conversation on intellectual topics was not despised. Here, free from the inhibiting possessiveness of his mother, he very quickly found himself at ease and able to shine, to be welcomed for his gifts of wit and mimicry, for all that he affected, as we have seen, a romantic indifference to social success. In Geneva he acquired the deportment and *savoir faire* of a man of the world.

But most of the qualities his family had hoped to see developed by this experience of travel and study had singularly failed to materialise. He showed not the slightest interest in politics or in the business of the great world, and confessed himself indifferent to the state of affairs between England and the American colonies, then at the very crisis of the war of independence.[6] Indeed he reacted with a sort of horror from the responsibilities of adult life. His ideal, adolescent and 'escapist', was summed up in another revealing passage from one of his Genevan letters to Cozens: 'Yes, that time may arrive when we may seek the green solitudes and roam about foreign Mountains, when we may sit together in such a Valley as I have described and gaze at the last gleams of departing Day. How should I delight to wander with you thro' remote Forests and pitch our Tents by Moonlight in a Wilderness. Then would we observe the Deer bounding over the Lawn and the Goats frisking on the margin of a Stream without a wish to disturb their happiness. Neither the Gun, the Arrow or the Net should be in our hands. We would cultivate some pastures and in the season gather ripe Corn sown by ourselves. Every week we would vary our abode and sleep upon Hills in the twilights of Midsummer, there to catch the Dream of inspiration from whence to presage the events of future Times ... Why might we not penetrate into unknown Regions, long concealed from the eyes of Man? Might we not arrive in new Countries by following the course of Rivers and tracing them thro' all their windings to their Source ...? Am I addressing myself to a Spirit that catches fire at my own Enthusiasm? If there exists one that would partake such a wild excursion it is yours ...'[7]

And those morbid thoughts, those exotic dreams that held for the Begum such warning of peril, had grown rather than diminished during his eighteen months abroad. Even at the Grande

C

Chartreuse in some lines he wrote in the visitors' book he
recalled that

> *the midnight bell*
> *Had toll'd each silent inmate from his cell;*
> *The hour was come to muse or pray,*
> *Or work mysterious rites that shun the day,*

as though the good fathers of St. Bruno might introduce a little
necromancy between Vespers and Compline.[8] This preoccupation
with mysterious rites (also a feature of the 'Long Story') had found
its setting in gothic castles or monasteries hidden on the slopes of
wooded hills which, in contrast to the Palladian symmetry of
Fonthill Splendens, encouraged all manner of extravagant or
fanciful reveries.

It was, therefore, not so much a budding politician as a professed Romantic who returned to England in November 1778,
steeped in the thoughts, proficient in the idiom, and master of the
attitude to life that characterised the movement then dawning in
Europe which drew its inspiration from the passions and emotions, which cultivated an awareness for poetry and the picturesque, and indulged freely in moods, whims and visions. He came
home, in short, less a disciple of Voltaire, whom he had seen
'sometimes', than of Rousseau, whom he had not seen at all. His
character was set in a pattern which would change very little for
the remainder of his life. 'I am determined to enjoy my dreams,
my phantasies and all my singularity, however irksome and discordant to the worldlings round me,' he noted that December, 'In
spite of them, I will be happy . . .'[9]

During the winter months he mooned about the estate at Fonthill living up to this romantic ideal. It was, of course, to Alexander
Cozens that he wrote of his determination to enjoy his dreams, and
over four thousand words were poured out on 4 December ('being
the full of the moon') to show that he could be taken at his word.

'The Dusk approaches,' he begins. 'I am musing on the Plain
before the House which my Father reared. No cheerful illuminations appear in the Windows, no sounds of Musick issue from the
Porticos, no gay Revellers rove carelessly along the Colonades;
but all is dark, silent and abandoned. Such Circumstances suit the
present tone of my mind. Did I behold a number of brilliant
Equipages rattling across the Lawn, or hear the confused buzz of
animated Conversation, or were a peal of Laughter to reach my

Ears or were they assaulted by shouts of hilarity and Joy, should I not fly to the woods for consolation and bury myself in their gloom to enjoy solitude in security? You are the *human Being* to whom I have discovered the strangeness of my fancies; for you can feel as well as myself the melancholy pleasures of wandering alone in the Dusk over Plains of green sward, bordered on one side by Hills of Oak and on the other by a broad River whose opposite Shore presents distant Glens and pastures, wild Copses and Groves of pines to which the Twilight gives an additional Solemnity. I surveyed my native prospects with fraternal affection and looked fondly at every tree as if we had been born in the same hour. The Air I breathed seemed nearer of Kin to me than that I had elsewhere respired; in short the hills, the Woods, the Shrubs, the very Moss beneath my feet entered into this general Alliance and I fancied myself surrounded by an assembly of my best friends and nearest Relations. Of what other Company then could I be ambitious?'

Lost in contemplation he leans against a tree before finally returning to the house while the bats flit before him and the owl 'according to the mythology of Birds, quitted his haunt and hastened to perform incantations'.

Back at Splendens he lapses once more into his imaginary world: 'I then ascended the steps which lead into a vast hall paved with Marble and seating myself, like the Orientals, on Cushions of Brocade placed by a blazing fire was served with Tea and a species of white bread which has crossed the *Atlantic*. Meanwhile my thoughts were wandering into the interior of Africa and dwelt for hours on those Countries I love. Strange tales of Mount Atlas and relations of Travellers amused my fancy. One instant I imagined myself viewing the marble palaces of Ethiopean princes seated on the green woody margin of lakes, studded in sands and wildernesses, the next transported me to the Rocks of *Carena* where Atlantes strove vainly to preserve Rugiero from the Perils of War. Some few minutes after, I found myself standing before a thick wood listening to impetuous waterfalls and screened from the Ardour of the Sun by its foliage. I was wondering at the Scene when a tall comely Negro wound along the slopes of the Hills and without moving his lips made me comprehend I was in Africa, on the brink of the *Nile* beneath the Mountains of *Amara*. I followed his steps thro' an infinity of vales, all skirted with Rocks and blooming with aromatic Vegetation, till we arrived at the hollowed Peak and after exploring a Labyrinth of paths, which led to its summit, a wide Cavern appeared before us. Here I surveyed landscapes of the most romantic Cast, tasted such fruits and scented such perfumes as ravished my senses. I was all Delight and amazement . . .' and so on for page after page of what he very truthfully described in the phrase: 'Such are my phantastic visions and such the flights of my fancy when Reason has abandoned it.'

How did Cozens respond to all these outpourings? Certainly not with a rebuke for had he done so the letters would have ceased, the relationship cooled. No word of reply, of advice, of praise or criticism has survived. His figure remains tantalisingly mysterious. But for Mrs. Beckford the sight of her son wandering listlessly about the park or lost in day-dreams by the fireside was provoking in the extreme. Why, she must have asked herself, was he not in the stables, or riding to hounds, or finding fault with the Government's policy in America, or even concerning himself with the problems of West Indian trade? What of the great career in Parliament that she had planned for him? He seemed hardly aware that with his coming majority two parliamentary seats would be dependent on his patronage; or if aware, he seemed wholly indifferent to the prestige and influence this conferred upon him. Was this proper behaviour for the heir of Alderman Beckford and the godson of Lord Chatham?

Another change of scene was all that the combined ingenuity of the Fonthill *camarilla* could suggest as an antidote to these strange moods. A tour of England was envisaged this time; a visit to some of the great country houses and to various relations scattered about the land as well as to some of the growing centres of industry. It was hoped that an introduction to the great houses, a closer glimpse at the patrician way of life that flourished behind their classical porticos or crenellated battlements might reconcile the heir of Fonthill to his fate; a fate very enviable in terms of wealth and opportunity as it must have appeared to most of those whom he was about to meet.

A comprehensive plan was drawn up for the young traveller to include the West Country, Plymouth, Exeter (from where he could visit his distant relations the Courtenays of Powderham), Bath, Gloucester, then Birmingham and Lichfield; Derbyshire with its famous noble seats would be a prelude to industrial Liverpool and Manchester; then Lancashire, the Lakes of Westmorland, and back via York to London and so home to Fonthill. Lettice, as usual, would travel with him.

They set out in the summer of 1779. Various adventures befell the pair as they travelled about the country. In Plymouth, tense with troops as the combined French and Spanish fleets cruised off the coast, they were nearly arrested for being spies and only the fact that Beckford was known to the military commander saved them from an awkward situation. At Birmingham they visited an engineering works and saw that wonder of the day, a steam engine used to power the factory. In Lancashire they crossed over Morecambe Bay on the sand at low tide, excitedly conscious that delay might cause them to be trapped in the great swirl of water that rushes up the narrowing estuary with the incoming tide. The lakes appealed at once to Beckford's aesthetic sense and he imagined himself leading 'a wild and savage life' there, fishing for sustenance, a notion that evoked only hesitating acquiescence from the prudent Lettice. Three months, he considered, was quite long enough for such a life among the Lakes. York Minster filled Beckford with admiration and 'the most religious sensations'. Overwhelmed by a sense of unworthiness he fled its walls and 'casting one more look at the Tombs of their revered Founders, left them to sleep in peace.'[10]

On the face of it the tour had been a success, but the Begum's plans, in so far as her son was concerned, had a way of going awry, for in the course of his progress round England Beckford had formed another sentimental attachment, innocent enough in its beginnings, which would in due time bring about his social ruin. The scene was Powderham Castle near Exeter where he had broken his journey in order to visit his Courtenay relatives.

It was a curious household. At the head of it was Viscount Courtenay, a merry but trivial-minded man who had considered it no disgrace to one of the most ancient lineages in Europe to take in marriage the hand of a Wallingford tavern-owner's daughter who had duly presented him with twelve daughters before producing an heir to his name and title. In this almost exclusively feminine nursery it is not surprising that the sole male inhabitant, named William after his father, was somewhat pampered and effeminate with the rather girlish good looks that did not quarrel with the nick-name of 'Kitty' that was soon to be bestowed upon him. The boy's mother, almost constantly in some stage of pregnancy, was in no position to dominate her household or family, and many of the wifely duties had devolved upon Lord Courtenay's sister Charlotte, then still unmarried. No sooner had Beckford set eyes on the young William Courtenay than he fell in love with him, while the boy's aunt Charlotte found much to admire in the undoubted attractions of their visitor. To be in love with the nephew and not to be unaware of the admiration of the aunt was a situation very much to Beckford's taste.

William Courtenay was at this time eleven years old. At the beginning there was nothing carnal in Beckford's feeling for him, and possibly never was at any period. His adoration, which was certainly deep though also very self-indulgent, is difficult to explain in view of the strange lack of personality shown by the object of his affection, both then and later. His character was shallow and he seemed to have few positive qualities; he was to develop into a singularly worthless individual. But Beckford at once discovered in him that much-needed characteristic—'you are the only person (yes, let me repeat it once more) to whom I can communicate my feelings'—a 'unique' quality that had already been admired in Alexander Cozens and was to be found later on in others.

Someone who must ever be the recipient of the poured-out feelings and impressions of another must of necessity be passive and faceless. At nineteen Beckford himself was still sexually am- bivalent and the element of physical love hardly applied to his relations with Courtenay; the latter, however, had another quality that Beckford prized but could not in himself possess—his childishness. As Beckford saw his own childhood recede he was caught in a sort of panic. He longed to regain the lost innocence, the freedom from moral responsibility that only a child can claim. 'How firmly am I resolved to be a Child for ever', he was signifi- cantly to write to Cozens a year later.[11] In Courtenay he saw an image of what he himself wished to be and was so much in love with the reflection that he failed to notice any defect in the mirror.

Back at Fonthill he committed to paper a long disjointed soliloquy addressed, but not sent, to the absent Courtenay, in which he attempted to give expression to the tumult of feeling which his new friend's image aroused in his soul.

After confessing that young William was the only person to whom he could communicate these feelings, to whom he could disclose 'the strange wayward passion' that throbbed in his bosom, he continued in a series of breathless sentences covering many pages: 'All those who surround me—view me pale—faltering—dejected—desponding—they know not why. What is the matter with you, cries my Mother—tell me for Heaven's sake what oppresses you? Have you not every circumstance, every means of happiness in your power—tell me what I can procure for your amusement—shall I instantly command a glittering equipage—shall I invite company—or will you accept the numerous invitations which lie scattered upon your table—speak, only speak your wishes and they shall be gratified . . .'

One has, indeed, a great deal of sympathy for the Begum who, after the failure (as it must have seemed to her) of the Geneva venture, now found her son returned from his tour of England in an even more dejected mood than that which prevailed before he set out. Her entreaty is brushed aside; the moment she turns away her son is again lost in reverie: 'my imagination bounds, not during these her holiday moments over the woods of Greece and Indian Solitudes, but flies to that western country—that blue river—and variegated shore where first I beheld the object of all my tenderness—and of all my present anxiety . . . Great power—who created us both, how rapid was the progress of our affection! Surely we must have been inseparable friends in some other existence. We must have doubtless shared the happiness and misery of some other world—or else why did we experience this sudden love for each other. Did it not increase each hour, and when I quitted his native castle—what expressive melancholy looks were cast after one down the long avenue . . . During the whole journey that evening no other object filled my mind . . . O Heavens, what conflicts—what unknown sensations tore me fifty different ways at once . . .'

He then describes a dream (a dream, it may be noted, that has some resemblance to his 'Long Story') in which he and Courtenay are sealed off from the rest of the world to enjoy a secret and perpetually youthful existence together. 'I seemed stretched in a dreary cave—across which ran several bubbling streams—no termination of the Grot was visible—its roof was lost in obscurity—heaps of cocoa-nuts were piled—to all appearances around me—so immense that whole nations I think could never have consumed them. You ask me perhaps how I saw these wonders in so profound and spacious a grotto into which no ray had ever penetrated. Recollect that internal—visionary light—which illuminates dreams—and your surprise will cease. I had not long surveyed this Realm of Darkness and silence before an Angelic Shadow issued suddenly from the depth of the cavern leading in its hand the one I love—he flew to me. I sprang forwards to catch him in my arms. Rest happy, said a thrilling voice—no one shall disturb you for ages. The great power—source of all felicity—has abstracted you both from the multitude of his creatures—as examples of perpetual tenderness—and has alloted this cave—sunk deep in the centre of the Earth, for your abode. These piles of nuts are destined for your nourishment—if ye freely renounce the lustre of the Sun for each other. Our transports proved how entirely we consented. The shadow vanished—all was still and silent —the form of my Courtenay alone was luminous—his voice the only sound which echoed thro' out the cavern. I awoke—just as I stretched out my hand for a nut—and behold no Courtenay was near . . .'[12]

One may wonder how young Courtenay himself responded to all this ardour. No doubt the constant attentions, the sense of being the chief object of the devotion of this handsome man eight years his senior was flattering to a nature already somewhat feminine. Beckford could talk in such a way that would hold a child spellbound, and the endearments, the embraces (there seems to have been little more), were perhaps not totally unacceptable to a child brought up the only brother of twelve doting sisters. That Beckford's influence on Courtenay might have been unwholesome or harmful never once occurred to him. He hoped to improve the boy's mind, to help him in every aspect of life as a means towards his lofty but essentially adolescent conception of divine friendship. It was a dangerous course he had embarked upon and he was totally unaware of the danger. For him Courtenay represented a type of spiritual love. Sensual love was soon to find expression in a more tempestuous but more 'normal' relationship.

The autumn and winter of 1779–80 were spent at Fonthill. There was the excitement of seeing the *Biographical Memoirs of Extraordinary Painters* through the press, and the discovery of Goethe's *Sorrows of Werther* which he found entirely to his mood. 'Read it', he urged Cozens, 'and tell me if every line is not resplendent with Genius.'[13] But for most of the time his thoughts were at Powderham. As a distraction he hoped that Cozens might be able to spend Christmas with them, but for once his friend was unable to oblige him. 'What are the Indian Apartments to me, now I am assured you cannot view them?' Beckford wrote to him on

Christmas Eve, 'You would pity me, could some Spirit transport you to this solitary Chamber where I lie stretched on the Carpets—pining.'

There was, however, another distraction at Fonthill that Christmas; one placed there, perhaps, by the assiduous Begum in her attempts to rescue her son from his gloomy and petulant fits. 'I have not spirits to write ten lines', a letter just after Christmas informed Cozens. 'My only consolation is to hear Louisa and her Sister sing.'[14]

It was significant that Beckford only mentioned the name of one of the sisters; the other, Marcia, clearly had little attraction for him. They were connections of his godfather Lord Chatham, the daughters of George Pitt who in 1776 had been raised to the peerage as Lord Rivers. Louisa was six years older than Beckford, and since 1773 had been the wife of his cousin Peter. Though Peter Beckford was a sympathetic man (his book on hunting had delighted Horace Walpole) the marriage was not a great success. Louisa found little in common with a husband fourteen years her senior whose interests lay in field sports, classical scholarship, and what passes generally under the heading of country pursuits.

She had a statuesque beauty, an ardent temperament, and an acute, rather feverish sensibility heightened by the early stages of tuberculosis. She was intelligent, preferred the town to the country but was compelled to spend most of her time in the latter, and was bored by the hunting squires who formed the chief society at her husband's country house at Stapleton in Dorset. Bored and frustrated, she was in the mood for amorous adventure. In her cousin William she saw, not the outgrown schoolboy she might well have expected to see, but a self-assured young man of handsome appearance, short but well made, grey-eyed and very conscious of his physical charm. In no time she had fallen passionately in love with him. It was to develop into an extravagant, consuming passion as far as her side of the affair was concerned. At first Beckford was no more than interested, a little flattered, and also in the mood for a flirtation. But if he intended it to be no more than another 'wayward passion' then he had seriously miscalculated the strength of the fire he had kindled in Louisa's breast.

There was more than a mutual boredom and frustration to draw them together. Both shared an interest in magic, and their talk was full of references to spells, talismans, incantations and sorcery, those strange paths along which Beckford may have first been led by Alexander Cozens and which, in a mild way, were very much *à la mode* just then. It was, after all, the age of Cagliostro, who had first visited London less than ten years before and whose mountebank career still flourished on the continent. Louisa, too, had the gift of catching her companion's moods, of listening in a rapt way to his monologues, and of returning his ecstatic utterances in the same coin. Did they read *Werther* together? Certainly they had soon cast themselves in the roles of star-crossed lovers, though only Beckford was playing a part. Louisa had no little Courtenay to distract her from her infatuation. There was a note of desperation in her need for sympathy and love, a suppressed hysteria which only later came to the surface.

Some sort of understanding had been established between them by the time Louisa's visit came to an end, the nature of which is clear from the letter Beckford sent to her from Fonthill in January 1780. 'Every day I have been waiting impatiently to hear from you, my lovely Louisa,' he wrote, 'and every Post has brought me some new disappointment. Fonthill is darkly shaded and all its charms overcast since no Letters have arrived from you. It is in your power by writing a Talisman to dissipate the gloom of its Cells, and will you refuse this consolation? I fancy I am not the least altered if you are not—the same genuine melancholy and thorough contempt of the World inspires me to remain in solitude and silence. Visions play around me and at some solemn moments I am cast into prophetic Trances. Lost in Dreams and majic slumbers my Hours glide swiftly away. I have none to awaken me —none to sympathize with my feelings. Those I love are absent. Thus desolate and abandoned I seek refuge in aerial conversations and talk with spirits whose voices are murmuring in the Gales. They are my Councellors—from them I hear of past and future events—they sing of departed Seers and Heroes and bring me Indian intelligence, but not one syllable have they whispered about you—why then are you the only superior Being who is deaf to me and silent . . .?'[15]

It was a very Beckfordian letter with its familiar imagery of dreams and visions, its references to melancholy and contempt for the world, but it was not the sort of letter to fall into the hands of a jealous husband. But then reticence and discretion had never been included in Beckford's complement of virtues.

In the quiet of his winter retreat at Fonthill in the early months of 1780 he could look back on a year in which his inclination for 'wayward passions' had been given a full rein. That anonymous Swiss youth was forgotten, though as late as August he had still recalled 'that voice, those thrilling accents sunk with such pleasing pain, such melancholy tenderness, into the inmost recesses of my existence.'[16] Those available recesses were now filled with thoughts of William Courtenay while the image of Louisa crept into such crevices as remained untenanted. But even so the need for 'the only Human Being who is worthy of our discourse' remained unfulfilled and still nagged at him, still left him feeling discontented and at a loss. 'How I long to see you to tell you a thousand things I cannot write', a letter informed Cozens early in February. 'Indeed, you are the only Being upon this Planet in whose bosom I can deposit every thought which enters mine.'[17]

6
Grand Tour

BEFORE THE FRENCH REVOLUTION changed the habits of the aristocratic classes the Grand Tour was considered an essential part of a young man's education, and at a period when neither Oxford nor Cambridge were noted for intellectual vigour, probably did more to open young eyes to the world of culture and civilisation than either university could have done. 'A man who has not been in Italy', as Dr Johnson remarked, 'is always conscious of an inferiority, from his not having seen what it is expected a man should see.'

The Begum's prejudice against the English seats of learning did not extend to the institution of the Grand Tour. Even the alarms she had felt during the latter months of her son's stay in Geneva were not sufficient to impose a ban on this more extended experience of foreign lands and customs. Perhaps, in her heart, she was glad to get rid for a time of the listless and melancholy youth who responded with such little enthusiasm to any of her suggestions for amusement or useful occupation. She must have noticed the growing sympathy between Beckford and his cousin Louisa, and though this was better than the sentimental attachment to the little Courtenay boy, it was clearly not to be encouraged. A change would be welcome and, who knows, perhaps her son might even yet develop an interest in public affairs and come back from his inspection of foreign courts and constitutions ready to take his place in the political life of his own country.

Meanwhile, until her son was ready to start on his travels in June 1780, she continued to press upon him her plans for his future; that career she expected him to pursue in parliament in accordance with the traditions of his family and (as she saw it) his clear duty as an English gentleman of influence and fortune.

From Beckford's point of view this was all so much waste

of time. Politics, party, war, peace, this was all the business of
'Frenguis' (he spelt the word various ways[1]) which for him meant
all people whose attitude of mind was foreign to his own way of
thinking. 'The news of the World affects me not half so much as
the chirping of a sparrow, or the rustling of withered leaves', he
confessed to Cozens in a letter of 13 March. 'What care I, who
pass my morning in groves and my evenings in a quiet cell,
whether this ship is taken, or t'other escape, provided the rout of
Frenguis squabble at a distance! Ambition at present lies dormant
in my breast and far from envying the triumphs of others, I
exult in my happy tho' inglorious leisure. I wish not to eclipse
those who retail the faded flowers of parliamentary eloquence. My
senate house is a wood of pines, from whence, on a misty evening,
I watch the western sky streaked with portentous red, whilst
awful whispers amongst the boughs above me, foretell a series of
strange events and melancholy times.'[2]

There are indications in Beckford's letters written while abroad
that before leaving England both Cozens and Louisa had been
admitted to the secret of his love for William Courtenay. It must
always have been something of an open secret, for Beckford had
still not learnt to dissemble his feelings, especially in the close
circle of his family. Everyone at Fonthill must have been aware
that his little cousin at Powderham was his particular favourite,
but only his mother, with her knowledge of the Genevan episode,
could have guessed that there was perhaps a dangerous element in
his infatuation. For this reason alone she must have been eager to
see him set off on his travels.

Cozens, first among the 'only' people to whom Beckford could
unbosom himself, must have received the news at an early stage.
He appears to have accepted it in his usual calm, amoral way.
There is nothing to indicate that he actively encouraged Beckford's 'wayward passions' in this particular case, nor is there
anything to suggest that he did not. His position remains enig-
matic. Later on, when the situation became more intense, he was
ready to act as a go-between and must therefore have given his
tacit approval to the affair, but whether because he sympathised
with the situation or simply because, as a man of the world, he
considered the intimate relationships of the man who was his
patron and former pupil to be none of his business (and it to be
very much his business to remain on good terms with him) is an
open question.

For Louisa to be told that however 'grand' their passion it must always take second place to her lover's affection for an effeminate schoolboy (for so Courtenay must have appeared to her) was indeed a bitter pill to swallow. If she had been less smitten herself by Cupid's dart this information alone should have opened her eyes to the fact that Beckford's feelings for her were not really deep, that he was still emotionally immature. To accept such a condition would be humiliating to anyone; that Louisa did accept it, even at this early stage when their relationship had gone little beyond the limits of a fashionable flirtation, shows that her feelings, at least, were already committed. If these were Beckford's terms for their continued intimacy then she was prepared to accept them. She was even able to put up some show of affectionate interest in the child who was soon to become 'Kitty' or 'the Dove' in her correspondence with the man she loved.

Thus as Beckford set off for London in June on the first lap of his Grand Tour he was leaving behind him a complicated emotional tangle. In Dorset, bored and irritated by her husband and finding, it would seem, little comfort in her children, Louisa Beckford fretted at his departure and longed only for his return while a more balanced temperament might have taken the opportunity of his absence to cure itself of a passion that had little hope of real fulfilment. In Devon, William Courtenay basked in the flattering attentions of an exciting friendship while his aunt Charlotte nursed the disappointment of an amatory attraction that had not been returned. To one of these two women Beckford was completely indifferent except in so far as she was a relation of his beloved Courtenay; for the other his feelings were no more than superficial, a dramatisation of romance rather than the reality of love. Only for the boy had he convinced himself of a feeling of genuine passion; for the boy who was unable, if only on account of his youthfulness and emotional inexperience, to return his love with anything like the same degree of ardour or intensity, or indeed of really comprehending what it was all about. It was fortunate for all concerned that Beckford was leaving the country.

London offered immediate and unexpectedly violent distraction to the travellers, for Lettice was once again Beckford's companion. Their arrival coincided with the outbreak of the Gordon riots, that strange manifestation of Protestant hysteria led by the eccentric and unstable Lord George Gordon, when for six days and nights the capital was given over to the tender mercies of the mob who pillaged and burnt Catholic churches and terrorised all who practised, or were thought to practise, the Roman religion. Beckford found a strange fascination in the scene of fire and devastation, confessing many years later to Cyrus Redding that apart from humane considerations he could have viewed the vast conflagration 'with the eye of an artist' feeling positive delight at the grandeur of the picture. Only the thought of the possible loss of life tempered these artistic sensations.[3] Meanwhile, he reacted in genuine horror at the savageness of the punishment visited on the offenders by Alexander Wedderburn, who had that very year been appointed Chief Justice of the Court of Common Pleas with the title of Lord Loughborough. It was a name that Beckford would later come to hate for other reasons.

A somewhat ludicrous sequel to his experience of the Gordon riots occurred a few days afterwards. Some old friends of his father's, members of the political opposition, suggested that they should put in an appearance at Court lest they should be accused of thinking too well of the rioters if they neglected this loyal duty.

Beckford went along with them to the king's levee, being introduced into the royal presence by his uncle, Sir George Howard, a general who had married his aunt Elizabeth after she had been left a widow by Lord Effingham in 1763. The king entered from his private apartments shortly after they had arrived and going up to General Howard, who had commanded some of the troops used to suppress the rioters, accosted him in his curious blustering way with the remark: 'Ah, Howard, glad to see you—peppered them well, I hope—peppered them well!' If the remark was not a model royal utterance it was also not unnatural in the context of the anxious and indeed alarming few days they had all just passed through, but Beckford later used it as an example of the lack of sensitivity and callousness of the monarch whom his father had once been bold enough to rebuke. 'This remark was thought coarse,' he commented when recounting the story, 'as many persons were killed and wounded . . . and in any case not a thing to be spoken lightly of by a sovereign in the hearing of so many persons. Sir George felt it, and gravely replied, "I trust your Majesty's troops will always do their duty." '[4]

In later life, for all his protestations of being on the side of the people (an opinion he owed to his father's memory), Beckford was not above thinking that the troops should be called out against the mob, especially during the troubled years following the Napoleonic wars. Had the remark he so affected to dislike been made by anyone other than George III he might well have recorded it without comment.

A more agreeable episode of his stay in London was an encounter with Samuel Johnson. John Lettice was responsible for introducing his young charge into the formidable presence, for he had made the doctor's acquaintance in Cambridge many years before. No record survives of the meeting beyond the fact of its having taken place.[5] As in the case of Voltaire, Beckford and Johnson met within a few short years of the latter's death and they never appear to have met again; the only significance of the event lies in the fact that the paths of the author of *Rasselas* and of the future author of *Vathek* did once briefly cross. There would, indeed, be little ground for sympathy between them. Johnson had a thorough hatred of slavery as a result of which, as Boswell declared, 'his violent prejudice against our West-Indian and American settlers appeared whenever there was an opportunity.' Alderman Beckford's son was probably lucky to have escaped without some resounding snub. As it was a few civilities were exchanged but the doctor remained morose and uncommunicative.

These London diversions were a mere prelude to the main business of the Grand Tour. Beckford and Lettice left the city on June 19, the former's mind in a whirl of romantic anticipation. He was determined to savour his new experiences to the full and offer his impressions to the world. Already he had felt the pride of authorship with the publication of his skit on extraordinary painters; now he hoped to offer a more serious work to the world—the 'dreams' and 'waking thoughts' evoked by the strange sights and novel adventures that lay ahead. While still on English soil the first notes were struck as he headed for Margate after visiting Canterbury cathedral: 'Don't ask me what were my dreams thither:—nothing but horrors, deep vaulted tombs, and pale though lovely figures extended upon them; shrill blasts that sung in my ears, and filled me with sadness, and the recollection of happy hours, fleeted away, perhaps for ever!'[6]

An extensive itinerary had been planned and the travellers were not to return until the following April, a period of ten months. They would visit the Netherlands, various German electorates and principalities, and parts of the Austrian dominions before reaching 'long-desired Italy' where they were to remain from the end of July 1780 until January 1781. The return journey took them by way of Augsburg to Strassburg, across France to Paris, and so back to England.

The crossing from Margate was stormy and they landed at Ostend 'in a piteous condition', which perhaps accounts for the poor view Beckford took of that famous port which he dismissed as being 'but a scurvy place', the whole atmosphere impregnated with the fumes of tobacco, burnt peat and garlic. It was a relief to pass on to Antwerp. They arrived there in the evening, which was Beckford's favourite hour for forming his first impressions of a town, for he usually planned things so that they reached the more important cities just as dusk was falling as he loved to discover new objects and places by 'this dubious, visionary light'.[7]

After the tumult and uproar of a London given over to the mob it was refreshing to find himself surrounded by the calm and profound repose of this Flemish city, and he indulged in one of those impressionistic passages which were to characterise his travel journals and make his accounts so different from the usual topographical observations of eighteenth-century travellers. 'As night approached,' he wrote, 'the ranges of buildings grew more and more dim, and the silence which reigned amongst them more awful. The canals, which in some places intersect the streets, were likewise in perfect solitude, and there was just light sufficient for me to observe on the still waters the reflection of the structures above them. Except two or three tapers glimmering through the casements, no one circumstance indicated human existence. I might, without being thought very romantic, have imagined myself in the city of petrified people which Arabian fabulists are so fond of describing. Were anyone to ask my advice upon the subject of retirement, I should tell them—by all means repair to Antwerp.'

These Arabian reflections, so curiously conjured up by the canals and gothic houses of Antwerp, were interrupted by the sight of another Beckfordian symbol which seemed to compel his attention; he found himself 'insensibly' drawn towards the cathedral whose stupendous tower shot up four hundred and sixty-six feet into the air. Fantasy now took another no less characteristic turn: 'The sky being perfectly clear, several stars twinkled through the mosaic of the spire, and added not a little to its enchanted effect. I longed to ascend it that instant, to stretch myself out upon its very summit, and calculate, from so sublime an elevation, the influence of the planets.'[8]

Though Beckford found many things to fascinate him in Holland and Germany, visiting collections of works of art, paying his respects to the shrine of the Magi in Cologne ('this step was inevitable; had I omitted it, not a soul in Cologne but would have cursed me for a Pagan'), watching a raft on the Rhine at least three hundred feet long on which ten or twelve cottages were erected, and wishing that he could build a similar floating village and people it with his friends, seeing the palace of Nymphenburg at Munich with its baroque pavilions 'all of a glitter with gilded Cupids and shining serpents spouting at every pore', it was always the thought of Italy that kept him hurrying south, giving no more than a 'transient look' at the treasures of the Emperor Maximilian's tomb at Innsbruck, eventually, in his impulsive haste travelling all night—'such being my impatience' he wrote almost breathlessly, 'to reach the promised land!'

Bolsano was reached on 29 July and Beckford began to notice a change in the landscape, the irrigation terraces thick with figs and melons, pomegranates and clusters of fruit hanging over garden walls; it was the first indication of approaching Italy. At dawn next day they galloped into Trent where a few hours sleep were snatched before pressing on with their journey after the worst heat of the day was over. On the last day of the month the great moment came and Italy lay before him in all its beauty. 'My heart beat quick', he wrote, 'when I saw some hills, not very distant, which I was told lay in the Venetian State, and I thought an age, at least, had elapsed before we were passing their base.'

Every educated eighteenth-century traveller was prepared by his training in the classics to appreciate the historical and artistic heritage of Italy. In this Beckford was no different from his contemporaries, and his volatile temperament responded at once to the architecture, the ruins of antiquity, and the great masterpieces of painting and sculpture which every Grand Tourist visited as a matter of duty though not all of them, alas, with the enthusiasm which Beckford genuinely felt for most of what he saw. Where he differed from others was in his response to the beauty of the landscape. He found as much to arrest his attention in the countryside which separated the various points on his route as he was to find in the galleries and 'cabinets' that came under his already critical observation in the towns and cities.

His very first impression of Italy, indeed, was of the physical
beauty of the land itself before he had so much as seen a picture,
inspected the frescoes of a church, or trodden the pavement of
some classical ruin; and it was this that made him feel instantly at
home there. 'It was now', he wrote as his eyes took in their first
sight of this promised land, 'I beheld groves of olives, and vines
clustering the summits of the tallest elms; pomegranates in every
garden, and vases of citron and orange before almost every door.
The softness and transparency of the air soon told me I was
arrived in happier climates; and I felt the sensations of joy and
novelty run through my veins, upon beholding this smiling land
of groves and verdure stretched out before me.'

This love of nature, which was so fundamental a part of his
character, was in fact almost certainly to be the saving of him in
the months that lay ahead, for in the course of his stay in Italy,
over and above the impressions made on a highly-strung nervous
system by all it had to offer in terms of cultural stimulation, he was
to involve himself in an emotional tangle of truly Beckfordian
complication from which (at least until he reached Naples) the
calming effects of nature formed his only means of escape. The
'visionary and Elysian' landscape was to be for him in Italy what
the woods of Fonthill had been in England, a symbol of sanity,
refreshment, and peaceful solitude.

Mestre was reached on 2 August and from there the travellers
continued by gondola across the lagoon to Venice, finding the
gentle motion of the boat an agreeable contrast to the jolting of
the post-chaise. It was evening, according to Beckford's custom,
and in the gathering dusk they passed by the islands of Murano and
St. Michele which he recognised from the innumerable prints
and drawings he had studied. Then the island city itself appeared
more closely to view and as the gondola glided forwards they
'every moment distinguished some new church or palace in the
city, suffused with the rays of the setting sun, and reflected with all
their glow of colouring from the surface of the waters'.

Venice, though long in decline, was still capital of the Most
Serene Republic whose penultimate independent ruler, Paolo
Renier, had been elected Doge only the year before. The state over
which he ruled had long ceased to have much international significance and the city itself had sunk into decadence, a last cadence of
luxury and pleasure-seeking before the ultimate crash of defeat
and humiliation in the face of revolution and military aggression

that lay less than twenty years ahead. The aristocratic and leisured classes, lost in *ennui*, had energy for little more than a game of cards; many lived in poverty or contrived to secure meagre pensions from an almost bankrupt state. The great navy that once policed the Adriatic and Mediterranean scarcely existed any more and the merchant fleet was no longer the feared rival of other commercial powers. 'One solitary galeass', Beckford wrote, 'was all I beheld, anchored opposite the palace of the Doge and surrounded by crowds of gondolas, whose sable hues contrasted strongly with its vermilion oars and shining ornaments.' It was a city that dreamt of the past, lived only to enjoy the present, and gave no thought at all to the future.

Beckford, in his romantic mood, discovered much to allure him in this place of faded charms and melancholy decay, but in more energetic moments found himself decidedly irritated by a people who seemed to have given themselves over entirely to 'cards and stupidity'. His chief guides to the pleasures of Venice were a rather *louche* couple, the Contessa d'Orsini-Rosenberg and her *cicisbeo* Count Bartolommeo Benincasa. The contessa, born a member of the distinguished Welsh family of Wynne, was then in her mid-forties, a former associate of Casanova and now the lively widow of a previous Austrian envoy to the Venetian Republic. The letter of introduction which Beckford presented to her came from Jean Huber who appears to have been one, but not the only one, of her former lovers. Not quite an adventuress, but not quite anything else, she was hardly the most suitable companion for a young man on the Grand Tour, and one wonders what the straight-laced John Lettice made of her. But presumably Benincasa, who had pretensions to culture, looked after Mr. Lettice. What else are *cicisbei* for?

Madame de Rosenberg was quickly enrolled by Beckford into that select company as one who could be the 'repository of his most intimate secrets',[9] for though much of her time was spent at cards, which were the chief means of her support and cause of her debts, she was also far from stupid. She knew how to flatter, entertain, and distract her rich young friend, taking him to the casinos (which bored him), introducing him to well-connected Venetians of his own age (which delighted him), or travelling with him to visit acquaintances in their country villas on the *terra firma*.

It was through Madame de Rosenberg's introduction that he

entered the Palazzo Cornaro and was soon involved in a situation
which, except for the depressing effect it was to have for some
months on his spirits, might have been taken from a farce by
Goldoni. Here he met two sisters and a brother. His ability to
charm both sexes was soon at work and in no time the elder
sister, ignoring the slight impediment of a husband, was declaring
her passion for Beckford while he, not only in self-defence but
speaking from the heart, replied that it was her brother for whom
he felt a passionate friendship. Unable to grasp the significance of
this the rejected lady immediately assumed that it was her sister
for whom Beckford felt a tender passion and swallowed, by way of
revenge but without ill effect, an extremely inadequate poison
which she had previously acquired for the purpose of disposing of
her husband. This dramatic scene, according to Beckford's much
later account, was played out at night to the accompaniment of a
tremendous storm.[10]

Recalling these scenes in old age Beckford played down the intensity of his feelings for the Cornaro youth. 'It was a passion of
the mind resembling those generous attachments we venerate in
ancient history and holy writ,' he then declared. 'What David felt
towards the brother of his heart, the son of Saul, I experienced
towards the person here alluded to.'[11] But at the time there can be
no doubt of the strength of his attachment or of the indiscretion
of his conduct in not concealing his inclinations. Louisa was
temporarily forgotten, for all that he had assured her from
Germany that he lived only by her remembrance, and even the
image of Courtenay began to fade. Gifts and vows were exchanged
and those romantic attitudes (of which Beckford was now so
much the master) were struck with a minimum regard for public
opinion in a society which had little to do, between card games
and coffee drinking, but indulge in the exchange of gossip.

Even those two worldlings, the Contessa d'Orsini-Rosenberg
and Count Benincasa, into whose sympathetic ears he poured the
full torrent of his emotions, began to take fright and feared an
open scandal. As a distraction they hurried him into churches,
conducted him round picture galleries and escorted him to concerts of music. Fortunately Venice, of all places in Italy, could
provide scenes calculated to divert the most distracted of sight-
seers, among which not the least for Beckford was the sight of
'Turks and Infidels' with whom he was able to ask as many
questions as he pleased about Cairo and Damascus; or the Greeks

who, in comparison with the others, he found 'by far a more lively generation, still retaining their propensity to works of genius and imagination'.

Nor did his sense of humour entirely desert him. His two friends accompanied him to the performance of an oratorio of which he left a lively description. 'The sight of the orchestra still makes me smile', he wrote. 'You know, I suppose, it is entirely of the feminine gender, and that nothing is more common than to see a delicate white hand journeying across an enormous double bass, or a pair of roseate cheeks puffing, with all their efforts, at a French horn. Some that are grown old and Amazonian, who have abandoned their fiddles and their lovers, take vigorously to the kettle-drum; and one poor limping lady, who had been crossed in love, now makes an admirable figure on the bassoon.'

But in spite of these distractions, the trips to islands in the lagoon by gondola with a group of musicians in attendance, listening to a serenade on the Grand Canal that 'stilled every clamour and suspended all conversation in the galleries and porticos', or visiting the island monastery of St. Giorgio Maggiore, 'by far the most perfect and beautiful edifice my eyes ever beheld', Beckford's heart was full of his latest infatuation and his mind disturbed by feelings of guilt and self-disgust. For the first time he began to realise the moral dilemma posed by his 'wayward passions' and saw an abyss open before him. The mental conflict began to affect his health and there was relief as well as regret when he left Venice to continue his travels early in September. It was refreshing for him to see the open countryside again. 'After breathing nothing but the essence of canals and the flavours of the Rialto,' he wrote, 'after the jinglings of bells and brawls of the gondoliers, imagine how agreeable it was to scent the perfume of clover, to tread a springing herbage, and to listen in silence to the showers pattering amongst the leaves.'

It was none the less a subdued and somewhat depressed Beckford who sailed along the Brenta, gaining what refreshment he could from the new scenes that opened before him, admiring the poplars that grew on either bank of the river 'with vines twining round every stalk and depending from tree to tree in beautiful festoons'.

Madame de Rosenberg and Benincasa were still with him, and their destination was the Cornaro villa at Fiesso, where they were engaged to dine. Was it here that he parted from his friend? In his account of the evening he only tells us that 'the Galuzzi sang some of her father Ferandini's compositions with surprising energy . . . I forgot both time and place while she was singing.' It was an evening full of charm, but full of melancholy too, reaching a climax of emotion both for Beckford and for 'one for whom I felt the most enthusiastic friendship' when Marietta Cornaro (presumably the unmarried sister of his friend) sang the aria 'Pur nel sonno almen talora' from Gluck's opera *Orfeo ed Euridice*. The words had a poignant application to Beckford's present situation:

> *When sleep its magic balm instils,*
> *The form I love my vision fills;*
> *Swift flies each torturing pain.*
> *Imperious God, Thy justice prove,*
> *Ah, realise the dream of love*
> *Or wake me not again.*[12]

It was in a desolate frame of mind that he continued his journey the next morning. Separated from his friend, but not from his feelings of guilt, for once he was unresponsive to his surroundings. 'I was too deeply plunged in my reveries to notice the landscape which lay before me;' he recorded, 'and the walls of Padua presented themselves some time ere I was aware.' In this abstracted and gloomy mood he first set eyes upon the shrine of the saint who was to become his patron; whom he was to hold, for the rest of his life, in a strange mixture of religious awe and superstitious veneration.

The origin of this devotion to St. Antony of Padua is difficult to place but seems to have gone back to his childhood or early adolescence. We have noted the joking reference to him in the *Biographical Memoirs of Extraordinary Painters*, but perhaps he was first attracted to the saint because he is the patron of the lower animals, those hunted creatures that Beckford himself always loved and tried to protect. He is also the saint who is usually represented as holding in his arms the infant Jesus, the very epitome of that childish innocence which had for Beckford so powerful an attraction. It was, therefore, already as something of a devotee that he now approached the church where the saint is buried.

Though he felt obliged to introduce a slightly mocking note into his account of his visit to the shrine, it is clear that he now in some curious way associated St. Antony with the emotional crisis he was passing through, that he half hoped to be able to shed the guilt feelings that weighed upon him as he gazed at the saint's tomb.

'You are too well apprised', his account begins, 'of the veneration I have always entertained for this inspired preacher, to doubt that I immediately repaired to his shrine, and offered up my little orizons before it. Mine was a disturbed spirit, and required all the balm of St. Anthony's kindness to appease it . . . The nave was filled with decrepit women and feeble children, kneeling by baskets of vegetables and other provisions; which, by good St. Anthony's interposition, they hoped to sell advantageously in the course of the day. Beyond these, nearer the choir, and in a gloomier part of the edifice, knelt a row of rueful penitents, smiting their breasts, and lifting their eyes to heaven. Further on, in front of the dark recess, where the sacred relics are deposited, a few desperate, melancholy sinners lay prostrate. To these I joined myself, and fell down on the steps before the shrine.'[13]

There was always an element of play-acting in these gestures of Beckford's; he loved to pose as a religious *exalté* (this would be particularly noticeable during his first visit to Portugal) but on this occasion there was almost a desperate note in his need for solace and purgation—alas, not to be fulfilled. 'I hastened to the inn, luckily hard by . . .' his account continues. 'Here I soon fell asleep in defiance of the sunshine. 'Tis true, my slumbers were not a little agitated. St. Anthony had been deaf to my prayer, and I still found myself a frail, infatuated mortal.'

A second visit to the shrine still found Beckford in an emotionally pent-up state: 'We found every chapel twinkling with lights, and the choir filled with a vapour of incense. Through its medium several cloth of gold figures discovered themselves, ministering before the altar and acting their parts with a sacred pomposity, wonderfully imposing. I attended very little to their functions; but the plaintive tone of the voices and instruments, so consonant with my own feelings, melted me into tears, and gave me, no doubt, the exterior of exalted piety.'[14]

The tour continued. In Verona he had an opportunity to indulge in 'recollections of perished ages' as he surveyed the Roman amphitheatre; for Bologna he only spared two hours, finding it 'sadly out of humour, an earthquake and Cardinal Buoncompagni having disarranged both land and people'; and he lost no time in posting on to Florence which he entered by the light of the moon.

In the Tuscan capital youth, vitality and curiosity came to his assistance and his spirits revived a little. He spent over a month there, interspersed with trips to Lucca and Pisa, and a letter to Cozens written on 15 October showed him back in his usual form. 'Be assured', he told his friend, 'you will find me ever the same romantic Being fond of the Woods and Mountains—the friend of sylvan powers and the Votary of Pan. Italy seems my native climate; it agrees perhaps too well with the ardour of my imagination, for I am ten times more enthusiastic than ever. I thought I should have gone wild upon first setting my feet in the Gallery and when I beheld such ranks of statues, such treasures of gems and bronzes, I fell into a delightful delirium which none but souls like ours experience, and unable to check my rapture, flew madly from bust to bust and cabinet to cabinet like a Butterfly bewildered in an Universe of Flowers.'[15] His mind was no longer entirely filled by thoughts of the friend he had left in Venice; after describing to Cozens the charms of the Boboli gardens he ends his letter with the confession that he never visits their shades without wishing for Louisa.

One of the causes for his renewed interest in life was that during a brief visit to Lucca he had encountered the great singer Pacchierotti whom he had first met, and heard sing, in London before he left on his Grand Tour. He had admired both the man and the artist and a friendship had been established between them. Gasparo Pacchierotti, twenty years Beckford's senior, very thin and surprisingly ugly, was the greatest castrato singer of the age, the acknowledged successor to the great Farinelli. Beckford's devotion to him even went to the extent of trying to force his own light tenor voice into the upper register of a male soprano, an affectation which was later to make him appear rather ridiculous in some London drawing-rooms. At Lucca, where Pacchierotti was engaged to sing, they went for walks on the city walls and even for rides into the countryside, as a result of which the singer caught a chill and his young companion received a severe rebuke from the town's musical enthusiasts for exposing him to such risks. Something of the effect this singer's voice had on him was recorded in a letter, probably intended for Fanny Burney, a copy of which Beckford left among his papers: 'Musick raises before me a host of phantoms which I pursue with eagerness. My blood thrills in my veins, its whole current is changed and agitated. I can no longer command myself, and while the frenzy lasts would willingly be devoted to destruction—These are perilous emotions and would lead me cruelly away.'[16]

Reports of an outbreak of malaria at Rome delayed his departure well into October, and it was not until the twenty-ninth of the month that he eventually entered the eternal city by the Porto del Popolo at his favourite evening hour, seeing the streets and palaces 'all glowing with the vivid red of sunset'.

Rome for most people was the climax of the Grand Tour but Beckford only spent the inside of a week there. He saw Pius VI returning in state from Vespers, and made two visits to St. Peter's where he imagined himself 'erecting a little tabernacle' inside the great church and living there with 'no other sky than the vast arches glowing with gold ornaments'. He would take his evening walks 'on fields of marble' and ascend the cupola instead of climbing a mountain. 'Music should not be wanting: at one time to breathe in the subterraneous chapels, at another to echo through the dome.' All his fantasies of deep vaults and dizzy heights seemed to be neatly contained within the compass of a single building.

But Rome did not delay him long; his gloomy mood had returned and he found himself too restless and dispirited even to deliver his letters of introduction. He decided that 'St. Carlos, a mighty day of gala at Naples, was an excellent excuse for leaving Rome and indulging my roving disposition.' In Naples he would meet his mother's cousin the genial and cultivated Sir William Hamilton and find a new friend and counsellor in the diplomatist's first wife. Her influence would be destined to have a lasting effect upon him; and it would be an influence, for once, entirely for the good.

7
Venice versus Naples

WHEN BECKFORD first visited Naples Lady Hamilton had been married for twenty-two years to a husband whose many duties as British envoy to the Neapolitan court often left her to her own devices. Her health was delicate and this prevented her from sharing her husband's official duties to the full, and she instinctively recoiled from the easy-going and somewhat dissolute atmosphere of the court. She was born Catherine Barlow, the daughter and heiress of a Pembrokeshire squire; her union with Hamilton had been a marriage of convenience but it had developed over the years into a relationship of mutual affection and esteem.

In spite of a considerate husband and a prominent social position her life was in many ways unfulfilled. Her husband's long absences on hunting expeditions with the king left her lonely and dispirited. She was naturally of a religious turn of mind and Sir William's frank indifference to religion caused her great private sorrow. Their marriage was childless, and her maternal instinct had been further frustrated when an adopted daughter had died tragically young. In her long solitary hours her chief consolation was in music; she was indeed a brilliant executant and generally considered to be one of the best harpsichord players of the day. It was to this lonely, cultured and sympathetic woman that Beckford now presented himself and to whom he found, suddenly, that he was able to open his heart.

Beckford and Lettice arrived in Naples on November 3 at the usual evening hour but the effect they had hoped to gain of seeing the famous bay illuminated by moonlight was shattered by a most tremendous storm which had sent everyone into hiding, so that they advanced 'with fear and terror' through deserted streets. It was some time before they could settle themselves into their inn and all that night Beckford could hear the waves roaring round the rocky foundations of the Castel dell' Ovo, onto which his windows looked, while vivid flashes of lightning kept him from sleep.

The next day offered a cloudless sky and after calling on Sir William Hamilton he was taken by the envoy 'in form and gala' to the palace where he was presented to the long-snouted Ferdinand IV of Bourbon, *Il Re Nasone*, and watched the courtiers rush to kiss the royal hand. 'Everybody pressed forward to the best of their abilities. His Majesty seemed to eye nothing but the end of his nose, which is doubtless a capital object.' Afterwards they re-turned to Sir William's palazzo where 'an interesting group of lovely women, literati, and artists were assembled', and it was here that he first heard Lady Hamilton play. 'No performer that ever I heard produced such soothing effects', he wrote. 'They seemed the emanations of a pure, uncontaminated mind, at peace with itself and benevolently desirous of diffusing that happy tran-quility around it; these were modes a Grecian legislature would have encouraged to further the triumph over vice of the most amiable virtue.'

The metaphor of vice and virtue Beckford employed was an un-conscious reflection of the conflict that was still taking place in his mind and had done so, in greater or lesser degrees according to his moods, since his amorous adventure with the Cornaro youth in Venice; for if that affair had more and more taken on the aspect of vice in his troubled conscience, Lady Hamilton was to become for him the very embodiment of virtue, yet a virtue that was ap-proachable and understanding unlike the stern, forbidding, all condemning type he associated with the harsh Calvinistic influences of his boyhood and early youth.

It was, of course, from these boyhood influences that his sense of guilt arose. In his earlier 'affairs' he had managed to escape the accusing finger because the various infatuations had never de-veloped to such a point that he was forced to ask himself certain fundamental questions about his sexual nature. He had always, as we have seen, been able to exert a strong attraction over people of either sex and in his adolescence this ambivalence had had no disturbing effect. Even before leaving England he could indulge his feelings of sentimental attraction for both William Courtenay and Louisa Beckford without being aware of any undue conflict, a situation which was made all the easier by his desire to prolong the state of childish innocence beyond its natural term.

But now he was twenty years old. He had broken away from the charmed circle of Fonthill with its escapes into fantasy and illusion; he was presenting himself as a man of the world. He had associated with cosmopolitan and cynical observers of the human comedy like Madame de Rosenberg and her friends who were very different creatures from the Methodistical dowagers who had dominated his youth. Though he would cry out to Cozens that he was resolved to be a child for ever he knew perfectly well that this was an impossible pose. In Venice his lack of reticence over the Cornaro business had caused a certain amount of unpleasant gossip and Beckford was no longer such a child as to be unaware of what the gossips were saying about him.

Now, in Catherine Hamilton, he found someone with whom he could discuss his problems with absolute frankness, not even hiding the nature of his feelings for the friend he had left behind in Venice. 'I can venture expressing to you all my wayward thoughts—can murmur—can even weep in your company', he was to tell her when he left Naples. 'After my mother you are the person I love best in the Universe. I could remain with you all my life, listening to your music and your conversation.'[1] Lady Hamilton did not approve of his unorthodox desires; not only did they transgress the moral code which she thoroughly endorsed, but she saw very clearly that if her young friend failed to control his impulses the result would be disaster, social as well as moral. Beckford, if strongly drawn to homosexual attachments, was still sufficiently bi-sexual (or just sexually immature) to feel that a choice lay before him, and in this frame of mind, stimulated by Lady Hamilton's affectionate encouragement, he could accept her assurance that to indulge in passions in this forbidden direction was indeed 'criminal'.

The choice seemed almost easy in the presence of this understanding woman who soon loved him like a son and could enter into his problems with so much sympathy and criticise, when she thought criticism to be necessary, without any hint of recrimination. But Beckford was to visit Venice again on his return journey. Would he be able to resist 'the insinuating whispers of a soft but criminal passion'[2] when temptation stared him in the face? It was in such moments that he felt most conscious of the injustice of his fate, that what for him seemed so natural should come under the moral condemnation of society and of the friends he loved the most. Was he wrong to follow an instinct which a blind or capricious fate had planted in him unasked? For Lady Hamilton the issue was painfully clear: 'Take courage, my Dear Friend, you have taken the first step. Continue to resist, and every day you will find the struggle less—the important struggle. What is it for? No less than *honor*, *reputation*, and all that an honest and noble soul holds most dear, while Infamy, eternal infamy (my soul freezes while I write the word) attends the giving way to the soft alluring of a criminal passion.'³ If his problem was not solved at least it was clarified.

Beckford himself realised that there was no easy solution to his dilemma, perhaps no solution at all that would be acceptable to the world at large. In moments of depression it seemed to him that fate had placed a burden on his shoulders too heavy to bear and he felt so miserable that he could tell Lady Hamilton how he 'would have given the Indies for one of those comfortable potions which lull us to sleep for ever'. But these were rare moods. Youth and vitality came to his rescue and he could look forward again to the Spring 'when I hope I shall have no cause to appear before you trembling and confounded'. Catherine Hamilton had at least given him the precious gift of hope. It was the thought of the loss of this gift, and the consequences that would follow from such a loss, that would occupy his mind when he came to write his Arabian tale of *Vathek*, a tale that grew from the depth of his own experience.

Of course not all their time in Naples or at the Hamilton's villa at Posillipo was spent in discussing Beckford's particular problem. They had so many interests in common in art, literature and music that the days passed as quickly as hours. 'The Sirens', Beckford wrote to tell Cozens, 'have been propitious and granted me, I am bold and vain enough to say, some few of their persuasive accents. Indeed I flatter myself I have gained considerably—how could I do otherwise—hearing Lady Hamilton every day, whose taste and feeling exceed the warmest ideas. I pass my whole time with her—she perfectly comprehends me and is more in our style than any woman with whom I am acquainted. My dear little Friend writes me the most affectionate letters I could desire—judge therefore whether I do not think Naples the Garden of Irem and see blue skies and brighter sunshine than exists perhaps in reality.'⁴

This passage is of particular interest in relation both to Cozens and to William Courtenay, the 'dear little Friend'. If there was one person before whom Beckford was incapable of dissembling it was Lady Hamilton. He was later to complain to her that in England he had 'no friend like you to sustain my spirits and receive my ideas except Mr. Cozens whom you have heard me frequently mention'.[5] Beckford would have been incapable of coupling Cozens' name like this with that of his ideal woman friend if there had been anything at all reprehensible in their relationship, and it is quite plain that he spoke of him to her with a clear conscience. The point is worth making as it would seem to rule out completely the suggestion that Cozens was in any way physically involved with Beckford's sexual activities, however strange or unusual his influence may have been in other directions.[6] The mention of Courtenay also, from whom Beckford must have been receiving these affectionate letters while he was unburdening his heart to Lady Hamilton about the Cornaro affair, shows that he had no feelings of guilt about this other relationship at the time, that it was still in all essentials innocent. There seems, in short, to have been no connection in Beckford's mind between what he felt for the Cornaro boy and what he felt for Courtenay, an indication that there was nothing physical in his relations with the latter.

Beckford was still very immature in spite of the experiences he had passed through. Lady Hamilton, who could meet him on his own social level, was one of the first people able to force him to face up to reality, who had nothing to lose by telling him the truth; nothing, that is, except the affection she felt for him, and this she was prepared to risk. In fact she did not lose it. She was to remain Beckford's 'good angel' until the end of her life, an event all too tragically near.

But his readiness to escape once more into the realm of fantasy is clear from another letter to Cozens written while he was still in Naples and still listening to Lady Hamilton's sound but disturbing counsels; the letter in which he declared his resolution to be a child for ever. 'The World grows more and more irksome to me every Day,' he wrote, 'and I am eagerly wishing for a Spirit like yours to comfort and revive my own. Nothing, I think, will prevent me daring to be happy in defiance of glory and reputation. Why should I desire the applause of Creatures I despise? rather let me enjoy that heartfelt satisfaction which springs from innocence and tranquility ... I am now approaching the Age when the World in general expect me to lay aside my dreams, abandon my soft illusion and start into public life. How greatly are they deceived how firmly am I resolved to be a Child for ever!'[7]

Significantly he employed the same adjective 'soft' to describe his ideal of childish innocence as he was to use in writing to Lady Hamilton of a 'soft but criminal passion'. All these efforts in which he struggled somehow to reconcile a langurous sensuality with the notion of the innocence of childhood, that saving and protecting innocence he so dreaded to lose, were now associated in his mind with the unwelcome thought of his approaching majority, a thought from which he recoiled with growing alarm as he started his journey back to England.

For return he must. Naples was the southern limit of his Tour. When he left there at the beginning of December for Rome he had secured a firm place in the affections of Sir William and Lady Hamilton, though in the case of the latter the affection was mixed with anxiety from all that she now knew about the problems of his complex temperament. 'I have been just taking a solitary airing during which you have entirely occupied my thoughts', she wrote to him on 6 December. 'Your singular situation and state of mind makes me feel the anxieties of a Mother and a friend and when I represent to myself the risks you run in *various* ways I tremble from head to foot. For Heaven's sake, My Dear Beckford, remember the harsh truths I have often told you; but at the same time remember the affection that dictated them; it was the most painfull effort of friendship to say what I have done, and yet I would again repeat it for *your* good tho' I felt and still feel *myself* the Wounds I gave you and, at this instant that I have your interesting, despairing figure before my eyes as if present. I call myself cruel and cannot refrain from tears, but let them flow. You know how much I have your interest at heart; your honor, reputation and peace of Mind are dear to me, and with a soul like *yours* I am sure you could not enjoy the latter without the former. What would I give to hear the delusion had ceased and that your mind was as calm as your unfortunate Sensibility would allow—but enough of this; it is in vain to reason with you at this distance . . .' Of Sir William she added at the end of her letter: 'He loves you sincerely, admires you, and will help me to take care of you.'[8]

Catherine Hamilton became for Beckford the ideal of all that was good and pure; in his better moments he aspired to be like her or at least to be worthy of her approval. In his struggle with the difficulties and dilemmas that faced him in the immediate future it was her example that he clung to, and even when he failed to live up to it (which would often be the case) she remained the symbol of goodness in his life. Half a century later, and almost as long after her death, he still spoke of her with loving respect. She was, he told Cyrus Redding, 'an angel of purity . . . I never saw so heavenly-minded a creature.'

At least her example seems to have kept him from falling into the arms of his Venetian boy friend when he passed again through that dangerous city at the close of the year. Pacchierotti was singing at the opera and perhaps this rival attraction helped to keep him on the straight and narrow path. From Augsburg, on 20 January 1781, he could write to his friend in Naples with an evident sigh of relief: 'At length, my dear Lady Hamilton, I am awake and see clearly around me. The gulf into which I was upon the point of being precipitated has disappeared and I am once more calm and happy. It is chiefly to you that I owe this enviable state. Your influence prevailed, your words never ceased to sound in my ears till the good work they had in view was accomplished. To express the transport I feel at my deliverance would be impossible.'⁹

It was the new terror that now possessed him: the responsibilities that must be assumed upon reaching his majority in the forthcoming autumn. A tangible reminder of this awaited him at Strassburg in the form of a packet of letters about his business affairs in Jamaica, letters that brought news of hurricanes, wrecks and devastation. In an agony of despair he wrote to Lady Hamilton expressing his longing to return to Naples and share with her his 'happy fantastic imagination'. But such an escape, as he knew, was impossible: 'I am fated, it seems, to return to a country where sober, sullen realities must put them all to flight . . . Not an animal comprehends me. At this disastrous moment, too, when every individual is abandoned to terrors and anxieties, which way can I turn myself? Public affairs I dare not plunge into. My health is far too wavering. Whilst I write my hand trembles like that of a paralytic Chinese. Strange colours swim before my eyes and sounds keep ringing in my ears for which I can hardly account . . . Would to Heaven I could find out some vale immured in the bosom of mountains to which I could transport my books and my instruments. I would send you the clue to enter my labyrinth, as soon as it was formed, but scarce any other being should know that it existed. For ambitious spirits this is not a period to shrink

D

out of the way. Dangers and difficulties are their pavements. But I no longer feel myself bold enough to tread such monsters under foot. Once upon a time I fancied myself filled with ambition. I looked this very morning and could not find a grain.'[10]

Early in February Beckford was in Paris. Here his Grand Tour was to end. Though he assured Lady Hamilton on 10 February that his frantic agitation over the Venetian boy was no more, he was thrown into a state of anxiety because no letter awaited him from Courtenay. Writing on the same day to Louisa (and disguising Courtenay's name and sex) he asked 'Why did the little Dove miss the opportunity of safely conveying her Letter when you offered to take care of it. This want of sensibility on her part makes me more miserable than I can express.' He told Louisa that he walked about Paris plunged in melancholy reflection, lost to the splendid tumult in which he lived, and added: 'You can define and pity the cause of this melancholy transfiguration.'[11]

In fact for most of the time Beckford was thoroughly enjoying himself in Paris. He resumed his oriental studies ('This is the Land of oriental literature,' he told Lady Hamilton, 'and I am once more running over my favourite poems . . .') and made a fine figure in various drawing-rooms in the company of the Duchess of Berwick, a daughter of the Prince of Stolberg-Gedern and sister-in-law of the Young Pretender. He also carried on a light-hearted flirtation with a certain Georgina Seymour whose father, a kinsman of the Duke of Somerset, was the enamoured friend and neighbour of the now middle-aged Madam du Barry. Unfortunately, as was so often the case with Beckford's girl friends, Miss Seymour, who was four years his senior, fell seriously in love with him and rumours of an engagement were whispered about Paris. This was embarrassing as Georgina was quite penniless, her father disreputable, and any thought of a marriage, even if Beckford had wished it, quite out of the question.

Still there was no word from young Courtenay. In his agitation Beckford wrote a long letter to the boy's aunt Charlotte confessing how he trembled lest the lad no longer loved him. It was a curious document, full of unguarded statements. It was the sort of letter which, fallen into hostile or unfriendly hands, could have had a very unwholesome interpretation read into it. 'Surely he will never find any other Being so formed by nature for his companion as myself', Beckford wrote. 'Of all the human creatures male or female with which I have been acquainted in various countries and at different periods he is the only one that seems to have been cast in my mold. When I first began to know him the pleasing delusion would often suggest itself of our having been friends in some other existence. You know he was never so happy as when reclined by my side listening to my wild musick or the strange stories which sprang up in my fancy for his amusement. Those were the most delightful hours of my existence. Twas then I grew sensible there was a pleasure in loving something besides oneself and there would be more luxury in dying for him than living for the rest of the Universe. Good God—were he to receive me with coolness and indifference I should desire to close my eyes for ever!'

The letter continued for many pages, one reckless phrase following another. 'I cannot understand why he has ceased answering my letters: explain this mystery if you are able or retain any regard for one who has so much for you. He used to write with the warmest affection and till he was silent I never thought myself unhappy tho' innumerable reasons conspired to warrant the idea. A languid chill moistens my forehead whilst I write upon this subject. Were I to continue you would imagine me upon the point of flying distracted. My chief treasure, my consolation, my last refuge is centered in William's friendship. The *possibility* of losing it gives me the most cruel alarms ... You are too well read in the Human Heart not to be sensible of the impatience with which I shall wait your answer.' And later: 'Even my dreams are full of his image. You know how it used to haunt me in the gloom of winter at Fonthill. If the wind sung in the crevices I seemed to distinguish his voice and if I took a lonely walk in the long avenues of the Temple plantation—his figure stood beckoning of me at the end of the perspective. How often has my sleep been disturbed by his imaginary cries, how frequently have I seen him approach me, pale and trembling as I lay dozing at Caserta lulled by my dear Lady Hamilton's musick and bathed in tears ... If anything could reconcile me to death twould be the promise of mingling our last breaths together and sharing the same grave. Should you perceive in him a pensive melancholy moment seize the opportunity and remind him of his friend ...'[12]

It was an extraordinary letter for a man of twenty to write about a twelve-year-old boy to a woman who was almost certainly in love with him. It was a perfect example of the sort of indiscretion Beckford was capable of committing when his emotions

got the better of him. It was so foolish a letter that one wonders
whether in fact it was ever sent, for only a draft of its exists. And
yet similar indiscreet letters were mounting up at Powderham,
letters that would later be used as ammunition against him.

Fortunately, some time in early March the much-longed-for
letter arrived. Louisa, who would no doubt have preferred a topic
of correspondence more personal to herself, was at once informed.
'Your Letter of the 6th March, my dear Louisa,' Beckford wrote
on the fourteenth, 'found me absorbed in Musick bent over my
instrument and dissolved in Tears. I had just received a few Lines
from my dearest Friend, and was recalling to my mind the tranquil hours we had passed together. Shall I ever be again so
fortunate, must I bid an eternal farewell to those enchanting
moments? Will he lose that amiable childishness we doat upon?
No—I flatter myself he will not—his Letters breathe its genuine
spirit and are tinted with our own beloved melancholy. Adieu,
remember next Summer we shall be wafted to Hesperia and enjoy
its fables and sunshine—Write me an answer however short. In a
month we shall probably meet—what consolation there is in that
idea—Goodnight—I will dwell upon it.'[13] Rarely had Beckford's
emotional complexities been so curiously intermixed in a single
letter addressed, as it was, to the woman he claimed to love upon
the subject of the boy whose childish image completely obsessed
him. And all the while, of course, his flirtation with Georgina
Seymour continued to divert his idle moments.

It is perhaps not surprising that Catherine Hamilton, with
whom his correspondence continued, detected in his letters 'a
degree of languor' (a word she used for all that alarmed her in his
character) that caused her to take fright. She urged him to return
to Fonthill. Mrs. Beckford had written her a letter full of anxiety
about her son. She had been ill and longed for his return. 'The
whole tenor of her letter convinces me,' Lady Hamilton concluded, 'that *you* are the only Physician who can give her relief.'[14]
Beckford took the hint and packed his bags.

There were other pressing reasons for his return apart from his
mother's health; for some time he had been involved in legal proceedings against his illegitimate half-brother Richard in the Court
of Chancery over complicated issues resulting from his father's
will which the unscrupulous Richard was exploiting in his own
interests. It was considered by his mother's and his own legal advisers that his presence was necessary in England before he came

of age in September, when many of these issues would come to a head, if not to a solution.

In a last letter to Lady Hamilton from Paris, written on 2 April, he summed up his feelings at the conclusion of his Grand Tour. It was hardly what his mother and guardian had expected of him when they had seen him depart eighteen months before; nor was it what Lady Hamilton herself had tried to instil into him during their long conversations in Naples. 'I fear', he wrote, 'I shall never be half so sapient, nor good for anything in this world, but composing airs, building towers, forming gardens, collecting old Japan, and writing a journey to China or the moon.'[15]

What effect did the Grand Tour have upon him? It had widened his appreciation of the arts and heightened his already acute sensitivity. In the notes he had prepared for his travel volume it had served to perfect a style already formed and characteristically individual. These were all things that might have been expected to result from such an experience. But from the point of view of developing his personality or of altering his capricious view of life the experience of the Grand Tour had effected little change. He remained as 'wayward' as ever; he was still self-absorbed and emotionally insecure, though on the surface precocious and assured.

Venice and Naples each offered him a key to life, neither of which he dared fully to grasp. His affair in Venice had forced him, if only for a moment, to acknowledge the inverted side of his sexual nature as something more than a childish aberration; while his talks with Lady Hamilton in Naples had offered him a glimpse of hope but had also left him in no doubt of the punishment society exacted from those who failed to observe its rules. For a time, at least, this lesson had been obeyed. The Neapolitan influence triumphed on the journey home and Venice was re-visited (though not wholly avoided) in a chastened mood. Yet even the sympathetic understanding of Catherine Hamilton left him trembling and bewildered. His problem remained and he continued to see himself as a person pursued by a relentless fate. If he were to express in a few words his state of mind upon returning to England it would surely have been in the phrase he had used, half in arrogance, half in despair, when he wrote to Lady Hamilton from Strassburg: 'Not an animal comprehends me.'

8

Prelude to the Halls of Eblis

BECKFORD'S SHIP landed at Margate on 14 April 1781. The returned traveller spent a couple of months in London, dividing his time between Wimpole Street and his mother's house in the more rural setting of West End, Hampstead, before going on to Fonthill for the summer. He threw himself into the social life of the capital (though affecting to despise its vanities), sat for his portrait to George Romney, and engaged a certain Zemir, described as an old mussulman born a native of Mecca, to tutor him in Arabic.

A letter from Lady Hamilton soon arrived begging him to blot out the remembrance of Venice for ever, and offering him some salutary advice now that he was back in England and soon to be master of a vast fortune. 'Try to forget what is past,' she urged him, 'lest the reflection should sully the lustre of your new born ideas and for Heaven's sake keep a perpetual watch over yourself or you will still be a lost man. Let not a word escape you that the World may take hold of. You are so exposed to envy from your situation, but above all from those talents and parts of which Nature has been so lavish to you, that you will find it more necessary than anyone to be upon your guard. If you are not, I repeat your reputation will be lost for ever, lost *never never* to be regained.'[1] It was wise advice, containing a grimly prophetic note of warning; but Lady Hamilton was now far away and Beckford was longing to cast off the fetters of his long tutelage, for all that he assured her in his reply that he was now much less exotic than he used to be and far more inclined to be reasonable.

Louisa was also in London, fretting at the responsibilities of marriage and also feeling the urge for freedom. The intimacy between her and Beckford now became closer, the one sighing under the oppression of a husband she increasingly disliked and failed to understand, the other longing to escape from the burden of an over-possessive parent. Beckford had another reason for wishing to resume this romantic attachment; it was an antidote to all that was summed up in the word 'Venice'.

A man who was about to come into the possession of one of the largest fortunes in the land was naturally in great demand and invitations lay at his door 'as deep as snow'. Every ambitious mother with a marriageable daughter on her hands was eager to attract his attention and it was perhaps not surprising that he found London 'sillier than ever and more ridiculously dissipated'. Every one was rushing to see the great ballet dancer Auguste Vestris, but Beckford, out of loyalty to Pacchierotti and the lyric stage, declared that he was indifferent as to 'how high or how lightly he capers'. When the ardours of the London season exhausted him he withdrew to the comfortable shade of a tent raised in his mother's Hampstead garden as a protection against the June sunshine. There, with half-closed eyes, he could imagine himself back with Lady Hamilton at Portici.

It was pleasant to know one's self to be the most eligible *parti* in the country and Beckford certainly enjoyed his triumph for all his pretended 'horror' of the social round. But he was not a townsman by nature and was genuinely glad when the time came for him to return to Fonthill. Louisa had already left. Her health was poor, she suffered from nervous disorders as well as incipient tuberculosis, and her husband wisely decided that Tunbridge Wells was better suited to her health than London. Other circumstances, unknown to Louisa, made Beckford glad to leave. Since quitting France he had been bombarded with letters from Georgina Seymour, and this persistent young lady had now announced her imminent arrival in London. Their flirtation had caused enough talk in Paris without his wishing for a further scene of the comedy to be played out nearer home. He had had quite enough of Miss Seymour, and early in July he fled to the safety of his Wiltshire estate.

When Beckford reached Fonthill he had the place to himself for a while and was able to revisit his old haunts in solitude and cultivate his favourite mood of melancholy without having his mother at hand to remind him that he should be preparing himself for a great public career. 'My arbitary mother not having yet made her much redoubted appearance,' he wrote to tell Louisa, 'I stray uninterrupted from morn till eve and feel a kind of melancholy pleasure in being at liberty to pronounce your dear name aloud in the free uncontaminated air unreproached and un-persecuted ... When shall I see you again moving about the slopes in all the flow of your beautiful antique drapery? Write to me Louisa even when you have nothing new to communicate. Were I not every day to hear from you I believe—without exaggeration—I could most willingly lay myself down—once and for all—and die.'[2]

Much as he wanted to see Louisa again (and they would soon be planning a meeting) nothing in fact was farther from his mind than the thought of death. He meant to enjoy himself while he could and before unwelcome responsibilities intruded themselves into his day-dreams. His time was spent in sorting out and pre-paring for publication the notes he had made on his Grand Tour. He also had the brilliant harpsichord player John Burton staying with him, a man then in his early fifties. Beckford described him as 'a mighty genius', which was no more than his public reputa-tion, but found even the highest musical power insufficient to rouse him from the state of languid depression induced by the thought of his twenty-first birthday. Nature itself was enlisted to pander to his moods: 'Oh, these long summer evenings, how they consume my soul away! The gleam of a setting sun is the very light to pine by.'[3]

Yet however much he cultivated this pose of pensive melan-choly, or what he termed in the same letter to Louisa as his 'mournful species of enthusiasm', there is no doubt that his dread at the thought of achieving his majority was quite genuine. He recoiled from the approach of adult responsibility with a real panic. 'What good can such a Being as me be in our boisterous Parliament?' he plaintively asked Lady Hamilton. 'No, let me be happy and flutter in the light a few years longer. Let me spread the wings of imagination a season. Age will soon draw on, and the gay texture be shrivelled. Then I will mump, growl, snarl, bite and be political.'[4] And when Madame de Rosenberg wrote to con-gratulate him upon the great event, he answered: 'Don't call me *illustre ami* and *homme unique*. I'm still in my cradle! Spare the delicacy of my infantile ears. Leave me to scamper on verdant banks—all too ready, alas, to crumble, but rainbow-tinted and flower-strewn!'[5]

But no one, not even a millionaire, can escape the process of growing up. In spite of the diversion of a visit to Bath to call on his uncle Charles Hamilton, or to Wilton, where he dined with

Lord Pembroke and was amused to observe the Marquis of Lothian 'buckram'd up in a capital pair of stays with a "soupcon" of rouge', the preparations for the inescapable birthday celebrations continued. To Louisa alone, at this period, could he turn for understanding and sympathy, and he began now to respond more passionately than ever to the appeal of this the nearest, most available, and most devoted of all those 'only' people to whom he could pour out his soul.

Louisa was now recklessly in love with him. There is no other word to describe the extravagant nature of her passion. She was prepared to make every sacrifice for his sake, to risk social ostracism, even to forsake her children. Beckford himself was no more than in love with the idea of being in love with Louisa. He was stimulated by the thought of her devotion and felt the need, as always, for someone who could offer him such willing and unstinted adoration and to whom he could communicate his own thoughts and fantasies with complete freedom. But his feelings for her, whatever they may have been, stopped short at the point where any real self-sacrifice might be required on his part. He had all the vocabulary of love at his command and in Louisa had found someone who could match his flow of romantic hyperbole, but while she was utterly committed in her devotion to him, Beckford's feelings for her were to remain on the surface only.

At the moment all they wanted was to have a brief time together at Fonthill before the turmoil of his birthday celebrations began. Peter Beckford, Louisa's unappreciated husband, had proposed a visit to his Wiltshire cousins in August and then to leave his wife at Fonthill for a few days while he attended to his own affairs. It was a plan entirely suited to the lovers' purpose, but the promise had been vaguely given, and much to his wife's irritation her husband showed no sign of fulfilling it. His dilatoriness in this respect threw her into a neurotic panic and desperate letters were sent off to Beckford as she moved disconsolately from Tunbridge Wells back to London and from London to Dorset, to a home only a tantalising sixteen miles from Fonthill.

Her letters to him left no doubt as to the intensity of her feelings though she managed somehow still to concede the first place in his affection to the boy William Courtenay, who was now to feature in their correspondence under the thin disguise of the name of 'Kitty'. But jealousy leapt up when she heard that the Bishop of Salisbury's young daughter had spent a week at Fonthill as Beckford's guest. 'A whole week with you— perhaps alone,' she wrote in anguish from Stapleton early in August, 'it is impossible but she must love you, yet if you return it not I am satisfied, and will flatter myself I have no reason to fear any rival save one. But do not for pity's sake my dearest William let me foresee a possibility of supplanting that one, and holding the first place in your affections. At present I am content to share them with another, but were I once to indulge the pleasing idea of possessing them alone, and find my hopes deceived, jealousy, disappointment, and misery would be the consequence. Your love is become absolutely necessary to my existence. Every fresh proof I receive of it binds me more strongly to you. Yet I fancy I can bear to share it—do I not deceive myself? I dare not ask my heart the question lest the result should turn out but very little to the advantage of my happiness. Adieu. I will write no more . . .'[6]

Her husband still delayed and she began to grow desperate as she longed for him to fix the date. 'When that happy period will arrive Heaven only knows', she wrote a few days later. 'I expect it with an impatience which is not to be expressed . . . I viewed the setting Sun with an unusual emotion. I fancied you were at that instant employed in the same manner, and tho' I dared not flatter myself that I was the subject of your meditations, yet the thoughts that our eyes were directed on the same object gave me pleasure. This sensation lasted not long. The consideration that we were too far apart to communicate our ideas to each other destroyed it. I walked to the summit of the Hill and there saw its last beams linger on the spot which you inhabit. The view darkened imperceptibly, till the black cloud of night hid it entirely from my sight . . .' Even her style was beginning to assume a Beckfordian tinge. Her lover himself was not always prompt in his replies. 'Adieu—it is late and the postman is getting impatient', her letter ends, adding on a slightly anxious note: 'To-morrow morning my eyes may perhaps open on a letter from you. Let me but hear that you are well, and that you love me—and I shall be happy.'[7]

Her husband at length relented and towards the end of August Louisa was at Fonthill. But there would be little opportunity on this visit for those melancholy walks in the park or the rapturous exchanges of confidences that had characterised her previous stay, for already the house was being prepared for the birthday celebrations and workmen were busy making arrangements for the entertainment of all Beckford's tenants and dependants as well as for a select gathering of relatives and close family friends. On 17 August Beckford had written a polite letter to the Lord Chancellor, whose official ward he would soon cease to be, expressing the 'pleasure and exultation' he would feel at seeing him among the guests, and Lord Thurlow had replied gravely that he would be 'much mortified' if any accident should prevent him from being present.[8]

Altogether the circumstances were not very propitious for a lovers' meeting, but at least they were able to snatch a few moments together and to sing duets to Burton's spirited accompaniment on the harpsichord. Reporting at the end of the month the presence of his 'beautiful cousin, Mrs. P. B., Lord Rivers' Daughter' to Lady Hamilton, and describing their musical evenings, Beckford confessed with unusual self-knowledge: 'Alas, it is very true—Musick destroys me—and what is worse, I love being destroyed. Rather had I die in this style than live in any other.'[9] It was not quite the style Lord Thurlow had had in mind when he wrote in his letter accepting his young ward's invitation that few had attained their majority more amply prepared than Beckford to take upon themselves their own government.

The celebrations of this important event in Beckford's life occupied the period from Friday to Monday, 28 September to 1 October, when Fonthill was given over to public and private festivities on a scale appropriate for the young man who now came into full possession of his fortune.

The Lord Chancellor headed the list of guests with Lord Camden, and from Powderham came Viscount Courtenay with his sister Charlotte, though his son William does not appear to have been included in the invitation for this essentially adult occasion. Whether Charlotte Courtenay still entertained tender feelings for Beckford is difficult to say; perhaps it was now, in all the splendour of Fonthill, that she realised that her hopes had little chance of fulfilment, for within the year she was to marry, as his second wife, the recently created Lord Loughborough, that same Alexander Wedderburn whose brutal sentencing of the Gordon rioters had so shocked Beckford the year before.

It was clear enough that she had rivals both in youth and beauty. Beckford took little trouble to conceal the admiration he felt for his cousin Louisa, while the devout Lady Euphemia Stewart had chosen this opportunity to introduce into the Fonthill circle her niece Lady Margaret Gordon, a daughter of the Earl of Aboyne. This nineteen-year-old girl had a fresh, blonde beauty and that innocent air of youthfulness that appealed so strongly to Beckford's senses. There was certainly the hint of a plot between Lady Euphemia and the Begum in producing this charming creature at such a moment, and they saw to it that Beckford led her out for the cotillion that opened the ball on the first evening of the party.

Over two hundred guests thronged the state rooms of Fonthill House. The tenants and local worthies, in as many thousands, had meanwhile been regaled with beef and beer in the park, bands playing for their enjoyment. As darkness fell lights shone out among the trees and twinkled from across the lake while the house itself was outlined with hundreds of lanterns. As a climax a fireworks display filled the sky with coloured stars and flashing rockets.

Within the house the privileged guests settled down on the Saturday evening for an entertainment more in keeping with the tastes of their host. The great Pacchierotti himself was to sing to them in a pastoral cantata called *Il Tributo* specially composed for the occasion by Venanzio Rauzzini, a former star of the opera now living in Bath. In this work the celebrated castrato was assisted by another male soprano named Tenducci who for many years had been a leading singer on the London operatic stage.

Shorn of their mellifluous Italian the words of this cantata sound a trifle banal in translation and it is not easy today to re-capture the charm of the piece as the singers, straining in the upper reaches of the treble clef, extolled the memory of the Alderman, praised the maternal sagacity of his widow and lauded the virtues of their fortunate son 'our amiable youth William' now 'in full Possession of his ample Inheritance'. In the late Alderman, Tenducci warbled in the rôle of Thirsis, 'magnanimity was con-spicuous and virtuous Principles regulated the Affections of his heart', while Pacchierotti, in the character of Philenus, saw in 'the amiable Mother of our Youth . . . the most rare and exalted Sentiments that can adorn the human Heart'. They then tunefully and in duet apostrophised her son not to refuse this grateful tribute of fidelity but to accept 'all that a poor Shepherd has to offer: Sincerity of Heart and true Affection'.[10]

Beckford himself was in ecstasy as his favourite singer offered him this musical encomium, and he later summed up the whole experience of his birthday celebrations in a letter addressed to the absent Lady Hamilton which showed that for all his horror at being twenty-one he had not lost his capacity for healthy enjoyment. 'My spirits are not sufficiently rampant', he wrote two weeks later, 'to describe the tumult of balls, concerts and illuminations in which we engaged here a fortnight ago. I will only say that Pacchierotti, Tenducci, and Rauzzini sung like superior beings in a little opera composed upon the occasion; that Burton played like one possessed, and all the world danced like demoniacs. It was a fine frenzy for three days, and not being able to sleep soundly the whole time I had not the misfortune of coming to myself, and was as gay as my neighbours.'[11]

The Sunday following this concert or cantata was observed with a proper quiet after the heady excitements of the two preceding days and the company was edified by an appropriate sermon preached in Fonthill Gifford church by Lettice who seems, as though in compliment to his former pupil's majority, to have somehow acquired the degree of Doctor of Divinity, for it is as 'Dr. Lettice' that his name in future appears. On Monday a cavalcade of carriages carried the guests away from the great house and Beckford, now absolute master of Fonthill and its domain, was left with a small group of friends for a further couple of weeks. The party consisted of Louisa, but not her husband, of Burton the harpsichordist, and of Pacchierotti and his ardent admirer and patroness Lady Mary Duncan, an eccentric amateur of music whose strange appearance, described by Fanny Burney as being of 'a manly stamp, and a manly hard-featured face' with her strange grotesque manners, made an odd companion for the celebrated castrato. She was, however, possessed of a kind and generous heart and she and Beckford vied happily with each other in their zeal and enthusiasm for the singer.

It was during this period, in the course of which the party visited Mount Edgecumbe where Beckford imagined himself on 'an isle of the Atlantic Ocean, to which if we believe Pindar and his poetic Brethren the Souls of Heroes are transported', and Pacchierotti did 'nothing but sing and thank Heaven' at having found a region so like his native Italy,[12] that the idea began to form in Beckford's mind of having a second party at Fonthill, one from which all alien spirits would be excluded and to which only his very closest friends would be bidden.

Other, more curious, thoughts were stirring in his mind, encouraged, perhaps, by the knowledge that he was now no longer answerable to others for the conduct of his affairs. For some considerable time Beckford had dabbled in the fashionable drawing-room cult of magic that occupied many idle minds towards the close of the eighteenth century; a reaction, in most cases, from the dry intellectualism of the *philosophes* and prophets of the Age of Reason. But in Beckford's case it had gone a little further than table-tapping and 'mesmerism'. His reading in Arabic sources and his love of oriental romance had kindled his imagination with tales of sorcery, necromancy and the black arts in general. The idea of gaining power over others by talismans, spells and conjuring fascinated him.

Now, with the thought of Fonthill emptied for a while of the dowagers, his mother and the censorious Lady Euphemia, Beckford seized upon the idea of putting some of his cabalistic knowledge to the test. He discussed the idea with Louisa. They had already made play with spells and incantations in their letters and it had become a stimulating element in their relationship. On Beckford's side his approach was half-joking, half-serious. There was a part of him that always remained sceptical and uncommitted, whether dealing with the spurious pretensions of thaumaturgy or with the more august claims of the Catholic Church. But his Calvinistic training had instilled a profound impression of the reality of evil in his mind, and it is only one step from belief in the power of Satan to belief in the power of Satanism.

Louisa, with a mind not only less sceptical but also totally obsessed by Beckford, caught on to the idea with almost frightening intensity as though she saw it as a way of binding him more closely to her in a sort of unholy matrimony. The letters that passed between them after the Mount Edgecumbe party broke up were dominated by the theme of the next gathering which they had planned to take place late in December. 'Stay a week,' Beckford urged her, adding the mysterious phrase: 'and then, Louisa, we must lie in wait for souls together.' Her reply was no less cryptic: 'William, my lovely infernal! how gloriously you write of iniquities. Not all the saints in Paradise could withstand your persuasive eloquence, and like another Lucifer you would tempt Angels to forsake their coelestial abode, and sink with you into the black infernal gulph. Converts to your faith would crowd from every starry world, and the wide expanse of Heaven be left desolate and forlorn.'[13]

Until his chosen guests were able to assemble Beckford divided his time between London and Wiltshire. The Courtenay boy was now at Westminster School. Beckford had commissioned Romney to paint his portrait as a companion to one of himself and both were able to meet at the artist's studio. The elder man's infatuation for the youth had shown no sign of cooling in spite of his close involvement with Louisa, and 'Kitty' Courtenay was to be one of his chief guests in December.

Another artist had been introduced into Beckford's circle at this time, a man who shared his occult interests and was later to be closely associated with Cagliostro. This was Count Philippe Jacques de Loutherbourg who had come to England ten years previously from his native Germany by way of Paris, where he had exhibited at the Salon and made his name as a landscape painter. In London he had also branched out into scene painting and had devised certain theatrical 'effects' by the manipulation of coloured glass and gauze in front of lamps. By this means he could produce 'necromantic light' which was just the sort of thing Beckford needed to create the right atmosphere of mystery and gloom in fulfilment of his present plans, and Loutherbourg's help was quickly secured to prepare a suitable *mise en scène* for the Fonthill party.

Shortly before Christmas everything was ready and Beckford drove back to Fonthill with Cozens and William Courtenay. All three were excited and looking forward with keen anticipation to the days that lay ahead. Beckford in particular was in a state of euphoria at the thought of realising in actual fact some of the curious and 'wayward' ideas that had long been drifting through his mind. It was an evening of unusual atmospheric brilliance for the time of year, glowing in colours more suitable to early autumn than the depth of winter. The experiences of that evening, the sky, the presence of his two close friends—the one, as it were, his mentor, the other his neophyte—the feeling of freedom and power, all combined to make a vivid and lasting impression upon him. He was to refer to it more than once in the future as a moment he would never forget, one of those flashes of heightened consciousness that occasionally confront a receptive mind and leave an indelible mark upon it; as though he had penetrated, for a moment, to the reality that lies beneath the sensuous perception of the exterior world. Cozens and Courtenay were also affected, or so at least it seemed to Beckford, and for a moment all three were caught up in a sort of ecstatic union.

Twice in the course of the next year he would recall this experience in letters to Cozens. 'I cannot banish from my thoughts those happy hours we past last Christmas at Fonthill', he was to write from Augsburg the following June. 'That Night in particular haunts my imagination when we arrived at Salisbury and seemed transported to a warm illuminated palace raised by Spells in some lonely Wilderness. Don't you remember the soft tints that coloured the Thames the preceding Evening? Alas, I cannot chase one circumstance however trifling, from my memory. Thank Heaven, you were with me; your image is now connected with the happiest recollections which rise in my mind.' And again, nearly two months later from Posillipo: 'How can you remain so long without telling me how you are? Do you fancy I am no longer anxious about you—do you imagine I have forgotten who accompanied me in the happiest journey I ever made? O those delightful days of Fonthill! When will they return? Do you remember the plains we traversed and the golden clouds that hung over the Thames at Staines in defiance of Winter? Do you recollect my little William's Transports? Alas, I remember all, all too well for my present happiness.' Ten months after that, in May 1783, he wrote to Cozens while actually on his honeymoon recalling once more 'the recollection of a certain journey to Fonthill' and the series of romantic conjectures it awakened.[14]

In retrospect, of course, the experience was bound up in Beckford's memory with the days that followed, the days of the secret gathering within the locked doors of Fonthill House. Beckford and his young friends spent the next three days sealed off from the world wandering through the rooms of the house which Loutherbourg's skill had transformed to resemble some mysterious grotto, a setting which might have been taken from Beckford's unfinished romance of Moisasour and Nouronihar and which hinted at those Halls of Eblis whose secret he was soon to unveil.

All the guests, save for Cozens and Loutherbourg and the three Italian musicians who had sung at Beckford's birthday and were once more present to provide music suitable to the strange setting, were young and, according to their host's later recollection 'lovely to look upon'. As well as Courtenay and Louisa they consisted of Beckford's two adolescent Hamilton cousins Alexander (later the tenth duke) and Archibald; Louisa's brother George Pitt, her sister Harriet and her great friend the beautiful Sophia Musters to whom George Pitt was passionately devoted. There were also present the highly respectable two daughters of Lady Dunmore. One other guest stood outside this charmed circle of youth, the Hamilton brothers' tutor Samuel Henley, but even this 41-year-old clergyman was not entirely out of place for he had an enthusiasm for oriental studies, and this in itself would have qualified him for Beckford's approval.

Only one account survives of those three days and nights and that was written by Beckford himself more than half a century later when as an old man he could look back upon a scene still vivid in his memory of people 'extremely youthful and lovely to look upon' wandering through the rooms 'too often hand in hand'. 'Delightful indeed', he recalled, 'were these romantic wanderings—delightful the straying about this little interior world of exclusive happiness surrounded by lovely beings, in all the freshness of their early bloom, so fitted to enjoy it. Here, nothing was dull or vapid—here, nothing resembled in the least the common forms and images, the *train-train* and routine of fashionable existence—all was essence—the slightest approach to sameness was here untolerated—monotony of every kind was banished. Even the uniform splendour of gilded roofs was partially obscured by the vapour of wood aloes ascending in wreaths from cassolettes placed low on the silken carpets in porcelain salvers of the richest japan. The delirium of delight into which our young and fervid bosoms were cast by such a combination of seductive influences may be conceived but too easily. Even this long, sad distance from these days and nights of exquisite refinements . . . I still feel warmed and irradiated by the recollections of that strange, necromantic light which Loutherbourg had thrown over what absolutely appeared a realm of Fairy, or rather, perhaps, a Demon Temple deep beneath the earth set apart for tremendous mysteries—and yet how soft, how genial was this quiet light.'[15]

It was the latter of Beckford's images, the 'Demon Temple', that was to be taken up by rumour when scandalised whispers of what was supposed to have taken place behind the walls of the house whose doors and windows had been so strictly sealed began to circulate first among the members of his family and then more generally in society. The 'Triumvirate at Bath', as Louisa had described the Begum and her two allies Aunt Effingham and Lady Euphemia Stewart, were soon thoroughly alarmed. What had passed during those three days, what orgies, what forbidden rites? Lady Euphemia, as usual, believed the worst, and even Beckford's long-suffering mother was forced to acknowledge that her son's majority had not brought her worries on his behalf to an end.

The account which Beckford wrote in 1838, looking back over the years to events so long past, in fact tells us virtually nothing about what actually happened during those three notorious days. It does not, however, give the impression that anything particularly evil took place. More positively, the contemporary references he made to this party, when the memory of it all was fresh, hardly suggest the Satanic orgies that both he and Louisa liked to hint at in their letters by way of titillation. One would not refer to acts of self-conscious wickedness as being 'happy hours' or 'delightful days'. No doubt they indulged in a little mumbo-jumbo and thought themselves very daring, but for the most part they probably did little more than make love, listen to music, enjoy a voluptuous ease and feel all the stimulation that the young can extract from a conscious flaunting of convention. This, indeed, was their chief crime in the eyes of their relatives. Louisa and her friend Sophia Musters were married women; neither was accompanied by a husband; both were attended by acknowledged lovers. It was the indiscretion of this that caused the main scandal.

Fortunately for Beckford the scandal was kept within bounds, thanks largely to the influence of his family and, one must assume, to an unusual degree of understanding or complacency on the part of Louisa's husband. The useful Mr. Henley, whom Beckford had interested in his literary projects, and who himself had no wish to be connected with scandalous rumours, was also helpful in calming the anxious fears of the Begum and her friends. It was the sort of minor scandal that a young man in Beckford's position could easily survive but to which people's minds would return, with much shaking of heads and raising of eyebrows, should he ever have the misfortune to be involved in a worse one.

Why then did he look back upon these few days as being of such importance in his life? It must be remembered that he was a person who suffered all the frustration of an artist without any obvious outlet for his creative drive. In this party at Fonthill during the Christmas season of 1781 he was at last able to find an expression for this pent-up frustration. He was like a theatrical producer directing his own play; and the sense of release this gave him set him upon a course that led him to find the true medium of his art. He was probably barely conscious of this at the time, but looking back upon it all from the vantage point of old age he saw the position clearly enough. 'No wonder such scenery inspired the description of the Halls of Eblis', he then wrote in concluding his account. 'I composed *Vathek* immediately upon my return to town thoroughly embued with all that passed at Fonthill during this voluptuous festival.'

9
A Strange Exotic Animal

THE NEXT FEW MONTHS were to witness one of the most creatively active periods in the whole of Beckford's life. Before half the year was out he would have completed work on the volume of Grand Tour letters, have composed the musical score and supervised the production of an operetta, and embarked upon the masterpiece for which he is still chiefly remembered, the story of the Caliph Vathek. All this was to be achieved against a background of hectic social activity, for it was the period when the young millionaire, so handsome, so talented and amusing, so eminently marriageable, was in constant demand in every fashionable drawing-room in London.

Already a legend was beginning to attach itself to his name, for as well as the vague hint of scandal resulting from the Fonthill 'orgy' there were tales to tell of his extravagance and profusion, of how, when travelling, he ordered the room of any inn where he would sleep to be specially decorated for his reception 'like Wolsey, who travelled with a set of gold hangings'.[1] Curiosity to see the rich young prodigy was general; even old George Selwyn, that connoisseur of bright young men, tottered out on a cold February evening to observe this latest example. 'I was last night at Lady Lucan's to see young Beckford who seems to possess very extraordinary talents', he reported. 'He is a perfect master of music, but has a voice, either natural or feigned, of an eunuch. He speaks several languages with uncommon facility and well, but has such a mercurial turn, that I think he may finish his days *aux petites maisons*. His person and figure are agreeable. I did not come till late, and till he had tired himself with all kind of mimicry and performances.'[2]

His skill as a mimic was much applauded. Lady Craven, of whom we shall hear more, described in her *Memoirs* a further extension of this talent. She and Beckford were at an evening party where they were able, from a safe distance, to watch Lord Thurlow in earnest conversation with a lady to whom he had just been presented. Beckford sat down at the harpsichord and proceeded to sing and improvise on the keyboard what he imagined might be the subject of their conversation. 'Music must be felt by others', declared Lady Craven, 'as it was by Beckford and me, who played by natural instinct, to conceive how highly laughable this musical conversation was. I laughed immoderately. Lord Thurlow and our friend were so taken up with their conversation, that they never suspected what we were doing.'[3]

The art of mimicry, however, is a dangerous talent to possess. It is very funny to watch but not so amusing to be the subject of the mirth it arouses. Beckford was fond of Lord Thurlow and we may assume that his mockery, on this occasion, was gentle, and at least neither the Chancellor nor his companion was aware of what was happening. But not all of Beckford's victims were treated so kindly. It has been said that Lord Loughborough, a very imitable character, was one of the people less mercifully caricatured and that when word of it got back to him he was in no way amused. Even Beckford's purely social graces, added to his immense wealth, gave rise to jealousy as well as admiration. If he made friends at this time he also, unsuspectingly, made enemies as well.

One friend with whom he was now in regular correspondence was the Rev. Samuel Henley, the Harrow tutor who had attended the second Fonthill party with Beckford's two young Hamilton cousins. Henley had had his academic career in America (where he had been a professor at the William and Mary College at Williamsburg, Virginia) cut short by the War of Independence, and in his early forties had found himself back in England with an obscure position and little chance of ecclesiastical preferment. His unfortunate plight must have seemed to him a poor recompense for his loyalty to George III, and like many indigent clergymen he had followed the course of attaching himself to the household of some nobleman or great landowner in the hope of catching such crumbs, or more than crumbs, that might fall from the rich man's table. In William Beckford, so lately come into his inheritance, he no doubt saw just such a patron as he needed.

There had obviously been a quick *rapport* between the two men. Henley's knowledge of oriental literature was a fortunate chance that offered an immediate means of approach. Eastern tales were exchanged and oriental lore discussed in the darkened recesses of the Egyptian Hall at Fonthill while the air was heavy with the fumes of incense, and Beckford discovered the existence of another sympathetic soul with interests close to his own. He had shown the clergyman the drafts he had already prepared for *Dreams, Waking Thoughts, and Incidents*, as his travel diary was to be called, and Henley offered to transcribe the text and see it through the press. He also suggested that the author might enlarge it here and there by the inclusion of some purely imaginative passages.

It was, therefore, with a head spinning with thoughts inspired by this flattering suggestion that Beckford returned to London. 'The spirit has moved me this eve,' he wrote to Henley before the end of January, 'and shut up in my apartment, as you advised, I have given way to fancies and inspirations. What will be the consequence of this mood I am not bold enough to determine. Good night. Pray for the soul of William Beckford.' And just over a week later he wrote again: 'You are answerable for having set me to work upon a story so horrid that I tremble whilst relating it, and have not a nerve in my frame but vibrates like an aspen.'[4]

The story upon which he was working was not *Vathek* but a lurid little gothic tale that appears at the end of Letter XXIII as it was finally given to the public in *Italy, with Sketches of Spain and Portugal*, the 'fearful narration' (as it purports to be) told him by an aged female recluse in whose hut, shaded by uncouth rocks and sharp-spired dwarf aloes 'such as Lucifer himself might be supposed to have sown', he had sought shelter from the heat of the sun. She proceeds to unfold a story replete with all the trappings of romantic fiction: curdled blood, agonising sighs, unbridled passion, murder, parricide and the double suicide of guilty lovers.[5] It is a story of no particular merit or originality, and indeed strikes rather a false note in the setting of Beckford's travel diary. It is interesting only in so far as it acted as a sort of detonator for the explosion of creativity that followed shortly afterwards when he threw himself into the composition of his Arabian tale.

But there was little enough time for literary work. In letters to Louisa pining away in rural Dorset where she was unable to escape from her husband—'my torment' as she now called him as she openly longed for his death—Beckford unfolded the catalogue of his social triumphs. 'All London,' the poor distracted woman had to read, 'notwithstanding ten thousand malevolent insinuations, is at my feet and all the Misses in array whenever I show myself. There is a general rising the moment I put one foot before another in a dancing attitude and mounting of chairs and tables to get a glimpse of my evolutions . . .' His whole time seemed to be spent in 'vaulting and pirouetting and mimicking this singer and t'other'. On the night of 21–22 March he danced until six in the morning at a great gathering of the Whig aristocracy celebrating the fall of Lord North's government. The Prince of Wales 'brighter than sunshine' was present. 'To me in particular,' Beckford informed Louisa, 'he was graciousness personified. So benign an example was sure to be followed and it became the rage to bestow upon my dress and my dancing and all I did and all I said the most wildly extravagant encomiums.'6

Time had somehow to be found in the midst of all this excitement for sittings to Sir Joshua Reynolds who had been commissioned to paint his portrait. The resulting canvas, which has often been reproduced, is probably the best known of the various pictures of Beckford that exist. There is a certain arrogance in the carriage of the head and the long sharp nose he had inherited from his father, but also a hint of immaturity and an almost feminine quality about the lips and eyes in which the artist had caught something of that fashionable melancholy that Beckford loved to affect. Looking back after the passage of five years, and in very different circumstances, the sitter would write his own account of how he saw himself at the time this portrait was painted. 'What a strange exotic animal I was in those days,' he wrote in his Spanish diary in December 1787, 'abandoned to all the wildness of my imagination, and setting no bounds to my caprices. Never was I quiet a single instant. I seemed like the antique Mercury perpetually on tip-toe on the point of darting through the air.'7

He was certainly exhilarating in his new independence and in the freedom he enjoyed from the control, if not from the criticism, of the dowagers. Young William Courtenay was at Westminster School and Beckford contrived various ways of seeing him, either at Romney's studio or at his own house. There are indications that their relationship entered upon a somewhat less innocent phase at this period. A curious fragment of a letter, probably meant for Cozens, may well refer to the boy: 'Why are we never to meet again? I am just at the moment a very extatic being and long to tell you so. Come early as you can this eve: Methinks I possess the pipe of Hermes, for all Arguses are laid asleep—Even the great Argus of all—the female, the mystic Argus slumbered last Saturday while I enjoyed the prize and revelled till ten in the morning.'[8] Cozens was already in the secret, Louisa was still in Dorset. What other prize than 'Kitty' did Beckford then wish to enjoy?

For Louisa, separated against her will from the man she loved, the strain was almost too much to bear. She longed to be rid of her husband and was hard put to it to conceal the jealousy she felt for Courtenay though she tried hard to master or disguise it. In a sort of frenzy heightened by the disease that was slowly gaining its hold upon her she saw almost any alternative as preferable to the ascendancy of her rival, the rival she dared not openly oppose. Invoking the memory of those secret days at Fonthill, she wrote to her lover almost on the same day he was making his cryptic references to the mystic Argus, offering her own son (another William) as a possible substitute in place of her rival: 'I am miserable now I have no little victim in training to sacrifice on your altar. I wish to God my William was old enough for it. He grows every day more and more beautiful, and will in a few years answer your purpose to perfection, but what an age it is to look forward . . . My William, can we ever forget each other, and if not William can it be—can our souls exist in an eternal separation? If it be permitted us after death to stalk invisible about this earth and haunt those places we once delighted in . . . never shall I quit your side . . . I would bear the pangs and tortures of Hell with resignation and even thankfulness at having contributed to your welfare. Were I certain of being thus always near you Death would lose all its horror and become welcome . . . but to be separated by the vast gulph of eternity is a thought I cannot endure.'[9]

New torments were to assail her. Beckford's family were anxious to silence once and for all the murmur of scandal that continued to follow him, the 'malevolent insinuations' of which he was himself very much aware, for however dazzling a figure he cut in society the shadow cast by those imprudent days at Fonthill continued to follow him. How else dispel them than by a brilliant marriage? Once again the name of Lady Margaret Gordon was being mentioned, that charming young niece of Lady Euphemia's who providentially had been safely at Bath with her aunt while the regrettable revels were taking place.

Louisa was thrown into despair by the thought of such a marriage, though it was as yet no more than a rumour, a subject for family discussion rather than a positive fact. 'I am on the rack of curiosity and impatience—and would give the Universe for one hour's conversation with you', she wrote. 'But why must Margaret be exalted to such a height of happiness? Why must she possess lawfully and eternally what I would suffer ten thousand deaths to enjoy one instant. William—it must not be, that cold-blooded disciple of pale-eyed chastity must not revel in your arms—pant on your breast—mingle her soul with your's, and under the sanction of virtue wantonly indulge all the luxurious fancies of vice. Since the dawnings of reason first illuminated my infant mind, never has it been torn by such a variety of distracting passions— Jealousy—fury—anger—revenge—and despair possess it by turns, and harass me out of all patience. For mercy's sake do not give yourself away yet—see me—speak to me—ere the cursed knot is tied—and let my longing arms be folded once more round the lovely form of my own William . . .'[10]

One cannot but feel sympathy for the poor woman who had staked everything upon the love of a man who could care deeply for no one but himself. Louisa, in a sense, is the only genuinely tragic figure who ever crossed his life, for there was no escape from her sad destiny once she had committed herself so rashly and impulsively to his affections only to discover (could she ever face up to the truth) that he was quite incapable of returning her passion.

Beckford wrote to console and reassure her but his letter shows that he looked upon the whole situation as little more than an escapade, a diversion from his London triumph. 'The Begum', he told her, 'is raving at a rate the prince of the abyss himself has no conception of, whilst Aunt Effingham blows up the flames, and declares it shall no longer be *her* fault if they do not envelope Peter and make him blaze. She tells everybody that comes in her way, royal and unroyal that *she*, at least, is completely scandalized and believes *all* the wild tales which were so charitably circulated of our orientalism last December at Fonthill. Be not alarmed Louisa. Let us defy their venom. The more it rankles—the more your soul will be rivetted to mine . . .'[11]

A few days later he drove down to Fonthill for a brief visit where he and Louisa were united again. But it would be almost the last time that he would see her. There would be another brief meeting in London, for Louisa, too, was sitting to Sir Joshua Reynolds and this gave her an excuse to escape up to town, but the truth of the matter was that Beckford was losing interest in her. A new feminine attraction, safely unromantic, was at present occupying all his time and energy. The letters to Louisa would continue, no formal break occurred, he would still from time to time address some romantic effusion to her when he needed such an outlet, but from now on she would gradually fade from his life, embittered, unreconciled to her fate, a sick and broken woman.

Beckford's new friend was a woman of remarkable character who but for the slight absurdity that accompanied so many of her actions might have figured as a pioneer in the emancipation of her sex. Elizabeth Lady Craven was almost exactly ten years his senior in age.[12] Her career had so far been capricious to a singular degree, and was to continue in the same pattern for many years to come, but charm, toughness of character, and sheer force of personality had always kept her just within the bounds of polite society despite her serene disregard for some of its most sacred rules and conventions.

A daughter of the fourth Earl of Berkeley she had been married to Lord Craven when only sixteen. After five or six years of marriage and a suitable complement of children she began to show signs of restlessness. She was intelligent and adventurous and her husband appeared rather dull to her when compared to some of the people she met in London society. She was constantly seen in the company of the French ambassador the Comte de Guines, and her husband's suspicions were aroused. During a masquerade ball in 1773 she was indiscreet enough to retire with the ambassador to a locked room with so little regard for secrecy that Lord Craven, who had followed them, forced the door and discovered the couple *in flagrante delicto*. For anyone but Elizabeth Craven it would have meant social ruin, but she managed to persuade her husband to forgive her and despite the scandal she was still received in society.

Though the marriage was patched up she continued to lead an independent life. In 1778 her play *The Sleep Walker* appeared (a translation from Pont de Vile) to be followed by *The Miniature Picture*, performed at Drury Lane in 1780, and *The Silver Tankard*, which was given the year after at the Theatre Royal, Haymarket. Horace Walpole, who claimed to admire her contributions to the drama, wrote of her: 'She has, I fear, been *infinitamente* indiscreet; but what is that to you or me? She is very pretty, has parts, and is good-natured to the greatest degree; has not a grain of malice or mischief (almost always the associates, in women, of tender hearts) and never has been an enemy but to herself.'[13]

If Lady Craven was somewhat easy-going in her private life she applied the strictest of aristocratic standards to the art of the theatre. Thus Beaumarchais' *Le Barbier de Seville* had come under her condemnation. 'The piece,' she declared, 'which made so much noise at Paris, is trifling. A barber should never be the hero of a play, though he may be the subject of a scene . . . A valet may be said to be naturalized on the critical theatre; the scene is as it were his native soil because he is always there in the suite of his master, who is generally the principal personage in the piece. A barber, on the contrary, is a stranger; he might be allowed to appear at intervals, if the author has need of him, but ought never to be the hero.'[14]

So much for the lower classes. Lady Craven clearly believed that they should know their place, at least on the stage. Whether she applied this rigid principle to the rest of life Lord Craven, at least, allowed himself to doubt. When he finally separated from her in the year in which she met William Beckford, he was reported to have said of her that 'she was become a democrat in love and had shewn marks of *complaisance* to the *canaille*.'[15] On this ominous note he left her to her own devices, which suited her very well, having meanwhile consoled himself with a mistress who was not conspicuous for the blueness of her blood.

Beckford and Lady Craven became staunch friends and allies. Their temperaments were very similar; they had the same *esprit*, the same mercurial intelligence, the same disregard for convention when it thwarted their designs or threatened their happiness. Both were relentless in pursuing their own ends and equally careless of the consequences, but whereas Beckford felt himself driven forward by an unrestrainable fate Lady Craven always knew just when to draw back and make the necessary, if often belated, sacrifice to the dictates of society. Their relationship was one of friendship and mutual appreciation without any of the amorous overtones or distorting dramatisations in which both delighted to indulge in different circumstances. A further link bound them together at this particular moment. If Beckford was aware of certain 'malevolent insinuations', Elizabeth Craven, thanks to her reputation for moral laxity, was also conscious of 'a certain film of shyness which was beginning to creep over fashionable faces at her approach.'[16]

It was to put a check to the embarrassment caused her by the circulation of 'spiteful old stories revived, and new ones disseminated' that Lady Craven conceived the idea of presenting an entertainment that people in society would be so eager to see that they would put on one side their prejudice against her in their eagerness to receive an invitation. Who better than Beckford to help her in this, who had his own reasons for wishing to placate the leaders of fashion? It was a brilliant idea. 'The scheme has succeeded to a miracle,' Beckford recorded, 'and everybody is begging and beseeching to gain admittance to our rehearsals. The starchest of the starch are fast relaxing into complacency, and the wisest of the wise are foolish enough to stoop down to all sorts of petty manoeuvres to curry an invitation.'[17]

Their plan was to produce an operetta or 'Pastoral' to be performed by children recruited from aristocratic families but assisted, where breeding was not allied to art, by strong vocal support in the background from professional singers. 'The words', Beckford wrote in his description of the affair, 'a farrago of her Ladyship's—the music a farrago of mine. Our actors and actresses, singers and songstresses, are all in their teens without any exception ... The "Spectacle" in the last scene will be "ravissant"—not less than twenty or thirty blooming girls and boys appearing together at one time on the stage.'

As a theatre for this presentation they managed to secure the use of Queensberry House,[18] though with only grudging consent from the duke. 'Would you believe it?' Beckford asked, 'For a long time our usually indulgent friend, the dapper duke, ran quite rusty and kicked at the idea of having his palazzo pulled to pieces. This was prophetic as it turned out, for we are all at work clearing away partitions and causing as thick a dust as ever was raised by coaches and phaetons on the grand day of Epsom and Ascot.' François Barthelemon, director of music at Vauxhall, was engaged to conduct the orchestra. Burton was once again at the harpsichord and the composer Ferdinando Guiseppe Bertoni, 'taking pinches of snuff in his quiet way and muttering blasphemies in an undertone against Handel', kept an eye on the young performers, 'drilling them apace'. To instruct the players in acting Beckford, who described himself as 'paymaster-general' of the undertaking, had secured the help of John Henderson, Garrick's former rival and successor at Drury Lane.

The piece was rehearsed during the first weeks of April. The composer was modest in his claims for both words and music. In the description written for his unnamed correspondent—perhaps Louisa—he noted disparagingly: 'When you recollect her [Lady Craven's] farce called the Silver Tankard and conceive that this same pastoral, although not half so vulgar, is ten times more insipid, you will not be surprised at my fits of impatience whilst adapting music to such lackadaisycal trumpery. Don't imagine I am much better pleased with my part of the performance than with that of her Ladyship. Not a single air do I think worth sending you. Lady Clarges, with one of her arch looks, told me fairly I did not shine. However, when she heard the finales, she exclaimed, "Thank God!—at least you have made a good end." '

The grand performance on 13 April was all that either composer or author could wish. 'Talk of the ark, indeed!' Beckford wrote, 'Never believe that *sacred* vessel sheltered half so incongruous an assemblage of curious animals as our profane little theatre.' Society had turned out in force, headed by the king's brother, the Duke of Cumberland, 'rattling away like a dice-box'. There was the Lord Chancellor and the Archbishop of York and as glittering an array of peers and peeresses as even the most ambitious of hostesses could hope to see under a single roof. But for Beckford the moment of triumph came in the last moments of the score when his idol Pacchierotti, who was present in the audience, slipped behind the scenes and added his matchless voice to the other singers in the finale. The young composer, overwhelmed by his emotions, hid his face in his hands and wept.

As though all these activities were not enough to occupy his time and energy, Beckford had been spending every spare moment he could snatch on his literary work. On 25 April, the excitements of the operetta production being at last out of the way, he was able to write to Henley to say that the story for inclusion in the travel diary was completed, and added a note which gives us the first hint that work on *Vathek* had already started: 'By the bye, my Arabian tales go on prodigiously, and I think Count Hamilton will smile upon me when we are introduced to each other in paradise.'[19] The mention of Count Hamilton was characteristic; it referred to Count Anthony Hamilton, a connection of his mother's family who had lived in France at the exiled court of

James II where he had written the *Contes de Feerie* and the *Memoires du Comte de Gramont*. Like his distinguished ancestor Beckford was writing his Arabian tale in French.

Just when he began work on the book cannot now be said with any certainty. Presumably it was already started while the rehearsals were in progress at the beginning of April as Lady Craven, with whom he must have discussed his plan, writing to say good-bye to him when he left for the continent in May, not only addressed him as *Etrange Arabe* but told him that she had been dreaming about the life of Vathek.[20] He must at least have shown her a rough draft of the book; perhaps it was the draft (for certainly no more can have been completed at this time) which he referred to many years later in the often quoted, and often misunderstood, statement made to Cyrus Redding when he declared that he had written *Vathek* in three days and two nights of uninterrupted work.

All we can say is that when he left England in the middle of May he took with him the manuscript of *Vathek* upon which he was still working and upon which, as we shall see, much work still had to be done. But the final form of the book was at least sketched out in his mind, if not actually on paper, for on 1 May, in the first definite reference to the book by name, he told Henley: 'My Caliph advances on his journey to Persepolis, alias Istakhar; but want of time, I believe, will force me to stop his immediate proceedings.'[21]

Beckford left England on 16 May. The reasons for this second continental tour were many. He needed a rest after the hectic life he had been living in London, and his family, always overanxious about his reputation, agreed that another absence from England would do him no harm and allow the tongue of calumny time to discover other topics for conversation. They were pressing him to make up his mind on the question of his marriage and his entry into the House of Commons; two subjects upon which he still had no desire to commit himself. He wished only to escape to Naples and the sympathetic company of his dear Lady Hamilton to whom he had written to say that if he remained another three months in 'this vile country' he would give up the ghost.

He was in a depressed mood as he went on board ship at Dover. He poured out his feelings in a letter to Henley, but it was young William Courtenay, his 'poor little animal', of whom he was thinking as the ship put out to sea. 'It is ten o-clock,' he wrote, 'and at

12 I must resign myself to my cabin, where I shall stretch myself out and cross my legs like a Knight Templar in one of our old cathedrals. Now had I much sooner been shut up in a dingy chapel, with velvet coffins and ruined altars, than breathe the soft atmosphere of Italy, if I might have one poor little animal that you have heard me speak of for my companion . . . My spirits are very low, as you may perceive by the stuff I scribble to you; therefore judge how the mighty are fallen. Lest I should sink you out of sight let me fold up my letter.'22

IO

The Caliph

❧❧❧

THE STILL INCOMPLETE MANUSCRIPT which Beckford carried
with him on his voyage to Europe would, before his return to
England in November, have taken the form of the book which he
would later describe as 'the only production of mine which I am
not ashamed of, or with which I am not disgusted'.[1] In its pages
were condensed not only the fruits of his oriental studies and wide
reading of Eastern texts, but also a projection of his own personality in its relationship to the people nearest to him in life or whose
influence most dominated his thoughts: his mother, Louisa,
William Courtenay and the memory of his father.

Various claims have been made for *Vathek*, some of which have
perhaps over-emphasised its unique position both as an oriental
tale and as a work of art. None of the claims that it is 'a completely
original composition',[2] a '*tour de force*, a flight of unregulated
imagination',[3] or that it 'stands alone, supreme, as the only tale
with a true Oriental glamour fashioned by an Englishman',[4]
though each contains part of the truth, in itself explains the
fascination of the book, a fascination that springs more from the
curious personality that created it than from the originality of the
form or subject. Beckford, as Dr. Oliver pointed out, 'with his
oriental enthusiasm, was almost bound to produce a full-dress
Eastern tale sooner or later'.[5] In this sense *Vathek* was in a tradition of oriental stories composed by Western hands that had been
popular, chiefly in France but also in England and Germany, for
the preceding twenty years.[6] *Vathek* differs from these only in
being more authentic to Western readers[7] and in being based on a
wider knowledge of Eastern literature and custom than most
other authors of spurious oriental tales possessed.

What may be said to make *Vathek* a unique book is the burning
sense of personal commitment that carries the reader from his first

introduction to the Caliph in the opening sentence to the final and terrible culmination in the Halls of Eblis. It was written in a crisp, terse French consciously modelled in style on Voltaire which is particularly effective for the ironic, epigrammatic character of the earlier passages. The pace never flags, and though the author's claim to have written it in three days was a typical Beckfordian exaggeration, the book none the less has the feeling of urgency and drive that suggest a rapid, 'inspired' mode of composition.

The original idea for the story had come to him, as we have seen, during the now notorious party at Fonthill the previous Christmas. There the sight of the great marble hall dimly lit by tapers with mysterious vaulted passages leading off in different directions, the whole scene veiled in clouds of incense and heavy with aromatic perfume, had inspired the idea of the Hall of Eblis. 'You could scarcely find anything like the Hall of Eblis in the Eastern writings, for that was my own', he confessed to Cyrus Redding fifty years later. 'Old Fonthill had a very ample, lofty, loud-echoing hall, one of the largest in the kingdom. Numerous doors led from it into the various parts of the house, through dim, winding passages. It was from that I introduced the hall—the idea of the Hall of Eblis being generated from my own. My imagination magnified it and coloured it with the Eastern character.'[8]

From this starting point his imagination carried him on, aided by his special knowledge of the exotic background and drawing heavily upon his own personal experience. The story is impregnated with the sense of predestination which the author had absorbed from the Calvinistic influences of his childhood and from which he was never completely to escape; it is the tale of a man caught in the prison of his own temperament and rushed headlong to destruction. There are moments of grace when the hero is offered the chance of salvation, but these are brushed aside and he is sped onwards towards his doom.

The Caliph Vathek was a historical character. His real name was Al-Wathek Billah,[9] grandson of the illustrious Haroun al-Rashid, the fifth Abbasid Caliph who reigned in Baghdad from the year 786 to 809, and around whose name the *Arabian Nights* has cast a perennial romantic glamour. But at this point any historical resemblance ceases, and the Vathek of the Arabian tale is in all else a creature of the author's fantasy.

The story opens at once with two Beckfordian traits: the terrible eye and the violent temper. These characteristics, both taken

E

from the author's recollection of his father, are described thus in the person of the Caliph: 'His figure was pleasing and majestic; but when he was angry, one of his eyes became so terrible, that no person could bear to behold it; and the wretch upon whom it was fixed instantly fell backwards, and sometimes expired. For fear, however, of depopulating his domains and making his palace desolate, he but rarely gave way to his anger.'[10] He is also shown as a sensual man who 'did not think . . . that it was necessary to make a hell of this world to enjoy Paradise in the next'.

Another characteristic feature is the tower which the Caliph builds 'from an insolent curiosity of penetrating the secrets of heaven'. It recalls Beckford's own impression of the tower of Antwerp cathedral which he saw on his Grand Tour when he described how he longed to ascend it 'to stretch myself out upon its very summit, and calculate, from so sublime an elevation, the influence of the planets'. For Vathek the tower is not only the symbol of knowledge and power (both gained through disobedience of conventional wisdom), but it is a place of escape from the responsibilities of the world. It is also the centre from which emanate the wicked spells of the Caliph's mother, who is the evil genius of the book.

This is Beckford's description of the Caliph's first ascent of his tower: 'His pride arrived at its height when, having ascended for the first time the fifteen hundred stairs of his tower, he cast his eyes below, and beheld men not larger than pismires, mountains than shells, and cities than bee-hives. The idea which such an elevation inspired of his own grandeur completely bewildered him; he was almost ready to adore himself, till, lifting his eyes upwards, he saw the stars as high above him as they appeared when he stood on the surface of the earth. He consoled himself, however, for this intruding and unwelcome perception of his littleness with the thought of being great in the eyes of others; and flattered himself that the light of his mind would extend beyond the reach of his sight, and extort from the stars the decrees of his destiny.'

This is the clue to the self-identification of Beckford with his hero. Two years before starting work on his Arabian tale he made the following note: 'My apartment shall be in the highest storey of the tower . . . from whence I may observe the course of the planets and indulge my astrological fancies. Here I shall esteem myself under the peculiar influence of the stars.' Nearly ten years later, still obsessed by the same image, he wrote: 'I am growing rich and mean to build Towers, and sing hymns to the powers of Heaven on their summits, accompanied by almost as many sacbuts and psalteries as twanged round Nebuchadnezzar's image.'[11] The result, as we know, was to be the great but unstable tower of Fonthill Abbey. It was for Beckford a symbol both of his revolt against society and his escape from its responsibilities, a refuge above the world from where he could contemplate the heavens and look down on the earth with a mixture of detachment and contempt.

The Caliph, then, is represented as a man who possesses some of the characteristics of both Beckford and his father the Alderman: violent, overbearing, sensual, unorthodox, given to curious learning and endowed with a lust for occult power. He possesses only their bad qualities, however. Apart from a grim sense of humour he is shown as having few endearing traits. 'He was fond of engaging in disputes with the learned,' we are told, 'but did not allow them to push their opinions with warmth. He stopped with presents the mouths of those whose mouths could be stopped; whilst others, whom his liberality was unable to subdue, he sent to prison to cool their blood, a remedy that often succeeded.'

Another character drawn unflatteringly from life is Carathis, the Caliph's mother. At the beginning of the story we are told that Vathek 'not only loved her as a mother, but respected her as a person of superior genius'. But as the story unfolds she is revealed as being the very personification of evil. It is she who urges him on his fatal course, propitiates evil spirits on his behalf, and strengthens his resolve when his course of ill-doing shows any sign of wavering.

Is this how Beckford now saw his mother, or is it simply a general revenge on the 'Methodistical dowagers' and the restrictions they represented in his life? Certainly at this time his mother was busily engaged in preparing a course in life for him which he had no desire to follow, and was doing everything in her power to discourage his artistic and literary hopes. It was she who was planning his marriage as a counterbalance to the unwholesome attractions of 'Kitty' Courtenay and the equally unacceptable situation of his affair with Louisa. But she hardly seemed to merit the fate meted out to Vathek's evil mother at the end of the story when her son reviles her for having perverted his youth and for having been the sole cause of his perdition. Carathis is a portrait of the Begum in reverse, with all her good qualities turned upside down. She is shown pursuing evil with the same single-minded-ness and determination that Maria Beckford devoted to the pursuit of her own narrow interpretation of the good. Perhaps Beckford only wished to show that either course, if followed without understanding or imagination, could result in the same chaos and confusion.

After establishing the characters of Vathek and his mother with a degree of dry humour the story begins when the Caliph is visited by a stranger who is described simply as the Giaour, a mixture of genie and magician, who is in fact an envoy of Eblis, the prince of Hell. The Giaour extracts a satanic pact from the Caliph and promises in payment to open the doors of the subterranean palace where are hidden the treasures and magic talismans of the pre-Adamite sultans. The stranger demands a terrible price and Vathek has to sacrifice the lives of fifty innocent children in return for his secret.

As soon as the children have been lured into the clutches of Giaour, Vathek, urged on by the evil encouragement of his mother, sets off with a magnificent retinue for Istakhar where he will find the ebony door to the Halls of Eblis. Various adventures overtake the cavalcade, and after being attacked by wild animals shelter is offered to them at the court of the pious Emir Fakreddin, and it is here that Vathek meets Nouronihar, the Emir's daughter, and the child-like Gulchenrouz to whom she is betrothed. The latter, modelled on William Courtenay, is depicted as an epicene creature still living in the harem where he is petted by the mis-chievous and strong-willed Nouronihar who treats him more like a younger brother than a prospective husband.

In Nouronihar we see Louisa Beckford transformed and 'orientalised' by the author's imagination. It is his eunuch's report of her wickedness that first attracts her to the Caliph's notice; the slave describes a trick she has played on him and adds: 'I wish this Nouronihar would play some trick on you; she is too wicked to spare even majesty itself.' Soon after this Vathek and Nouronihar are in love and she pledges herself to join him in his evil quest.

The good old Emir is in despair at the thought of losing his daughter to the Caliph, whose own wickedness is now manifest. In an attempt to save both his daughter and Gulchenrouz he has a secret drug administered to them which brings on all the appear-ances of death. They are then spirited away to a secluded valley where, upon recovering from their trance, they imagine themselves to be in the next world. Nouronihar, however, is not taken in for long by the Emir's pious deceit and, after herself having a vision of the Giaour, escapes to join her lover. Gulchenrouz stays in the secret retreat where he remains in a state of perpetual pre-adolescent innocence.

Vathek and Nouronihar now continue their journey, committing many acts of sacrilege on the way. At length they reach the vast ruins of Istakhar; here they find the staircase of polished marble cut in the solid rock of the mountain at the bottom of which stands the vast portal of ebony. 'Upon each stair were planted two large torches . . . the camphorated vapour of which ascended and gathered itself into a cloud under the hollow of the vault.' The Giaour is waiting for them; he welcomes them 'in spite of Mahomet and all his dependants' and the door flies open to admit them into the domain of the prince of darkness.

Within the Halls of Eblis the evil destiny which has pursued the Caliph reaches its consummation. Though the treasures and magic talismans are now at their command they discover that they are doomed never to escape. They must join the multitude of silent people who wander in the vast subterranean chambers each with his right hand pressed to his side beneath which his heart is consumed in undying flames.[12] This terrible revelation removes all joy from the fulfilment of their quest, and at the awful and irrevocable decree of Eblis their hearts also take fire and they lose for ever 'the most precious gift of heaven—HOPE'. The Caliph's fate is contrasted in the final paragraph with that of the boy they left in the secret valley: 'Thus the Caliph Vathek, who, for the sake of empty pomp and forbidden power, had sullied himself with a thousand crimes, became a prey to grief without end, and remorse without mitigation; whilst the humble, the despised Gulchenrouz passed whole ages in undisturbed tranquillity, and in the pure happiness of childhood.' Here the characters of Vathek and Gulchenrouz have become fused to represent the two unreconcilable aspects of Beckford's own personality: the temperament flawed (as he still saw it) by homosexual and other 'wayward' passions which threatened to make him an outcast from society, and the irrepressible longing to regain the lost innocence of childhood.

The character of Eblis himself is shown in an almost sympathetic light. He is a Miltonic devil; a fallen angel rather than the fire-and-brimstone figure of traditional myth, and prefigures a whole convention in romantic fiction. 'His person', Beckford wrote, 'was that of a young man, whose noble and regular features seemed to have been tarnished by malignant vapours. In his large eyes appeared both pride and despair: his flowing hair retained some resemblance to that of an angel of light.'

Other aspects of the book throw a strange light on the personality of the author. All the female characters, with the single exception of Nouronihar's old nurse, are evil in one form or another, from the Caliph's wicked mother whom he blames for his fate to Dilara, the only one of his wives to be mentioned by name. Gulchenrouz is represented as almost trans-sexual; when he wears Nouronihar's clothes 'he seemed to be more feminine than even herself'. He appears more androgyne than catamite; though a boy his masculine qualities are never once stressed. The whole book, written and developed after the initial creative burst in London as Beckford travelled across Europe, reveals different aspects of his curious nature on almost every page. It is no wonder that he was always to hold it in a special place in his affections and to resent any criticism levelled against it. It is a profoundly autobiographical work, and as time went on Beckford would come to identify himself with his creation of the Caliph Vathek more and more closely. Thus criticism of the book seemed to him like a criticism of himself and could result in one of his outbursts of uncontrollable rage. 'To abuse *Vathek* he deemed a personal insult,' Cyrus Redding wrote of the author at the end of his life, 'his pride took the alarm and he could scarcely restrain his anger, so fierce when aroused, though evanescent.'[13]

When Beckford set out on the second phase of his Grand Tour the book was, of course, still unfinished. He managed to work away at it as he moved from place to place and references to its progress appeared in his letters to Lady Craven and Lady Hamilton as well as to Samuel Henley. He was overflowing with creative energy, at least at the beginning of his tour (the reaction would come later) and travelled in a style suitable to a young heir who had just come into possession of his fortune. It was no longer the case of a callow youth accompanied by his tutor: Beckford now travelled *en prince* with a cavalcade of three carriages and outriders, and his suite consisted of his personal physician Dr. Ehrhart, his harpsichord player Burton, Lettice the former tutor now acting as chaplain and secretary, and Alexander Cozen's son, the thirty-year-old John Robert, an artist of genius, whose business it was to make a pictorial record of their journey. No wonder the procession was once mistaken for that of the Emperor of Austria who was thought to be travelling incognito in the same neighbourhood. The bystanders watched them with wonder; it was as though the Caliph Vathek himself had passed by.

The route they followed was very much the same as before: Ostende, Brussels, Cologne, Innsbruck, Padua and on to Venice, Rome and Naples. But the situation Beckford had left behind him in England was very different. Though his infatuation for 'Kitty' was unabated his feelings for Louisa were rapidly cooling. Her health was beginning to fail but Beckford, with the insensitivity of the self-centred, refused to recognise the seriousness of her condition. He continued to write to her in much the same style, for as always he needed someone to whom he could pour out his feelings. Memories of the three magic days at Fonthill continued to haunt him. In early June he wrote to Cozens from Augsburg: 'Your son is well and grows every day in my esteem. Burton falls into delightful reveries upon the Harpsichord, but often touches certain chords which bring all Fonthill before my Eyes and make me run wild about the Chamber ... My langour is such that I can write no more.' And in much the same mood he addressed Lady Hamilton in Naples by the same post: 'Let me entreat you to send a Letter to Rome as soon as you receive this wretched scrawl which I have hardly spirits to put together; for, to confess the truth, I am still very languid, tho' *perfectly freed* from *illusions*. I bring you an ample treasure of musick and many a strange Arabian tale which I sooth myself with the idea of reading to you under my favourite cliffs of Posilippo.'[14]

The melancholy and languidness at this stage was no more than his usual reaction to the problems he avoided or postponed facing up to, his marriage, his future career in parliament—all that had to be faced when he returned to England. Otherwise his health was still good. In Padua he once more paid his respects at the shrine of St. Antony and described in a letter to Henley the impression made by the multitude of tapers hovering about the altar 'like floating exhalations' and where he again 'grew very devout and melancholy'.

Both devotion and melancholy were banished when Venice was reached and old scenes (though not, it would seem, old temptations) were recalled. A slight but not disagreeable nostalgia overcame him when he saw its domes rising out of the water and found himself back in familiar surroundings. 'A fresh breeze bore the toll of innumerable bells to my ear', he wrote. 'Sadness came over me as I entered the great canal, and recognised those solemn palaces, with their lofty arcades and gloomy arches, beneath which I had so often sat, the scene of many a strange adventure.'[15] Was he thinking of the Cornaro youth and his love of almost two years ago? There is no evidence that they met on this second visit to Venice though his old friends Madame de Rosenberg and Count Benincasa had joined him again.

Beckford reached Rome in time for the feast of St. Peter and St. Paul (29 June). From here he wrote to Louisa making only passing reference to her illness ('take care of yourself, Louisa') and suggesting that anyway it was no more than a 'veil policy' so that she might leave England for a more temperate climate and perhaps also for his own company—this despite the fact that both Lady Craven and Louisa herself had warned him of the seriousness of her state. He could only see her sufferings as they might affect himself: 'I could not live and see your lips pale, your eyes sunk, and the bloom of your cheeks annihilated.'[16] He did not conceal from her that the chief pleasure her last letter had given him was contained in the postscript which was written in the hand of William Courtenay. From now on he became increasingly unresponsive to her love for him, as though, like his own expressions of love for her, it was merely a question of hyperbole. He seemed quite unaware that her heart was broken (or else he refused to face this unpleasant fact) and that this, as much as the tuberculosis from which she suffered, was the cause of her rapid decline in health and spirits.

Meanwhile he wrote a most unguarded letter to Courtenay from which it is clear that both the boy's father (his mother had died the previous summer) and the aunt who had once been so much Beckford's own admirer were now united in trying to keep the two apart. 'I read your letter with a beating heart, my dearest Willy,' he wrote on 1 July, 'and kissed it a thousand times. It is needless for me to repeat that I am miserable without you. You know I can scarcely be said to live in your absence. No words can express my feelings when I read the afft. lines you wrote in our dear Louisa's letter. At this moment I am ready to cry with joy. Do not forget me my own William. Do not forget the happy hours we have spent together. Your poor Mother loved you not better than I do. At any time I would sacrifice every drop of blood in my veins to do you good, or spare you a moment's misery. I shall never enjoy peace again till I know whether I am to be with you when I return. I am certain your Father is set against us, and will do all in his power as well as your cruel Aunt to keep us asunder; but it will be your fault, if you entirely abandon me. What have we done, William, to be treated with such severity . . .' After much more in the same style the letter ends: 'Why cannot we be friends in peace? Is there any crime in loving each other as we do? You will hardly be able to read this letter: it is blotted with my tears. My William, my own dear Friend, write to me for God's sake: put all your confidence in Louisa who loves us both.'[17]

It was a foolish letter to write. Though it is clear that Beckford was in a somewhat hysterical state when he wrote it he should at least have paused to consider what would be the consequences should it fall into the hands of the unsympathetic father or the 'cruel aunt', the very aunt to whom he had written a no less indiscreet letter from Paris at the end of his previous trip abroad. Its tone is characteristic of the recklessness with which Beckford, like his Caliph, rushed almost open-eyed to his doom. It was indeed a personal dilemma which he expressed when he asked what crime there was in a love like his for Courtenay; but he knew perfectly well what the answer of the world would be, what answer Lord Courtenay or his sister Charlotte (now married to the formidable Lord Loughborough) would make if the letter should ever come into their possession. The boy to whom it was addressed would be fourteen years old at the end of the month. To write to him in such terms was quite extraordinarily irresponsible; it was little more than courting disaster.

What makes it all the more sad is that Beckford, when he chose, could write such charming letters to children. Only the day before he had written to the twelve-year-old Archibald Hamilton of the whizzing of rockets and thundering of cannon and prattling of prelates that he had witnessed at the religious festivities. 'My dear little Archy,' the letter continues, 'if you know a Witch, borrow her Besom, mount it and be at the Fireworks this evening; but be sure to get back into your nest—it is much more comfortable than Rome with all its Fountains and Amphitheatres. Your letter I have just received, and it is just like yourself, short and entertaining. I hope you will grow taller and your letters in proportion; but if you was no higher than Thomas Thumb I should love and

esteem you.'[18] How much more sensible had he written to young
Courtenay, who does not appear to have been advanced for his
age, in this same amusing fashion. And how much better for himself if he really wished, as he had confessed to Lady Hamilton, to
be perfectly freed from illusions.

Possibly he was already beginning to sicken for the malarial
fever which attacked him soon after his arrival in Naples. His
nerves had been at full stretch since leaving England; now the
reaction set in. Both he and John Robert Cozens caught the infec-
tion but the latter soon shook it off. Beckford, exhausted in mind
and body, took much longer to recover. He had gone, shortly
after his arrival, to visit the studio of the Welsh landscape painter
Thomas Jones, a friend of J. R. Cozens, but the artist was out and
the two did not meet. On 10 July Jones had recorded the visit in
his diary, noting of the rich prospective patron 'though he is said
to have expressed his great satisfaction and pleasure in terms most
extatic, I never was able to procure a sight of that Gentleman.'
Four days later Jones called on Sir William Hamilton, hoping to
meet Beckford there, but 'saw nobody but Mr. Lettice the Tutor,
Mr. Burton the Music Master, and poor little Cozens, who was ill
in bed of a fever, as was likewise one of the Grooms.'[19]

Beckford must by that time also have been laid up with the
fever, for on the day before visiting Jones's studio he had written
to Louisa a letter full of loving references to Courtenay, now
once more disguised by the female gender ('Tell her all my follies
upon her account and let me know if she is glad I am her Slave'),
which ended: 'My head swims—the Room whirls round, the Sea
I am looking upon seems to my fascinated eyes to assume a
thousand fantastic colours. Strange Islands appear rising from the
Woods. Pity me Louisa—sustain me for God's sake . . .' Ten days
later, rebuking her for her silence, he writes, 'a fever occasioned
by the fatal vapours of this unwholesome Country has reduced me
very low. Like a sick child I cry after you and William.'[20]

The Hamiltons took him off to their villa at Portici for his con-
valescence. Here he was able to lie in the shade of a grove of
myrtles and pine and devote his time to the composition of his
Arabian tale, perhaps starting work on the 'episodes' which were
intended to form a part of it. This peaceful scene with 'the Sun
setting in a sea of gold and Vesuvius flushed with purple' was
described in a letter to Samuel Henley in which he was told that
Arabian tales were springing up like mushrooms, but a hint of the

shadow that was soon to fall upon both Beckford and Sir William
Hamilton was contained in the last sentence: 'Adieu, my dear Sir.
I write in haste, poor Lady Hamilton being much indisposed.'[21]

This is the first reference to Catherine Hamilton's fatal illness.
She had been in sadly declining health for some time but the
hastening of her end, if we may believe the report of the artist
Thomas Jones, was indirectly due to the young man who had
taken the place of a son in her heart. 'Mr. Beckford,' Jones confided in his diary, 'whose exquisitely delicate habit of body obliged
him frequently to change his situation and air, was at this time
accommodated, by the great attention of Sir W. Hamilton, with
the use of his palace or villa at Portici. Dr. Drummond, a Scotch
physician who resided at Naples, was frequently sent for to attend
him, but unfortunately, one day, refusing the convenience of Mr.
B's coach, he must needs ride one of his high-spirited English
hunters and attended by a groom set off full gallop for Portici.
The horse taking fright, the Doctor, I suppose, not being much
in the habit of the management of such animals, was thrown and
bruised in so dreadful a manner that he expired the next morning,
being the 13th of August 1782. On the 25th Lady Hamilton who
had been long in a declining state dyed of a billious fever, rather
prematurely, as it was thought, owing to the sudden shock she
received at hearing the news of that fatal accident which befell her
confidential physician Mr. Drummond.'[22]

Whether in fact it was for himself that Beckford had sent for
Dr. Drummond is a matter for conjecture as he had his own confidential physician in his suite, and he was certainly not to blame
for the fact that the doctor refused his carriage and chose the
hunter instead. Jones was doing no more than report the gossip
of Naples. Whatever the immediate cause of Lady Hamilton's
death it was a bitter blow for him, removing one of the few
people who had managed to influence him for the good without
losing her hold on his affections or being classed among the pious
dowagers who surrounded his mother. No one would replace her
in his life.

An air of sadness pervaded the atmosphere at Portici. Sir
William, to distract his thoughts from a loss that affected him
deeply, flung himself into his hunting expeditions with the king
while Ferdinand IV, for once using a little imagination, saw that
plenty of sport was provided for him. Beckford was left to his
own melancholy thoughts, still weak from his illness. Then

tragedy visited him again. Early in September John Burton, the brilliant musician whose harpsichord playing had so delighted his young patron, succumbed to the same disease, dying about the third of the month. According to Jones his last hours were spent 'execrating in a most shocking manner the person who was incidentally instrumental, as he thought, in bringing him to this deplorable situation'. For Beckford this was the last straw; he packed his bags and on 10 September set sail for Leghorn leaving J. R. Cozens behind him in Naples 'a free agent', in Jones's unfriendly words 'and loosed from the shackles of fantastic folly and caprice.'[23]

His chief preoccupation now was to get home as soon as possible. On board ship he started to translate his *Vathek* into English, but the work was left incomplete; an unfortunate circumstance as time would prove. From Leghorn he made his way north towards the Swiss frontier. He was still feeling far from well, but the ague from which he suffered responded to an extract of bark ('a rare stinkabus as strong as old Nicholas's Scratch' he told Sir William Hamilton) and by the time he had reached Turin his spirits were beginning to revive.

There was a happy reunion in Geneva where he met the Huber family again. The younger made sketches from the adventures of the Caliph while the elder held forth in his inimitable way 'telling stories, the best imaginable'. Meanwhile Beckford had been buying some *objet d'art* while still in Italy; to Sir William, that seasoned connoisseur, he wrote in a letter aimed at cheering the bereaved diplomatist: 'In the course of my Peregrinations I picked up a rare old Japan Porringer which came out of the Medici Lumber Room; but hunted for some Bronze Deities in vain.'[24] It was the beginning of that collecting mania which would grow with the years.

Towards the end of October he left Geneva and was in Paris by the twenty-eighth. His stay there was brief for by 9 November he was at Dover having spent a miserable week in Calais while contrary winds howled dismally and prevented him from sailing. 'I landed by moonlight under the Cliffs and walked to and fro a few minutes in spite of the cold,' he wrote to an unnamed correspondent, possibly Alexander Cozens, as soon as he was back in England, 'My dear Friend . . . you are the only Being to whom I write.'[25] He then left for London and the uncertainties of the future.

11

Marriage

BECKFORD RETURNED HOME to a somewhat muted welcome. The family were laying plans for his marriage and evolving schemes designed to settle him in a more conventional mode of life. They showed no enthusiasm for his literary efforts; their ambition was still to see him safely seated in parliament. On reaching his house in Wimpole Street he found letters awaiting him from Louisa which must have depressed his spirits. Her illness had taken a turn for the worse and she would soon be leaving England for the milder climate of the south. 'My William, I must leave you,' she had written on 23 October, 'the gates of Death are open before me, and whilst a meagre spectre drives me on towards the dark and silent Habitation, I fancy I hear at an aweful distance the busy murmur of the world I am quitting. I can distinguish your voice, and strive to linger in it till I have once more beheld you. Must that blessing be denied me, and must I perhaps in this letter bid you an eternal adieu ?'[1] Though she did not leave the country for some weeks Beckford made no attempt to see her.

He soon moved to Fonthill where Christmas was spent in an altogether more simple way than had been the case in the previous year. He had brought some oriental manuscripts with him[2] and assembled a group of scholarly companions including Henley and an Arabic scholar, probably his old tutor Zemir, who could guide them in their studies and regale them with Eastern stories. 'We are very clean and quiet at Fonthill,' he wrote to tell his cousin Alexander Hamilton, 'ride out every Morn, and translate Arabic every night.'

We know from a letter sent to Henley on 13 January 1783, after the party had broken up, that Beckford was now busily working on the 'episodes' of *Vathek*.[3] These were to occupy him off and on for some considerable time between the years 1783 and

1786, and were three in number, though a fourth, suppressed by its author as being improper, had existed at one time.[4] They are the stories of the 'four young men of goodly figure and a lovely female' whom Vathek and Nouronihar discover in the Halls of Eblis 'holding a melancholy conversation by the glimmering of a lonely lamp'. Like the Caliph and his companion they have all found their way into the power of the Prince of Evil. The episodes, which Beckford originally meant to insert into the narrative at this point, relate how they each came to find themselves in their sad plight, awaiting the moment when they will be deprived of hope and their hearts consumed by undying flames.

All the stories explore the less orthodox aspects of human relationships. The first (though probably, owing to the nature of its subject, the last to be written) gives us a glimpse of Beckford's view of his affair with Courtenay seen from a later point in time to that which influenced the picture of the boy when the story of *Vathek* was written, for a note of disillusionment is now very evident.

It is called *The Story of Prince Alasi and the Princess Firouzkah*. The theme is frankly paederastic, but propriety is saved in the nick of time when it is discovered that the boy prince Firouz has been a girl all the time, the princess Firouzkah, though after the discovery is made she loses no time in getting back into male dress again. In spite of this device it is in fact a story of homosexual love in which the young boy, or boy-girl, is represented as the corrupting influence who leads the older man astray, and the whole presentation of the character of Firouz (Courtenay), deceitful, devious and predatory, suggests that it was written after the scales had fallen from Beckford's eyes with regard to the real-life Firouz. It is a character that bears little resemblance to the child-like and innocent Gulchenrouz. Originally Beckford seems to have written the episode as a straightforward story of love between a man and a youth, for its first title was *Histoire des deux princes amis, Alasi et Firouz*. Through this story, as through *Vathek* itself, there runs the theme of predestined doom. Despite marriage, the prince Alasi is bound inescapably to the other and must share in his fate. It ends on a note of despair: 'O Mahomet! O Prophet beloved of the world's Creator, thou has forsaken me utterly and without hope! What refuge have I, save with thine enemies?'[5] It is the desperate cry of one whose passionate desires, so natural to himself, are condemned by a hostile and unsympathetic world.

The second episode, *The Story of Prince Barkiarokh*, takes us into dark regions of the subconscious where themes of violence, masochism, murder and necrophilia are found lurking in the gloom. It is also an essay in the arts of hypocrisy, the tale of a man who veils his vices from the sight of the good as the only resource of those who are not blind and who know the vicious nature of their own personalities. To know oneself, in other words, means that one must always wear a mask. But to know oneself is not to be liberated from the torturing lashes of conscience. In this episode the criminal progress of the prince towards his inevitable doom is interrupted periodically by visitations from the 'wand of remorse', represented in physical form by the Peri who appears without warning and administers violent punishment to the recalcitrant prince. The episode gives a chilling view of the depravity of human nature and again ends on a note of despair as the prince meets his fate in the knowledge that it is self-inflicted: 'hurled down into the crowd of the damned . . . to be whirled about forever, bearing in my heart the fearful furnace of flame which I have myself prepared and ignited'.[6]

The third and last episode remains incomplete, breaking off in the middle of a sentence as the princess who is the narrator of the tale is about to enter the realm of Eblis. It is called *The Story of the Princess Zulkais and the Prince Kalilah*. The theme here is the forbidden love of a twin brother and sister for each other; a near-incestuous relationship (they are not depicted as being actually physical lovers) that could stand for Beckford's affair with William Courtenay or equally for that with Louisa, for while he and Louisa were not blood relations, as his first cousin's wife she stood almost within the prohibited degree, a fact which added to the scandal of their relationship. Once more fate, this time in the person of their father, intervenes to drive the lovers apart; once more they cry out against the injustice of fate's degree: 'Alas . . . all is over. Our blissful moments will return no more. Why accuse me of perverting Kalilah? What harm can I do him? How can our happiness offend my father? If it was a crime to be happy, the Sages would surely have given us warning.'[7] The autobiographical reference requires no emphasis. In this episode the children's father, the Emir Abou Taher Achmed, bears many characteristics in common with the Alderman and the description of the rigorous upbringing prescribed for the young prince has parallels with Beckford's own strictly regulated childhood.

In all three episodes, as in *Vathek*, a strongly autobiographical theme persists. They are all, in a sense, essays in self-justification or self-explanation. In every case doom awaits the protagonists because fate has implanted in them traits or characteristics which set them at variance with their environment. Though their final fall from grace may be brought about by their own conscious volition, the force that drives them to it is innate, as essential a part of their personality as life itself. They see themselves, therefore, as victims of injustice who cry out helplessly against the cruel chance that has destroyed them. If they are driven into the clutches of Eblis it is only because the Creator, who made them as they are, has manifestly forsaken them. In the *Episodes of Vathek*, as in the story of which it was intended to form a part, Beckford was giving literary expression to the dilemma which had confronted him first in Venice more than two years before and which he was still unable to resolve.

While Beckford, in the calm retreat of Fonthill, was engaged in work on these episodes and busy also with translations of the Arabic manuscripts he had with him, the family, led by his mother, were planning their campaign for his social rehabilitation, an operation they considered overdue. Their reasons for this belief were not hard to find. The rumours which the Christmas gathering of the previous year had started were still in circulation; the affair with Louisa was well-enough known to cause the Begum anxiety; and other rumours of an uglier nature, which his openly expressed admiration for the charms of young William Courtenay did little to disperse, were being repeated about him with increasing relish by those who wished him no good.

At Powderham, too, there had been a change in feeling towards the heir of Fonthill. Young Courtenay's mother had died the previous summer. Viscount Courtenay was easily led, and his wife's death had increased the influence of his sister Charlotte who could no longer be ranked among Beckford's friends. Furthermore her marriage to Lord Loughborough had introduced another unfriendly presence into the family circle, a man wholly out of sympathy with everything Beckford stood for and one who must have regarded the effete and epicene boy who now became his nephew by marriage with a mixture of revulsion and disgust.

The time has come to take a closer look at Lord Loughborough. It is not a pleasant task. Alexander Wedderburn was born in Edinburgh in February 1733, the son of a Senator of the College

of Justice. He was educated at Edinburgh University where he
enjoyed the friendship of David Hume and Adam Smith. Their
influence, however, does not seem to have produced a philosophic
calm in the bosom of the young man who followed his father's
footsteps into the legal profession: after an altercation with a
Scots judge he had flung off his gown and walked out of the court,
determined to try his luck in England.

He was called to the English bar in 1757, became a protégé of
the Earl of Bute, and was elected to the House of Commons in
1761. Though initially a supporter (like Alderman Beckford) of
John Wilkes, he changed sides as often as it suited him and in
1771, after 'one of the most flagrant cases of ratting recorded in
our party annals', was appointed Solicitor-General, to be promoted Attorney-General seven years later. As a lawyer he
notoriously defended the most brutal forms of punishment then
in use and even produced specious arguments in favour of the
public burning of women offenders found guilty of coining.
There was something about him, as 'Junius' noted in 1771, 'which
even treachery cannot trust', while the satirical poet Charles
Churchill summed him up in four devastating and often-quoted
lines:

> Mute at the bar, and in the senate loud,
> Dull 'mongst the dullest, proudest of the proud,
> A pert, prim prater of the northern race,
> Guilt in his heart, and famine in his face.

More unfortunately from Beckford's point of view Wedderburn
was the avowed enemy and rival, both in politics and in the law,
of the former's friend and political patron Lord Thurlow. Wedderburn now sat in the House of Lords as Baron Loughborough
and Chief Justice of the Court of Common Pleas. It was no secret
that he had his eyes on the Woolsack which his rival Lord
Thurlow then occupied.

Unreliable as a friend, unrelenting and vindictive as an enemy,
Lord Loughborough was a dangerous man to anger or oppose.
Beckford, with his whimsical view of life, his enthusiasm for art
and music, his flippant contempt for the political attitudes of the
day, was hardly the man to endear himself to this grimly ambitious
and dourly humourless Scots lawyer with whom he shared but
one common attribute, a Calvinistic sense of guilt. Loughborough
was one of those men for whom Beckford's very considerable

charm had no effect whatsoever; it affected him, in fact, in quite
the opposite way; he disliked Beckford profoundly, was possibly
also jealous of him, and strongly distrusted the influence he still
exercised over the mind and character of his nephew William
Courtenay.

Beckford was soon aware of this source of enmity. Courtenay
himself would seem to have warned him of the hostile element
that now existed at Powderham and threatened to disrupt the
calm course of their friendship. Henley was in their confidence,
and in mid-February received a note in which Beckford gave
voice to his fears. Only initials were used to identify the enemy,
but there can be little doubt as to whom the letters 'L.L.' referred:
'I have seen Wm. again and again since I saw you, but we both
live in horrors of that malicious fiend L. L.'[8]

Altogether Beckford was feeling threatened or harassed from
more than one quarter. Not only did he have to contend with the
critical observations of his mother and the dowagers, with the
new threat to his friendship with Courtenay, but Louisa, though
no longer in England, continued to send him letters full of passion
and reproach. 'Not the reviving beams of the Sun, the hopes of
returning health, nor the change of objects, can dissipate for an
instant the gloom that hangs over my mind', she wrote to him
from Avignon in December 1782. 'In vain I strive to think on a
less interesting subject—your image ever recurrs and renders me
miserable . . . My only hopes are in your letters. They will afford
me some consolation. No words can express how I languish
after them.'[9]

He wrote to tell her of the troubles that threatened his relations
with 'Kitty' and she replied in January 1783 to say how miserable
she was to know that he was being persecuted. But her own
troubles dominated her mind and must have accused his conscience: 'I abhor the sight of human beings, and loath every thing
allied to mirth. Under the pretext of illness, I retire to my apartment, and there without interruption retrace every happy hour I
have spent with you. These gleams of happiness are passed, they
flew before me like shining meteors, not a trace have they left.
The immediate space is dark and gloomy as night. Write often,
tell me you are happy. That alone can render my existence
supportable.'[10]

He was very far from happy. All these various threats to his
peace of mind only served to increase his sense of insecurity. It

was at this moment, when he was least able to offer any resistance, that his mother confronted him with her plans for the future.

The first thing to be dealt with was the book of travel diaries, *Dreams, Waking Thoughts and Incidents*, now ready for publication. The family had decided that the edition must be suppressed. Their reasons for this now seem absurd. The book, though presented in the conventional contemporary form of a series of letters, was otherwise totally unlike the usual eighteenth-century travel book. Beckford's approach was subjective, he sought to convey sensitive impressions rather than to produce cold facts; he allowed his fancy to wander and devoted more space to descriptions of his feelings than to the delineation of architectural monuments or the cataloguing of works of art. It was an unusual book and very much ahead of its time.

His family were indifferent to the significance of all this; what they worried about was the impression the book gave of its author, an impression they considered to be wholly unfavourable. John Lettice led the attack, the same Lettice who had encouraged the publication of the *Biographical Memoirs* and had always been so docile in his attitude to his brilliant but capricious pupil. But now the former tutor was seriously alarmed at the accusations of 'decadence' that were being whispered about his young friend and thought, in his timid and unimaginative way, that the publication of the travel diaries would only serve to add fuel to this fire.

The Begum seconded the tutor's objections and added more of her own. She still clung obstinately to her ambition of seeing her son in parliament. She entirely failed to recognise that it was not a politician but an artist that she had brought into being. And what would the political world, she asked herself, make of a book composed of whims and fancies and that began with the phrase: 'Shall I tell you my dreams? To give an account of my time, is doing, I assure you, but little better. Never did there exist a more idle being . . .' She had no doubt that to publish such a book would compromise her son's reputation among her Whig connections beyond hope of redemption.

The book must go, they decreed, and so must all the whimsical nonsense it represented. But this was merely clearing the decks for more positive action. The rumours of his clandestine love affair with his cousin Louisa, not to mention the more unthinkable rumours that connected his name with young Courtenay's, must be silenced once and for all by marriage. As for the bride, they had

a perfect candidate ready and waiting whose suitability they had
already canvassed, the same 'cold-blooded disciple of pale-eyed
chastity' as a jealous Louisa had once unfairly described her,
Lady Margaret Gordon. It was true that she had little or no
dowry, but as the niece of Lady Euphemia Stewart she was already
almost one of the family, her background was impeccable, her age
(two years his junior) just right, and her character simple and
unaffected. If it was a 'marriage of convenience' there was nothing
unusual about that in the year 1783, and if she was not an heiress
that hardly counted if she was to marry one of the richest men in
England. It would be unreasonable, they argued, for Beckford to
raise objections. Once safely married he could then take his place
in the House of Commons. He owned two boroughs himself and
family influence, if necessary, could offer other openings; there
was no problem about finding a seat. But first the tongue of
calumny must be silenced.

Beckford did not object. He accepted their conditions with an
extraordinary meekness. One can only guess at the reasons that
made him capitulate so completely to their demands. Perhaps he
saw in marriage a way out of his entanglement with Louisa,
though he shrank from the task of breaking the news to her. He
must also have realised that society would expect him to marry
sooner or later and he had no particular objection to Lady
Margaret Gordon. He did not love her, of course, but she had a
fresh beauty and charm to which he was not indifferent, and to
marry the daughter of an Earl of Aboyne whose brother would in
due course succeed to the Marquisate of Huntly had a definite
appeal to a man who was both a romantic and a snob.

His agreement to suppress *Dreams, Waking Thoughts and Incidents* is almost harder to understand. It was his first mature work
to be published, and he had put in long hours of work on its
preparation. But since completing it (the last few 'letters' were
finished in Naples in the summer of 1782 but the bulk of it was
written before his second continental journey had started) all his
creative energy had been concentrated upon the writing of *Vathek*,
and this work now occupied the first place in his thoughts. Perhaps he was prepared to sacrifice his travel diaries so long as he
could keep the precious manuscript of his Arabian tale safely in
his own hands to publish at leisure when he thought fit.

All the same it must have cost him some considerable effort to
kill the publication of a book upon which he had set so many

hopes. It was an experience not dissimilar to that traumatic episode in his childhood when he had been forced to destroy his
collection of oriental drawings. He had learnt then to present a
stoical face to the public whatever the nature of his private feelings
may have been. The lesson was not forgotten. There was no trace
of emotion in the businesslike letter he wrote on 13 April to
Samuel Henley who had been supervising the publication of his
book and had seen it through the press: 'I have been considering
and reconsidering, and cannot reconcile myself in the least with
the idea of committing my *Dream* to the wide world, therefore
must beg you will stop advertisements, entries at Stationers Hall,
etc. etc. Don't too imagine I shall change my mind any more.
This determination is as fixed as the sun. As for the copies I shall
have them locked up like my title-deeds. Not one shall transpire,
so Hamilton must go without his *large paper* for some years to
come. I have desired Mr. Wildman to settle everything concerning
expences.'[11]

It was not, in fact, quite the end of his *Dream*, but very many
years were to pass before it would re-emerge, trimmed and edited
and with much additional material added, as *Italy, with Sketches of
Spain and Portugal* which would achieve a belated success for its
author fifty-one years later. For the present all hopes for a literary
success had to be abandoned in another fruitless sacrifice to Dr.
Lettice's beloved 'shrine of good taste'.

Beckford's next concern was to convey the news of his forthcoming marriage to Louisa. Always hysterical in her reactions it
would not have been an easy undertaking at the best of times, but
now, with her health shattered and her spirits crushed, the task
seemed almost brutal. Both he and Courtenay had written in
March[12] a letter full of foreboding and gloom when Beckford declared that his nerves quivered 'like the wings of an expiring
moth' and 'Kitty' had complained that they had been so persecuted
that they seemed to have been living in hell, but beyond dark
references to 'L' and a typical Beckfordian cry of: 'Pity me Louisa
—the path is at present bordered with flowers, but too soon will
it lead me to barren wildernesses from whence I can never return', he lacked the courage to break the fatal news.

His wedding day had almost arrived before he told her.
Louisa's reply is dated the day before the event and only reached
him after the fatal knot was tied: 'William William what have you
done—cast a look into futurity—and see ... Your wife must

detest me—she will persuade you to abandon me, and I shall never more behold you but thro' the cold medium of a formal relationship. How is that idea to be borne. The tortures of Hell are pleasant to what I feel. O Memory Memory what a curse art thou become! Must hope be for ever excluded from thy pleasing recollections, and must I look for happiness only in annihilation . . .? For mercy's sake write immediately, 'tis I that ask you for consolation. Tell me that I am not entirely forgotten—that you sometimes cast a thought on a being whose whole Soul is devoted to you . . .'[13]

There was to be little consolation for poor Louisa for the few remaining years of her life. His reply reassured her, for her next letter begins: 'Yes my William—I love—I adore you, no bosom ever glowed with a purer and more disinterested affection than that you have kindled in mine', but in fact Beckford's marriage meant the end of everything for her. They continued to correspond, messages of affection reached her, but all her proposals to effect a meeting were evaded. She would still try to maintain her hold on his heart in a desperate and losing battle against her own failing health and her lover's increasing indifference, but it was a battle already lost, lost even before Beckford's gradually growing affection for his young wife made any hope of victory impossible.

Beckford and Lady Margaret were married on 5 May 1783. The ceremony was performed by special licence at Lady Euphemia Stewart's London house. It was not a romantic occasion. The only couple who could congratulate themselves were the bridegroom's mother and the bride's aunt for both had achieved an ambition: the former to see her son safely married and the latter to see her niece united to the owner of so large a fortune. Few marriages have had so inauspicious a beginning, and the fact that it turned out better than anyone could have hoped owed little to the bridegroom. Up to the date of her marriage Margaret Gordon had shown no very distinct personality, but time was to prove that her rival Louisa had been very mistaken in dismissing her so crudely and contemptuously in words prompted more by jealousy than by any true judgement of character. In fact Beckford had met in his wife the only other person who was to come anywhere near to taking the place that Catherine Hamilton had once occupied in his life.

Though Beckford entered into his married life without love he at least from the beginning treated his bride with kindness and showed an appreciation for her innocence and sweetness of character. On the day following their wedding, resting at Tunbridge *en route* for the continent, he gazed out of the window of the house where they were staying on to a scene of rain and hail wholly uncharacteristic for the month of May. He was in the middle of a letter to Alexander Cozens. These gloomy circumstances, he wrote, 'serve only to set off the sweet smiles of Lady Margaret's countenance. She looks happy, and that sight gives me more joy than sunshine ever imparted.' His own mind, however, still lingered on the past and on experiences unconnected with matrimonial bliss. The evening before, the evening of his wedding day itself, had ended with a glowing sunset. He had wished, as he gazed upon it, that Cozens could have been with them: 'The lights we saw twinkling amongst distant Woods and in shady hollows would have awakened a series of romantic conjectures. Perhaps the ruddy tint which lingered in the West long after the sun's going down might have revived too strongly in our minds recollections of a certain journey to Fonthill.'[14]

So it was that he embarked on married life, not looking forward into the future but glancing back to the past, evoking nostalgic memories of those three days when his house had been transformed into an enchanted palace and he had wandered through its rooms in a romantic trance with Louisa and his beloved William Courtenay.

12

Honeymoon

BECKFORD AND HIS WIFE spent most of the next twelve months
abroad, not returning to England until the spring of 1784. Before
leaving the country he had entrusted the precious manuscript of
Vathek, the only copy that existed, into the hands of Samuel
Henley who had undertaken to translate it into English, a task
that the author himself had abandoned after his first attempt the
year before, following Lady Hamilton's death in Naples. Henley
also offered to add notes to the text in elucidation of some of the
more esoteric passages, and the problems arising from these or
from the translation itself were to be the occasion for a considerable correspondence during the next three years or so.

Married life began for Beckford in a state of disillusion verging
almost into cynicism. He and Lady Margaret settled for the first
months of their life together on the shores of the lake of Geneva
where memories of his happy and carefree adolescence confronted
the reluctant bridegroom at every turn. The contrast between
those days of freedom and adventure and his present frustrations
did not help to create an atmosphere of happiness. His mother (as
he discovered in a letter from Louisa) had not been content merely
with his marriage; she had discovered or intercepted letters of
Louisa's addressed to him and was threatening the poor woman
with disclosure unless she broke off all relations with Beckford
and promised never to meet him again.[1] But it was less of Louisa
than of William Courtenay that he thought as he wandered about
his old haunts in a mood of self-conscious melancholy.

Gradually, however, as spring advanced into summer, his spirits
began to revive. At first Lady Margaret was an alien influence,
someone outside his elaborately constructed if artificial world of
romantic images and dreams, but as time progressed and he became more used to her company he began to see that she offered

him a haven of quiet security that he had not previously known. This slow awakening to the realisation of potential happiness is reflected in a series of letters sent to Alexander Cozens between the months of June and August; to Cozens, the only contact he had in England who was a link with Courtenay, with Louisa and with his old life in London and at Fonthill.

On 8 June he writes: 'My Friend, I have been fifty times on the point of writing to you, and as often have I been interrupted. I lead a quiet uniform stupid sort of life on the banks of the Lake; but never angle like the rest of my neighbours. Not a soul except old Huber has the least idea why I should be discontented in the midst of smirking faces and spruce habitations. Every now and then the recollections of past times and happy moments for ever gone, rouses me from my torpid state and forces me to run wildly about on the shore. Sometimes I lie down in an open meadow and observe the clouds rolling along the sky and casting their shadows on the Mountains. 'Tis then innumerable fancies rush upon me. Strange hopes and as strange fears! During these moments I dream of William and of Fonthill whilst the confused murmur of leaves and water lulls me to sounder rest. Lady M walks about gathering flowers from the Shrubs which almost dip their boughs in the Lake. Why am I not happy?—Is it not my own fault that I am miserable?'

On 28 July he writes again. He is just returned from 'the Region of Ice and Crystal' and from 'the silent retired valleys at the base of Mont Blanc'. But even here, he confesses, the image of his dearest William pursues him. He has spent three days in a larch forest totally abandoned to his reveries. 'Would to God you could share them!' he tells Cozens, 'would to God I might converse with you once more upon the subject nearest my heart!' The next day he leaves for Evian where he proposes to wander 'like a melancholy Ghost too full of the remembrance of the World it has left to taste the pleasures of that into which it is entering.'

In the month that followed a change took place. There is no mention now of William, or indeed of Louisa whose name does not, in fact, appear in the correspondence. The melancholy Ghost has, after all, tasted the pleasures into which it is entering and is no longer melancholy any more. 'My Friend, what can have prevented your writing to me?' Cozens is asked on 26 August. 'Do you imagine I am grown insensible to your regard, and that I am dead to our World of Ideas? You are quite mistaken. I am what I have ever been. The Woods, the Mountains, the wild flowery hills, have not ceased to appear delightful in my eyes. I am not lost; but restored to myself. The consciousness of a secure tranquil happiness has recalled these sportive fancies which were wont to form our dearest amusements. I can give myself up to Dreams of India and antient times without fearing to wake with a dreadful start to misery and agitation. I shall return happy and contented with a Companion I love and who loves everything that amuses me. You, of all others, may reckon upon her affection, for she knows how long and how sincerely you have been my Friend. Farewell—convince me by writing immediately, that you likewise are what you have been.'[2]

Bit by bit Lady Margaret had been able to assert her personality. She never tried to rival her husband or to compete with him in extravagant declamations of rapture as Louisa had done; that was not her style at all. She preferred to remain in the background and allow her husband to enjoy the limelight, but just occasionally she would surprise everyone as when, on an expedition up some snowy peak, she had amazed her husband and their guides by her skill in crossing the glaciers without making a false step. In the evenings, too, she would be content to laugh at old Huber's anecdotes or listen to him while he read them extracts from Goldoni's comedies.[3] After a while her husband began to see her with new eyes, and Louisa was sent a letter that can hardly have been pleasant reading for her, in which Lady Margaret's charms were compared not unfavourably with her own.[4]

Life, all the same, was not easy for her. Her husband was all the while in correspondence with Louisa, for though in fact he evaded his former lover's constant pleas for them to contrive a meeting, he was unable to break the habit of confiding in her and feeding his vanity on her continuing protestations of devotion. To make matters worse the meddling Begum, having failed to put a stop to Louisa's correspondence with her son, now tried to fan Lady Margaret's jealousy by revealing to her the unpleasant information that she still had a rival. That Maria Beckford was ready to risk her daughter-in-law's happiness at this early stage in the marriage she had done so much to bring about gives one a disturbing glimpse at the lengths she was prepared to go in order to impose her will on the lives of others, albeit she had no doubt convinced herself that she was doing it only for the best.

It would indeed have surprised and distressed the bride (as it would have scandalised the Begum) had she known what was passing in the letters between her husband and Louisa.[5] The latter, constantly moving from one spa or health-resort to another, was desperately fighting to keep alight the last few dying embers of an affair which, like her own health, was fast sinking into a fatal decline. She could not reconcile herself to the thought that all was over between them, while Beckford himself, with a cruelty which one must hope was unconscious, alternatively raised or dashed her hopes according to the tone of his replies. He was unable to make a clean break with her; he could not resist the impulse to carry on a correspondence that had lost all connection with reality. This resulted in periodical outbursts of irritation when Louisa took his fantasies at their face value and allowed herself to believe that there was still hope.

Her letters sometimes overflowed with endearments, at other times bristled with angry reproaches. She staked everything upon the possibility of a final meeting. Beckford neither agreed nor disagreed with her suggestions, keeping her often in a state of anxious suspense ('I am in a state of hope, fear, impatience and expectation that is not to be expressed') but when it came to the point he always found excuses. Sometimes she indulged in bursts of grim humour. When told that Lady Margaret had been bitten by a dog she showed little sympathy but replied with a story of the witty Duke of Buckingham who had turned on a dog that had splashed his stockings with the remark: 'I wish you was married and settled in the country!' Beckford, she added bitterly, was 'too domestick to feel the force of that curse.'

The extent of her mounting disillusionment was expressed in a letter to which this story was a postscript. 'Tomorrow William I leave this place without having seen you, and without any prospect of seeing you', she wrote. 'This long, long while, surely there is some strange fatality prevents our meeting. Yet pardon me when I say that had you chose, we might have evaded it, and passed a few days at least together in comfort.' She had hit on a truth which at other moments she refused to accept: that Beckford would never meet her again and no longer had any real desire to do so.

Perhaps even sadder than these moments of justifiable anger were those other occasions when Louisa tried to convince herself that the old days could return and that they could all meet happily together as had been the case when she had gladly shared her love for Beckford with William Courtenay. 'Could I but persuade Lady M. to lay aside her fears and judge me impartially,' she wrote at the end of November, 'I flatter myself I might in time gain her friendship and be restored to that place in her good opinion which I once fancied I possess. In short, let me but see you sometimes and I care not how dearly I purchase that pleasure. How I shall love a little Ganimede *de votre façon*! tho' I must ever regret it was not my fate to give it birth . . .' Such passages show a deeper anguish than any of her invectives, her pleadings, or those sudden unguarded cries as when, in a previous letter, she asks: 'Do you and Lady M. occupy the same Room? Gods! what a question! Fool that I am. Why do I dread the answer—what difference will it make in my situation—can it be more wretched?'

By the end of the year Louisa had at last come to realise that she had lost all hold over her former lover's affections. A dull sense of resignation possessed her. 'The insipid uniformity of life is become tiresome to a degree I am unable to express', she wrote to him from Nice on 12 December. 'Time hangs like a dead weight on my Soul. I go to rest—rise—eat and drink—the same dull round of occupations employ my hours—the same set of un-interesting objects strike my eyes without reaching my heart. My passions are calm—yet my Soul is joyless, like a Pool of long stagnant water covered with weeds—its death-like tranquility re-mains unruffled. Even musick has lost the power it once had over me. I feel it for a moment—then sink again into a calm more terrible than the storm of contending passions . . . William, I feel every hour more and more that the aching void of my heart can be filled by none but you—yet I must never hope to live with you in comfort. The deluding meteor that led me to destruction is extinguished. The path before me is dark and silent as the Tomb—its cold dews benumb my Soul.'

Only the belief that she and Beckford might be joined together in some sort of after-life, 'an undescribable something within' that 'speaks us immortal', gave her any comfort. This was now the last shred of hope left in her. 'My William, I will be comforted', her letter ended. 'I will rekindle the flame of hope at that comfort-ing idea—tho' I should never more behold you on this Planet—we shall exist together on some happier. If such happiness is reserved for me how I shall bless the hour when my eyes will close for ever on this scene of sorrow and disappointment!'

So the 'infernal' love of Louisa and her 'lovely Daemon' that they had flaunted before a shocked galaxy of aunts and cousins and paraded in defiance of the not over-strict social conventions of the day, now petered out in bitterness and despair. Louisa's fate seems all the more cruel in that her health was shattered and she was left not only to the remorse of unrequited love but to a gradual fading of her beauty and strength which was to result in her death a few years later at the early age of thirty-seven.

All this was to show up Beckford's treatment of her in the worst possible light. And yet the blame for the unhappy situation in which Louisa now found herself was not entirely to be laid to his charge; it sprang from defects of character on both sides, in the over-intensity of her own feelings and in Beckford's emotional immaturity which could respond to such a whirlwind of passion only on a surface level of heightened language and self-dramatisation. And how could any affair flourish that had to be shared on so equivocal a basis with another? How could Beckford provide Louisa with the reality of what her soul craved for when his own sexual ambivalence was still an unresolved problem? His obvious selfishness makes him appear in a less agreeable light than Louisa, abandoned as she was to a lonely and lingering death, though she, too, had deserted her husband and children in a selfish pursuit of adventure. In fact both were victims of the 'vicious mole of nature in them' and both were unable to escape from the consequences of it.

One reason for Beckford's growing tenderness for his wife was that she had suffered a miscarriage some time in October. It had been caused, it would seem, from the shock she had suffered as a result of the attack by a dog which had occasioned in Louisa an outburst of misplaced humour. Beckford was also worried by a long silence from Henley, the man into whose hands he had placed the manuscript of *Vathek*. Was this book, too, to suffer the same fate as his travel diary? The author reassured himself. 'Thank God', he wrote to his chosen translator, '*Vathec* [*sic*] at least has produced no misunderstanding, and I may still dwell upon its recollection with pleasure; but how can I endure my book of *Dreams* when I reflect upon what disagreeable *waking thoughts* it has occasioned me? If you have a mind to reconcile me to it, let me be assured you are not less my affectionate friend than when you silenced the hiss of serpents at Fonthill . . .'[6]

Neither Beckford nor his wife were in the best of health that autumn and they delayed their departure from Switzerland until the end of the year. January 1784, however, found them in Paris and Beckford himself restored to his usual vitality and able to respond with characteristic zest to the stimulations offered by *la ville lumière*. He even wrote to Lord Thurlow declaring (in relation to his political patronage) how happy he was for the opportunities that presented themselves for him to show his zeal for the government, and added that, his health being greatly re-established, he felt much inclined to sit in parliament.[7] It was a letter that would have warmed the Begum's heart.

He was to leave vivid accounts of this visit to Paris in the period of *la douceur de vivre* just five years before the outbreak of revolution, but the reader must approach his record with caution. Though presented as letters to Louisa, the accounts were in fact written many years later when, in the years 1838–9, he copied them out, possibly from contemporary letters and diaries, and would read them aloud to privileged visitors to his tower on Lansdown Hill above Bath, such as Samuel Rogers and his physician Dr. Gairdner. They must therefore be treated as the recollections of an old man recalling his youthful days, with all the embellishments and lapses into fiction which Beckford loved to add to the bare bones of history, rather than as factual reporting written soon after the events described.

For him Paris was 'this glittering, flaring, noisy, racketing place (Lucifer's own metropolis)' which 'teems as usual with every sort and kind of amusement conceivable and inconceivable'. It was 'more festive, more glittering, and more abominably depraved than it ever was known to be since the *pious* era of Henry the third and his *chaste* mother Catherine of Medicis'. It was a place where Beckford could enjoy himself thoroughly and he proceeded to do so, behaving often in a brash and adolescent way that made few concessions to his new status as a married man. He was still very much the spoilt child of fortune. Lady Margaret was pregnant again and forced often to remain in her rooms while her husband romped about Paris as though still an irresponsible bachelor with more money than sense, butting an intolerable bore in the stomach with his powdered wig and upsetting a glass of water '*accidentally* or the *reverse*, whichever you like best to conjecture' over the richly brocaded lap of Madame Necker.[8]

In spite of his own rather boorish behaviour he avoided the company of his friend Lady Craven who had arrived in Paris all too closely attended by her footman and who was about to launch

herself into a succession of rather more acceptable liaisons that
were to lead her, all in good time, into the arms of the Margrave
of Ansbach. 'I will never come within glare again of her magnificent eyes, if I can help it,' he declared, 'they scorch me up . . .'
For all that she led so domestic an existence without the help of a
husband he considered that she had gone too far. Later on, when
he himself was banished beyond the pale of society, their friendship would be renewed.

Lady Lucan, another visitor he encountered in Paris, presented
problems of a different sort. With this eccentric but rather more
respectable peeress, whose ambition it was to produce an illustrated edition of Shakespeare, he was whisked off to the Biblio-
thèque Royale. Unfortunately, her devotion to literature did not
extend to the physical treatment of the books themselves which
were sadly mauled in her hands. When later she was about to
scratch one of Beckford's own illustrated volumes, a rare purchase
he had just made, with her sharp pointed fingernail, he made a
snatch at the book and 'bore it off like a whirlwind to her speech-
less astonishment'.

It was during this visit to Paris that Beckford made the first
purchases for what was later to be a very remarkable library, perhaps one of the best collections ever made by a single buyer. He
had the true collector's love for rare or fine editions, but at the
same time bought primarily for subject-matter and content; it was
the library of a voracious and informed reader and, as his many
annotations were to show, of a very critical one as well. This was
to give to his collection of books a peculiarly individual flavour.
The beginning of this great library, later to be the glory of Fonthill Abbey and the Lansdown Tower, was made now at the sale
of the Duc de Vallière's collection where Beckford had to contend
with the competition of agents buying for the Emperor Joseph II
and King Louis XVI. The manuscript which Lady Lucan's predatory fingernail had so nearly ravished was bought in the teeth
of these royal bidders. 'It glitters', the proud purchaser wrote,
'with golden letters and curious miniatures where amongst other
nonsensical figures shine Jupiter and Juno married by a mitred
priest before the image of our redeemer.'

Beckford's visits to book sales and the interest he took in the
work of contemporary artists show that his time was not spent
entirely in frivolous pursuits. At this period the first timid attempts were being made to establish a public gallery at the

Louvre (not to be fulfilled in any real sense until the time of Napoleon) and Beckford made this place one of his favourite haunts and delighted in 'hunting out the artists it harbours'. Here he made the acquaintance of Hubert Robert, the charming painter of romantic landscapes and ruins, who was the first curator of the gallery. This artist, whom he described as being industrious as a spider, he discovered 'spinning a most beautiful web, light aerial enfilades of palaces, bowery trees, fountains and waterfalls, gay as Watteau, but more classical. It is astonishing with what facility these creations grow under his pencil.' Though he acquired at some time a study of ruins by Robert (and sold it in 1807) the works he now saw being painted were not destined for the walls of Fonthill House; they were all commissioned by the King's brother, the Comte d'Artois.

It was in the company of Hubert Robert that Beckford, if we may believe his much later account, had an adventure with a lioness in the Jardin du Roi (now the Jardin des Plantes) which he claimed made him the talk of Paris. He was always proud of his 'way' with animals and like many an animal-lover liked to boast of the sympathy he evoked in them. According to his story he became on such intimate terms with the captive lioness in the Jardin du Roi that he could enter her cage and stroke her enormous paw 'leisurely and deliberately touching one after the other the terrific talons with which it was adorned' while the wild creature half-closed her eyes in ecstasy. This extraordinary performance attracted many spectators, so he assures us, and when report of it was related at court 'nothing else was talked of at Versailles during the whole evening'. How much of the familiar Beckfordian exaggeration went into the telling of this tale the reader must decide. Certainly, for all the tattle of Versailles, the episode is mentioned by no one else, though Beckford names a distinguished list of witnesses.

Another Parisian adventure, also recorded much later, has been received with a good deal of scepticism by posterity, and even Beckford himself would sometimes relate it as a dream rather than as an actual occurrence.[9] In the story as it took its final shape in his papers some fifty years later, after many preliminary drafts, Beckford was taken by the architect Charles-Nicolas Ledoux through many obscure streets and several passages to the temple of some sect of Illuminati where he witnessed strange and chilling sights—'the frightful shapes, the unaccountable phantoms'—and

heard the brethren solemnly and sonorously chanting their ori-
sons. On leaving the temple he was assured by his companion, an
adept of the secret fraternity, that by declining to take part in 'a
slight ceremony' he had missed an opportunity of gaining knowledge that might never return.

The story contains many of the characteristics of Beckford's
earlier fantasies, a vaulted temple reached by tortuous subterranean passages, a grim-visaged old man endowed with magical
qualities, a rite of initiation into an esoteric cult, the murmur of
distant voices chanting psalms, all of which relate to scenes described in *The Vision* or to those acted out during the secret party
at Fonthill. It is true that Paris had many secret societies flourish-
ing behind locked doors in the years immediately preceding the
revolution and Beckford, with his eager curiosity, may have witnessed some of their sessions. But the story of 'The Mysterious
Visit' (as he marked the folder in which he kept the manuscript)
has all too much the character of one of his stories, like that
'gothic' tale which he added to his travel diaries at Henley's
request and later published, without revealing its fictitious origin,
when the suppressed diaries were finally revised and issued to the
public in 1834. This story of his visit to the temple of the Illuminati must surely be placed beside it as a work of fiction.

The arrival of the penitential season of Lent made very little
difference to life in Paris. The archbishop's Lenten exhortation,
placarded all over the city, was pelted with rotten eggs. 'Nothing
so vulgar as religion', Beckford noted, 'is ever alluded to at those
select great dinners and *petits soupers* where the new light of
doubly refined philosophy is shedding its beams in profusion. The
insects it has hatched are acquiring fresh vigour every day. Some
lull all terror of the future asleep by their soft drowsy hummings,
others are sharpening their stings, and even threaten to use them.'

Altogether he was beginning to tire of Paris and turn his
thoughts towards home. Everything seemed tawdry or artificial.
'Rousseau's prose poems in praise of nature have been sung in
vain', he wrote. 'Nature is forgotten or unknown. I am sick to
death of the pedantic gabble in such vogue here at the present
moment in the highest circles about political wants and political
miseries, admiration for rebellious America and contempt for
Cathedrals and palaces, Versailles and Rheims certainly not ex-
cepted. The turgid display of sentiment, not one of those titled
praters and prateresses actually feel, is to me perfectly nauseous.

F

The reality of their liberal wishes and good will to the people at large is so problematical that I am more than persuaded this pretended milk of human kindness would turn to the deadliest poison at the first evident appearance of a patriotic thunder storm.'

He had other reasons for wishing to be home again. Lady Margaret was now well advanced in her pregnancy and he wished for her confinement to take place at Fonthill. He was also concerned about the future of William Courtenay. That young man, now rising sixteen, was still a pupil at Westminster School but Beckford, who took a keen interest in his intellectual development, was not at all satisfied with the progress he was making. It would be better, he considered, if the boy could be placed under the care of Samuel Henley, who had previously acted as tutor to the two Hamilton boys.

In February he had written to Henley from Paris: 'I pray God to inspire Ld. C's decision, as I firmly believe you are the only person who can allure William into the paths of elegant literature, to expatiate in which I am certain nature originally intended him. For my sake and William's, remember that a little condescension at present to the father's caprices may ensure the success of some future plan, which all parties will approve of . . . I need not say how much I long to see you, nor how anxiously I wait to hear whether William is to be brightened and polished, or left in the mire like a long series of his noble indolent forefathers . . .'[10] A month later he tried to enlist the help of a neighbour of Viscount Courtenay's, Sir George Younge, in the same plan. He hoped that Sir George would convince the father that 'a twelve months of uninterrupted study in Suffolk is far preferable to flattering dissipation and sistering at Powderham Castle.'[11]

In the early spring of 1784 he was back in England. He was at last reconciled, if not positively eager, to taking his seat in the House of Commons; he looked forward to the birth of a son and heir; he expected to renew his relationship with William Courtenay whom he hoped to see advancing under Henley's guidance from pampered childhood into maturity as a cultivated and reasonably educated adult. Upon the whole the prospect was pleasing and he could look into the future with some degree of complacency and confidence.

13
Scandal

UPON HIS RETURN to England Beckford set about the business of his political career. His boyhood friend William Pitt, still more or less a Whig, had 'made surrounding nations stare' by becoming First Lord and Chancellor of the Exchequer the year before at the age of twenty-four, and was now head of the administration with Lord Thurlow restored to the Woolsack which he had been compelled to vacate during the brief ministry of Fox and North. The warmth of friendship which had subsisted between Beckford and the younger Pitt in childhood had not survived into adult years; the cold and ambitious young minister viewed his old friend with an indifference which later froze into hostility, and it was to Thurlow that the other now turned for political advice.

As his two 'pocket' boroughs Hindon and Saltash were already filled to the satisfaction of the government Beckford had to look elsewhere, taking his seat for Wells in Somerset, a constituency which had previously been represented by his maternal grandfather George Hamilton. As an indication of his arrival on the political scene he made his appearance at Court where Lady Margaret was presented in her new character as a married woman, wearing her court dress and plumes for all that she was in the last stages of pregnancy.

Beckford was bored by political life and from the first took no part at all in the business of the House of Commons. He had no desire to emulate his father and become involved in the hurly-burly of party strife; he resembled the Alderman only in his firm loyalty to the principles of the Whig cause. He looked upon membership of the lower house of parliament as no more than a necessary step to membership of the upper, for his one and only political ambition was to be created a peer.

His claim to a peerage was not so astonishing as might at first appear under the system of patronage then operating and generally accepted by those in whose hands the bestowal of such prizes lay. With his vast wealth, the position he occupied (largely through the memory of his father's services and his mother's family connections) in the Whig oligarchy, and his virtual control of two parliamentary boroughs, he was in many ways an obvious candidate. People had achieved their coronets on less than this. The only real impediments were his comparative youth and George III's reluctance to increase the numerical membership of the House of Lords. Both these obstacles could be overcome by influence and persuasion in the proper quarter. Such influence Beckford fully believed himself to possess.

It was as the political protégé of Lord Thurlow that he hoped to secure this end. The Lord Chancellor had known him for many years, liked him enough to wish to help him, and was eager to have a say in the representation of Beckford's two boroughs, especially Hindon where one of his nominees already sat. A list of new peers had been drawn up when he wrote on the subject in April, but he promised to do his best to get Beckford's name included, though at the same time expressing his surprise that his young friend should wish to quit a more active political scene so soon. However, he declared his readiness to help: 'I should certainly be happy to second your wishes (whatever I think of them) because they are yours, and I have attended to them as well as I know how.'[1] With such powerful help it seemed only a matter of time before the barony was conferred.

While these negotiations were under way Beckford was continuing those other negotiations, started while he was still in Paris, that concerned the future of William Courtenay. On 18 March, the very moment he had landed in England, he had written to Alexander Cozens what was destined, in fact, to be his last letter to this old friend. 'After dozing and dreaming strangely for four hours,' he wrote, 'I landed in a black melancholy twilight at Dover . . . I am very impatient to see you once more, my dear friend, and to assure you I am as Indian as ever. With respect to Wm. I have been for this fortnight past in total darkness. How I long for the sight of his lovely countenance.'[2] But Cozens, aging now, and tired, perhaps, of all that was meant, and whatever was meant, by the word 'Indian', that realm of the imagination into which he had himself initiated his friend so many years ago, was no longer to be drawn on this or any other subject.

Back in London, when sight of the lovely countenance was vouchsafed him at last, Beckford received a shock. Courtenay was no more the seductive child he had formerly loved or even a virile adolescent; he had developed into an effeminate youth interested only in 'millinery', wholly lacking in any enthusiasm for those literary or artistic tastes which Beckford had hoped to stimulate in him. It was a moment of disenchantment. So much had been built on the hopes he had entertained for the boy's future, for the friendship that he longed to see continuing for many years to come, that he could not believe that this was the true character of the youth he had set apart from all others and placed on a pinnacle of loving devotion. He blamed the school, the influence of a home overflowing with doting sisters, anything other than the nature of the boy himself. He returned with more determination than ever to his scheme for Henley to take over young William's education and to wean him from these epicene ways.

To Henley he wrote in some agitation, as much to convince himself that the scheme would prosper as to persuade the other to undertake the task. 'William has been long returned from Devonshire,' he wrote from his house in Portman Square on 19 May, 'and wastes away in the warm sun of idleness. Don't imagine that I have indulged him as much as appearances a year or two ago might have tempted you to believe. Of late I have rated him soundly and done my utmost to check and ridicule his *milenary* dispositions ... How impatient I feel to know your opinion of my friend after a week or two's scrutiny. I am in hopes it will not be very difficult for you to fix his attention to objects more worthy of it than balloon hats or silvered sashes. He has, I am convinced, the most affectionate regard for me, and the most perfect confidence in what I say to him. You may conclude, therefore, he will come into Suffolk with the strongest prejudice in your favour and the utmost readiness to follow your instructions.'[3]

Beckford, as Courtenay's future history was to show, was pinning his hopes on a false conception of the boy's character. However much he might respond momentarily to the older man's ridicule of his effeminate tendencies or obsession with the trivialities of fashion, his character remained irredeemably weak and shallow. To what extent Beckford was himself responsible for this lack of development in the boy whom he had so caressed and flattered a few years earlier is a matter of opinion; what is clear is that he now made every attempt he could to remedy the harm done. Gradually the scales were beginning to fall from his eyes. He began to see the reality that lay behind the romantic vision he had created in his own imagination and he did not greatly like what he saw, a youth (as an earlier letter to Henley had depicted him) 'quite lost in flowers and foolery . . . still more girlish and trifling than you are aware of.'[4]

That Beckford, upon his return from his marriage tour, was deeply disappointed, if not actually disillusioned, by what he saw in Courtenay is beyond dispute. Their friendship, in any case, had reached a critical stage. What Beckford had loved in Courtenay was his childishness, his boyish innocence, characteristics to which the name 'Kitty' could be used, as applied to a child, without the obvious homosexual overtones which the same nickname would carry when applied to an adolescent or adult. But Courtenay was now no longer a child; he was between sixteen and seventeen years of age, not much short of the age Beckford himself had been when he went to Switzerland to complete his education. The boy had physically outgrown his former *persona*, the androgynous qualities which appealed so strongly to Beckford and had inspired the character of the boy-girl Gulchenrouz in *Vathek*. He had therefore ceased to be an object of passionate love in Beckford's eyes (though Beckford's awareness of this was slow to dawn) and his continuing to adopt the pose of 'Kitty', to be 'girlish and trifling' when he was approaching manhood could only seem grotesque, and ultimately decidedly unappealing, to the critical gaze of his former lover.

Beckford realised, of course, that 'Kitty', unlike Gulchenrouz in his novel, could not be expected to pass 'whole ages . . . in the pure happiness of childhood'. But this did not mean that he wanted an effeminate youth in place of the child; such a transformation appalled him. His plan to send the boy to Henley was a last attempt to make something reasonable out of Courtenay and to justify, in his own eyes if not in others, the devotion he had lavished on him in the past. Perhaps the plan might have succeeded. In fact it had no chance. Other influences were being brought to bear on the life of the heir of Powderham, and these did not include any interference from Beckford. They were, as would soon transpire, decidedly hostile to him.

The change in feeling of the once friendly household at Powderham to Beckford's excessive interest in young William dates from a couple of years before, from two events which occurred in 1782, the death of Courtenay's mother and the marriage of his aunt Charlotte to Lord Loughborough. During much of this period Beckford had been abroad, showering his beloved friend with indiscreet letters, but too far away to sense any change in atmosphere, though he had long recognised Loughborough as an enemy. It was only now that he was back home again and actively interfering once more in the boy's life that he began to be aware of the extent of the hostility. Lord Courtenay was an easy-going but weak man. While his wife was alive and his sister was still under the spell of Beckford's charm he had raised no objections to the latter's intimate relationship with his son.

But now the scene had changed. Charlotte no longer loved Beckford—indeed she had reacted strongly, jealously, against him —while her husband cordially detested both the man and his way of life. For him the famous Beckfordian charm had never worked. He was opposed to his political advancement (was not Beckford the protégé of Loughborough's hated rival Thurlow who blocked his own ambitions for the Woolsack and made sport of his defective legal abilities in the House of Lords?) and he deplored, as we have already seen, the unwholesome interest, as he interpreted it, that Beckford so openly showed for young Courtenay.

Neither Lord Courtenay nor his sister (even had she so wished) was proof against the determined authority of this formidable man. Very soon he was the dominating influence in the family. But he was a lawyer and a politician; he played his hand with care. There was no sudden break. He moved slowly, deviously, but with deadly effect. He made no attempt yet to crack the façade of intimacy between the two families, even less that which existed between the two friends; he simply warned the boy's father against Beckford, making good use, no doubt, of the reputation for 'decadence' which still clung to him despite his marriage, and managed successfully to frustrate all the plans made for young Courtenay to become Henley's pupil. A new tutor was provided and arrangements were made for him to take up his duties at Powderham. For Beckford it was both a snub and a warning; a warning he failed to heed.

With the spring the Beckfords returned to Fonthill. The sight of his old home and its associations with earlier days turned his mind momentarily to Louisa to whom he wrote on 20 May: 'I have been so hurried and jaded of late, that I have neither had time nor spirits to tell you how often my soul is transported to the regions you inhabit, and how eagerly it longs to converse once more with yourself.' Why did she not spend the summer with them at Fonthill? Lady Margaret, he assured her, 'will harbour no prejudices, nor suffer herself to look upon such a graceful, lovely being as yourself in the light of a malignant friend'. He must have known that Louisa was in no state of health to accept such an invitation nor would be in much of a mood to do so, even had her health permitted it, when she read his last sentence: 'In about a month I expect a *young one*. Will you not be highly curious to see another little animal *de ma façon*, for I flatter myself it will turn out a true William.'⁵

This hope, alas, was not to be fulfilled. Another disappointment was in store for them. In June Lady Margaret gave birth to a son but the child was born dead. It was a bitter blow for Beckford. With his peerage soon to be announced he had naturally looked forward to the birth of a son, not merely as another 'true William' but as heir to the man who hoped soon to be able to style himself as Lord Beckford of Fonthill.

On top of this he received a grumbling letter from Henley who was clearly irritated at the prospect of losing the chance of having a nobleman's son as his pupil. He hastened to assure Beckford that it was only to oblige him that he had agreed to take on young Courtenay, though 'confident I could have done him *some* good', but the general tone of the letter was designed to make his rich patron feel rather uncomfortable: 'The immediate emolument upon very accurate calculation would but have barely paid my expences, without compensating at all for my time devoted to him. So that I have but little regret on that score, only that perhaps the connexion might be of service to my family, if I should be taken from it before they are fixed in life—and that by acceding to Lord C's application, I have since rejected a proposal that would have been very advantageous.'⁶ Beckford took the hint and sent him two hundred pounds. If it did not compensate for the loss of Courtenay at least it might encourage the tutor in his work on the translation of *Vathek*.

Relations with Powderham Castle were still sufficiently normal for Beckford and his wife to receive an invitation for a month's stay there at the end of September and beginning of October. The Begum, when consulted, strongly advised her son not to go, being convinced, as she later told the artist Benjamin West, that

the Loughboroughs and probably also Lord Courtenay were determined to injure her son's reputation and somehow 'lower his
importance'.[7] Beckford took no notice. Even though the attractions of William Courtenay were now on the wane for him, if they
had not, in fact, ceased altogether to affect him, he could not
resist another visit to the house where they had first met, where
memories of the earlier 'Kitty' still lingered. No doubt he was also
curious to see the tutor who had been chosen in opposition to his
own plans for the boy, and to discover whether he had been able
to affect any improvement.

So Beckford walked into the trap that his enemy had set for
him. But it did not go off with quite the snap that Loughborough
had intended. The wily lawyer had been working on the boy
hoping to find incriminating evidence against Beckford. He does
not seem to have succeeded, though Beckford found his young
friend, as he told Henley after the visit was over, 'more to be
pitied than any reptile that crawls the earth . . . mangled, bruised,
and smashed every day'.[8]

Loughborough hoped to catch his victim in some compromising situation, and later spread the rumour that this in fact had
happened, that Beckford had been caught in Courtenay's bedroom
in circumstances that offered no reasonable explanation. But did
such an episode occur? Though the visit was obviously a thoroughly disagreeable one the Beckfords stayed until the end and
it was not until at least two weeks later that the Courtenay family
began to make complaints about his conduct. If he had indeed
been caught, as the story was later to be spread, in his young
friend's room with the door locked, then surely he would have
been ordered out of the house at once and threatened with immediate criminal proceedings. In fact he left quite normally with
his wife at the end of their stay and was able to write, in a great
state of irritation but with no sense of any guilty secret, in the
letter to Henley already quoted, that he had been 'wonderfully
vexed and griped with L pills' but had no more to report of his
visit beyond the fact, hardly to be wondered at, that it had been
passed in 'one perpetual worry'.

Beckford returned to Fonthill unconscious of the storm that
was soon to break over his head. The newspapers had already announced the list of new peers about to be created and his name
had been included among those to be made barons. His wife was
again pregnant and hopes for an heir were revived. It was then

that complaints of his 'unnatural' conduct with Courtenay came from Powderham Castle. Since his departure Loughborough had continued to put pressure on the boy and some sort of confession had been dragged out of him. Worse still, for Courtenay's confession, whatever it may have been, still fell short of anything warranting a criminal charge, some of Beckford's letters to the boy, those passionate, romantically expressed, extravagant and heedless letters, had fallen into Loughborough's hands. The letters were dynamite and Beckford must have known it. Suddenly he found himself face to face with disaster.

For the moment the scandal was confined to the immediate families concerned, though the damaging evidence against Beckford had somehow been revealed to Lady Margaret's brother. The fiery young man, at this time styled Lord Strathavon, came storming down to Fonthill determined to rescue his sister, but Lady Margaret, whose loyalty to her husband was the only good thing to come out of this sorry episode in their lives, flatly refused to be rescued. No one was in a stronger position than she to know of her husband's innocence of the gross charges made by Loughborough, and she stood by her husband throughout. Unable to persuade his sister to fly away with him Strathavon then slapped Beckford's face, hoping to provoke him to fight a duel, but this clumsy stratagem also failed and the young man was forced to leave Fonthill unsatisfied and unaccompanied.

Strathavon's visit had at least demonstrated to the family the gravity of the situation, and a council was hurriedly called. It consisted of Beckford, his wife, his mother, Lord Thurlow and John Lettice. Of these his mother and possibly also John Lettice were aware of his bisexual nature and therefore of his vulnerability to any charge of homosexual behaviour, even when based on evidence as slender as that which his enemies now seemed to possess. A charge, if legally pursued, would be one of buggery, as defined under an act of Henry VIII then still operating and which, if proved, could result in a sentence of death.[9] What was Beckford to do? He denied the fact of any particular episode at Powderham such as Loughborough now claimed had taken place, but he realised, or if he did not Lord Thurlow would soon have convinced him, that even if acquitted by a court of law through lack of evidence the publication of his letters to Courtenay, read in such a context, would damn his reputation for ever.

Such was his unenviable dilemma. The Begum's solution had

something of the earthiness of the early eighteenth century about it. Let her son go up to London and parade about with half a dozen Covent Garden whores. This, she claimed, would do more to remove suspicion than anything else.[10] The suggestion was hardly one to appeal to Beckford and he rejected it, not so much from pride (as his mother seemed to think) as from fastidiousness of temperament. He could see no point in acting so obviously out of character.

The only other course the family council could suggest was that he should leave the country until the storm had blown itself out. This was the advice of Lady Margaret and it was strongly endorsed by Thurlow and Lettice. It meant, of course, that he would have to go alone, for his wife, pregnant once more and having previously had two miscarriages, was in no state of health to submit to bumpy roads and the hazards of a channel crossing in late October. If the plan offered nothing else it at least meant that Beckford, once abroad, would be safe from arrest, and meanwhile his family would have time to negotiate with Loughborough. As no other scheme seemed feasible, Beckford reluctantly agreed to go.[11]

By 29 October he was at Dover. But for the eighteenth-century traveller contrary winds or other causes often prevented an immediate embarkation and it was not unusual to spend anything up to a week in a channel port waiting to sail. Such was the case now, and Beckford had time to reflect once more upon his predicament. To leave the country alone, without his wife, must have all the appearances of a sudden flight; and flight immediately implied guilt. If he had indeed been caught at Powderham *in flagrante delicto* with Courtenay then he would have had every reason to fly, and the sooner the better. The fact that now, upon further consideration and with the means of escape ready to hand, he decided to return to Fonthill, is surely proof that nothing happened at Powderham beyond those usual indiscretions of language and expression in which he had always indulged.

If any further proof were needed it lay in a letter which Lady Margaret sent to her aunt Lady Gower shortly after her husband's return from Dover. 'I flatter myself,' she wrote, 'you cannot dissaprove of the part I have taken, nor of my conduct; sure, I was not to abandon *a man* who had always *behaved* to me with the *greatest tenderness and affection.* The satisfaction I feel at having acted in the manner I did, is not to be expressed; I every hour see fresh proofs of gratitude and affection from my dear husband. The affection you have always shewn, my dear Lady Gower, makes me believe you will now shew it and stand forth as my friend, now that I want your assistance; and shew by your goodness to me and my husband [that] you do not believe the half of what has been said. I wish it was in my power to persuade you to come down here. I am not well enough to write, and yet have so many things I wish to inform you of, relative to Lord L[oughborough]'s behaviour, that I should take it as the greatest favour in the world; would you but come and see me, I am apt to think I should convince you how much to blame my brother has been.'[12]

Beckford's return to Fonthill was in a sense calling Lord Loughborough's bluff. It was now up to him to prosecute or to withdraw his charges. In fact he had no intention of doing either. He had insufficient evidence for legal action but it was still in his power to wreck Beckford's character, and this he now proceeded to do. On 27 November the following paragraph appeared in the *Morning Herald*: 'The rumour concerning a *Grammatical mistake of Mr. B——* and the *Hon. Mr. C——*, in regard to the genders, we hope for the honour of Nature originates in *Calumny*! For, however depraved the being must be, who can propagate such reports without foundation, we must wish such a being exists, in preference to characters, who, regardless of Divine, Natural and Human Law, sink themselves below the lowest class of brutes in the most preposterous rites.' Other newspapers took up the tale, and similar reports were to feature in their columns over the next month, including slighting references to the Ministry that was to give the offender a peerage, and even dragging in offensive remarks, purporting to be sympathetic, about 'the young and beautiful wife of one of the Monsters'.[13]

Beckford was completely helpless against this onslaught of vilification and abuse. If he denied the insinuations or brought an action for libel what would happen? Lord Loughborough would produce letters, those fatal pages full of expressions of endearment and love, that would show up the writer's character in a far from 'normal' light and would appear as ample corroboration of the conduct described in the offensive paragraphs. Loughborough's triumph was complete, and he probably cared little that his wife's nephew was also a casualty of the press campaign he had inspired with such success. He had caught Beckford in a trap from which there was no escape.

The whole of London buzzed with the scandal. Beckford's peerage was quietly dropped and no more was heard of it. The self-righteous critics who had clacked their tongues at reports of the Fonthill 'orgies' three years before now congratulated themselves that their worst prophecies had come true. One dowager, carried away by her virtuous indignation, declared that after Beckford had 'extravagantly and ridiculously addicted himself to music all prospect of his becoming great or respectable was over', though she expressed surprise that 'his conduct was vicious'.[14] Lord Pembroke, writing to his son from Italy, was eager to know all the details, 'the exact business, how, when, & by whom, & with whom discovered? Who passive & who active . . .?' and later on, with all the special interest of a country neighbour, enquired 'Is Beckford at Fonthill, and is he chassé or still received in company?'[15]

Sir William Hamilton at his embassy in Naples received a highly inaccurate account of the affair from his nephew Charles Greville (who was also a relation of Beckford's through his mother) which ended with the comment: 'His promised honors will be witheld; he probably will be obliged to vacate his seat, and retire to Italy to make up the loss which Italy has sustained by Lord Tilney's death, unless he aspires to the office of G. Chamberlain to the K[ing] of P[russia].'[16] Lord Tilney, it should be pointed out, had suffered a similar scandal a generation previously and the King of Prussia's homosexual tendencies were well known.

Greville's letter is interesting as it gives an account of the Powderham affair as it was being circulated round London, and may be taken more or less as the story that Lord Loughborough had concocted. 'It seems', he wrote, 'young C. was put to a school with a clergyman near Fonthill; he [Beckford] went over very early one morning before they were up & into Courtenay's room; Mr. Moore, the tutor's name, heard a creeking & bustle, which raised his curiosity, & thro' the key hole he saw the operation which it seems he did not interrupt, but informed Lord C. and the whole was blown up.'

The inaccuracies in the story as recounted by Greville (and by countless other club gossips no doubt) are obvious enough. It was not near Fonthill but at Powderham that the episode was supposed to have occurred; the tutor's name was not Moore but Taylor; Beckford was staying in the house and did not 'go over' anywhere. The change of *venue* from Powderham to 'near Fonthill' in this version of the story is interesting, however, in view of the chief weakness in Loughborough's whole calumny. As has been pointed out, if Beckford had actually been spied through a keyhole at Powderham in the manner described here then he would certainly have been turned out of the house on the spot if not actually arrested. By changing the whole circumstances of the affair, as this bogus report does, Beckford's enemy managed to avoid the one weakness which, upon reflection, would have made his whole story untenable.

The version of the affair as related by Greville had, none the less, sufficient currency for Mrs. Beckford (who had not been present at Powderham) to feel it necessary to produce her own version of it in an attempt to exonerate her son. According to a story she told Benjamin West the Courtenay boy had been acting as a go-between, carrying love letters between his aunt and Beckford, that one of these missives had fallen into the wrong hands, and that Beckford had gone to the boy's room, locked the door, and proceeded to administer a horsewhipping. It was at this moment that the tutor had clapped his eye to the keyhole. The Begum's motives were no doubt for the best in trying to counter one story with another, but her account is no more reliable than Greville's, if only for the reason that Beckford never showed any indication of being in love with Courtenay's aunt, however much that lady may at one time have felt a *tendresse* for him.

For all the Begum's ingenious stories and Beckford's own strenuous and continual assertions of innocence the mud which Loughborough had thrown at him was to stick for the remainder of his life. Though nothing had been proved against him society accounted him guilty and turned its back on him. Lady Hamilton's warning that if he did not keep a watch upon himself he would become a lost man, that his reputation would be lost 'never, never to be regained' had now come terribly true. For the rest of his long life, and he had sixty years still ahead of him, he would never escape from this imputation in the public mind. When Hester Thrale six years later was reading *Vathek* she claimed to discover 'Beckford's favourite propensity' on every page,[17] while twenty-five years after the event he would appear to Byron as the 'great Apostle of Paederasty' if also as the 'Martyr of prejudice', which was perhaps the more just title of the two.[18] Even towards the close of his life, after he had left Fonthill and was building the Lansdown Tower, there was a moment when the workmen struck,

refusing to work for a 'bugger', and Beckford was only persuaded by the master builders from leaving Bath in a fury.[19]

The question remains as to why Loughborough pursued Beckford so relentlessly and humiliated him so completely. Jealousy
lay at the root of the matter. Jealousy of a man who had all the
ease of wealth and natural talent from one who had had to struggle
for his success in a hard and competitive world; jealousy of the
tender feelings his wife had once felt for this much younger man;
jealousy of the political patronage which Beckford could command without effort and of the honours he could claim without
any very obvious merit. All this rankled in Loughborough's mind
and was fed by a strong personal antipathy which amounted to
real hatred. To this must be added the fact that in ruining Beckford he was also damaging his rival Thurlow whom he disliked
almost as much. If by hurting the one he could score off the
other, so much the better for him. When he found that he had
Beckford at his mercy nothing could stop him from taking his
revenge.

How completely successful Loughborough was to be in destroying Beckford's reputation even he himself might have been
surprised to learn. Years later Sir William Hamilton, who had
always championed Beckford, would still be discussing means for
his 'getting into the world again', pointing out that 'no direct
accusation lies against him, and it is now 20 years since an unfortunate suspicion arose and was maliciously encouraged'.[20] It
was all to no avail. The verdict of society had gone against him,
and from that sentence there is no appeal.

14
Exile

LORD LOUGHBOROUGH had certainly hoped to drive Beckford out of the country as is clearly indicated by the campaign he inspired and organised in the press. On 1 December the *Public Advertiser* hinted that both Beckford and Courtenay had fled to Italy, adding that 'Florence is the place of destination fixed on for the eccentric couple', and on the thirtieth of the same month the *Morning Herald* plainly and wrongly announced that 'The Fonthill fool is ere this in Italy. Are we, if possible as foolishly to suffer the money that was his, to go after him.'

Beckford's fortune, luckily for him, was beyond the predatory grasp of his persecutor but was not the least, as the paragraph in the *Morning Herald* shows, of the causes of Loughborough's hatred and jealousy. The extent of this fortune, as we know, had always been a subject for exaggeration by Beckford's forebears, and their policy had sufficiently succeeded for the rumours of his own wealth always to err on the side of excess. Ten years later the artist Joseph Farington, quoting the architect James Wyatt, noted in his diary that Beckford's income in the last three years from Jamaica alone, not counting his English interest, 'has not been less than 120,000 [pounds] a year'.[1] This statement represents the prevailing report of gossip but in fact, during the years of his greatest wealth, Beckford's income from all sources rarely exceeded £45,000 a year; and the average, before his building and other extravagances greatly reduced the sum, was between £27,000 and £29,000.[2] Severe inroads were made on this annual income by the almost constant litigation concerning his West Indian properties and the plunder of his legal advisers, but even so, if not as rich as rumour would have him be, he was certainly a man of considerable wealth, and unlike the great landowners of the day, it was money that was easily negotiable and not tied up in farms and acres or complicated by entail. In this sense, as has been shrewdly pointed out, his fortune was more like that of a modern American millionaire than of an eighteenth-century magnate.[3]

It was no doubt behind the protection of this fortune that Beckford hoped to hide himself, and with its aid that he expected in due time to be able to buy his way back into the favour of society. But this was not to be, or if it was so, then only in a limited sense. For the next decade all that his wealth could do for him was to mitigate the severity of an almost continual exile abroad.

At first he hoped to be able to brazen out the attack on his character by remaining at Fonthill with Lady Margaret and behaving, as much as possible, as though nothing had happened. But the great rooms of Splendens echoed to no footsteps but his own. Society kept its distance; even the servile Henley, while still ready to assist in his patron's literary work, found unconvincing excuses for evading an invitation to stay, his offspring suffering from 'one of the thousand evils that children have to contend with' and his wife, to judge by the string of ailments listed, almost upon the point of losing all natural means of locomotion, so that his declining a journey to Fonthill was a hard necessity against which, so he averred, he had no remedy.[4] Only Beckford's immediate family came to visit him, his mother, Lady Euphemia, his sister; all people whose company, just at this moment, he would quite as well have done without.

It was only natural in the circumstances that he should look for a scapegoat, someone upon whom he could vent his rage and blame for all the frustration and humiliation which his ostracism was causing. It was upon the once beloved head of William Courtenay, the 'Dove' and object of such extravagant devotion in former days, that his wrath was now to fall. To his belief that Courtenay had betrayed him was added all the irritation he had felt before the catastrophe at the boy's overt femininity and the disillusion caused by his having outgrown the childlike charms that had once been such a potent cause of attraction. 'Let it suffice for me to assure you', he wrote to Henley, 'that a certain young person I once thought my friend has proved himself the meanest traitor and blackest enemy. You may guess who moved the wires and made this miserable puppet dance to its destruction.'[5] The spell which had once enthralled him was now entirely broken. Courtenay would never be forgiven; three years later

Beckford could still only think of him as 'that cowardly effeminate fool'.[6]

His rage, and the violence of his reaction against Courtenay, sprang not only from his feeling of betrayal but from the fact that now, at long last, he saw Courtenay as he really was, no longer the seductive ephebe of his imagination but a pathetic, weak, crushed and spiritless youth lacking in both loyalty and strength of character. That he himself had done much towards the creation of this image, or that the unfortunate youth had been terrorised and broken by the relentless Loughborough, mattered to Beckford not at all. With his exalted view of friendship he could see nothing to mitigate the disloyalty of the friend who had been the cause of his fall. He cast him off completely and in the future, when he spoke of him at all, did so only with contempt. They never saw each other again.

Courtenay's subsequent career was to end in tragedy and disgrace. He succeeded his father as third viscount in 1788, but once his own master his character, never very strong, gave way completely and his ill-concealed homosexual activities soon made him notorious. By 1811 things had reached such a pass that he was threatened with a criminal prosecution. At first he tried to brazen it out, saying that he would elect to be tried by his peers who were all like himself and would not decide against him, but when the stark reality of his situation was finally brought home to him, his resolution collapsed. He 'wept like a child, and was willingly taken abroad on a vessel . . . and passed there under a false name'.[7] His exile was permanent. He died in Paris in 1835 at the age of sixty-six, having four years previously been declared Earl of Devon when his relations in England, with an eye to the succession, had called the earldom out of abeyance.

If Beckford's return to Fonthill after his flight to Dover had been something in the nature of an act of defiance, his complete isolation there, as one month followed another, began to prey on his nerves. He who had been used to finding himself always the centre of attraction, who had enjoyed every moment of his freedom, of the choice of company and of interests and activities so varied and exciting, soon began to chafe at the restrictions now imposed on his life. Though he loved the woods, lakes and groves that surrounded his great house their confines quickly began to appear restricted to someone who had so recently been ranging all over Europe. He had had his fill of his mother's

warnings and advice while Lady Euphemia Stewart's pious reflections always drove him to distraction. But his wife's confinement was drawing near and after their past disappointments
there was no question of their moving until the child was born.

To while away some of these idle and boring hours Beckford
set to work transcribing his letters, in particular those which he
had addressed to Louisa, into a red leather-bound copy book. The
work had been started some time before when he had entrusted it
to Madame Anne-Marie de Starck, a former nun who had taken
refuge in England and was one of his circle of oriental enthusiasts; but now he took the work in hand himself with all the
thoroughness of a gardener busy with his pruning-hook, im-
proving sentences here and there, leaving out certain passages and
redrafting others. He was eager to present a better picture of his
life than the letters might show if left to speak for themselves, but
as a result of his labours he was to create many problems for his
biographer. However, he could congratulate himself that he was
in good company, for had not Alexander Pope done just the same?
Beckford was to continue this work of editing and transcribing his
letters at various stages during the rest of his life, always with a
view to showing off, to its best advantage, the character in which
he hoped to present himself to posterity.

For the present, however, the work was also a sort of therapy,
a process of rehabilitation for himself, if not yet for the public, of
a self-esteem which had received a very severe mauling. The blow
to Beckford's pride had been a shattering one. In former times he
had wandered through the Fonthill woods in an agreeable state of
fashionable melancholy; now, as he took the same solitary walks,
he had very real reasons for giving way to the spirit of despair.

Into this gloom there flashed a welcome ray of light in February
when Henley sent the first portion of his translation of *Vathek*. It
had, the author declared, 'all the spirit of the Caliphes and their
Daemons', and he longed to see the remainder of the work. His
curiosity was gratified a month later. On 21 March he wrote to
Henley: 'You make me proud of Vathek. The blaze just at present
is so overpowering that I can see no faults, but you can depend
upon my hunting diligently after them ... Were I well and in
good spirits I should run wild among my rocks and forests telling
stones, trees and labourers how gloriously you have succeeded.
My imagination is again on fire. I have been giving the last
trimmings to some Episodes and sown the seeds of another

which I trust will bring forth fruit in good season. I eagerly hope
you will one day or other introduce those plants to our English
soil . . .'[8] The new Episode upon which he now began to work
must surely have been the story of Prince Alasi and Princess
Firouzkah, originally cast as a straightforward homosexual tale
under the title of *Histoire des deux princes amis*, in which he explored again the history of his relationship with Courtenay as seen
after the mist of romanticism had evaporated or been blown away
by the Powderham scandal, and in which the boy-lover is no
longer the childish and devoted Gulchenrouz but the cruel,
capricious and destructive Firouz.

The correspondence with Henley quickened as one question of
interpretation after another cropped up over the text. Should not
Carathis suffer a different and more conspicuous punishment than
the rest on account of her 'superiority of wickedness' the translator
asked, in ignorance, it must be hoped, of the parallels between
that character and the author's mother; a reference to the Bis-
millah was anticipating history by a hundred years and must be
discarded; mention of 'Watering Pots' also worried the erudite
clergyman as being out of place. He was concerned, too, about the
fate of Nouronihar; should not some discrimination of punishment be shown between her fate and Vathek's? 'No doubt she
deserves to be damned,' Henley considered, 'but Vathek deserved
the heavier damnation.'[9] All these points Beckford hoped to discuss with him in person, but Henley thought it more prudent to
continue his enquiries by letter.

Reading the English translation of his book had had a tonic
effect upon Beckford's despondent spirits, but he still felt in-
hibited and humiliated by the social isolation into which he had
been forced by Loughborough's accusations and innuendoes. On
9 April Lady Margaret was safely delivered of her child, a daughter who received the names of Maria Margaret Elizabeth, and at
least one of the reasons that had tied them to Fonthill ceased to
exist. But now that she was able to get about again his wife would
also begin to feel the sting of the ostracism that must necessarily
include them both. Yet they were free to travel, so long as it was
outside England, should they wish to do so. It was six months
since the fatal visit to Powderham had taken place. Beckford was
beginning to feel that he could now safely leave the country
without it thereby implying any acknowledgement of defeat.

[He was still in something of a quandary, however, and another

three months passed before he reached a final decision. To Lettice
he complained that he was fretted to a skeleton by the suspense
and torment in which he lived. When that faithful friend coun-
selled patience he exploded with anger: 'Confused as I am, your
letters make me *more confounded* and then to talk of patience and
quietness at Fonthill. Great God! do you comprehend me so
little. Rather advise some retirement amongst the Alps surrounded
by the few friends who are yet left me than the remaining wrapped
round with the dismal winding sheet of Salisbury Plain, tormented
with paragraphs and scared by unknown terrors and phantoms but
half discovered. Who are these slumbering spirits whose repose
my Mother has lately learnt I could only at my peril violate? Pray
inform me and dream not Ld. Loughborough has taken lodgings
at Shaftesbury to read my letters or placed marksmen on the road
to shoot every mail flying that brings intelligence to Fonthill.'[10]

Gradually the longing for freedom began to assert itself. He
would rather, he declared, sit in the pillory a mark for all the
rotten eggs and oranges in the capital than remain at Fonthill
pestered with the 'snivling advice' of his family. 'And can you
suppose', the unfortunate Lettice was asked a fortnight later, 'I
will stay here with my hands crossed on my breast—and my
mouth pursed up into a demure simper—whilst my heart inspires
nothing but revenge, and all uncharitableness. You ought from
your knowledge of me to be certain such caution, quietness and
moderation is quite out of my character . . .'[11] All the same, in
spite of this fine bravado, he was aware that if he left Fonthill it
could only be for the continent for an unspecified period of self-
imposed exile. For him, thanks to his enemies, there was no
longer any chance now to 'shine forth in London—appear at the
Opera—at Robsons—at the Exchange—at Lord Exeter's concerts'. The only things that remained sure in the wreckage of his
life were the support and devotion of his wife and the book into
the narrative of which he had woven so many strands from his
past existence.

The Beckfords eventually set out on 23 June, Henley still
having failed to pluck up enough courage to visit Fonthill. He
was all apologies, 'much mortified' indeed, but assured his patron
that his wife's unspecified complaint was 'rather worse than
better'. Beckford returned him the translation of *Vathek*, which
still required revision, so that when he sailed from Dover Henley
had in his possession the only copies that existed of both the

French and English texts. Fortunately Beckford retained his manuscript of the Episodes, which were as yet incomplete, as he had no second copy.

Switzerland was once again their destination. They settled near Vevey at the Château de la Tour de Peilz where Beckford had to make the best he could of what was in fact little more than unofficial exile. Impatience, spurred on by that irascible temper of his, had driven him to this extreme when more prudent advice, Lettice's in particular, had encouraged him either to remain where he was or to embark on a prolonged tour of his West Indian estates, which at least would have had the appearance of business rather than flight. But Beckford had reached the end of his patience, a virtue which for him was always in short supply; furthermore he knew that there was no way of reaching any sort of an accommodation with the Loughboroughs. Whatever he did, whether he remained in England or went abroad, his action could be construed to his disadvantage. If he remained a social outcast at Fonthill it would look like defeat; if he 'fled' abroad then it would give the impression of an acknowledgement of guilt. At least the latter course gave him more freedom and an escape from constant reminders of his plight or exposure to the snubs and strictures of society. It was really (short of going to Jamaica) the only course open to him.

In Switzerland, too, he had friends who were less likely to be censorious, nor would there be the same social pressure to resist the splendid hospitality that his fortune enabled him to offer people. Upon the whole he was received in a friendly spirit in the circles where he was already well known, only the English demurring at his presence among them. His old friend Jean Huber showed a typical tolerance, though somewhat despairing at the prospects for the future. 'This fellow Beckford really is a subject for a moralist', he wrote to Germaine de Staël. 'Extravagant conduct, arising from a Don Quixote-like character rather than depravity, has lost him beyond hope—however exemplary a life he later leads.'[12]

Exemplary his life now became. 'Calmly resigned to my present situation,' he wrote to inform a friend, 'I cling fast to my tutelary Mountains . . . We continue the favourites of Heaven in respect to weather, having violets and wallflowers in profusion. Flies buzzing a summer song almost every day on the Terrace and now and then a butterfly by way of regale. Are you not astonished and have we not reason to adore the great Mithra . . . ?'[13] For a moment, indeed, they basked in sunshine after the stormclouds of England. The trials through which Beckford and Lady Margaret had passed had drawn them closer together. Gratitude for the support which she had given him in his ordeal was allied on Beckford's side by a genuine and growing affection, while his wife never seems to have wavered in the love she felt for him. Soon she was pregnant once more and hopes grew that this time she would present Fonthill with an heir.

During the summer and autumn of 1785 Beckford devoted much of his time to work on the Episodes which he now saw as an integral part of *Vathek*, the tales within the tale which would complete the artistic whole of the work, building up a still more inexorable sense of doom to underline the final catastrophe in which the protagonists of each story, led by an inescapable destiny, share an identical fate. Henley had been pressing for the publication of his translation on its own, both before Beckford left England and since by various hints in the letters he sent out to Switzerland, but the author was in no hurry. He wished the French text to come out first, and also wanted to hold up the publication of any version until the Episodes were finished and the entire work could be issued as a single volume.

He made his position quite clear on this subject in a letter he wrote to Henley on 9 February 1786. 'The publication of *Vathec*', he wrote, 'must be postponed at least another year. I would not on any account have him precede the French edition . . . The episodes of *Vathec* are nearly finished, and the whole work will be completed within a twelvemonth. You must be sensible that, notwithstanding my eagerness to see *Vathec* in print, I cannot sacrifice the French edition to my impatience. The anticipation of so principal a tale as that of the Caliph would be tearing the proudest feather from my turban. I must repeat, therefore, my desire that you will not give your translation to the world till the original has made its appearance and we have touched more on the subject . . .'[14] It would have been difficult for him to have made his intentions any plainer. In spite of this warning letter, however, with its clearly expressed wish, Henley (now that Beckford was safely out of the country) was already planning the publication of his translation without the author's knowledge or consent. Of this treachery Beckford would only learn later.

Apart from his literary work Beckford kept up a fairly busy

social life, a welcome change after the months of virtual solitary confinement at Fonthill with only his immediate family for company. Among his friends was Dr. Frederic Schöll, a scholarly physician a few years his senior in age who acted as doctor to Edward Gibbon as well as to Beckford and shared some of his literary interests, as did François Verdeil, another learned physician, a native and leading citizen of Lausanne who was later to attach himself to Beckford's entourage as his personal doctor during his visit to Portugal in the following year. Lettice also came out to join the household where he could act as an intermediary between Beckford and his relatives in England, a very necessary post in view of the latter's delicate position, and one where Lettice's much tried loyalty and discretion were of especial value.

It was, however, upon the whole a calm and tranquil life that they lived, at least in comparison with their previous visit when Lady Margaret had been a bride and Beckford was still behaving very much as though his marriage had not taken place. Now all that was changed. His wife had moved from the perimeter to the centre of his existence and at last there was some indication that in the protection of this growing relationship he might find the basis for a more relaxed and secure life, that the 'wayward' side of his personality might give place to those other more positive qualities that he certainly possessed. But this opportunity, if such it was, for a more settled and domestic way of life, was cruelly snatched away from him. On 14 May Lady Margaret gave birth to a second daughter to be christened Susan Euphemia. At first all seemed well, but the young mother failed to recover her strength. Twelve days later, on 26 May, she died of puerperal fever. She was only twenty-four years old.

For Beckford the shock was terrible and his grief overwhelming. On many occasions in the years to come he would look back on this sad time and recall, often with tears, the dreadful days of 'sunshine and spring without, death and gloom within'. His grief was all the more bitter because he knew in his heart that his loss was irreparable, that never again would the circumstances of his life present him with a similar chance to restore the wreckage and damage which fate had brought on him, or again offer him the vision of a happier and more reasonable future. Lady Margaret's death, coming so soon after the Powderham débâcle, seemed to emphasise more than ever the sense of doom, of being at the mercy of a blind and malignant fate, that had always haunted him.

For a time at least he was a changed man. Even Lady Euphemia Stewart's cold heart was melted at the sight of his unhappiness. She arrived at Vevey on the very day of her niece's death, too late for the dying girl to recognise her. From Lettice and the servants who were in attendance she learnt that Lady Margaret had died in peace with all the world and with no resentment against anyone. Something of the same forgiving spirit took possession of her own usually untroubled conscience. 'Poor Mr. B. is inconsolable', she wrote to Lady Gower. 'I hope, my dear, you will get the Chancellor and Lord Stafford, my brothers and brothers-in-law to forget the past, as he is certainly quite changed and cares for nothing but what she valued.'[15]

Lady Euphemia even encouraged Beckford to brave the 're-vengeful opposition' and return to England when his wife's re-mains were sent for burial at Fonthill. But in that country the press campaign which Loughborough had inspired broke out again in an even more unworthy and vindictive attack upon his character. He was now accused of direct responsibility for his wife's death. On 9 June the *Morning Chronicle* came out with the statement that 'Poor Lady Margaret Beckford's illness which brought so much merit and elegance to a grave was a broken heart.' Other papers followed its lead.

This time his enemies had sufficiently overstepped themselves for the newspaper to have to withdraw the statement and make an apology, while in Switzerland his friends were so angered by the injustice of the attack that they issued a testimonial to his merit, praising his general conduct as a man of honour and his virtues as a husband.[16] But in spite of this reaction in his favour, for Beck-ford himself this wholly unmerited attack left a festering scar that never entirely healed and was to embitter his feelings towards his native country for many years to come. The wound was still fresh four years later when he recalled the sad events of these days in a letter to Lady Craven: 'You was in Turkey or in Lubberland when the storm raged against me, and when I was stabbed to the heart by the loss of Ly. Margaret. And what was the balm poured into my wounds? A set of paragraphs accusing me of having occasioned her death by ill usage. Allowances were to be made for former attacks but none for this, and I will own to you that the recollection of this black stroke fills me with such horror and indignation that I sigh for the pestilential breath of an African serpent to destroy every Englishman who comes in my way.'[17]

He left Vevey and the Château de la Tour de Peilz, now so redolent of despair. For a month or so he wandered about the territory of Geneva and Savoy looking for consolation in the mountains and natural scenery that had always appealed so strongly to his senses and helped so often to calm his jaded nerves. In his sadness at the loss he had suffered news of another death, which can hardly have left him unmoved, passed almost without notice. On 23 April Alexander Cozens had died in England. He was nearly seventy and for some time had been out of touch with his former pupil, the youth whose eyes he had opened to a strange exotic world and whose life and career now seemed to be laid waste in ruins. With the slow rate at which news then travelled it would be three weeks or so before the report reached Geneva, and by then Beckford was lost in his greater grief. What he thought on this occasion we do not know, but a year later he dreamt that his old friend was with him again: 'I seemed to behold him seated at my feet, examining the sprigs of citron I had gathered, and saying with a smile: "Shall I give them to Lady Margaret?" I woke from my trance in tears . . .'[18]

It was some time before Beckford could summon up enough energy or interest to return to work upon his book and finish off those Episodes which had been so near to completion before the tragedy of his wife's death had banished all thought of such work from his mind. But by the beginning of August he was able to return to the subject, if only to reiterate to his translator (who had written to condole with him upon his bereavement) the ban on any premature publication which he had already issued in February. 'I fear the dejection of mind into which I am plunged,' the letter declared, 'will prevent my finishing the other stories, and of course *Vathek*'s making his appearance in any language this Winter, for I am resolved to launch them into the world all together. I would not have him come forth without his companions upon any account.'[19]

The letter, written on the first, reached England on the eighteenth of August. There was no reply to it, for what could Henley say in answer? Ignoring the instructions he had received in February he had gone ahead with his plans to publish the translation, and the book had made its appearance in London on 7 June, ten weeks before. Not only had he published *Vathek* without the author's permission, indeed in direct opposition to his wishes, but in an introduction which he had been careful not to submit to Beckford's notice he had claimed that the work was the translation of an original Arabic manuscript 'collected in the East by a Man of Letters', thus effectively suppressing any reference to Beckford's authorship and taking upon himself all the credit for the work.

It was a complete betrayal of the trust that had been placed in him, and after all that had happened to Beckford over the past eighteen months came upon him as a final blow of fate. But the shock had also a certain therapeutic effect, for it jolted him out of his state of melancholic lassitude and self-pity and galvanised him into action.

First he set his solicitor Thomas Wildman on to Henley, but all the lawyer could do was to hope to extract most of the edition from the publisher and so prevent its circulation as much as possible. From Henley all Wildman obtained was a letter[20] in which deviousness, impertinence and servility were mixed up with plain untruthfulness and even, in veiled references to the Powderham affair and to his patron's 'reputation', a hint of blackmail. He declared, quite correctly, that Beckford's letter of 1 August had reached him too late, but made no reference at all to the much more explicit letter of 9 February. He also claimed to have apprised Beckford of his plans to publish and to have sent him a 'large paper copy' which he presumed would be 'gratifying him in the highest degree', but no such letter and no such copy of the book ever reached Switzerland and presumably were never dispatched. He had, he declared, 'in consideration of a late unhappy occurrence' really wished to suppress the work altogether, but as things were he failed to see how his publishing the book would detract from Beckford's reputation—that indeed it would have a contrary effect. No mention at all was made of the author's wish to delay the issue until the Episodes were finished and could be included as an essential part of the work.

As it was obvious that no real satisfaction could be obtained from Henley, Beckford had now to set about bringing out a French edition and making his authorship of it clear. One problem was that he had no copy of the French text, as the only manuscript of it had been left in Henley's keeping. He was able, however, to obtain a copy of the published English version from London and this was handed over to a certain David Levade, a professor of theology and former Anglican clergyman, who re-rendered it into French. This new French version, far from perfect in matters of style and idiom, was then published by the Lausanne bookseller Hignou with a preface which began with the sentence 'L'ouvrage que nous présentons au public a été composé en Français par M. Beckford', and went on to denounce the claims made by Henley in his introduction that the work was a translation from an original Arabic source.

It was all done in something of a rush, but at least Beckford had established his claim as author and denounced the edition pirated by Henley. He was, however, distressed by the clumsiness of Levade's rendering of his text which was full of anglicisms and had all the marks of a hurried and inexpert piece of work. He could not let his reputation rest on such a version and so another translation into French was undertaken for publication in Paris. This time he worked with his friend François Verdeil, and between them they produced a text that met with the author's approval. Both the Lausanne and the Paris editions were published before the end of 1787 and Beckford at last had the satisfaction of seeing his masterpiece in print, albeit in a manner that fell short of his original intentions. The Episodes, of course, were not included. They remained in manuscript, occasionally to be read to privileged friends, but never published in the author's lifetime. Thanks to Henley's treachery Beckford never saw a complete version of *Vathek* in the way in which he had always hoped to see it published, 'the proudest feather in his turban'. That had to wait until many years after his death.[21]

15
Portugal

In the autumn of 1786 Beckford slipped back to England, but he was not allowed to remain there for long. This time the chief voice advising further absence abroad was Thomas Wildman's, the man who had managed Beckford's affairs since his coming of age. There was a somewhat sinister note in this advice which was far from being disinterested. Wildman had already established his brother James in Jamaica, ostensibly to look after the Beckford interests there, but in fact the gradual but systematic plunder of the great fortune which was placed in their trust had started, and over the next twenty years the Wildmans were to feather their nest very effectively at the expense of their wealthy client. The elder brother had no wish for Beckford to remain at Fonthill where there was always the danger that he might decide to take over the management of things himself, or at least begin to look more closely into his business affairs; but the Powderham scandal could still be evoked, the machinations of his enemies appealed to as a potent reason for his continued residence abroad. The plan for him to visit his Jamaican estates was revived.

Beckford accepted the advice without enthusiasm. The West Indian climate he believed would give his constitution a shock from which it would probably never recover, and his imagination recoiled with horror at the thought of tornadoes, hurricanes and earthquakes. He showed no concern at all for his possessions there. But it was made clear to him (perhaps wrongly) that England was still no place for him, and as he must needs go somewhere he might as well go to Jamaica as anywhere else, and the fact that he was known to have great business interests there would at least give to his departure, to any curious enquiries, less of the appearance of a retreat than would a return to Switzerland.

A somewhat bizarre detail of the preparations for his voyage

was the introduction of Robert Drysdale's name among the suite
of travelling companions, which also included the Swiss physician
Verdeil who was to remain with Beckford for the next year.
Drysdale's re-emergence into Beckford's affairs was probably the
Begum's doing. It was eighteen years since he had last been seen
at Fonthill when he had so impressed her by his stolid Presbyterian earnestness. Now forty-five years old and not a whit less
serious he still obviously looked upon himself as a sort of moral
policeman. 'There is something very disagreeable in his history',
he observed of his former pupil, 'but I am certain he means to behave well or he would not have chosen me for a Companion, as
he knows full well from a boy the uncouth inflexibility of my
temper.'[1] It is no surprise to learn that he did not remain long
with the party. Beckford at twenty-six was a different proposition
from the sprightly but amenable child of seven or eight, nor was
the rather pedestrian Scot likely to prove much of a match to the
quick-witted and sceptical Swiss. After Falmouth (where they
were delayed by contrary winds) we hear of his name no more.

Falmouth was reached early in March 1787. The *Julius Caesar*,
one of his own fleet of merchantmen that brought the precious
cargoes of sugar and rum to England, lay at anchor in the bay, but
the wind either refused to blow at all or built up into a gale. With
each day that passed Beckford grew less and less keen at the prospect of the long voyage that lay ahead of him. He sought distraction by visiting various sights of interest in the neighbourhood,
but all the time his mind was occupied with his future prospects
and in these speculations Jamaica seemed to play no part. A feeling
of ennui descended on him. 'How tired I am of the language of
compass,' he wrote, 'of wind shifting to this point and veering to
the other; of gales springing up, and breezes freshening; of rough
seas, clear berths, ships driving, and anchors lifting. Oh! that I
was rooted like a tree, in some sheltered corner of an inland valley,
where I might never hear more of salt-water or sailing.'[2]

As the days passed and still the wind remained contrary he
began to hint that perhaps he would only go as far as Madeira.
Jamaica was altogether too far away, its climate too deadly. Meanwhile he regretted ever having quitted Switzerland. 'What a fool I
was to leave my beloved retirement at Evian!' he wrote on 11
March. 'Instead of viewing innumerable transparent rills falling
over the amber-coloured rocks of Melierie, I am chained down to
contemplate an oozy beach, deserted by the sea, and becrawled

with worms tracking their way in the slime that harbours them.'[3]
He became thoroughly depressed: 'Tho' I do my utmost to keep
up my spirits, I cannot help confessing that no one ever embarked
even for transportation with a heavier heart.'[4]

Towards the end of March they were able to embark. Even the
thought of being on board ship made Beckford feel seasick and
to add to the general nausea he found his cabin infested with
cockroaches. It was an inauspicious beginning to the voyage.
Nature made up for the rest: rarely had there been such a stormy
crossing of the Bay of Biscay and the misery of the passengers
was complete. So frightful an experience was not to be repeated.
When the Rock of Lisbon was sighted and the ship crept into the
shelter of the Tagus Beckford resolved to go no further. Better,
he decided, to spend his time in some Portuguese monastery eat-
ing oranges and worshipping his beloved St Antony than submit
himself again to the mercy of the sea.

Though the mere chance of his hatred of sailing and his
determination not to risk any more storms or seasickness was
responsible for his disembarkation at Lisbon, his stay in Portugal,
which lasted from March until December, was to be one of the
most important periods in his existence. It was to produce a
Journal which contains some of his best writing and was to give
him his first real opportunity to come to terms with life after the
two shattering experiences of the Powerdam scandal and his wife's
death. In fact this strange man (or 'animal' as he would have
described himself) who lacked the capacity genuinely to fall in
love with other human beings, was to fall permanently in love
with the country he now first visited as it were by sheer fortuity. It
was to become 'beloved Portugal, my own true country'[5] and for
no other place would he feel the same affection except for his
native Fonthill.

Beckford reached Lisbon thirty-two years after the great
earthquake that had destroyed thirty thousand of its inhabitants
and so shattered the complacency of mid-eighteenth-century
thought, and a mere ten years after the fall from office of the
Marquis of Pombal. He was to discover a country slowly relapsing
into slumber after the invigorating experience of that reforming
minister (who still had a few adherents in office) and a city that
even yet showed the scars of the terrible disaster of the first of
November 1755 despite the passage of so many years.

Portugal was ruled by Maria I, the delicate thread of whose

sanity had not yet snapped and who, in true Bragança fashion, had married her own uncle. She presided over a court famous for its patronage of music and a government in which the influence of the Church and the Inquisition had almost completely ousted what remained of the reforming spirit of the previous reign. There was much in all this to appeal to Beckford's imagination. 'Portugal', it has been pointed out, 'to such a mentality as his, possessed all those qualities that he admired; a rich aristocracy, with that feudal antiquity to which he aspired and to which he could not really, with his semi-plebeian origin, attain; and, in the opposite extreme, a docile population well schooled in their landowners' canons of obedience and submission.'[6]

Even so, his first impressions of Portugal were not favourable. He found the merchants and traders who formed the British colony decidedly hostile and unwilling to welcome someone whose scandalous reputation was not unknown to them, nor did he himself go out of his way to court their sympathy. He treated them with considerable disdain, referring to them as the 'scrubs and scrubesses of the English Factory'. This was a mistaken policy for it quickly led to an open feud with the British Minister, Robert Walpole, who refused to present him at the Portuguese Court. Walpole, a nephew of the great Whig minister and cousin of the master of Strawberry Hill, was probably ill-disposed to Beckford in the first place, but the latter's contemptuous treatment of the English 'Factory' sealed his fate with him, for the envoy, twice married, had chosen both his wives from among the daughters of the English merchants settled in Lisbon. The remainder of Beckford's time in Portugal was to be taken up in a protracted intrigue which was soon to split the society of the capital into two factions, those who supported him in his endeavours to force the Minister's hand or to circumvent his authority, and those who concurred with the latter's implacable refusal to introduce a man of Beckford's reputation (the details of which Walpole did everything in his power to disseminate) into the presence of the Queen.

Viewed from the last quarter of the twentieth century it may seem absurd that anyone should devote so much energy and ingenuity over so minor a point, but seen from the same point of time in the eighteenth century the situation was very different. It was much more than a mere question of etiquette. A man of Beckford's station in life, visiting a foreign country, would not be

William Beckford aged twenty-one. Engraved by T. A. Dean
after Sir Joshua Reynolds

'The Begum' Mrs. Beckford, by Benjamin West

Alderman Beckford, Lord Mayor of London. Mezzotint by
John Dixon

William Beckford in 1791. Engraved by S. Freeman after P. Sauvage

William Courtenay as a boy. Photogravure after G. Romney

Fonthill Splendens. Engraved by Thomas Higham after a drawing by J. Buckler

Fonthill Abbey, south-west view. Engraved by H. Winkles after G. Cattermole

The Octagon, Fonthill Abbey. From J. Britton's *Illustrations of Fonthill Abbey*, 1823

William Beckford in middle age, by John Hoppner

Lansdown Tower, Bath. Lithograph by G. C. T. Richardson after
Willes Maddox

The Sanctuary, Lansdown Tower, Bath. Lithograph by
G. C. T. Richardson after Willes Maddox

William Beckford in 1842, by John Doyle

able to move in society, meet his social equals, or engage in the round of official, diplomatic, or indeed ordinary 'society' functions until he had made his bow at court properly introduced into the royal presence by his sovereign's envoy. By withholding this privilege from Beckford, Walpole was in fact placing a social embargo on him and also, in a community so small, inter-related and prone to gossip as was the Lisbon aristocracy, branding him as being in some way socially unacceptable. Walpole was, in short, doing Loughborough's work rather than his royal master's, and continuing on foreign soil the campaign of innuendo and subtle persecution that had already driven Beckford from his native land. That the envoy was acting without any official mandate soon became clear, but to make him change his policy of exclusion was another matter.

Beckford might well have given up the struggle in the first months of his stay had not two circumstances peculiar to his curious temperament brought about a change in the situation and greatly strengthened his position *vis-à-vis* the unaccommodating Minister. These were his devotion to St. Antony of Padua and his fondness for the ritual and music of Catholic worship. St. Antony, despite his adoption by the people of Padua (where he had died), had been born in Lisbon and was one of the patrons of the city. With his devotion to the cult of this saint and his fascination by splendid ritual, especially when this was embellished by the music of Jommelli, Beckford was often to be observed on his knees in the Patriarchal and other great churches of Lisbon.

To see an Englishman and a heretic so obviously rapt caused something of a sensation in more genuinely pious bosoms. Among those to observe the phenomenon and be edified by it was the Abbade Xavier, a sprightly and somewhat garrulous priest who could still savour the zest of life though already in his ninety-second year. This cleric, for whom Beckford was to develop a warm affection, had spent most of his long life as confidential adviser and close friend to the Marialva family, one of the great noble houses of Portùgal and one that by influence and prestige was very much a power to be reckoned with. The Abbade, having made the acquaintance of the young devotee of St. Antony, lost no time in introducing him to his master and patron Diogo, the 'young' Marquis of Marialva.

The Marquis was distinguished by the epithet 'young' to differentiate him from his father the 'old' marquis who enjoyed

G

the same title, but for all this the Marquis Diogo was not in his first youth, being twenty-one years senior in age to Beckford. Their meeting was a fortunate occasion for both men; for Beckford because it was to change the whole character of his stay in Portugal; and for Marialva because he was to meet in Beckford someone who would become, for him, his greatest friend and one whose personality would hold a strange fascination over him for the rest of his life.

The Marquis fell completely under the spell of that allurement by which Beckford could so easily bind people to him. Nothing quite like it had happened to him before. It was like a love affair except for the fact that the whole relationship was devoid of any sensual element. There is nothing at all to suggest that Marialva was a homosexual, or even conscious of such feelings in relation to his friendship for Beckford. He was a happily married man devoted to his wife and children and his one desire was to integrate his new friend into this close family group. He was, none the less, totally infatuated by Beckford, longed only to be of service to him, and was prepared to use his immense influence both in society and at court to help his friend and to frustrate the designs of the British Minister. It was his conviction that it was God's will that he should admit Beckford into an 'unlimited, unreserved friendship', and he declared his belief that an 'unaccountable impulse' had driven him to this conclusion, and to the uniting of his friend's salvation and welfare with his own.[7]

For Beckford the friendship was on a less exalted level. He felt no physical attraction for the Marquis who was neither of the age nor the type to appeal to him. Any such attraction of this nature as he felt would be reserved for Marialva's thirteen-year-old son Dom Pedro, and even here his feelings would veer quickly from fascination to exasperation as he blew hot and cold in his reactions to this awkward and rather gauche boy. The member of the family for whom he seems to have felt the strongest friendship was Marialva's illegitimate uncle Manoel, the Grand Prior of Aviz, whose geniality and slightly cynical humour agreed with Beckford's own turn of mind. He was, Beckford wrote, 'a good, portly prelate-like figure, very cheerful and cordial. I like him extremely.'[8] The Marquis he saw more in terms of a father, referring to his 'parental fondness' but adding, which was no more than the truth, 'I much doubt if I ever had a more zealous or affectionate friend.'[9]

The Marialvas occupied a powerful position in Lisbon and
were inter-related with many other of the leading noble families.
The 'young' Marquis filled the court appointment of Grand
Master of the Horse, which was hereditary in his family, and was
also a Gentleman of the Bedchamber and Councillor of War.
These offices brought him into daily contact with the Queen and
the leading members of the government, in particular Martinho
de Melo, the Chief Minister, and Archbishop Inacio de Sao
Caetano, who held the probably even more powerful posts of
Inquisitor-General and Confessor to the Queen. It was the
Marquis's ambition, through his influence with these powerful
ministers and by the mobilisation of all other means at his disposal, either to compel Walpole to withdraw his opposition and
present Beckford himself, or failing that, to get his friend introduced into the royal presence in some less formal but equally
effective way.

In this task, which he took up with dedicated enthusiasm,
Marialva enrolled the help of his entire family and made it clear
that those of his more distant connections and mere acquaintances who failed to support him in his endeavours did so at the
risk of his continued friendship. Beckford himself joined in the
fray with spirit, heaping invectives on the head of his adversary
who now became 'that malevolent cuckold Walpole' and was
likened to a blundering puppy or a venomous reptile.[10] For a
while all Lisbon could talk of nothing else, everyone felt compelled to take sides in the dispute, and even the Queen's irresolute
interest was momentarily aroused by the contest.

Nothing stimulated Beckford so much as a good fight. The
ennui and disgust he had felt on first landing in Portugal (much
of it a legacy from the stormy sea passage) quickly left him. His
interest in life and in his surroundings revived. 'The thought of all
those manoeuvres in the Marialva family keeps me employed', he
wrote in his Journal on 19 June. 'My curiosity is never off the
stretch. I long to know when and in what manner Her Majesty is
to give my audience.'[11] He was to wait a good deal longer before
he realised that the audience would never take place, that Melo
and the archbishop, wishing to offend neither the Marquis nor
the British Minister, were playing one off against the other and
doing their best to prevent a confrontation.

Meanwhile he began to take stock of his situation. His acceptance by the Marialvas had another significance for him outside

the context of his feud with the British envoy. They were the first family of his own social rank to welcome him with open arms on a footing of complete equality since the scandal at Powderham had made similarly placed people in England turn their backs on him. In their friendly circle Lord Loughborough might not have existed; the lurid stories spread by Walpole were brushed aside as being beneath contempt. As Beckford reflected on this fact his feelings of antagonism against his native country rose up again with all their old force, but he also began to realise that England was not the only country in the world, and that if he chose to settle abroad he could well afford to make his own life where he pleased and ignore the fulminations of his enemies at home.

These ideas were linked up in his mind with memories of Lady Margaret whose influence, had she lived, might have opened up another path leading him back to social rehabilitation. Just over a year after the first anniversary of her death an entry in his Journal reveals his thoughts clearly enough. He had been for a drive through Lisbon and the sight of the Tagus with the range of distant mountains visible in the coolness of the air brought back sudden and sad memories of the Lake of Geneva. 'That dreadful gulf which now is fixed between us arose before my imagination in all its terrors', he wrote in a significant passage. 'I returned home gloomy and comfortless, calling in vain upon her who can hear no more, the companion of my happiest hours, once so lively and blooming, now lying cold and ghastly in the dark vaults at Fonthill, the loveliest and most unaffected of beings who doted on her poor William with such excessive fondness, and pardoned with such a sweet endearing cheerfulness his childish errors. That tutelary angel it has pleased the Great Being to take away from me, and I am now left almost without a friend wandering about the world, the object of the vilest calumnies and the most capricious persecutions. But it is Englishmen alone who behave to me with such malevolence: the first characters in other nations know how to excuse my past faults and respect my present conduct. In Portugal particularly many persons in the highest stations and of the worthiest as well as the noblest families treat me not only with politeness but affection.'[12]

There was much to tempt him to remain where he was and settle permanently in Portugal, for Marialva, anxious not to lose his fascinating friend and seeing, perhaps, that Walpole would never give way on the matter of the presentation, made tempting overtures and hinted at rich rewards if his friend should decide to adopt Portuguese nationality. The Queen, Beckford was assured, would confer a title upon him and make him a grandee, while the unfortunate fact of his not being a Catholic would be ignored. St Antony, no doubt, would sort that problem out in his own good time. Meanwhile, as an indication of his affection and good will, the Marquis offered Beckford the hand of his daughter Henriqueta, for all that it was well known that her betrothal to the Duke of Lafoes, a close relative of the Queen, was virtually settled.

Beckford was flattered by the offer but knew perfectly well that he would never marry again. He was still attracted by fresh young beauty in girls, especially if they were well-born and could thus appeal to his snobbish romanticism as well as to his senses, but he knew now beyond any shadow of doubt that his real tastes lay elsewhere. It was not by mere chance that he had linked the memory of Lady Margaret with recollections of the endearing cheerfulness with which she had pardoned his childish errors. In this last phrase was summed up all that was contained in his paederastic urges, urges in which he not only longed for the love of boys of twelve or thirteen years of age, but liked, in the context of such a relationship, to feel himself a 'child' of the same age. When he was in the throes of such a sentimental attachment we find him using phrases like 'No child of thirteen ever felt a stronger impulse to race and gambol than I do',[13] or 'Of all the favours gracious Heaven has bestowed on me, the one I esteem the most is the still retaining the appearance, the agility and the fancy of a stripling,'[14] while the word 'childish' is employed again and again in association with the objects of his affection as applying to himself no less than to them.

Bitter experience had taught him of the dangers to which this temperamental weakness could lead. He had learnt to be on his guard but he was still capable of remarkable indiscretions, indeed, the very 'childishness' which he cultivated laid him open to it. But a better understanding of his feelings, a more true awareness of his nature than had been the case in the days of his infatuation for William Courtenay or the Italian youths had at least schooled him to exercise a better degree of caution. 'I shall get into a scrape if I don't take care', he wrote early on during his time in Lisbon when some of the more reprehensible pleasures of the capital were revealed to him: 'How tired I am of keeping a mask to my countenance. How tight it sticks—it makes me sore. There's metaphor for you. I have all the fancies and levity of a child and would give an estate or two to skip about the galleries of the Patriarchal with the *menino* unobserved.'[15]

It was, therefore, not so much for Donna Henriqueta, whom he described as a lovely girl with eyes full of youthful gaiety, as for her rather solemn and self-conscious brother Dom Pedro that Beckford felt a kindling interest. At first the youth made a poor impression, he had 'a countenance as long as one's face in a spoon' but showed encouraging signs of sharing his father's fondness for their exotic new friend. But he was laconic and rather dull except when Beckford's piano playing roused him to action. 'My singing, playing, and capering subdues every Portuguese that approaches me,' the proud performer boasted, 'and they cannot help giving way to the most extravagant expressions of their feelings.'[16] Upon such occasions he and Dom Pedro would dance together, the father often looking on with a complacency that would have astounded Lord Loughborough and his allies in England.

For the Marquis no doubt it all seemed a matter of youthful high spirits; he would, indeed, quite often join in the dancing himself. He looked upon Beckford as a prospective son-in-law and even hoped to see his own son married in due time to one of Beckford's daughters. Nor could he fail to approve the genuine interest his friend showed in Dom Pedro's education and general welfare. But Verdeil, more worldly-wise and with no illusions about the complexities of his patron's nature, occasionally had reason to feel alarmed. He was well able to interpret the blushes that rose to youthful cheeks and after an escapade some time later that had left Beckford confiding breathlessly to his diary: 'He loves me, I have tasted the sweetness of his lips; his dear eyes have confessed the secret of his bosom', the doctor felt obliged to warn him of the serious consequences that might follow. He tactfully suggested that the attachment was only on the boy's side but his meaning was clear enough. 'He has staggered me,' Beckford wrote somewhat disingenuously, 'I am lost in an ocean of perplexities.'[17] He took the hint, however, and allowed things to cool.

There were various reasons that combined to hold him in check with regard to Dom Pedro. There was the respect and affection he felt for Marialva and the need to remain on good terms with his family; there was the boy's own character, secretive and unsophisticated like many adolescents', where sulks or blank stares would often follow the hectic dances and meaningful glances; and there was also the fact that a good deal of Beckford's time was taken up by another emotional skirmish in which he was involved with a seventeen-year-old musician from the Patriarchal choir school. This was Gregorio Fellipe Franchi, a youth of considerable musical talent and great charm of personality, whose life was later destined to be associated with Beckford's in London and at Fonthill.

The appearance of this young man in his life was another of the fortunate circumstances that resulted from his chance landing in Portugal on a voyage intended for so different a destination. The boy was the son of Italian parents, though born in Lisbon, and had been a pupil at the Patriarchal musical seminary for the past four years. Their friendship began casually enough. Beckford, assiduous in his attendance at Mass (there was, he declared ironically, no conversation in Lisbon but of his piety), would escape during the sermon to the musicians' gallery, and it was there that he first set eyes on Franchi, having already been attracted by his brilliant playing of Haydn on the harpsichord. An introduction was made by the leading tenor of the Queen's chapel, Polycarpo da Silva, who hinted archly that Beckford's pianoforte would set off the young player's talents to even greater advantage. Beckford was immediately attracted, but fear of scandal kept him for a while 'in prudent silence and gravity'.[18]

He need not have worried. His relationship with Franchi was to be one of the few in which there would be neither scandal nor remorse, though the youth's later arrival in England occasioned some sneering references to the presence at Fonthill of a 'Portuguese orange'. Franchi had a cheerful disposition, an amusing manner, and was to become genuinely devoted to Beckford and his interests, which he shared in every respect. Shortly after their first encounter he began to make regular appearances at Beckford's house. 'I got home just as it was dark,' the latter noted in his Journal on 1 July, 'and in came Gregorio Franchi, the boy who played so delightfully on the harpsichord . . . I think his eyes are grown larger than ever, and fix themselves so inveterately upon me that I cannot help colouring. He caught my style of playing instantaneously and flourished away several overtures and sonatas at sight perfectly in my manner. The Portuguese youths are composed of more inflammable materials than other mortals. I could keep them spellbound for hours at my side, listening to the child-ish notes of my voice, and dissolving like snow in the sunshine.'[19] In no time the boy was being loaded with 'childish caresses' and his visits to Beckford, sometimes by invitation but often by way of surprise, became a regular feature of life.

It was, therefore, to a background of these amorous escapades conducted with a good deal of adolescent skipping and jumping in which the twenty-seven-year-old man rather than the teen-age youths took the lead, that Beckford's life in Portugal, whether in Lisbon or in the cooler air of Sintra, was to be lived. In one aspect at least it differed from the more intense atmosphere that had prevailed in his previous attachments. He no longer hoped to find in his young friends that exclusive, unique personality to whom alone he could communicate his feelings. He had learnt to be more relaxed, more aware both of the possibilities and of the limitations of his emotional entanglements. The experience of life had taught him to be more cautious in his responses, more guarded in his language, and more generally cynical in his assessment of his fellow human beings.

Meanwhile the battle with Walpole continued. Marialva was unsparing in his efforts and visited his friend almost every day with news from the palace designed to raise his hopes and per-suade him to remain in Portugal a bit longer. The Grand Prior was all encouragement and the Abbade prattled away at length on the glories of the Marialva family and the potent advocacy of blessed St. Antony. The Prince of Brazil, heir to the throne, had expressed (so Beckford was informed) the liveliest impatience to see him, but etiquette and diplomatic intransigence still inter-vened.[20] After a while it became plain that no progress was being made, that the British envoy's obduracy was not to be assailed. Beckford's patience was exhausted. After spending the hottest months at Sintra, away from the heat and turmoil of Lisbon, he began to make preparations to leave for Spain.

The Marquis was heartbroken. A desperate rearguard action was fought and it was in fact almost the end of the year before Beckford crossed the Spanish frontier leaving the despised but triumphant Walpole, for the time being at least, in possession of the field. On 27 November he went to the Marialva palace to take leave of his friends. He embraced the Marquis and the Grand Prior, and bid Dom Pedro and his sisters an 'eternal adieu'.

The old Abbade, who had first introduced him to this kindly and pious family, was in despair and made 'a piteous moaning'. 'I fear', Beckford wrote, 'I have seen him for the last time and that his days will not be long in the land.'[21] In this he was correct, but for the rest of the family the adieu was fortunately not destined to be so eternal after all. Beckford would return to Portugal six years later and they would all meet again.

It was 12 December before he reached Madrid. As he travelled on the long overland route between the two capitals, often enduring very primitive conditions ('Not a wink of sleep did the Musquitos allow me', he noted in Badajoz), Beckford, in such moments as he allowed for reflection, had some reason to be pleased with himself in spite of the harassment he had suffered at Walpole's hands. He had arrived in Portugal very much a fugitive, acutely conscious of the sense of persecution which Loughborough's vicious campaign had caused him to suffer, and still acting very much at the beck and call of his family whose advice, not always wise, he lacked the spirit or resolution to oppose.

Nearly ten months in Portugal had given him time to reassess his position, and the result was a return of self-confidence and a re-awakening of that zest for life and interest in all that went on around him which would not desert him again. He had also shed a lot of the romantic self-absorption and melancholic moods which had always had something in the nature of a pose about them. He was less prone to escape from reality and could see himself with more veracity and clarity; could even indulge in a little criticism at his own expense. 'I could not help saying a thousand things which ought never to have been uttered', he had recorded in his Journal after some hours of idle, unguarded chatter: '*Faire sans dire* is an excellent maxim, and it would have been better for me had I paid it a stricter attention. I have more profligacy of tongue than of character and often do my utmost to make myself appear worse than I am in reality.'[22] Such moments of truth were a new and welcome sign of maturity.

For this recovery Beckford owed a great debt to the Marquis of Marialva. Had this friend not come to his rescue in Lisbon he might well have accepted defeat and escaped yet again with an even bigger grudge against his fellow countrymen and a sense of persecution more crushing than ever. It was only after meeting this friend that Beckford was able to throw off the depression that had haunted him since the death of his wife, and see all the consequences of the Powderham affair in a clearer and more sane perspective. Almost literally he turned over a new leaf, for it was on the day that he met Marialva that he began to write his Portuguese Journal, a work which reflects a scene of unending fascination and gives us the most revealing insight into his strange and curious personality. It marks the moment of his real recovery from Loughborough's attempt to destroy him.

16
The Wall

THE SIX MONTHS spent in Madrid were passed in a whirlwind of flirtations, fandangoes, musical parties and amorous intrigues. The time passed like so many scenes from an *opera buffa* to a score by Pergolesi or Cimarosa, sweeping Beckford along at such a pace that after little more than a month he abandoned his diary with the characteristic remark that he had acquired a confirmed habit of going to Mass, an observation into which it was clearly unnecessary to look for any religious significance.

What he most dreaded was to find himself involved in another 'Walpolean contest'. Early in his visit he called on the British envoy Robert Liston, but left no account of their conversation. Liston was a more amenable man than Walpole and he had no feelings of personal vendetta against Beckford; he made himself quite helpful, introduced him to the American Minister and raised no objections, as Walpole would certainly have done, when he dined or danced at various ambassadorial houses. All the same, Beckford was not presented at court, and the unfortunate Venetian ambassador was in consequence 'upon thorns' whether or not to ask him to a solemn diplomatic dinner in spite of all the rules. In the end he went, and Liston turned a blind eye. Beckford was, none the less, in an invidious position, for though the British Minister showed no hostility to him personally he obviously felt himself obliged to support the line taken up by his colleague in Lisbon. But if feelings of professional solidarity dictated the conduct of the envoy with regard to Beckford, others in Madrid saw no necessity to ape their opposite numbers in Lisbon by taking sides upon the issue. He appears to have moved very freely in society and especially in diplomatic circles, being on a friendly footing at the Portuguese, French and Venetian embassies, and meeting at dinner the Swedish Minister whom he found 'a lusty young man with a broad countenance shining with the oil of gladness',[1] a picture which hardly summons up a vision of diplomatic outrage or disdain.

His stay in the Spanish capital was reminiscent of that hectic season six years before when all London had been at his feet. It was as though, following the reappraisal of his situation in life that had taken place in Portugal, he was throwing himself into a last fling of recklessness before the undercurrent of disillusionment forced him to come to terms with grimmer realities. For the last time the pages of his Journal would be embellished with such phrases as 'I danced till three in the morning', 'I sat down at the pianoforte and ranted and roared till my throat was parched up', or 'I am so worn down with late hours that I can hardly keep my eyes open.'[2] Youth, like the cherished illusion of childishness, was slipping through his fingers though he was only in his twenty-eighth year.

There was a note of feverishness in his pursuit of love, and as always with Beckford he pursued it simultaneously on various opposing fronts. Very soon he was to meet the family of the French ambassador, the Duc de la Vauguyon, and find himself strongly attracted by his daughter who already, at only eighteen or nineteen, had been found a husband in the Prince de Listenais. If the Princess's gay personality caused his heart to beat faster he had also to confess to feelings of a little more than interest in her youthful husband, 'a smart stripling with wild hair and a low grecian forehead, who has not yet entered his fifteenth year'. And to add to the confusion there was the ambassador's son, the twenty-year-old Prince de Carency, whose comments on Madrid and its society kept him in constant amusement.[3] It was the familiar Beckfordian situation, one of those complicated entanglements which he found so stimulatingly irresistible. 'I must take care,' he was soon confiding to his Journal, 'or I shall kindle a flame not easily extinguished. I am surrounded with fires; it is delightful to be warmed, but unless I summon up every atom of prudence in my composition I shall be reduced to ashes.'[4]

A safer encounter, and one very much to his liking, was with Ahmed Vassif Effendi, the Sultan's ambassador to the Spanish court. He met this cultured and distinguished Turkish diplomat and historian on 14 December after catching sight of some of his staff in their caftans and turbans and enquiring who such 'picturesque animals' could be. A presentation to the ambassador followed and they soon became friends, Beckford later supplying him with rolls and brioches from his own kitchen, declaring: 'I have quite won his heart by these attentions and he will miss me when I depart.' In return he was entertained with oriental music and dances whenever he visited his new friend.

It was a friendship inspired on Beckford's side by his absorbing interest in all things oriental, but even these innocent pleasures had their risks. On the first of January 1788 when visiting Ahmed Vassif he found him in conversation with the Tripolitan ambassador who was himself only twenty-two and who was accompanied by his twelve-year-old brother, a boy in whose eyes Beckford at once discovered a languid tenderness. It was as though Gulchenrouz was suddenly seated in front of him. 'The little boy's name is Mohammed . . .' he wrote in his Journal, and such was the tumult of his emotion that he recorded that they 'conserved' instead of 'conversed' together in lingua franca: 'I was seated on the carpet like an Oriental, to the great delight of Ahmed Vassif, who has hopes of alluring me to Constantinople; but still more to that of little Mohammed, who kept whispering to me with a tone of voice that went to my soul, and pressing my hands with inconceivable tenderness. I thought myself in a dream —nay, I still think myself so, and expect to wake.'[5]

It was perhaps just as well that the relationship remained in this dream-like state for very soon another whirlwind affair was under way, this time with the Marquesa de Santa Cruz, a daughter of the Prince of Lichtenstein, and four years his senior in age, demanding in her attentions, possessive in her love, and violently jealous of the young Princess de Listenais and all her family. Her letters would pursue him for many months after he had quitted Madrid where their behaviour provided plenty of material for the gossips. With all these entanglements, male and female, to cope with it is hardly surprising that his Journal began to suffer, petering out in a splutter of disjointed phrases: 'My Journal is in sad confusion. I have no time to write. From the moment my eyes open to that in which they close, I think confusedly of Mme de Santa Cruz, the Turks, Mohammed, Listenais etc . . .'[6]

Of course Beckford's time in Spain was not spent entirely in the role of philanderer; his interest in books, pictures and architecture was not forgotten. He visited the Escorial, though December was hardly the best time of year to see that austere palace-monastery. He found Raphael's *Holy Family*, once the pearl of Charles I's collection, in a sad condition, but admired the monastic church 'heavy as if hewn out of rock'. He was constantly popping in and out of churches either to admire the architecture, enjoy the music, or assist on his knees in the service, though he no longer posed as a *dévot* as he had done in Portugal. He haunted printshops and booksellers looking for manuscripts, travel books and accounts of curious voyages, subjects that would be well represented one day in his great library; and he had his portrait painted by a cousin of Angelica Kauffmann and presented it to the Marquesa de Santa Cruz who afterwards discovered, much to her chagrin, that its duplicate had been given to a choir-boy.[7]

In the midst of all these activities there suddenly appeared, in May 1788, the young musician Gregorio Franchi from whom Beckford had parted, with many tears on the boy's part, six months before in Lisbon. He now arrived in Madrid carrying a letter from his father: 'Excellency, with tears in my eyes I commit my son Gregory to Your Excellency, and recommend him to you, believing and hoping that your protection may be the true beginning of his fortune. All Lisbon envies his luck ... I only desire that he may show himself worthy of your incomparable protection, and I remain, with all imaginable respect, Your Excellency's most humble and obedient servant.'[8] It was the beginning of a long partnership that would end only in Franchi's death forty years later by which time he had become a trusted confidant and friend, the only person, perhaps, with whom Beckford would be able to communicate with complete freedom.

By this time Beckford was beginning to tire of Madrid. When the court moved to Aranjuez the French ambassador departed in the wake of the king taking his son, daughter, and son-in-law with him. Certain rumours had reached his ears about the young friend they all shared with so much enthusiasm and he was glad to have an excuse to go. Beckford, not having been presented, was unable to follow. Madame de Santa Cruz was left in possession of the field, triumphant and desperately in love, but it was a love he could not return and had no wish to anyway. He was in danger of becoming bored and decided to leave. A month after Franchi's arrival the bags were packed once more, the coaches loaded with his purchases and his growing train of dependants (which now included a dwarf) and he set out on the road to Paris indifferent to the broken hearts he left behind him.

Before he left Spain he had written to Lady Craven a carefree and amusing account of his adventures: 'And so I have been in Spain and have been in love over head and ears, which is still more extraordinary ... Don't let your imagination loose upon Spain—it is a hideous parched-up Country, with only here and there a tolerable spot like the Temple of Jupiter Ramshorn in the deserts of Lybia. Where are you, Superior Being? when shall we meet? When will the hour of entire Confidence arrive, when the secrets of both our hearts will be mutually laid open? I long to see your glorious eyes once more, and talk to you about Portugal —a pleasanter region than Spain and in which I was also up to the neck in adventures ... What are you about?—gathering roses perhaps or composing pastorals full of grace and sprightliness. I am ten times more musically given than ever, and quite wild with hearing Seguidillas and Fandangos ...'[9]

In spite of the bantering tone of his letter Beckford was not quite so free from anxiety as his style might suggest. All the time he had his eye upon England and was eager for news either from Wildman or from his sister as to the state of affairs there, and in particular to the state of his own reputation. Was it safe to return? How would society receive him? Behind all the dancing, flirting and frivolity that went on in Madrid this question was always nagging at the back of his mind. His spirits had risen the previous June in Portugal when word had reached him that Lord Courtenay had taken certain dangerous papers 'out of the talons of Beelzebub' (the name he had devised for Loughborough), but a month later the hopes raised by this encouraging information were dashed: 'I have just heard from Wildman that Lord Courtenay has been once more overawed by old Beelzebub, and like a contemptible coward suffers the most obnoxious papers to remain in old Beelzebub's clutches. I cannot yet discover any decisive method of smoothing my way home to England.'[10]

Beckford settled down in Paris and awaited events. In the autumn came news of Lord Courtenay's death on 14 October at the early age of forty-six and of 'Kitty's' succession to the family honours as third viscount. There was little to be hoped for from either event, and anyway Loughborough still had the 'obnoxious papers' in his possession and the new peer was even less likely to be able to extract them from his grasp than the father had been. Beckford had to content himself with the thought that his family, Lord Thurlow and the solicitor Wildman were doing what they

could for him. In the spring of 1789 his impatience got the better
of him and he wrote to the latter suggesting that the time had
come for his return home but Wildman sent such a discouraging
and devious reply that (as Beckford noted at the foot of the page)
his blood curdled and every nerve in his frame quivered as he read it.

For the present there was nothing he could do but remain where
he was, fuming meanwhile at the ineptitude of that 'infernal rascal'
Wildman and the malignancy of fate. Paris, at least, was seething
with excitement and mounting frenzy as the delegates to the
States-General began to gather. Beckford at this period was full
of enthusiasm for the ideas which were very soon to boil over
into revolution. Dissatisfied with his lot, conscious of injustice,
and full of indignation and frustration as a result of his rejection
by his own social class in England, he was just in the mood to
identify himself with the attack being launched against entrenched
privilege in France. He witnessed the riots that followed the over-
throw of Necker (into the lap of whose wife he had once spilled
a glass of water) and claimed he saw the mob rush the fortress of
the Bastille on 14 July. 'Mr. Beckford watched the events of the
Revolution with a keen eye', Cyrus Redding would write many
years later, having heard the story often enough from the old
man at Bath; 'Some of the pictures of the scenes at that stirring
time represented an Englishman on horseback, an apparent
spectator of them, and that spectator was Mr. Beckford.'[11]

But Beckford would not have been Beckford had he allowed his
other interests to lapse in the intoxication brought on by the sight
of this seeming dawn of freedom. France had not changed much,
the time of the terror was some distance away, Louis XVI ruled
at least in name and Paris was still an agreeable place for a young
man of taste and wealth to find himself living in. 'I read from
Morn till Night,' he wrote to tell his sister, 'having purchased at
the Soubise Sale a number of original out-of-the-way Authors
which delight and surprise me beyond measure. I have thirty or
forty volumes in Latin, Spanish and Portuguese, about China and
Japan, full of the rarest stories imaginable of Castles, Treasures
and miracles.'[12] Not only did the collecting mania grow, but he
discovered a useful fact that he was later to exploit more fully,
that a period of political upheaval and inflation can fill the art
market with very desirable and relatively cheap objects for someone like himself whose source of wealth was unaffected by either
contingency.

As autumn approached and the revolutionary crowds became more unruly Beckford decided that the time had come for another move, and set off for Germany. His object was to visit his old friend Lady Craven who for the past three years had been living as the *chère amie* of the Margrave of Brandenburg-Ansbach-Bayreuth, a nephew of Frederick the Great and ruler of one of the smaller German states. As she was still encumbered with a husband and her lover with a wife she demurely described herself to anyone bold enough to enquire into the nature of their relationship as the Margrave's 'adopted sister'. In this improbable role she had established herself at Ansbach, ousted the reigning mistress (a French actress called Mlle Clarion), founded a literary club and taken over the management of the court theatre for which she provided plays from her own busy pen. One would have enjoyed Beckford's description of this comic opera scene but unfortunately he was not destined to see it. After a few weeks at Lausanne news reached him from Wildman that the way was clear for him to return to England and he left at once for Ostend.

He reached Fonthill in October accompanied by the dwarf and by Franchi, the 'Portuguese orange', whose inclusion in his entourage had already, according to reports from Wildman, given rise to unfriendly comment even before they had arrived in England. Verdeil, an ardent protagonist of liberty, equality and fraternity, remained in Paris from where, in due time, he would return to his native Switzerland with a pension from his patron of £100 a year. Whatever interest Beckford's return may have caused, his former friends and neighbours made sure that they did not betray it by calling upon him. If there was no outcry against him, if, as his sister rather patronisingly informed him, his name could now be mentioned in polite society without offence, his presence at Fonthill was none the less ignored by everyone; his social isolation remained complete. It was a decidedly chilly homecoming.

The family, as usual, were generous with offerings of unacceptable advice. His sister Elizabeth Hervey had wisely advised him to send a substantial donation towards the restoration of Salisbury cathedral, work entrusted to the architect James Wyatt and destined to earn for him, rightly or wrongly, the nickname of 'the Destroyer'. The bishop had shown his appreciation of Beckford's generosity by offering, through Mrs. Hervey's mediation, his own particular exhortation to her erring brother. 'He enquired much after you,' she wrote to him at Fonthill, 'and expressed a wish that you might marry and settle in England.'[13] The bishop did not, however, include an invitation to the Palace in returning his thanks, nor was Beckford likely to be tempted to purchase this privilege at the additional expense of a second marriage. When his sister also urged him to find himself a wife he answered her very frankly: 'I shall not suffer myself to be led to the Galloway Market. I am not matrimonially disposed.'[14]

From these irritating counsels he turned, as he had so often done in moments of childhood misunderstanding or depression, to the woods and parkland that surrounded his house. In the natural beauty of the landscape he could find a solace that he was clearly not going to discover in the society of his fellow beings, not, that is, so long as he chose to remain in his native country. The planting of shrubs and saplings that he had ordered and supervised in the past had grown during his absence and the domain was beginning to show promise of even greater beauty and seclusion, a retreat from which all discord, all emnity and malevolence could be banished. If his red-faced neighbours chose to ignore his existence, despise his tastes and ridicule his manner of life, let them do so. He could do without them. He was uninterested in them or in their passion for destroying all wild creatures in their senseless orgies of hunting and shooting. Let them pursue their sport elsewhere. Neither he nor the animals and birds he loved would be their quarry. He would show his contempt for them and for their opinions. He would build a vast wall round his estate and keep them out of it.

It is dangerous to read too much significance into the building of the great Fonthill wall, though its symbolic character cannot be denied. It ran for about six miles, enclosing over five hundred acres, thick and strongly built, and was sufficiently high to prevent anyone from climbing or jumping over. The top was adorned with *chevaux de frise* as an additional deterrent to would-be trespassers, constituting, as an early account puts it, a sort of fortified barrier.[15] Entrance to the enclosure was provided by strong double gates, and these were later guarded by attendants who were forbidden to admit any strangers. It was a grim and formidable fortification presenting a forbidding aspect to the exterior world.

Beckford later in life played down the idea that he had built it to exclude his neighbours and the vulgar world in general from his secret retreat. 'Some say I built the wall before I built the house to cut myself off from mankind', he told Cyrus Redding almost half a century later. 'Why, I had always from one to two hundred workmen with me, and I superintended all myself. I built the wall because I would not be intruded upon by sportsmen. In vain were they warned off. Your country gentlemen will transport a pauper for taking a few twigs from a hedge, while they will break it down without ceremony themselves. They will take no denial when they go hunting in their red jackets to excruciate to death a poor hare. I found remonstrances in vain, and so I built the wall to exclude them. I never suffer an animal to be killed but through necessity. In early life I gave up shooting because I consider we have no right to murder animals for sport. I am fond of animals. The birds in the plantations of Fonthill seemed to know me—they continued their songs as I rode close to them; the very hares grew bold. It was exactly what I wished.'[16]

He was not exaggerating his love of animals when he spoke to Redding but in other respects the passage of time had mellowed his mind and healed, to some extent, the ache of the wound that still festered when the wall was built. At that time his feelings of bitterness and resentment were still acute as a contemporary letter shows. 'I cannot yet pretend to have taken the Road of acquiring popularity,' he then wrote to Lady Craven, 'for I have just stopped the career of Fox hunters by a wall not quite so long or so high as that of China—but better built I dare say. Vathec you recollect was spoiled by Carathis and will have his way tho' it lead to the Devil. I am extending my forests and sticking them full of hideous iron traps and spring guns that snap legs off as neatly as Pinchbeck's patent snuffers snuff candles. In the process of time, when my Hills are completely blackened with Fir, I shall retreat into the center of this gloomy circle like a spider into the midst of its web. There I will build my tower and deposit my books and my writings and brood over them till it please Heaven to close my eyes on this strange medley of mischievous Beings and open the doors of a pleasanter existence. Few people have right or reason to hold this dismal language; but I have been hunted down and persecuted these many years. I have been stung and lacerated and not allowed opportunities of changing that snarling, barking style you complain of, had I ever so great an inclination. No peace, no respite have I experienced since the first license was taken out at Nebuchadnezzar's office for shooting at me. If I am shy or savage you must consider the baitings and worryings to which I allude—how I was treated in Portugal, in Spain, in France, in Switzerland, at home, abroad, in every region.'[17] It was the most bitter outburst he had ever allowed himself to make since the Powderham scandal had marked him as an outcast, and it ended with the account, already quoted, of the wounding attack made on his character at the time of Lady Margaret's death.

This letter very clearly shows Beckford's state of mind when he gave orders for the wall to be built, and it encompassed a good deal more than kindness to animals. The resolution sprang from the deep resentment he felt at the way society had treated him, a resentment that had been lulled to some extent while he was abroad but now came back with all its old force when he returned to England and found the attitude of society unchanged against him. It was also bound up with the symbolic notion of the tower as a place of mysterious sanctuary and magic power and of his growing self-identification with the character of the Caliph Vathek. It shows also that the building of the wall was a conscious act of defiance directed against his persecutors and not just a device to frustrate their hunting of the fox. It was Beckford himself who was the hunted animal.

And so James Wyatt was sent for from his work at Salisbury where chance had so conveniently placed him, for all that Mrs. Hervey had warned her brother how the bishop had been fretted to distraction by the architect's unreliability and 'provoking delays'. Plans were discussed and drawn up and preparations made for the work to begin. Beckford did not supervise it himself as he later told Redding; that was a reference to the time when the great Abbey itself was being built. Now he simply gave his orders and then made plans for another visit to France, only stipulating that the work should be finished within a space of twelve months, a vain request as things turned out, for thanks to Wyatt's dilatoriness the work was not completed until after Beckford left for his second visit to Portugal three years later. But the wall would be built, that was the main thing. When and in what manner he himself would ultimately retire behind its protecting embrace was another question, and one that he would settle in his own good time.

17
Paris and Revolution

It must seem strange that Beckford should want to return to Paris in October 1790 at a period when many French nobles had already decided that their safety depended upon flight and were busily making tracks in the opposite direction. There was something in the revolutionary air of Paris that attracted him, just as he had confessed to a fascination in the scenes of violence that had accompanied the Gordon Riots in London a decade before. There were other reasons, too, that made Paris attractive. The emigration of sections of the nobility had filled the art market with even more treasures for the discerning collector, and the inflation that came in with the issue of paper money, the notorious *assignats* that had first appeared in the previous December, greatly increased his purchasing power, especially at a time when Wildman was assuring him that he was richer than ever. Furthermore, the acceptance of the constitution by Louis XVI in July 1790 on the anniversary of the storming of the Bastille may have deceived Beckford (as it did many others) into believing that a period of stability and constitutional rule was about to begin. He was to remain in France until the following June when the attempted flight of the royal family and their capture at Varennes brought an end to this brief and uneasy alliance between the monarchy and the revolution.

He seemed cheerfully indifferent to the political and personal dramas that surrounded him—or so at least a letter to Lady Craven would suggest, written only a month after his arrival. 'I never amused myself better at Paris in all my days', he told her. 'The whole town is at my devotion and I live in a perpetual Vapour of Incense—which—*entre nous* be it spoken—we fiery beings are rather inclined to snuff up our flame coloured nostrils . . . No sooner had I taken possession of my Appartments than I waved my wand and behold—a garden as green as in the month of May, full of wall flowers and Laurustine, primroses and violets started up on the Terrace, upon which I go out *de plein pied* from the large glass door of my saloon. Is not all this quite in our own way? What care I for Aristocrates or Democrates. I am an Autocrate, determined to make the most of every situation . . .'[1]

This feeling of euphoria seems to have remained with him during this whole visit. It was inspired partly, perhaps, in reaction to the sense of restriction that he still found himself faced with in England. It owed a good deal to the enthusiasm that he felt at the time in favour of liberty, though this, as he later admitted to Cyrus Redding, would be checked by subsequent events.[2] It also, we may be sure, sprang from the excitement of the collector who finds many desirable objects suddenly within his grasp. So much was happening to keep his interest at full stretch that what occurred elsewhere hardly entered his consciousness. Did he even know that Louisa had died that April of 1791 in Florence? He was busy then writing to Sir William Hamilton, that 'first of connoisseurs, not only in the fine arts but in the science of human felicity', telling him that 'the reign of grim Gothic prejudices is nearly over, and people begin to serve God and themselves in the manner they like best',[3] a premature judgement as events would show, but indicative of his feelings at the time with regard to what was happening in France.

His letter caught Sir William *en route* from Naples to England where, among other things, he planned to marry his mistress Emma Hart with whom he had been living for the past five years. Beckford himself returned to England shortly afterwards and invited them to visit him at Fonthill, but before they came he had a visit from another couple whose unconventional relationship had made the rest of society eye them coldly, his old friend Lady Craven and her German prince. It was an indication of Beckford's social isolation in England that he could only invite couples who, like himself, were for some reason or other *hors de société*, and a reminder also that things were not so for him abroad. He found the Margrave to be 'all goodness, meekness and resignation', and Elizabeth Craven 'all eyes, nose, fire and fury, exclaiming against relations who will not allow her to live as she likes, and against beastly Germans who accuse her of leading their gentle Sovereign out of his senses and out of his dominions'.[4]

It was a situation he understood and sympathised with only too well. Lady Craven and the Margrave were about to go to Portugal and he was able to tell them many things about the country he had himself only recently left. He must, indeed, have hinted to them that he might yet marry and settle there, for barely had his friend arrived in Lisbon than she wrote begging him to make no such mistake. She clearly disliked Portugal as much as he loved it; their songs to her were 'Horrid negro airs—miawling of cats, door hinges or anything horrible is preferable to such diabolical noise', and she urged him not to think of allying himself to 'Jewish, Moorish blood . . . Do anything for God's sake but misally yourself thus—use them to your purpose but never *tie* yourself to Negro Land.'[5]

Possibly she felt in a stronger position to give matrimonial advice from Portugal than had been the case while she was at Fonthill, for in Lisbon she was at last able to marry her prince, who had been a widower for some months. 'Lady Craven', Horace Walpole was to record, 'received the news of her Lord's death on a Friday, went into weeds on Saturday, and into white satin and *many* diamonds on a Sunday, and in that vestal trim was married to the Margrave of Anspach by my cousin's chaplain, though he and Mrs. Walpole excused themselves from being present.'[6] Beckford, however, was in no need of her advice, either as to marriage, which did not seriously interest him any more, or as to Portugal, which he would soon be visiting again despite the new Margravine's strictures on its songs and its society.

The visit of the Hamiltons was a more placid affair. Beckford was all attention and flattery to Emma out of respect for his genial and kind-hearted cousin to whom he had every reason to be grateful, but in private he found her loud and vulgar, 'not at all delicate, ill-bred, often very affected', and a devil when in a temper; in fact no substitute at all for the previous Lady Hamilton whose character he had admired so ardently. For once Emma had met a man whose judgement of her was not swayed by the impact of her physical beauty; indeed he later declared that he found her somewhat masculine and her countenance agreeable but no more than fine, 'hardly beautiful, but the outline excellent'.[7]

With Sir William he had family affairs to discuss. Beckford's illegitimate brother Richard had been in financial trouble and had appealed to Hamilton to act as an intermediary between himself and the Fonthill family. This Sir William had done with his usual tact and understanding as a result of which Richard had received a payment of five hundred pounds down and the promise of an

annuity of the same amount. After the envoy's return to his post
at Naples he received a letter from Richard describing a reception
at Fonthill 'not only friendly but affectionate'. William Beckford,
he declared, 'received and recognised me as his brother, assured
me that he was now satisfied of the falsity of all the reports he had
heard of my ill will towards him, and promised me his friendship
and support for ever'.[8] It was an act of magnanimity on Beckford's part for he was well aware that his brother had been one of
the leading opponents of his father's will and had been working
against his interests for many years.

In spite of these visits and family reconciliations Beckford must
have been bored by his solitary life at Fonthill and his pride hurt
by the continued determination of the local 'county' to cut him.
To while away the time he made a translation of J. K. A. Musaus's
fairy tales *Volksmarchen der Deutschen* which John Murray published anonymously later in the year as *Popular Tales of the
Germans*. It was a free adaptation with many characteristic passages from the translator's pen, including a self-portrait which
shows us how he saw himself in the summer of 1791 while still in
his thirty-first year: 'He is shrewd, whimsical and fickle, petulant
and rude; proud and vain, and so inconstant that he will be today
your warmest friend, and not acknowledge you tomorrow; the
distressed have sometimes found him kind, generous, and feeling;
but he is at such perpetual variance with himself, that, like an egg
put into boiling water, he proves hard and soft in a couple of
minutes: and you will report him frank or reserved, mulish or
pliant, just as the ignis-fatuus of his fancy whisks at first sight.'[9]
Drawing up verbal self-portraits was a favourite drawing-room
game of the late eighteenth century, and this one makes it clear
that the growing cynicism with which Beckford viewed the
human race was applied as much to himself as to his fellow
creatures. Though still describing himself as 'whimsical', the old
romanticism of the earlier years, all that was implied in the cry 'not
an animal comprehends me' had now vanished and a more down-
to-earth, unflattering assessment of character taken its place.

In November 1791 he was back in Paris, again lured by the
thought of the spoils he might pick up in the glittering debris
left in the wake of revolution. He seems to have given little
consideration to the plight of those whose former possessions he
now hoped to pick up at bargain prices, and what time was not
spent in the sale rooms was passed, if we may judge from a letter

sent to Wildman shortly after his arrival, entirely in the pursuit of pleasure with a fine indifference to those whom the revolution had dispossessed or of interest in those whom it was supposed to have liberated.

'Happy, aye, thrice happy,' Wildman was informed on 29 November, 'are those who in this good Capital and at this period have plenty of money—their Kingdom is come, their will is done on Earth, if not in Heaven. By St. Anthony, my dear Friend, I never was better amused since I existed. I have the most delightful apartments, and the best wine and the best Bristol waters, and the bed, everything . . . The finest dinner which ever Flanders or Saxony produced is scarcely thought worthy to garnish my side-boards, or be spread under my boots when I return in all the majesty of mud from dashing in the most invincible manner thro' the sloughs of the Bois-de-Boulogne attended by half-a-dozen Captains and Lieutenants of the Garde Nationale. Don't suppose I wait one instant for my carriage at the Opera (where by the bye I have taken possession of the Prince de Condé's box)—not a bit—down drives my coach upon the slightest signal, to the admiration and desolation of penniless Dukes, Counts and half-pay Ambassadors. I neither cant nor whine nor wear out the cushions of St. Sulpice with kneeling—St. Anthony having given me leave of absence from such sort of places, till he had settled things in Portugal to my wishes.'[10]

The letter does not conjure up a particularly pleasant impression of Beckford at this time. Indeed, Paris rarely brought out the best side of his character; in former days flattering his vanity as a spoilt and precocious young man, now pandering to his power as a millionaire. We can see him at this period in a portrait by J. P. Sauvage, a medallion in profile, his hair falling in a queue at the back and caught in a ribbon according to the fashion of the day, a picture which shows that at thirty-one he still preserved his youthful appearance. The long sharp nose and rather fleshy chin are much the same as in the Reynolds portrait painted a decade before, but there is more confidence and assurance in the pose.

Books and pictures were still his main interest, and he became a very valuable customer to the bookseller Auguste Chardin, a contact highly profitable to them both. Chardin was a man whose political principles were in accord with the revolutionary spirit of the times but who was by no means averse from doing business with this rich patron from England. They soon became friends, a

fortunate circumstance for Beckford, for the time would come
when the friendship of this stalwart republican would help him in
a moment of danger.

But Beckford's collecting interests were never confined to one
or even two aspects of art; the range of his knowledge and enthusiasm was always expanding. Furniture also claimed his attention and it was probably at this time that he bought the bureau
made for King Stanislaus Leczinski of Poland, father-in-law of
Louis XV, which was later to be one of the glories of the grand
drawing-room at Fonthill Abbey. He also commissioned new
furniture from the royal cabinetmaker and goldsmith R. J.
Auguste. 'I think you will be enraptured with the furniture I am
having made under his direction in the true spirit of Corinth and
Athens', he told Sir William Hamilton.[11] His taste in Japanese
lacquer was already established, and in this, too, he may have had
opportunities to indulge, though his main purchases belong to a
later period when the Bouillon Collection was sold in 1797. In
due time he would assemble one of the greatest collections in this
particular genre, but as with so many items in his possession at
different times it is easier to discover when they were sold than
when they were bought.

By December some of the ebullience which had characterised
his letter to Wildman was beginning to wear off and he started to
show a little more awareness of the political situation. Paris in
winter, and in revolution, had its drawbacks after all and his
thoughts turned to Naples, that haven of sunshine and calm. 'A
thick cloud hangs over Paris at this moment, fraught with some
confounded crackers', he wrote to Hamilton on the fifteenth. 'I
expect an eruption every minute. The assembly know not which
way to turn themselves, and publick credit is at the lowest ebb.
In short, I wish myself a thousand leagues away, and would set
forth in depths of hail, snow, sleat, or rain . . . Notwithstanding
the confusion of the moment, all my baggage, plate, books,
horses, carriages, etc., have been admitted duty free & I must own
nothing can exceed the civilities I meet with from the nation; but
there is no living in comfort with a sword suspended over one's
head by a thread; I take the dear nation itself to be in that disagreeable predicament . . .' At least he took the precaution of
keeping on good terms with France's new rulers. 'Two or three
Deputies', his letter concludes, 'are chattering at one end of my
room and swilling tea, and observing that, since the introduction

of this English beverage, *on pense plus librement*, etc., etc., a deal of French stuff . . .'[12]

Beckford remained in Paris until July 1792. This was the period of the Duke of Brunswick's manifesto threatening 'exemplary and never-to-be-forgotten vengeance' against Paris in the event of harm coming to the royal family, a threat which had the opposite effect of rallying the more moderate Frenchmen to the support of their government and rendering more uncertain and unwelcome the presence of foreigners in the French capital. On 8 July France declared war on Prussia and on Sardinia ten days later; Prussian and Austrian troops would soon be invading French territory. Beckford decided to remove himself to Savoy, conveniently near the Swiss frontier, taking with him in his suite a band of musicians who had formerly all been in the king's regiment of guards.

He travelled in Vathek-like style despite the unsettled state of the country. In an earlier letter to Sir William Hamilton he had mentioned the need, should he settle in Naples, of having 'terraces and gardens, with views of the sea, and capabilities of placing pavilions, tents, and awnings in an Oriental fantastic style'. Now, in a letter from Evian on the Savoy side of the lake of Geneva dated 31 July, we get a glimpse of him in this exotic encampment: 'I left Paris just in time to avoid a scene of the most frightful confusion, and am quietly established in one of the wildest forests of Savoy, on the borders of the lake. My pavilions are in a style you would like, and Lady Hamilton be in raptures with. They have been planned, executed and adorned by the finest artists of Paris, who are all here in my suite . . . It rains at this moment, which deranges my encampment a little. I wish you could take a peep of it by the aid of some miraculous telescope without stirring from under your canopy of soft blue sky.'[13]

Just how long he continued living in this *al fresco* manner is not clear; not very long, we may be certain, if the weather continued wet. By September he had been compelled to cross the lake to Lausanne 'in a violent hurry' (as he told Hamilton) because 'all Savoy is bedivelled and bejacobinized, and plundering, ravaging, etc., is going on swimmingly'. The town itself he found 'in sad confusion, its government half crazy with alarms, suspicions, etc.'[14] He planned to remain there a few days before continuing his travels on the Swiss side of the lake.

According to another account, that of the Irish traveller Thomas 'Buck' Whaley, Beckford had been ordered to quit

Lausanne by the Bailiff of the town on pain of being taken into custody if he did not comply. The reason Whaley gives for this extraordinary conduct was 'that Mr. B. was suspected of having, by means of a considerable sum of money, favoured the escape of a prisoner, who had been confined upwards of twenty years on conviction of being the chief in forming a conspiracy at Rolles, the object of which was that of detaching this bailiwick from its dependence on Berne and of delivering it into the hands of France'.[15] Beckford makes no reference to this strange story in his correspondence or in his later reminiscences (when surely he would have elaborated so picaresue an episode for the entertainment of his listeners), and nothing in his letter to Sir William Hamilton suggests that he left Lausanne under any constraint.

Buck Whaley was one of the few people of Beckford's own class who was prepared to defend him in the face of the cold hostility which mention of his name could still inspire. This was perhaps because, as an Irishman, he was less susceptible to the sort of hypocrisy that men of Loughborough's stamp knew so well how to exploit in their own countrymen. Whatever the reason, he was ready to remind people that Beckford was condemned on no more than a suspicion, and that nothing was proved against him; he even went so far as to record Beckford's denials of the charges held against him in his published *Memoirs*. It was an attitude he was prepared to defend against very formidable opposition. When Edward Gibbon, in the presence of the Duchess of Devonshire, rebuked him for visiting a man 'who lay under such an imputation as Mr. B. did', and added that even if he were innocent 'some regard was due to the opinion of the world', Buck Whaley answered the historian in his own way: 'The only reply I made to his impertinent animadversion was, that I did not look upon this little piece of history as anyway deserving the attention of so great a man. The Duchess complacently smiled: the rest of the company looked grave; my pedant was dumb, and I took my leave.'[16]

It is through the eyes of another Irishman, the young Viscount Cloncurry, that we get an impression of the manner in which Beckford travelled at this time. His 'travelling *ménage*' consisted of about thirty horses with four carriages and a corresponding number of servants, a cavalcade, as Cloncurry pointed out when he came to write his recollections many years later, that 'would astonish the princes of the present degenerate days'. Beckford also had a yacht on the lake, and his lavish hospitality quickly attracted the young peer and his companions. But even here Beckford did not escape from the long shadow of Lord Loughborough. 'In the course of a few weeks,' Cloncurry recorded, 'letters came from England . . . as a result of which our visits to Mr. Beckford ceased.'[17] Buck Whaley would have responded less meekly to this warning from home but Cloncurry, it must be admitted, represented the more usual attitude that Beckford still had to face.

During the last months of 1792 he was lost from sight. It is clear from his correspondence with Sir William Hamilton that he planned to go to Naples, and his band of musicians, seven in number, actually set out and got as far as Milan, but his own wanderings remain mysterious until, more surprisingly than ever considering the growing danger and confusion there, he turned up in Paris again at the end of the year. A legend claims that he was present in the Place de la Concorde on 21 January 1793 and witnessed the execution of Louis XVI,[18] an act that symbolised the end of an age.

What could have brought Beckford back to Paris at so perilous a moment? Less than six months previously, as we have seen, he had left the city 'to avoid a scene of the most frightful confusion', and yet now he was back there again when the situation had deteriorated even more, when the most innocent citizens lived in fear of denunciation and when foreigners were more unpopular than ever. Though he could still pass himself off as a friend of liberty, even as a republican, his revolutionary enthusiasm was beginning to wear a bit thin; it was not in this rôle, which he would only assume by way of self-protection, that he now revisited Paris. It must surely have been his desire to save the collection of books, pictures and *objets d'art* that brought him back. As a foreigner (and the subject, as he became on 1 February, of a country at war with France) his collection was in danger of confiscation by the state, and at a time of revolutionary confusion it could just as easily have been looted or destroyed. He could only feel secure if he was there himself to supervise its protection and to plan, if possible, for its ultimate shipment to England or to some other less dangerous locality.

He was able to persuade Chardin to look after his treasures, a fact that was to be included in the indictment against the bookseller when he was arrested and briefly imprisoned by order of the

Committee of Public Safety a year later.[19] Meanwhile Beckford himself was in serious danger of being denounced and imprisoned, and for a while, thanks again to Chardin, went into hiding, working for several weeks disguised as a clerk in Merigot's bookshop. The extent of his gratitude to the friend whose prompt action saved him at this moment is an indication of the danger in which he stood, for after returning to England he was to pay the bookseller an annuity which the latter would enjoy for the rest of his life. For a brief spell Beckford found himself a fugitive from terror if not from justice; it was a change indeed from the days when deputies from the National Assembly had met to drink tea in his drawing-room and make elegant discourse on the fashionable topic of liberty.

Soon he found himself faced by another threat, this time from across the channel. On 15 March William Pitt passed the Traitorous Correspondence Act through Parliament which made Beckford's position as an Englishman living voluntarily in enemy territory liable to a treasonable interpretation, all the more so in his case as he was still a Member of Parliament. Urgent appeals reached him from Wildman to return home at once as any delay would only serve to make things look worse, nor can Beckford's own hopes have been raised by his boyhood friend's decision to suspend the law of Habeas Corpus at the same time as passing the act which made correspondence with the enemy treasonable. Beckford set off at once for the coast, but at Arras he was arrested on the absurd charge of dressing his man-servant in green livery, which was considered to be a symbol of feudalism, and he was packed off back to Paris, there to clear his character and go once more through the tiresome and often risky business of applying for a passport.

The anxiety made him (as he confessed in a letter to Wildman) 'miserably uneasy' at finding himself still in France. 'My conscience however cannot take alarm,' his letter continues, 'and when I reflect upon the justice and Laws of England, my mind is at ease. There never existed at Paris a single scrap of my writing in which any political opinion was conveyed. I cannot therefore be accused of traitorous correspondence. I have neither aided or assisted the Enemies of England. As to my remaining here—it is not my fault and perfectly against my will. I have been for more than these ten days past in a constant course of solicitation in order to obtain my passports. The laws are positive against their being granted to any subjects of countries at war with France and it was not without the most perseverant exertion that I have at length procured an exception in my favour ... I am tired and jaded to death; all my anxieties redoubled by the thought of those you endure upon my account, but there was no remedy—not an hour's idle delay—and I may think myself in luck to have obtained my passport at all.'[20]

The passport was finally issued, he declared, by producing a letter from Wildman which proved that his fortune would suffer from a longer stay in France, but even so he had to traipse from his section or parish to the local Revolution Committee, then to the Surveillance or Police Committee who in turn referred him to the Committee of Public Safety, and then, after 'tedious, tumultuous and desultory debates at all these assemblies' to the Hotel de Ville, where he had to take his place with 'a thousand strangers, English, Dutch, Spaniards, etc', who had all been waiting up to six weeks in vain for their passports. It was a grim and disillusioning experience, for someone not wholly out of sympathy with the new régime in France, of liberty, equality and fraternity in action.

At last he was able to set out once more for the coast, but even now his troubles were not at an end. The over-zealous officials at Calais took it upon themselves to question the validity of the passport which had cost him so much in trouble and, in all probability, in bribe-money as well, for all that it was signed by the Foreign Minister and its holder described as *étranger que Paris voit partir avec regret*. His case, they insisted, must be referred again to the Committee of Public Safety, and while waiting for a reply they took the opportunity to requisition two of his horses for the army. In due course his clearance came, his love of liberty was suitably vouched for, and he was permitted to leave. He was back at Fonthill before the end of May.

Beckford's visits to Paris during the period from 1789 to 1793 present certain problems to which no definite answer can be found. To what extent, for example, was he really committed to that revolutionary love of liberty which his passport proclaimed? Who were his political friends in Paris, and what particular faction in the many different clubs and fraternities did he mostly support? That he had political friends in influential places we know from the later period when the Directory took office and his name was put forward from the French side as a possible negotiator for peace with England. As men who rose to the top at this later time they were clearly moderates in opinion and removed from the Jacobin extremists, but even so Beckford was careful to leave no record as to their identity at the time, nor did he throw any light on this aspect of the matter later on, and was at pains (possibly in view of his attempts to establish his political respectability in England) to leave everything in a perplexing state of mystery.

As to his radical views, these he would profess to hold for some time yet, not only for their own sake but as a mark of hostility against his former friend Pitt, whose gradual shift from the Whig standpoint of Chatham and the Alderman to the leadership of the Tory interest was to evoke Beckford's animosity and contempt.

But to what extent his sympathy with the ideas of 1789 was genuine is difficult to say. He liked to play one set of ideas off against others, as when, at the time he was toying with the notion of securing a Portuguese title, he could write to Wildman: 'Suppose Mary Portugal should hesitate, I shall accept the propositions of the National Assembly and fix myself in France',[21] a sentence which raises the whole question of Beckford's political sincerity. Furthermore, at the time under discussion he was an outcast from England and in particular from English political life, a scene where Lord Loughborough and his friends still held the stage, and much of his flirting with radical ideas in France (where he found himself socially accepted) must be seen as no more than a reaction against his rejection by the political and social 'establishment' at home.

Beckford probably gave the key to his real and somewhat superficial political views when he wrote the lines quoted earlier in this chapter: 'What care I for Aristocrates or Democrates. I am an Autocrate, determined to make the most of every situation.' This cynical judgement, however, did not exclude a sympathy for those less fortunate than himself; he had a paternalist view of social problems which was no different from that of other Whigs. 'I would not have the rich live much worse than they do,' he wrote later, 'but I would have the poor supported a great deal better', a sentiment that belonged to Whiggish London rather than to Jacobin Paris. But Beckford's temperament was fundamentally that of an artist and not of a politician, and it is perhaps absurd to expect to find him conforming to any pattern of political consistency. He was, indeed, to take a very different political line just over two years later after his second visit to Portugal.

18

The Wanderer

Back once more in England Beckford began to concentrate his attention on the Fonthill estate. If he was to live there in social isolation he might as well make the isolation as splendid as possible. Work was hurried forward on the building of the barrier wall and James Wyatt was commissioned to undertake some alterations and improvements at Splendens. It was now that Beckford's idea for some sort of retreat within the enclosure of the wall began to take more positive shape in his mind. The conception was not new. He had told Lady Craven during his last visit to England that one day he would retire to the centre of his gloomy circle like a spider in its web, but the notion of a secluded cell or refuge among the woods round Stop's Beacon can be traced back to his very early years.

At the age of seventeen, while he was living in Geneva, he had first conceived the idea of a sanctuary dedicated to nature and art to which he gave the name of the Dome of the Setting Sun. He imagined it, at that romantic period of his life, as a place where he could indulge in fantasies and pursue the chain of enchanting fables. 'It suggested itself to me,' he wrote, 'that a Dome might be erected in which Painting and Sculpture should embody these delightful Ideas and recall, as presented by classic Poets and Historians, the Description of ancient "Afric and Ind" those countries most favoured by the Sun.'

It was to be a place to which he could resort as a shelter from the turmoil of the world. 'The Dome shall be situated upon some sequestered hill', his description continues. 'Three parts of its circle shall be girt with the thickest foliage: the fourth alone freely open to the West shall receive the mild Rays of the declining Sun. Its Western Slope shall command a still retired landscape confined to Woods and Waters, where ancient Persians met to pay their

H

adoration to the departing God. Rapt in that calmness and serenity which this sober Hour inspires, I will enter the consecrated Dome and reposed in luxuriant leasure describe the Scenes which it presents all round me as if my Artists had already executed them.'[1]

Thoughts similar to this adolescent fantasy had never entirely left him and would emerge from time to time in various forms, often linked with the idea of the tower. It nearly always presented itself in the form of a retreat, a place of retirement to which he could withdraw with his books and favourite possessions and sometimes, though more rarely, with a chosen companion. It usually also took the form of a place of study and contemplation; an eminence from which he could watch the movements of the planets or look down and 'survey the vast range of countries beneath'.[2] These ideas, examples of which we have already noted, would now at last take on a concrete form in the woods of Fonthill.

The conception of the tower and the sanctuary at first took separate forms. The foundations of the tower which the Alderman had planned but never finished still remained on Stop's Beacon and Beckford now discussed with Wyatt the possibility of completing what his father had left unfinished. As well as the tower, but distinct from it and set apart, Wyatt was also to construct in the gothic style a 'folly' that would be part chapel and part convent with the slightly ruinous aspect that was just then beginning to come into fashion; a building in conformity with the new cult of the picturesque with its insistence upon 'splendid confusion and irregularity'. There was no question at all at this period when the ideas were first germinating, or indeed for a good many years to come when the convent actually began to rise on a different site, of its being in any sense a substitute for Fonthill Splendens as a place of residence. It was to consist of no more than a chapel, parlour and dormitory, contrived by the inclusion of a small cloister to give the appearance of the remaining fragment of a ruined abbey. It was to be a place for study or amusement, for day-time occupation, as much an embellishment of the landscape as a rather grandiose and gothicised garden pavilion.

This was the original idea from which the vast fabric of Fonthill Abbey would one day grow, to astonish the traveller who caught a passing glimpse of the great gothic tower rising nearly three hundred feet above the tree tops. The link between the convent in the woods and the abbey as finally built is tenuous enough,

but behind both lay the unifying motive that so possessed Beckford's imagination, and which he had expressed in another letter
to his kindred spirit Lady Craven written three years before: 'I
am growing rich and mean to build Towers, and sing hymns to
the powers of Heaven on their summits, accompanied by almost
as many sacbuts and psalteries as twanged round Nebuchadnezzar's image.'[3] The convent as envisaged at this time was in
fact destined to remain in the realm of fantasy, at least in so far as
it was originally intended for a sight on Stop's Beacon. So too
was the plan to complete the Alderman's tower. But it was from
these unfulfilled dreams that all the rest was to follow. The
partnership with James Wyatt was launched, a collaboration that
was to result in so many delays and frustrations but was to bear so
exotic a fruit. Their association would end only with the architect's untimely death twenty years later.

Having left his architect with instructions to proceed with
plans along these lines Beckford set off once more upon his
travels. His restless spirit could find no fulfilment in his native
country; the winter was approaching, and he began to think of
warmer and sunnier lands. France was no longer a possible scene
for either pillage or adventure, except for adventures of a type he
had no wish to experience again, and so it was to Portugal that he
now returned, knowing that he would find a welcome there in the
same privileged circles he had frequented during his previous
stay. He set out in November 1793. He had not yet completely
abandoned the idea of settling there, and between his two visits to
the country Franchi had been sent on a mission to enquire on his
patron's behalf whether the offer of a title and grandeeship as a
reward for a change of nationality could still be counted upon. It
is difficult to believe that he seriously contemplated such a change,
particularly in view of all the plans he was making at Fonthill,
but he was eager to know that the proffered titles had not been
withdrawn. The Marquis of Marialva, anxious to see his friend
again, had been full of hopeful assurances.

He was to remain in Portugal until October 1795. Once again
he was taken up by the Marialva family and his routine in Lisbon,
where he rented a house near the Marialva palace, continued
much as it had done before, though he no longer expected any
help or protection from the British Minister, whose presence he
now ignored. The Grand Prior of Aviz was waiting to welcome
him, as genial and friendly as ever; and Dom Pedro, no longer a

gauche fifteen-year-old, but now rising twenty, was beginning to win a reputation for gallantry at the royal court where the wife of the heir to the throne was to prove herself far from indifferent to his charms.

The old corrupt paternalistic régime still prevailed in 'this land of parroquites and oranges', as he described it to Sir William Hamilton, but various subtle differences could be observed since his previous visit in the years immediately before the French revolution, and the sense of uneasiness was emphasised by the sight of French warships cruising off the mouth of the Tagus. 'This country is by no means quiet,' he told Sir William, 'the priests are chop-fallen, the oracular images of our Lady and St. Anthony are mute as the fishes to whom he preached, and the ministers scared by the terror of France out of the scanty remains of their senses.' The nervous state of the country seemed to be reflected in the sad plight of the Queen, who was now completely bereft of her sanity. 'Poor Mary Portugal fancies herself damned to all eternity,' the letter continues, 'and therefore, upon the strength of its being all over with her, eats turkey and oyster sauce Fridays and Saturdays, and indulges in conversations of rather an unchaste tendency. Were there ever such times, such vertigos, such bedevilments? Society is almost totally disolved in every part of Europe.'[4]

Whether society were dissolved or not, Beckford decided to set himself up in style. His establishment consisted of no less than eighty-seven people at its full complement and, in his own phrase, exceeded in splendour and talents that of any prince in Europe. The old free-thinking Verdeil no longer accompanied him, his physician was now Dr. Ehrhart, a native of Alsace once in the service of Louis XVI, but a man of similar stamp to the Swiss whom he had replaced. There was also a maître d'hotel, a band of musicians, a French cook of splendid reputation with all the attendants required by an acknowledged culinary genius, a valet de chambre and any number of footmen, coachmen and stable boys, while the now indispensable Gregorio Franchi continued to act as a sort of confidential secretary as well as musical accompanist. It was a household assembled as much to impress others as to serve the not over-elaborate requirements of the solitary being who presided over it; it represented a fine sense of ostentation in the best tradition of Beckford's paternal ancestors.

He still cultivated an excessive devotion to St. Antony of Padua as a means of ingratiating himself with the powerful faction that surrounded the court. 'I am a pattern of sanctity,' he told Sir William Hamilton in February 1794, 'and have set St. Anthony a going again so effectually that the patriarch, the Inquisitor, and the Heads of religious houses stuff me with sweetmeats and smother me with caresses.'[5] News of this effusion of piety even reached England and caused great alarm at Fonthill where Wildman, dreading the thought of anything so rash as a conversion to Romanism, wrote to his employer in obvious concern. Beckford's reply must have set his fears at rest: 'The gravity with which you write of my having changed my Religion from Protestant to Roman Catholic takes away all gravity from me. I laughed as if I had been seeing the farce of the Agreeable Surprise or Tom Thumb—I change indeed! Pray when did you know me adhere to the Sect I am supposed to have relinquished? How can a man who was never at Wapping be said to have gone from Wapping to Rome?'[6]

Yet in spite of his hot denials and the patent insincerity of much of his religious posturings in Portugal, there was still an element of genuine devotion in this curious but persistent cult he had for St. Antony. The saint was more to him than a mere mascot if less than a heavenly advocate. He still clung with the same mixture, as of old, of superstition and uncommitted religious homage to this figure who somehow symbolised the Christian conviction he would have liked to possess himself but was unable to grasp hold of; a spiritualised being who might assuage the sense of guilt that hung over him. For all the blatant use he made of St. Antony in Portugal his attitude was not wholly hypocritical, as was to be shown by the oratory he was later on to build in the saint's honour at Fonthill Abbey.

The idea of such an oratory or sanctuary in fact first took shape in his mind during this visit to Portugal. Beckford decided to build his own house in Lisbon, buying a site near the Necessidades Palace in the rua da Cova da Moura, and drew up some sketch plans in December 1793 for the main floor which show an interesting parallel with the future layout of the galleries at Fonthill Abbey. His plan incorporated an enfilade of connecting apartments, one leading into another, with an anteroom, gallery, octagon and Turkish saloon all leading the eye on to the apsed sanctuary that completed the vista and would house the statue of the patron saint. It was almost exactly the same plan that he would adopt on a much grander scale at Fonthill, with the oratory of St. Antony, glowing in the light of many candles, terminating the three-hundred-and-twelve-foot vista of the galleries of St. Michael and King Edward III.[7]

To this visit to Portugal belongs the excursion to the monasteries of Alcobaça and Batalha which in old age Beckford was to write up from contemporary notes into what many people consider to be his best literary work, the brief but sparkling *Recollections* he published in 1835. The diary he kept at the time shows certain discrepancies when compared with the version he finally published.[8] The latter account begins with a typically Beckfordian flourish: 'The Prince Regent of Portugal, for reasons with which I was never entirely acquainted, took it into his royal head, one fair morning, to desire I would pay a visit to the monasteries of Alcobaça and Batalha, and to name my intimate and particular friends, the Grand Prior of Aviz, and the Prior of St. Vincent's, as my conductors and companions.' In fact Beckford was not presented to Prince Joao (later King Joao VI but not then actually regent) for another year, so the idea of the excursion must have been his own, and owed nothing to any royal command; but in 1835 the seventy-five-year-old author was anxious to impress upon his readers the notion of the easy footing upon which he would have them believe he stood with the royal family and government of Portugal. The contemporary record also shows that the Prior of St. Vincent's, though a friend of Beckford's and his host on part of the journey, did not actually accompany him to the two monasteries, nor did the Grand Prior of Aviz stay with him the whole time but returned to Lisbon a day ahead of him.

The diary also shows that the twelfth day, the famous interview with the regent at the royal palace of Queluz, never took place at all, or at least not upon that occasion. The passage describing the royal audience is one of the best that Beckford ever wrote. He describes how the Grand Prior (who in fact had already left him) and the Prior of St. Vincent's (who did not come with him at all) were already in conference with the prince when he arrived at the palace. He takes a stroll in the gardens and there encounters his old friend Dom Pedro who introduces him to the Spanish infanta who was the wife of Prince Joao. He finds her 'surrounded by thirty or forty young women, every one far superior in loveliness of feature and fascination of smile to their august mistress'. The princess has heard of his athletic prowess and decrees that he must run a race with Dom Pedro and two of her 'donzellas'. It might be a scene from Lancret or Fragonard. Scarcely has Beckford finished his sprint than the Marquis of Anjeja appears to summon him into the presence of the regent; the princess looks 'rather blank' at this interruption in their sport but graciously holds out her hand for him to kiss.

He finds the prince standing alone in a vast room, thoughtful and distracted, but he visibly brightens on Beckford's approach, and a perfunctory discussion takes place upon the subject of the monasteries he has just visited. He is dismissed by the prince with one of 'those affable expressions of regard which his excellent heart never failed to dictate', and rejoins Anjeja in a neighbouring room. The marquis discourses on the melancholy gloom of the prince, pressed down as he is by an accumulated weight of sorrows which spring from the affection in which he holds his mother and from the sorrow which her sufferings inflict upon him. The queen's pitiable mental state is described in harrowing detail and this leads the marquis on to the subject of Portuguese politics and the aspirations of the Marialva family, of which house he was himself a member. 'At this moment,' Beckford wrote in his account of 1835, 'the most terrible, the most agonising shrieks—shrieks such as I hardly conceived possible—shrieks more piercing than those which rung through the Castle of Berkeley, when Edward the Second was put to the most cruel and torturing death—inflicted upon me a sensation of horror such as I never felt before. The Queen herself, whose apartment was only two rooms off from the chamber in which we were sitting, uttered those dreadful sounds: "Ai Jesous! Ai Jesous!" did she exclaim again and again in the bitterness of agony.'

Beckford leaves his reader with these horrible screams ringing in his ears after recounting, in the previous eleven chapters, all the excitements and merriments of his visit to the monasteries, scenes packed with amusing and ironical episodes such as only he could describe. It is a brilliant literary contrivance and all the more sad to think that this dramatic final scene never took place. This is not to say, however, that the incidents described in such detail all flowed from Beckford's imagination. He was finally presented to the prince in May 1795, nearly a year after his journey to Alcobaça and Batalha. He may have had more than one audience before he finally left Portugal, and the account he concocted for the fictional twelfth day of his excursion, so right from the literary if not from

the historical point of view, was probably evolved from various
incidents he had experienced himself or had heard about from
others at a later date. But at the time his visit to the monasteries
came to an end, on Friday 13 June 1794, he had still not met the
prince, and on 14 June, instead of dancing attendance on the royal
family at Queluz he was back in his house at Lisbon.

The excursion to the monasteries was one of the last really carefree moments in a life that was growing increasingly cynical and
embittered. It was as though the freshness and enthusiasm of
youth had suddenly, fleetingly returned. He seemed to throw off
all his worries and frustrations as he rode with the amiable Prior of
Aviz through the Portuguese countryside, always on the look-out
for some interesting building, some quaint or eccentric individual,
some piquant or unusual scene. His fascination with everything
he saw at the monasteries themselves was such that he had no time
for detailed descriptions in the diary he kept at the time; a few
staccato jottings have to suffice, though the entry ends on a
characteristic note: 'This evening a sleek friar with wanton eyes
accompanied Franchi on the Jew's harp; I hear him twanging
away at this moment.'[9]

Only twice does he allow a melancholy or cynical note to appear. On the second day the Prior of St. Vincent's, whose guests
they were, organised a fishing party for their amusement, but
Beckford found himself unable to join in. 'I turned with disgust
and sorrow from the poor unfortunate animals rudely thrown
upon a bare sandy bank and gasping for life', he noted in his
diary. 'We children of Adam should be justly punished were some
gigantic inhabitants of another planet permitted by the Great
Disposer of all things to fish us out of our element into some other
where our lungs would be useless and we should try to breathe in
vain.' When he came to transcribe this passage forty years later he
added: 'Men have in general such wide-open appetites for the objects of their individual pursuit, that, only render the bait sufficiently tempting, and I promise they swallow it, hook and all.'[10]

The other passage gives us some insight into the true nature of
his love for Portugal and the reasons which still could prompt him
into believing that he might settle there. After describing a scene
where vast spaces of wild mountain pasture divide the cornfields
and vineyards 'and still retain the verdure of spring', his 1794
account continues: 'These are the spots I peculiarly delight in,
where I seem to breathe with greater freedom, and which the

goats and sheep, whose bells I heard tinkling at a distance, love
not better than I. How often, contrasting my quiet situation with
the horrid disturbed state of almost every part of Europe, did I
bless the hour when my steps directed me to Portugal. I looked
round with complacency on a roof which sheltered no politician,
on tables upon which perhaps no newspaper had ever lain, on
neat white pillows which had never propped up the heads of
financiers and schemers. The air was genially warm, and every
breeze wafted the perfume of thyme, wild roses and honey-suckle
from the hills.'[11] The passage was only slightly modified in 1835.
By then the financiers and schemers had become 'those assassins
of real prosperity—political adventurers'.

It is tempting to guess at the effect these two gothic buildings
had upon Beckford's imagination and to what extent they influenced the work he was later to inspire at Fonthill. The first
version of Fonthill Abbey, as we shall see, owed something to the
spire of the mausoleum of King Joao I at Batalha, but this design
would seem to have been no less familiar to Wyatt than it was to
Beckford. The detailed account of the monasteries in the published version of the excursion, which includes the description of
the great kitchen at Alcobaça (where he saw, perhaps making its
first appearance in the European *cuisine*, Chinese food being prepared by a lay brother from Macao) and the first impression of
Batalha with 'its rich cluster of abbatial buildings, buttresses, and
pinnacles, and fretted spires, towering in all their pride, and mark-
ing the ground with deep shadows that appeared interminable, so
far and so wide were they stretched along', all belong to the
recollections of old age.

What may be said more certainly to have influenced Beckford's
later architectural ideas was the house he took in the country near
Sintra just after his excursion to the two monasteries was over.
This was the villa or quinta at Monserrate which Byron later
described as 'the most desolate mansion in the most beautiful spot
I ever beheld'.[12] When the poet saw it the house and gardens had
fallen into decay and the desolate scene was to inspire his somewhat specious reflections on the theme of 'England's wealthiest son':

> *Here dist thou dwell, here schemes of pleasure plan,*
> *Beneath yon mountain's ever beauteous brow:*
> *But now, as if a thing unblest by Man,*
> *The fairy dwelling is as lone as thou!*

Here giant weeds a passage scarce allow
To halls deserted, portals gaping wide;
Fresh lessons to the thinking bosom, how
Vain are thy pleasances on earth supplied;
Swept into wrecks anon by Time's ungentle hand.

The house was built in a commanding position amidst rolling, wooded hills, and consisted of a central crenellated, tower-like block with two wings each ending in smaller circular towers with pointed 'pepper-pot' roofs. More interestingly, the internal arrangements all radiated from a central octagon, as would be the case at Fonthill, offering long vistas to the eye. Not only did the quinta of Monserrate have its influence upon Beckford's architectural taste, but it was here also that he first conceived some of those ideas in landscape gardening, of blending architectural mass with natural settings, as it had first confronted him at the Grande Chartreuse and as he was later to develop and exploit it more fully at Fonthill. Though gardens were planted and pathways cut to give views of the surrounding countryside all was done to conceal the hand of the gardener so that an impression of naturalness was achieved. Straight lines were eschewed and the formal design of the parterre banished. Everything must appear spontaneous and 'natural', hiding the frontier between the cultivated and the wild. As Horace Walpole said of William Kent, whose ideas in gardening Beckford followed and expanded, 'he leaped the fence, and saw that all nature was a garden'.

In the autumn of 1794 he was startled by a summons to return to England and attend to his duties in the House of Commons. The request came from the government but Beckford, oversensitive to attacks, saw in it a plot by his enemies to do him further damage. Loughborough, he believed, would not rest until he had ruined him totally, and rather than comply with the demand he resigned his seat, applying for the Chiltern Hundreds. It was a decision that can have cost him little anguish. He had taken no active part in politics before the Powderham affair except to scheme for a peerage, and since that unhappy business had wrecked his life he had of necessity been a stranger to politics completely. The wonder is that he hung on to his parliamentary seat for so long. His resignation merely meant that the electors of Wells would at last have a chance of being adequately represented at Westminster.

There was also unfinished business still to attend to in Portugal.

His presentation at court, as we have seen, did not take place until the spring of 1795. What bribery, what intrigue was involved in achieving this end is not related, but it was done behind the back of the British Minister who had proved so stubborn and un-compromising on Beckford's previous visit. When Walpole learnt that he had been bypassed and that the presentation had been made without his intervention his fury was great, and he wrote a curt note to the Portuguese Foreign Minister demanding an explanation. But the envoy had overstepped himself; the Foreign Minister referred the matter to London where his am-bassador, in an interview with Lord Grenville, received an assurance that the British envoy was not acting officially and Wal-pole was compelled to withdraw his protest and offer an apology. There the matter was allowed to rest.

If this was a triumph for Beckford he showed no inclination to glory in his victory. In fact he was beginning to get restless again and by the end of September was making plans to visit Sir William Hamilton in Naples. Much depended, of course, upon the sort of reception he might expect to receive there. Fortunately he had already been presented to King Ferdinand but even so he wanted to be sure that he would be treated with due respect. 'I mean to be quiet and prudent in Naples,' he told Sir William, 'and shall most chearfully follow any advice you may bestow upon me. I think it would be fair, however, to let the King know that I am *worth* humoring, and that no person in Europe can spend more money in his country, *if I am properly cherished and attended to* . . . I bring very little baggage, and only wish for a pleasant airy appartment at the Albergo Reale, or any other Al-bergo, wherever you think best. The less I spend in show the more I shall have for collecting and real comfort, so *trêve de parade* till times change for the better, or his Neapolitan Majesty should animate me to a display of magnificence by *peculiar* graciousness and distinction.'[13] Once again it was the voice of the Alderman speaking through his son in this rigmarole of threats and promises.

He was at pains, earlier in the letter, to make it plain that his flirtation with the goddess of liberty was now a thing of the past. 'You may most securely answer for my never meddling with Neapolitan politicks,' Sir William is assured; 'if my taste lay that way I might indulge it at home with a vengeance. My purse, my pen, and my lungs might do wonders in England at this eventful moment. No, my dear Sir William, you may assure his Majesty of

Naples that a more loyal subject, a more hearty well-wisher to established forms of Government than myself exists not in all Europe.' In proof of this assertion he cites, apparently with no sense of irony, the support 'from principle' he has given to his own king and government at home and the 'distinguished and unprecedented manner' in which he had been received by the court of Lisbon. It was all a very far cry from the attitude he had adopted in Paris not so very long before and was to assume again, to some extent at least, after his return to England. Was this the effect Portugal had had upon his never very deeply held political principles or was he merely window-dressing for the benefit of the reactionary court of Naples? More probably he simply wished to tone down the no longer fashionable reputation he had earned as a friend of France and its republican form of government, for, as he would now have Sir William believe, 'of all the calumnies which have been floating about the world to my prejudice this is the plumpest'.

What that seasoned diplomatist Sir William Hamilton made of all this we do not know, but at least he must have reported encouragingly on the chances of a favourable reception in Naples, for in October Beckford had set out once again on his wanderings. He had reduced his following of attendants as much as he was able; he had with him no more than his physician Dr. Ehrhart, his maître d'hotel, baker, cook, valet de chambre and three footmen, something less than his usual eighty-seven, but with any fewer he felt quite unable to travel. With this diminished household he set out for the coast and, with his usual misgivings at the prospect of a sea voyage, boarded ship for Italy.

Before setting sail he had dispatched to Naples a cargo of packing-cases containing his linen, servants' liveries, wines, a forte-piano and many other necessities together with a copy of his daughters' genealogy carefully drawn up and engrossed in Indian ink. 'It is a very curious work,' he told Sir William Hamilton, 'strictly historical, in which I have no fabulous embellishments, and as it partly concerns your own family, may interest you for a moment as well as amuse; pray take care of it till I come, or the cargo is reshipped.'[14]

With this shipment of household and heraldic oddments safely taken care of he then embarked himself. But whatever gods watched over Beckford as he travelled from one country to another seemed always to abandon him when he put to sea; scarcely had his ship passed through the straits of Gibraltar than a violent storm overtook it. No sooner was this unpleasant hazard circumvented than one if possible even worse threatened; a Barbary corsair hove into sight and proceeded to give chase. The pirate was almost within gunshot range when a sudden change of the wind saved them, 'a miraculous sort of a St. Anthony jerk round of the wind' as Beckford described it, well aware what a splendid catch he would have made for the ransom-hunters of Algiers or Salee. 'I was prettily heavily laden with the good things of this world, so I have had a narrow escape', he commented wryly to Sir William.

They were forced to seek shelter in Alicante and Beckford, unwilling to risk any more adventures, promptly went on shore and remained there. The perils of the voyage had induced a state of fever and the mere mention of another fortnight or three weeks at sea was enough to bring on a relapse. All thoughts of seeing Sir William and Lady Hamilton were put aside, and the traveller continued his journey by land to Valencia and Barcelona in the hopes of recovering his jaded spirits. He may have thought of embarking again at the latter port but if so his courage must have failed him for in fact he turned inland and set off in the direction of Madrid. At one point he had thought of wintering in the neighbourhood of Valencia, 'this sweet-looking, soft-smelling, dull region of Melons and Cauliflowers', but the impression he gained there of 'such stiff nobility, such frowsy females, such grimy priests' had decidedly deterred him.[15]

By the beginning of December he had reached Aranjuez where the confluence of the rivers Tagus and Jarama had enabled the Bourbon kings of Spain to create a park and garden of cool fountains and shady walks sheltered by avenues of trees rare enough in the arid countryside south of Madrid. It was in this elegant pink and white palace that the great Italian castrato Farinelli (whom Beckford had met in extreme old age) had sung without pause to soothe the melancholia of Philip V, always repeating the same four arias. Ferdinand VI, no less musical and, at the end of his life, no less melancholic, had built a theatre here with a ceiling painted by Raphael Mengs in which the same artist had performed. Beckford was eager to see this masterpiece, but only to find it in the process of demolition in order to form new apartments for the Infant of Parma. 'No mercy was shown to the roof . . .' he recorded sadly, 'the workmen are hammering and plastering at a great rate, and in a few days whitewash will cover all.'[16]

It all seemed to him symptomatic of a decadent court in which the influence of the favourite Manuel de Godoy (the Duke of Alcudia as Beckford calls him in his account later published at the end of *Italy, with Sketches of Spain and Portugal*), was everywhere to be seen. This opinion was obviously shared by the guide who showed him round the palace, 'an old snuffling domestic of the late King', who when asked if some new buildings were to be for the king or the favourite, replied tersely: 'For both, no doubt; what serves one serves the other.' More sympathetic to Beckford was the altar to his favourite saint in the royal chapel. He found himself 'immediately attracted ... by the effulgence of glory amidst which the infant Jesus is descending to caress the kneeling saint, whose attitude, and youthful, enthusiastic countenance, have great expression'.[17] It was a treatment of the subject after his own heart.

By the time he reached the Spanish capital all thoughts of going on to Naples had left him. The prospect of a wintry Mediterranean infested with storms, pirates and hostile warships was a sufficiently strong argument against any further moves in that direction. He would go back to Portugal as a prelude to returning to England. For the past ten years he had been almost constantly upon his travels, only visiting his native country for periods of a few months at a time, but now the spread of the revolutionary wars was making continental travel ever more unpleasant and un-predictable, even for a millionaire. The time had come for him to go home; but first he must revisit Portugal to settle his affairs there and await a more suitable season for undertaking so long a journey. And so he found himself applying to the same Duke of Alcudia whose influence he so thoroughly deplored for the docu-ments necessary for his departure. His passport, signed with a flourish 'El Principe de la Paz', was issued to 'Don Guillermo Beckford, Caballero Inglés' at the end of December and he left Spain with the dying year.

19

Unavailing Diplomacy

BEFORE BECKFORD quitted Portugal in the spring of 1796 he must have had further meetings with the Regent for he left the country, so he claimed, entrusted with a special mission from that prince to King George III. Just how this came about he does not make clear but we may be sure that Marialva had a hand in the matter, for the Marquis had never ceased to work on his friend's behalf.

Beckford attached great importance to this mission. He had never allowed himself to believe that the ban against him at home was permanent and always hoped that he would be able to scramble back to the position of influence and authority from which he had been pushed by Loughborough's evil machinations. What better opportunity was there to begin this process of re-instatement than to arrive in England bearing letters from the Regent of Portugal to the British Court? That he saw the business in this light is clear from a letter he wrote to Sir William Hamilton some months after his return home: 'You cannot imagine the favors and distinctions with which I was loaded in Portugal, nay, charged with a particular mission to the King, which his Majestie's ministers have not yet thought fit I should deliver; but the King is fully aware of my attachment and loyalty, and I make no doubt in a short space of time I shall again climb the eminence to which I was born, and from whence I was so maliciously and foolishly precipitated.'[1]

The British government unfortunately did not share in the feelings which Beckford entertained with regard to the gravity of his mission. After all, they had a Minister in Lisbon and the Portuguese court was diplomatically represented in London; what need was there for Beckford's intervention? His approaches were received with considerable coolness, and though he managed to secure an interview with the Duke of Portland, who was Home Secretary, this was not until July, three months after his arrival in England. It was plain that a government in which Pitt was the presiding genius and Loughborough the Lord Chancellor was not going to make any gestures of friendliness or forgiveness to the returned outcast. After his interview with Portland all further attempts on his part to obtain a hearing were firmly rebuffed.

Beckford took a high line over this treatment, complaining to his mother that he had been shamefully trifled with. 'I have received no answer to that important communication with which I was entrusted,' he told her angrily in August, 'no invitation to consult upon them, no mark of attention or gratitude. Things at Lisbon are advancing to such a Crisis that I shall be forced to confess my inability of recording the Prince's most excellent dispositions towards this Country—the consequence will be confirming the triumph of the Spanish Faction to the utter destruction of our commerce with Portugal and its dependencies.'[2] But his anger sprang not so much from the affront to Portugal as from the affront to himself; from a realisation that he was still *persona non grata* with the official world; that nothing had been forgotten.

To his friends in Portugal he somehow contrived to give the impression that he was still an influence to be reckoned with in England, that his social position there was as impregnable as he would have had them believe and himself would have wished it to be. The talks with the Home Secretary, when reported to Lisbon, elicited an ecstatic response from the Marquis of Marialva who urged him on behalf of the Regent to continue the good offices he was performing in the interests of their country. 'I read your letters to the Prince my Master,' he wrote on 15 August, 'and saw in his expression a certain pleasure which showed me a great esteem for your person, and he charged me several times not to forget to convey to you that he was your cordial friend, and if you were to return to this country he would show you in a practical way how much he esteems you.'[3]

In spite of the failure of this manoeuvre as a step towards social rehabilitation, and in spite of the coldness with which his overtures had been received, Beckford was soon to propose himself again to the attention of the government, this time in the rôle of a negotiator between Great Britain and the French Republic, who had been at war with each other since 1793. In the April of 1797 preliminaries of peace had been signed between France and

Austria at Ioeben and there were indications that a more general peace might follow. In July the Directory (of which Talleyrand had just become Foreign Minister) put out peace feelers to Britain and Lord Malmesbury was sent to Lille to meet representatives of the French government. Negotiations were eventually to break down, due more to the defeat of the Constitutionalists in the *coup d'état* in Paris on 4 September than to anything that was happening at Lille, and Lord Malmesbury had to return home, but in the summer of 1797 there were hopes among reasonable people on both sides of the channel that the war might be coming to an end.

When the negotiations started Beckford's agent Nicholas Williams was already in Paris trying to secure his employer's property there and in particular to collect the work done by the cabinetmaker Auguste, who was proving somewhat difficult. Beckford himself had been unable to go over for fear, on the one side, of the Traitorous Correspondence Act, and on the other by the fact that his name had been placed on the list of *émigrés* and his appearance in Paris would have resulted in his instant arrest. That Williams should have been allowed to visit France in time of war must seem strange to the modern reader, but in fact he had had little or no difficulty in obtaining the necessary permission.

The notion that Beckford should intervene in the delicate peace negotiations seems first to have come from Williams, conveniently placed as he was in Paris and having various unspecified contacts with the ruling clique. In a long rambling and rather confused letter written as early as 25 June he put this view to Beckford after first commenting sadly on the 'debauchery, low manners and vulgarism' which he found to be the fashion of the times in Paris. 'The Arts, cultivation of manners or education are altogether neglected,' he complained, 'and the rising generation will be little superior to the Beaste creation.' The bulk of France, he was convinced, wished for peace, but opinions were so various that even the government and the Assembly were divided on the issue.

'Lord Malmesbury who it is now positively asserted is coming has not the public opinion much in his favour,' the letter continues, 'and when I am convinced from every observation I have made that the future prosperity and perhaps existence of our country depend upon the present negotiation, which you are so well calculated to enter into with this Country and are so acceptable to them, I do not hesitate to write in this open manner, nor do I care whose hands it may fall into: I shall yet assert that you are the man from a hundred circumstances in your favour . . . This choice should have come from our side who should have thrown aside all prejudices when the public good was so concerned; besides, why should persons in power here be interested whether a proper man comes from England or not when they are indifferent about peace or war. Indeed, the latter is become their trade and the very brutality I mention in the former part of my letter make them the most formidable of enemies; in fact Agriculture and Arms are the employment of the whole nation.'[4]

Beckford responded immediately to his agent's suggestion. The Portuguese affair, though disappointing in its results, had whetted his appetite for diplomatic intrigue, and he was more than ready to make another attempt to re-establish himself in society and perhaps even achieve that other ambition which he had never been able to abandon despite all he had suffered at the hands of his enemies, the peerage he had so nearly won thirteen years before. As the year advanced and no progress was made in the conversations at Lille he began a campaign in the *European Magazine* and certain other newspapers putting forward his own name as the most proper person to secure peace with France,[5] while Williams kept him posted with information from Paris, declaring that the Foreign Minister himself had expressed to him his repugnance for Lord Malmesbury and had assured him of his preference for Beckford or Lord St. Helens.

At this point the unfortunate agent was thrown into the Temple prison by the French authorities, the egregious but enterprising Auguste having denounced him as a British spy. He languished there for twelve days, consoling himself with the thought that his cell had formerly been occupied by Louis XVI and that he had Admiral Sir Sidney Smith, another reluctant guest of the Republic, as a neighbour. His release followed an examination by the police which ended, so he informed Beckford in a letter of 1 November, in establishing both his character and Beckford's as being patriots of their own country while not enemies to France, and in the judge declaring that 'you have shewn you have had no view but a wish of being instrumental in restoring the blessings of peace to the two Nations.'[6]

The terms which Beckford hoped, at Williams's prompting, to offer the British government must have been common knowledge in London by this time, for the artist Joseph Farington was able to record them fairly accurately in his diary on 11 November.

They were equally well known to the cabinet for, as the diarist noted, all the letters had been opened and read at Dover by the government examiner before being forwarded on to Fonthill. 'The contents of these letters were', Farington wrote, 'that Mr. Williams had been with the [French] Secretary for foreign affairs and with others, that it had been proposed to him that if the government of England would privately advance £6,000 to be made use in *feeing* certain persons, and would give security for a million being paid for the *use of the Directory* as it was understood, *peace* should be agreed to, England retaining the *Cape of Good Hope*, etc., etc., in short better terms than perhaps were looked for. Beckford is so confident of the ground of this proposal, as to offer to risk the £6,000 from his own pocket.'[7]

Beckford presented his proposals to the Duke of Portland on 28 November, calling Williams over from Paris to bear witness to the authenticity of the documents he brought with him for the Minister's scrutiny. The Duke received him as courteously as he had done before, and as had happened before nothing resulted from the meeting but a portentous silence. Beckford, restless and anxious about the fate of his scheme, refused to read the omen, and when no letter or proposal came from Portland wrote directly to Pitt, again sending Williams as his emissary. The Minister, after another considerable delay, replied on 17 December. He did not address Beckford personally; the note was directed to Williams. 'Mr. Pitt presents his compliments to Mr. Williams,' it ran: 'He has received his Note inclosing a letter from Mr. Beckford, but as he does not think any advantage likely to arise from the Communication proposed, He will not give Mr. Williams the trouble of calling on him; and begs the favour of him to convey the Contents of this Note to Mr. Beckford.'[8] Once again the official world, speaking in the person of his childhood friend and the son of his godfather Chatham, had expressed the peremptory opinion that it wished to know nothing of William Beckford.

Their victim's own immediate reaction was to write an angry letter to Lord Thurlow: 'I addressed Administration in the first instance thro' the Duke of Portland, and in the second thro' Mr. Pitt, but without being able to procure from the noble Secretary any due degree of Attention, or from the Minister anything better than a haughty Indifference towards myself, and an affected Contempt for Overtures, the foundation of which he has not condescended to examine. As I am confident of the firmness of the

Ground on which I have proceeded, it seems impossible to account for the manner in which my Intelligence has been received, but from it contradicting, so pointedly, the constant assertion of Ministry, that the French Government are averse to peace. From the very moment of the Expiration of Lord Malmesbury's late Mission to the seventeenth day of the present month, I have received repeatedly the most positive assurances of the readiness of the French Ministry to treat for Peace upon certain Considerations and thro' the medium of certain Persons whom they have named; for I may add, that Lord Malmesbury, as a Negotiator, was highly obnoxious to them.'[9] This was, however, just so much bluster. There was nothing he could do but accept defeat once again, and a letter full of justifiable fury and contempt intended for Pitt was, on Thurlow's wise and friendly advice, reluctantly abandoned. He would make no further attempt to storm the citadel by direct assault. In the autumn of the following year he slipped away quietly to Portugal where he remained for the next six months lost to the world outside.

During the period of these abortive attempts to regain admittance into official circles Beckford found an outlet for his feelings of political and social frustration by writing two anonymous novels which were published respectively in 1796 and 1797. Looking back to the style and manner of his *Biographical Memoirs of Extraordinary Painters* he allowed his gift for irony and satire to run wild, but while that early work had a certain youthful innocence about it, the two books he now produced, each issued under a female pseudonym, fail to conceal the bitterness and disillusion of his life on the threshold of middle-age, despite a surface veneer of parody and ridicule. His authorship of both books was kept a closely guarded secret at the time of publication, and though both were received with some success, no one thought of attributing them to their true author. Indeed, had not Beckford himself admitted the fact to Samuel Rogers, and later on to Cyrus Redding, the real identity of 'Lady Harriet Marlow' and 'Jacquetta Agneta Mariana Jenks' (in whose style contemporaries thought to detect the work of Robert Merry or Charlotte Smith) might never have been discovered at all.

The first novel, described on the title-page as 'a Rhapsodical Romance interspersed with Poetry' is the less politically vicious of the two, having been written before the author's hopes of fighting his way back into favour with society had received their final check. It appeared as *Modern Novel Writing or the Elegant Enthusiast* and purported to be the work of Lady Harriet Marlow. In recording the 'interesting emotions' of Arabella Bloomville the book was a broad parody of the romantic, sentimental novel of the day, a genre in which Beckford's sister Elizabeth Hervey had made her name as an authoress. It was replete with mysterious grottoes, dramatic assignations, lambent tears and swooning heroines; and Mrs. Hervey when reading it, though unaware that her brother was the author or she herself was being lampooned, none the less showed some uneasiness and was heard to murmur 'Why, I vow and protest, here is my grotto', with other equally puzzled exclamations.[10] To preserve his anonymity Beckford inscribed his own copy of the book with the legend: 'W.B. Presentation copy from the divine authoress', and no doubt hoped that his sister would see the intriguing inscription and be confused even further.

Though the book was not so overtly political as its successor, Beckford allowed himself some sharp criticism both of the government and of the continuation of the war with France. In an address by the 'authoress' in ironical praise of the *British Critic*, a journal that fully supported Pitt and his policies, the sarcasm was clear enough: 'To your virtues, liberality, and candour, the whole nation can bear testimony, for I defy the most impudent of your detractors to shew a single instance amongst all your writings, where you have spoken favourably of any work that was base enough to vindicate the hoggish herd of the people, that was mean enough to object to any measure of the present wise and incorruptible administration, or that was cowardly enough to censure the just and necessary war in which the nation is now so fortunately engaged. No, ye worthy magistrates of the mind! you have exerted your civil jurisdiction with meritorious perseverance, and if at any time you have stepped forth as warriors to defend the exclusive privileges of the FEW, against the vulgar attacks of the MANY, your demeanour has been truly gallant . . .' The passage ends with the prayer of the 'authoress' that the enemies of the recipients of her ironic eulogy may all speedily be cast into dungeons or sent to Botany Bay, while they themselves may become 'placemen, pensioners, peeresses, loan-mongers, bishops and contractors'.

Modern Novel Writing was followed by *Azemia*, 'a Descriptive and Sentimental Novel interspersed with Pieces of Poetry', written, so the reader was asked to believe, by a certain Miss Jenks of Bellegrove Priory in Wales who very appropriately dedicates her work to Lady Harriet Marlow. It is the story of a Turkish girl captured by a British warship and brought back to England where she is separated from the young naval officer with whom she has fallen in love. The situation is a sort of reversal of a favourite eighteenth-century theme epitomised by Bretzner's *Belmont und Constanze* from which Mozart had derived the theme of his comic opera *Il Seraglio*, but by bringing his heroine to England instead of having her rescued from imprisonment in the harem Beckford gave himself an opportunity for some cutting social criticism and satirical comment on the curious habits and customs of the islanders among whom the fair Azemia finds herself.

Pitt again is his main target, but Beckford manages to take a critical glance at some other institutions about which he had himself cause to complain, not least the Court of Chancery and the notion of equality before the law: 'You may as well say to the wretched pauper who beseeches in the street your charity to relieve his hunger, "Friend, why are you hungry? There is a tavern open on the opposite side of the way, where you may eat your fill." Would not this be a barbarous insult to the poor mendicant's distress? Yet it is precisely thus people talk who urge to the oppressed in common life the excellence, the equality of the English law.' As to the Court of Chancery (of which Beckford had bitter and costly experience) a Chancery suit is 'ranked as an evil of as great magnitude as a fire, an inundation, a descent of the enemy, or an earthquake; and really as to the ruin they produce, I see but little difference—what difference there is, is rather against a chancery-suit: the invasion, inundation, earthquake, may render a family houseless and desolate at once; a Chancery-suit keeps them in lingering misery for years, and leaves them beggars at last.'

The essence of his attack upon Pitt's character and administration is distilled in a long poem again written from an ironic point of view, and attributed in the novel to the sycophantic pen of a certain Mr. Puffwell, 'now an under-secretary of state'. There are many verses but one need only glance at a few to get an impression of the general effect.

> *Ye, who places hold, or pensions,*
> *And as much as ye can get,*
> *Come, and hear the praising mention*
> *I shall make of Mister Pitt.*

All he does is grand and daring,
All he says is right and fit;
Never let us then be sparing
In the praise of Mister Pitt.

Who, like him, can prate down reason,
Who so well on taxes hit?
Who detect a plot of treason
Half so well as Mister Pitt?

The cold, misogynistic temperament of the still single statesman, celebrated more for his devotion to port wine than to
women, was too tempting a target to be missed by the man whom
society had branded for unproved sins against its sacred conventions:

You ne'er see him love a wench, Sir,
Driving curricle or tit;
He attends the Treasury-bench, Sir,
Sober, honest *Mister Pitt.*

Nor could Beckford forget that this man who stood so firmly, as
it seemed to him, on the side of reaction and repression, who had
suspended Habeas Corpus and imposed the Traitorous Correspondence Act, who appeared always to turn a deaf ear to the
growing cry for reform, had once been the hope of the Whigs and
was the son of the great Lord Chatham who with Beckford's
father had always stood forth as the champion of liberty. How did
the land of liberty fare under the guidance of this son?

Two thirds of that nation starving,
Now of meat ne'er taste a bit;
For his friends he still is carving,
This great statesman—Mister Pitt.

The other verses continue in similar vein. The tone of the poem
is one of sustained malice, but it sprang from the chill, almost contemptuous attitude which the Minister had adopted to his former
friend whom he now steadfastly refused to see and with whom he
would not deign even to correspond directly. Beckford's enmity,
considering the long persecution he had suffered, and the new
impetus just given to it by the reminder that his 'past' was neither
forgiven nor forgotten, is not difficult to understand.

What is more difficult to account for is the sudden switch from
the reassuringly mild sentiments expressed only a year before to

Sir William Hamilton when he had described himself as supporting 'in principle' the king and his administration. That letter, of
course, had been written while Beckford was still under the spell
of Portugal, and Portugal, where he was accepted, fêted, flattered
and admired, brought out the feudal, paternalistic, would-be
patrician side of his character. It was only when he returned home
to England and felt the keen cold wind of criticism and social rejection that he remembered that he was a radical. It is interesting
to speculate whether, had the Powderham scandal never occurred
and Lord Beckford of Fonthill taken his seat in the House of
Peers, he would have sat with the government or the opposition.

   Before leaving for his final visit to Portugal in October 1798
Beckford had been engaged in other negotiations which have an
air of comic opera about them. Taking up the offer in Marialva's
letter of August 1796 that the Regent would show 'in a practical
way' how much Beckford was esteemed in Portugal, the latter
now asked, through the marquis, that the prince should confer the
Order of Christ upon Gregorio Franchi. It was a somewhat impertinent request; the order was highly esteemed, its members
were jealous of its honour, and neither they nor the prince could
see how this honour would be in any way enhanced by bestowing
the order on a former choir boy whose only claim to distinction
was that he lived in questionable circumstances with an eccentric
English millionaire.

   Marialva was deeply embarrassed. He did not wish to offend his
friend, whom he longed to see again in Portugal, by refusing the
request, nor did he wish to insult the other members of the order
by granting it, knowing, as they would, that the prince would be
acting on the marquis's recommendations. Between February and
October, when Beckford arrived in Lisbon, letters on the subject
passed backwards and forwards with Marialva desperately trying
to satisfy his friend, placate the other knights of the order, and
save the prince from compromising himself in a situation he
clearly found distasteful. It was to honour Beckford, the marquis
made plain, that Franchi would be given the order, though this
was quite against the regulations. The prince would indeed confer
the decoration but did not wish to do so in person: 'with reference
to Franqui he wishes to give you the Order so that you yourself
may place it on his breast to show you in some way that he is
bestowing the Order only to satisfy you'. That Franchi eventually
received the coveted decoration was a tribute to Beckford's stub-

born persistence and to Marialva's devoted friendship. At least there was some consolation for the marquis. Early in the correspondence he insisted upon two conditions: Beckford must come to Lisbon to thank the prince, while as for the new Chevalier, 'he must leave without delay as soon as the Prince has invested him'.[11]

If Beckford went to Portugal on this last visit partly to recompose himself in this, to him, always therapeutic air after the shocks he had received to his self-esteem and hopes of re-establishment, another reason prompting a further retirement abroad may have been the death of his mother, which occurred at her Hampstead house on 22 July, in her seventy-fifth year. The relationship between them had not always been easy, but there is no reason to believe that Beckford was lacking in affection for her, despite the rather patronising attitude he sometimes adopted towards her, especially in the character he had bestowed upon her as the Begum.

He certainly never lost the desire to justify himself in her eyes. At this period, as we shall see in the next chapter, he had been busily engaged in the early work on the structure of 'the Abbey in the Woods', what would soon become known as Fonthill Abbey; in describing these operations to his mother in June 1796 he had felt the need to make excuses both for his extravagance and for his withdrawal from society, even though the latter course was not of his own choosing. 'I need not tell you,' he wrote in a note of self-defence, 'that I have the satisfaction of giving constant Employment to some hundreds of People in one way or another. If this is doing any good or Service with my Fortune, and that you know is my meaning in most of these occupations, I may, I suppose, content myself with my own interior approbation; but do not think me so ridiculous as to imagine I am doing myself half the Credit with the World in general, which I should do by keeping a Pack or two of Hounds, giving Hunting Dinners and bumpering port and Madeira with Country Squires, in running for the Sweepstakes at Salisbury Races, figuring at a County Ball or a Mayor's Feast. From many Intimations and indeed a Disposition which has plainly shewn itself towards me since my return I perceive I might acquire much Consideration and Consequence in the course of the Winter by asking and being asked to eight o'clock Dinners and Morning Suppers either in Town or Country, and above all by a little Exercise of my Elbows at the Gaming

Table. But what, my dear Mother, is to make it worth my while to quit my quiet habits, to injure my health and risk my fortune for all this unmeaning Whirl? Am I to set so lightly by all my own internal resources, and surely I have some to value, that I should make such Sacrifices to Fashion?'[12]

This is how Beckford hoped to present himself to his mother and to justify himself in his own eyes. Neither can have been deceived by his plausible reasoning. Few, if any, invitations reached Fonthill; no one, if asked, would have dared risk an acceptance. Shortly after writing to his mother Beckford had appeared at some public function in Salisbury. The Bishop and Dean, hearing that he would be present, declined to attend, and Lord Radnor, meeting him unexpectedly, cut him dead.[13] This was the true disposition shown to him since his return. After giving his mother a splendid funeral at Fonthill with all the pomps due to the great Lord Mayor's widow it is not surprising that her son withdrew quietly from the scene to the country where at least he did not feel himself an outcast.

20

The Abbey

❧❧❧

In the period between his return to England in March 1796 and his final departure for Portugal in the late autumn of 1798 Beckford's building activities at Fonthill began in earnest and the foundations were laid of the structure, already described as 'the Abbey in the Woods', which over the next twenty years was to develop into the most astonishing private house ever to be built in England. Beckford's name is so completely associated with Fonthill Abbey, which absorbed most of his creative energy between 1797 and 1818, that it comes as something of a surprise to realise that out of the eighty-four years of his long life only fifteen were spent actually living under its roof, and that except for the effort expended in supervising the work and pursuing a dilatory and usually absent architect, and in collecting the treasures of every variety that embellished its galleries and rooms, they were singularly unproductive years. All the literary works upon which his fame rests, from the *Biographical Memoirs* and *Vathek* to the *Recollections of an Excursion to the Monasteries of Alcobaça and Batalha*, were written either before the Abbey was built or after it had passed out of his hands.

Yet it is right that his name should always be linked with this most splendid of follies, for it symbolised so much in his personality that sought for expression in some physical shape; the compelling urge to erect towers, the desire to dazzle and defy his enemies, the need for a retreat, at once secret and hidden and yet at the same time startlingly flamboyant, into which he could creep to lick his wounds and brood over his destiny. Fonthill Abbey was created because in some curious way he saw it as his fate to build it. 'Some people drink to forget their unhappiness,' he was to write to his friend Franchi in 1812, 'I do not drink, I build.'[1]

Like others before and after him (one thinks in particular of the eccentric Earl-Bishop of Derry and the 'mad' King Ludwig II of Bavaria) building became an obsession, an outlet for a frustrated artistic temperament, but in Beckford's case the urge to build was always coupled with the desire to see the work completed. His sharp temper and irrepressible impatience were in this respect to serve him ill, for his impetuosity caused the work to be carried on with dangerous haste, hundreds of workmen often toiling by day and night, so that much of it was botched and had later to be rebuilt or, more alarming in its consequences, faults in construction were passed over unchecked and foundations skimped or inadequately laid. All this gave to the whole structure an air of impermanency, as of a theatrical set, and to its ultimate disappearance a sense of the inevitable. Like much else in Beckford's life Fonthill Abbey, for all its array of towers and pinnacles, was to assume the quality of a dream.

Beckford was both fortunate and unfortunate in the architect he had chosen to interpret this dream. Fortunate in that James Wyatt was the leading architect of his day and probably the only man then practising his art in England who could have produced designs to satisfy so exacting and imaginative a client; but unfortunate in almost every other aspect of their relationship, for the initial enthusiasm with which Wyatt drew up his designs was quickly dissipated and followed by long periods of indolence. He rarely answered letters, was usually absent from the site for long periods at a time and unavailable when his advice was needed, and took little or no interest in the detailed supervision of the work in hand. He drove his clients almost to despair by his dilatoriness but generally managed to win them over by his charm and affability when once they had managed at last to capture his fleeting attention.

Wyatt was the most distinguished member of a remarkable family, being himself the son of an architect and builder; and of his six brothers, three practised the same profession, as did two of his sons and three of his nephews, not to mention other less close relations. He was born in 1746 and as a youth had spent five or six years in Italy, studying in Venice and Rome. Success came early in his career with the building of the Pantheon in Oxford Street, which had won the praise of Horace Walpole, and he was elected an Associate of the Royal Academy when only twenty-six, becoming a full Academician in 1785. Like most architects of his generation he had been brought up in the classical tradition, but

he had also considerable experience of the gothic style before he
started working at Fonthill, not only in the controversial restora-
tions at Lichfield and Salisbury cathedrals, at Milton Abbey and
Windsor Castle, but in work of his own at Sheffield Park in
Sussex, Sandleford Priory in Berkshire and, shortly before undertaking the commission from Beckford, at Lee Priory in Kent. He
possessed the sort of versatility that could excel in almost any
style, but his essays in gothic showed a knowledge of structure
that went beyond the mere gothicising of classical forms that had
been practised by some of his fashionable contemporaries.

In their personal characters Beckford and Wyatt could hardly
have been more different. The architect's nature was bucolic; he
loved his wine and was a great womaniser (Beckford soon nicknamed him *Bagasse*—the Whoremonger) and his business affairs
seemed always to be in a state of chaos. He failed to keep appointments or would slip away when he was needed and be discovered
sitting gossiping at some fireside in the neighbourhood with his
bottle of wine. He drove Beckford distracted as he did his other
clients, and the letters from Fonthill are full of such expressions as
'Who can ever rely on such a person!' 'I can't stand all this annoyance', and 'Would to God that he had never been born.'[2] At the
same time Beckford knew that he could not get on without him.
'Tell Wyatt', he wrote on 29 June 1808, 'that unless he wants to
irritate and torment me to death he must come. The confusion
into which everything will be thrown, and the impossibility of
finishing anything (either the Octagon or the rooms) if he doesn't
come at once, is not to be borne,' and again in July 1810, 'Without
Bagasse I'll lose heart.'[3] It was from a collaboration of such disparate temperaments that Fonthill Abbey was created.

The idea of a semi-ruined convent with a separate tower on
Stop's Beacon had already been abandoned when serious work on
the Abbey began early in 1796. A new site had been chosen to the
north-east of the Beacon on Hinkley Hill, less high than Stop's
Beacon but nearer to Fonthill Splendens and commanding extensive views to the south and west. Beckford chose a ridge on the
southern slope of this hill for his gothic retreat (for it was not yet
thought of as a place for permanent residence) which was to be
considerably larger than the previous plans had allowed and was
to incorporate the tower as an integral part of the design. The
surrounding territory, already planted with carefully selected
trees and shrubs, was to be developed according to his own scheme

of landscape gardening, following and developing the ideas he had first tried out at Monserrate in Portugal.

At the beginning work must have gone forward at a brisk pace, for a letter written to his mother in November 1796 (the same letter in which he had tried to justify his extravagance as providing employment to some hundreds of people) gives the impression of steady progress, while also glancing at some of his other activities within the enclosure of the barrier wall and in the surrounding woods: 'You are mistaken, my dear Mother, in supposing the approach of Winter to have relaxed the vigour of my proceedings at Fonthill. Everything is going on with the same alacrity as at the time when you and my dear Children were here. I have extended the front of the Abbey in the Woods from the dimensions you saw us working upon, to near two hundred feet, and a good part of the building has already reached the first floor. The Conservatory and flower garden, which are to surround it, are begun. My Walk, which you will recollect is, according to the Plan, to be carried considerably more than twenty miles thro' and round the Woods (to which I have just made an addition of ground by the completion of a new purchase), has already proceeded to nearly the length of nine miles. The Season proves admirable for my planting and, if it continues as open till Christmas, I think Vincent [his gardener] will by that time, with all the hands allowed, have got above a million Trees into the ground for this year's work.'[4]

One reason for the rapid progress, apart from Beckford's own impatience and the large work-force he employed, was because the Abbey was constructed of very flimsy material. At this stage he was not thinking of raising a permanent structure in the sense of someone building with an eye to posterity. He was simply indulging a whim and reproducing, on a somewhat larger scale, an example of the many 'convents', ruins, hermit's cells and grottoes that were springing up on noblemen's estates in many parts of the country. For this reason Wyatt did not use stone facings but relied upon wood and compo-cement, a patent substance in which he placed an unwarranted confidence. Beckford was still in raptures with his architect and had told his agent Williams in October: 'Wyatt has been doing wonders according to his custom, and he has given the great Hall another push 20 feet or so; we shall reach Knoyle before we have done.'[5]

By February 1797 things were further advanced and Sir William Hamilton was sent a few details: 'I am staying my stomach with a little pleasure building in the shape of an abbey, *which is already half finished*. It contains appartments in the most gorgeous Gothic style with windows of painted glass, a chapel for blessed St. Anthony—66 ft. diameter & 72 high—a gallery 185 in length, & a tower 145 feet high.'[6] What Beckford here describes is the main layout of what was to become, after many alterations and additions, the south and west wings of Fonthill Abbey, containing the West Hall, joined by the octagon to the south (later St. Michael's) gallery, with a suite of living rooms at the southern extremity. These living quarters, which projected slightly to the west, were connected to the West Hall by a cloister, and over the octagon was a pointed spire with flying buttresses. The chapel was situated in the octagon which, until the north wing was thrown out later, terminated the view from the south end of the gallery.

The spire that proudly, but only fleetingly, crowned the octagon was closely based upon that which Beckford had seen over the mausoleum of King Joao I of Portugal at Batalha, and which Wyatt may have known from the drawings made in 1788 by the Irish antiquary and architect James Cavanah Murphy. Murphy had made the drawings[7] at the request of a Colonel William Burton Conyngham for whom Wyatt had worked in Ireland, and he must surely have seen some drawings there, for the Colonel had also visited Portugal and was familiar with the monastery. Certainly the spire at Lee Priory, where Wyatt was engaged between 1782 and 1790, bears a certain, though less detailed, resemblance to the Batalha original.[8] In 1795 Murphy's drawings had been published with an introductory discourse in collaboration with a Portuguese priest, Father Louis de Sousa, and the name of William Beckford had featured in the list of subscribers.

When Beckford left for Portugal at the end of 1798 he was satisfied that all was progressing well and he was able to turn his mind to other matters, in particular to the satisfaction of his mania for collecting. While still in England, towards the end of 1796, he had made one of his most curious purchases; curious, that is, in so far as he took little or no interest in the transaction (which cost him £950) and did not set eyes on his purchase for another five years. This was the library of Edward Gibbon, which had remained in Lausanne after the historian's death, and had been offered for sale in accordance with the directions left with his executor.

In ignoring so important an acquisition, indeed in treating it with a sort of contempt, perhaps Beckford was taking his revenge on Gibbon for the slighting remarks made at his expense years before. Eventually, in 1801, while passing through Lausanne, he at last had a look at the collection. 'I shut myself up for six weeks from early in the morning until night,' he recorded, 'only now and then taking a ride. The people thought me mad. I read myself nearly blind.'[9] Even then he did not take the books back to England. Except for a few volumes they remained in Lausanne gathering dust. At length, after many years, in an even more uncharacteristic gesture, he gave the entire library to his friend Dr. Schöll who had been responsible for negotiating the purchase.

Now, while he was in Portugal, negotiations for another important purchase were under way. This concerned two paintings by Claude Lorraine, *The Landing of Aeneas* and *The Sacrifice of Apollo*. Beckford had seen them in Rome as a young man in 1780 when they still belonged to Prince Altieri. If Altieri himself had shown him round the picture gallery it must have been a strange experience, for though he knew each picture and could describe its merits he was unable to see any of them, for the prince was blind. When the dangers of a French invasion threatened Rome in 1797 the prince had sold the pictures, and after various vicissitudes due to the precarious times, they had reached Palermo where the painter Charles Grignion had so impressed Lord Nelson of their importance that the admiral had agreed to their shipment to England in a man-of-war.

Despite a narrow scrape with a French frigate off Brest the Altieri Claudes reached England in safety. In April 1799 they were seen by the painter Henry Tresham who at once got in contact with Beckford's agent Nicholas Williams, assuring him that there could be no doubt of the importance of such an acquisition for all that the owner was asking the then fantastic sum of seven thousand pounds for the pair. 'Give me leave now to state my opinion of the pictures', he wrote to Williams on 14 April. 'I have seen them this morning with a fresh and dispassioned eye, and they far surpass the opinion I entertained of their merit, and their preservation is extraordinary. I have insisted that no varnish shall be put on them, nor no tricks, nor attempts at cleaning until I have relinquished the treating for them . . . I waited on Mr. Wyatt this morning requesting him, in case the pictures are mentioned in his presence, to appear cold about them, as objects of Mr. Beckford's research; he advised me to send you immediately a letter thinking no time should be lost. 'Tis a matter that requires confidence, and I will forfeit all my hopes of Mr. Beckford's patronage (which I look up to) if I do not conclude the affair to his satisfaction, the pictures, in my opinion, being invaluable, and the opportunity such as nothing but the extraordinary revolution of things could have brought about.'[10]

Beckford was so eager to obtain the pictures that he was said to have been prepared to bid up to ten thousand pounds for them,[11] and presumably left Williams with instructions to that effect. In fact, after a good deal of haggling by Tresham who at first offered five thousand, the two masterpieces were acquired for £6,825, and became Beckford's that same April while he himself was still abroad. He was to sell them, at considerable profit, in 1808, but at the time of the purchase he was well content, for that December, home once more, he wrote to Sir William Hamilton, 'I am warming myself by the Altieri Claudes which have found their way to Fonthill, and being magnificently framed, well-placed, and tenderly washed by Tresham, appear in the utmost glory and perfection.'[12]

When Beckford returned from Portugal in the summer of 1799 he was irritated to find that virtually no progress had been made on the Abbey building during the nine months he had been away. Wyatt, profiting by his patron's absence, had abandoned it while he attended to his other clients, who had no doubt been clamouring for his attention; for at this time, among other commissions, he was engaged in work for the king at Windsor Castle, for the Bishop of Durham at Bishop Auckland, as well as at Felbrigg Hall in Norfolk, Dodington Park in Gloucestershire and Norris Castle on the Isle of Wight. He was also just about to start work on the gothic cloisters and rooms for Lord Pembroke at Wilton House, a commission that was to result in a good deal of conflict with the no less pressing claims of neighbouring Fonthill. No wonder Wyatt was a difficult man to pin down.

Beckford was particularly angry for it was now that his plans for the Abbey really began to expand and his architect's advice was all the more urgently needed. New wings, longer and more impressive vistas, a higher tower with a spire to rival that of Salisbury were among the visions that flashed through his soaring imagination. It was to be a cathedral dedicated to the arts, a site for splendid ritual and solemn music, a shrine for the work of the best English painters and craftsmen of the day, and a special

I

'Revelation Chamber' with a floor of polished jasper would in due time shelter the tomb of its founder.[13] Wyatt was instructed to draw up new designs and an imaginative picture of the proposed building as it would be when completed, with its tower and spire rising precariously into the sky, was commissioned from the artist Charles Wild.[14]

Wyatt's fresh plans were exhibited at the Royal Academy in the summer of 1799, but work on his drawing-board had not been followed up by any new additions on the site. Beckford fumed and fretted in his impatience and the architect drafted more workmen to Fonthill, actually sending some of those who had been engaged on the work he was doing for George III at Windsor, a point that would have pleased his other patron's sardonic sense of humour. Beckford's enthusiasm now returned and in December he wrote triumphantly to Sir William Hamilton: 'The abbey will astonish you.' The old diplomatist was due for recall next year and Beckford was eager to show off his new pleasure dome to his friend and the sprightly Emma, the news of whose liaison with Lord Nelson, only recently reaching England, gave hope that an even more distinguished visitor might possibly accompany them.

With the turn of the century a new setback had to be faced. In May 1800 violent storms lashed the fragile structure of the tower, still encased in its scaffolding and with a flag flying from the top. A mighty gust caught the fluttering standard and in an instant flag and scaffolding came crashing down, to be followed by Wyatt's buttresses and spire with their delicate framework of timber and compo-cement. 'The fall', declared an early historian of the Abbey in the best picturesque jargon of the period, 'was tremendous and sublime, and the only regret expressed by Mr. Beckford upon the occasion was that he had not witnessed its destruction.'[15] Despite the bravado of the remark the fall of the tower was a humiliation for Beckford no less than for Wyatt, and laid him open to the ridicule that he had always feared and sought so strenuously to avoid. It was more than just a check in his building programme. The tower, which he had dreamed about for so many years, meant a good deal more to him than bricks and mortar, or even compo-cement; it was for him like the tower which Vathek had raised 'not . . . to escape being drowned, but from the insolent curiosity of penetrating the secrets of heaven'. Its fall was like an insult to his most veiled thoughts and secret aspirations. It must therefore be rebuilt, and rebuilt even higher than before.

He preserved a front of splendid indifference in the face of the public. Thus to Sir Isaac Heard, the Garter King-of-Arms, who had been helping him in his heraldic researches, he wrote: 'We shall rise again more gloriously than ever, provided the sublime Wyatt will graciously deign to bestow a little more commonplace Attention upon what I supposed his favourite Structure. The Crash and the Loss sound magnificently in the Newspaper; I neither heard the one, nor felt the other.'[16]

To Wyatt himself, however, he did not mince his words. He reproached him in a long letter for the collapse of the tower and for the other derelictions of duty, and warned him that if he did not mend his ways the Abbey would be renounced and every account concerning it closed immediately. 'Determined to sink no longer from disappointment to disappointment,' the letter ended, 'I give you this plain and decided warning. If you take it as it is meant I shall soon see you at Fonthill. If not—the whole shall be stopped, every workman discharged, the reasons which have compelled me to adopt so violent a measure stated at large in the Morning Chronicle and every other Chronicle, Morning or Evening, which appears in London.'[17]

This rebuke had the effect, at least for the moment, of galvanising the lethargic architect into a spurt of furious activity. Workmen, sometimes as many as five hundred, toiled in relays upon the building so that there was no break in their activity. As night fell torches and lanterns were lit and from the distance the Abbey presented a magic spectacle of twinkling lights glittering like giant fireflies in the dark recesses of the woods, a scene which added a new note of mystery to the tales that were already circulating in the neighbourhood about the latest extravagances of the strange owner of Fonthill. The presence of so many people working in his service stimulated Beckford's ideas of feudal splendour. He hurried about urging them on in their labours and dispensing food, beer and blankets in the manner of a *grand seigneur*. He was all the more eager for the present phase of work to be completed, for the promised visit of Sir William and Lady Hamilton was now fixed for December, and the victor of the Nile, unable to separate himself from his enchantress, would definitely be one of the party.

Beckford was himself deep in intrigue with Emma, but on a

subject that would have caused no pang of jealousy in the susceptible heart of Lord Nelson. Ever since the Powderham scandal
sixteen years before he had never been able to reconcile himself to
the loss of the honours that had so nearly been won at that
moment, and always believed, as had been the case at the time of
his abortive negotiations with the government and would be the
case again whenever he thought the opportunity offered, that he
would somehow manage to secure the peerage that had slipped
through his fingers in 1784. Considering the circumstances of his
life, and the constant reminders he received of official hostility, it
was a curious ambition to foster, and showed that at forty he was
as capable of self-deception as he had been when still a child.

The scheme which he now hoped to bring to success with the
help of Emma was ingenious enough, but a little too far-fetched
to commend itself to those powers by whose aid alone it could be
achieved. After thirty-seven years *en poste* as British envoy in
Naples Sir William Hamilton had some claims to the grant of
a peerage, but his energies, now he was retired, were more usefully
engaged in trying to get a tight-fisted Treasury to compensate him
for his 'extraordinary expenses' and other financial losses he had
incurred in the king's service. It was a discouraging undertaking,
and Sir William must often have wondered whether he was ever
to get any satisfaction. It was here that Beckford stepped in. In a
letter from his agent Nicholas Williams written on 15 November
it was proposed to Hamilton that he should give up his attempts
for a financial settlement and ask for a peerage instead. Beckford
himself would make up by way of a life annuity whatever sum Sir
William needed, on condition, in the words of the agent's letter,
that 'a peerage should be offered you and you could arrange it so
that the grant may be made to yourself with remainder to Mr.
Beckford and his heirs.'[18]

Sir William showed no very great liking for the proposal and
only gave a grudging consent to the scheme because of his
genuine financial embarrassment. It was unlikely, anyway, that the
idea would be entertained for a moment by the government.
Quite apart from their antipathy to Beckford personally, special
remainders were most unusual and in any case Sir William had
closer relations than Beckford (his nephew Charles Greville,
former possessor of Emma's affections, for one) who might well
think that they had a prior claim. Considerations such as these
made Hamilton's response to the idea no more than lukewarm,

and only Beckford, who coveted a title, and Emma, who fancied herself as a peeress, pursued it with any enthusiasm.

Beckford enlisted the help of his other Hamilton relations including his cousin Alexander, now, since the accession of his father to the family dukedom, Marquis of Douglas and Clydesdale. Lord Douglas was not sanguine, largely, as he later confided to Sir William, from 'the final clause in the object in question being of so peculiar a nature, and so little consonant with the feelings and tempers of people'. In other words, Beckford's reputation still stood in the way, though Douglas was too tactful and indeed too well disposed towards his cousin to say this to Beckford himself.

Meanwhile Emma bustled about in London canvassing the support of her influential friends, urged on by encouraging letters from Fonthill. 'How unaccountable that there should be the smallest difficulty in the business, so energetically ready as I am to come forwards with something solid in exchange for a mere Vapour,' Beckford wrote to her on 24 November. 'I can scarcely persuade myself that any of these Satraps however callous, however obdurate, would stand plump in Sir Wm's way; or that the King if properly informed on the subject, would allow cold water to be thrown upon so reasonable a proposal, because I happen to be distantly, and, I hope, very distantly interested in its success. We shall see, and they shall see and hear too, if they are determined to put Knives and Ratsbane under my Pillow whenever I attempt at any Stage of this troublesome business to lay down my Head . . . We must not give up easily. If baffled one day—rise again the next and pursue your object with those omnipotent looks, words and gestures, with which Heaven has gifted you.'[19]

The scheme, alas for Beckford's ambitions for a coronet, eventually came to nothing, but it was still very much in the air when his guests arrived at Fonthill on 20 December 1800. They were in an elated mood, having made a triumphal progress across England, and came now from Salisbury where the hero of the Nile had been presented with the freedom of the city and their little cavalcade had been escorted on its route by a detachment of yeomen cavalry. Sir William was now seventy years old and somewhat subdued by the loss of part of his great collection of Greek and Etruscan vases which had sunk to the bottom of the sea with the loss of the *Colossus* the previous year. The loss of his wife's affection probably troubled him less, though he can hardly have

been insensitive to the ridicule that came his way as a result of
Nelson and Emma's blatant parade of their attachment. The
lovers themselves, both middle-aged and Emma now immense in
size though still beautiful of face, were enjoying their provincial
triumph after a rather cold reception by the official world in
London. Lady Nelson was conspicuously absent.

Beckford's social isolation was demonstrated by the company
he had assembled to meet his distinguished friends. Even with the
man whom most of them would have regarded as the saviour of
their country present at Fonthill none of the neighbouring
'county' cared to cross its threshold. There was no visit from
Wilton, from Longleat or from Stourhead; no local magnate rode
over to pay his respects. Instead Beckford had to fall back on his
artistic and literary friends, most of whom were in fact executing
commissions for him at the time or were in some way or another
in his pay. They consisted of James Wyatt, Benjamin West,
President of the Royal Academy, Henry Tresham, Madame Banti,
a celebrated singer who had known Emma in Naples, and the
satirical verse writer Dr. John Walcot, a man who in the past had
lampooned both Sir William and Emma under his pen-name of
'Peter Pindar'.

The party stayed at Splendens, but the climax of the visit,
which lasted several days, was an entertainment at the 'Abbey in
the Woods' devised by Beckford with elaborate care and dramatic
effect. This was a 'monastic fête' held on the evening of the
twenty-third. As dusk began to fall a procession of carriages and
soldiers from the volunteer regiment Beckford had raised set out
from the great house, passing through the woods to the Abbey by
the winding paths and clearings created by their host. Special
lighting effects had been achieved by placing torches and flam-
beaux among the trees while bands of musicians, some close by
and others placed farther away, provided a musical accompaniment to the ride, the more distant players providing an eerie echo
effect which reverberated in the darkness. 'Everything', as a
chronicler of the evening reported, 'was provided to steal upon
the senses, to dazzle the eye, and to bewilder the fancy.'[20]

Arrived at the Abbey the party wandered along the gallery or
explored the panelled rooms whose 'mediaeval' gloom was only
relieved by the scarlet, purple or crimson of the hangings. In one
room on the ground floor a special banquet was provided, the
food 'unmixed with the refinements of modern cookery' to give it

an authentic monastic flavour. Those unprepared for this simple repast may have been glad to know that a more orthodox supper was awaiting them back at the great house.

After tasting this refreshment the company moved upstairs to where the chief rooms so far completed were situated. As they climbed the staircase Beckford produced his most daring effect; instead of lighting the stairway with silver sconces, as in the rest of the Abbey, he had provided 'certain mysterious living figures, at different intervals, dressed in hooded gowns, and standing with large wax torches in their hands'. After this weird experience it was no doubt a relief for his guests to sit down and digest their monastic fare while Emma, transformed into a plump Agrippina, diverted them with a demonstration of her famous 'Attitudes'.

Finally, to induce a suitably solemn note before returning to Splendens, they were conducted to the octagon, still without its north and eastern wings, where they could admire Rossi's statue of St. Antony of Padua placed on an altar and surrounded with reliquaries and other jewelled objects, the whole illuminated by several clusters of silver and gold candlesticks and candelabras which 'exhibited a scene at once strikingly splendid and awfully magnificent.' So the evening ended. 'On leaving this strange nocturnal scene of vast buildings and extensive forests,' the chronicler ended his account, 'now rendered dimly and partially visible by the declining lights of lamp and torches, and the twinkling of a few scattered stars in a clouded sky, the company seemed, as soon as they had passed the sacred boundary of the great wall, as if waking from a dream, or just freed from the influence of some magic spell.'

This was precisely the effect that Beckford had hoped to produce and was one of the reasons for which his Abbey had been created. Its great galleries, stretching, in their completed form, for many hundreds of feet with their panelled or vaulted ceilings and dazzling display of artistic treasures, were intended as the setting for elaborate and colourful entertainments. But in fact this one evening of strange enchantment was the only occasion of its kind that the Abbey, still far from complete at the time it took place, was ever destined to know. Though it was possibly upon this evening that Beckford finally decided to move, in due course, from Splendens into the Abbey his existence there, once he was installed, was to be entirely solitary except for visits from his daughters and later on from his son-in-law. His wealth enabled him to surround himself with a retinue of paid retainers, but after the Christmas season of 1800 Fonthill Abbey would never again be filled with the laughter of guests or echo to the sound of music for anyone to hear except its lonely owner and the rare individual who might somehow, upon very exceptional occasions, be permitted to pass through the closely guarded gateways in the great barrier wall and enter the sacred precinct.

21
Crimson and Gold

THE IDEA of the Abbey as a cathedral of art with its founder's tomb waiting to receive him in a jasper-floored 'Revelation Chamber' did not survive for very long; more practical ideas took its place, especially after Beckford had made the first move towards taking up residence there by selling some of the contents of Font-hill Splendens in 1801 and removing himself into one of its pavilions until such a time as the Abbey would be ready to receive him. Further sales took place in 1802 and 1807. Among the pictures he parted from, either because he was tired of them or because they were unsuitable for the new gothic setting, were works by Nicholas Poussin, Canaletto, Murillo, and Sebastiano del Piombo, as well as Dürer's *Presentation of the Virgin*, Hogarth's series of the *Rake's Progress* and Rembrandt's *Christ at the Column*.

In 1803 the first major extension to the Abbey was undertaken when work began on the northern wing, which was to balance the existing south wing on the opposite side of the octagon and to end in a sanctuary and apsidal oratory to which Rossi's statue of St. Antony would be moved from its present home in the octagon. Pointed arches would open from this central space into both wings or galleries so that a person standing with his back to the oriel window at the southern end of St. Michael's Gallery would have an uninterrupted vista to where the altar of St. Antony glittered in the darkened oratory that terminated the northern or, as it was to be called, King Edward's Gallery. The new tower, now planned to rise some 276 feet into the air,[1] would soar above the central octagon, itself increased in height and lightened by three vast gothic windows inspired in design, like the previous tower, from the monastery of Batalha.

The final realisation of this phase in the Abbey's progress was delayed for some years, however, by two unforeseen circum-

stances: the decay of Wyatt's compo-cement which failed to withstand the rigours of the climate and began to show signs of rapid
dilapidation, and a temporary (or, as would soon be proved, in
fact recurrent) crisis in Beckford's financial affairs. The deteriora-
tion of the compo-cement meant a virtual rebuilding of the
existing fabric, which now had to be faced in stone at immense
expense, and all further building had to be suspended until the
work of renovation was complete.

For the same reason Beckford's own plans to move into the
Abbey had to be put off until it was made more habitable, and
the opportunity was taken to modify and improve the design of the
chief reception rooms adjoining the southern end of St. Michael's
gallery which were flanked to the north by the cloister or fountain
court. These consisted, on the main or first floor, of the Yellow
Withdrawing Room, so named from the yellow silk damask of its
walls, and the smaller cabinet room, hung in green silk and with
a ceiling decorated in elaborate fan tracery. Below these rooms,
on the ground floor and connected with those above by the staircase that had been lighted by those romantically hooded figures at
the time of the 'monastic fête' for Nelson and the Hamiltons, was
a dining-room panelled in dark oak and lighted by eight pointed
windows. These were to be Beckford's chief living apartments
until the east wing was completed and ready for occupation
in 1817.

While the Abbey was still in this incomplete state it was
already beginning to attract attention, particularly among artists
and connoisseurs. The President of the Royal Academy, Benjamin
West, who considered Beckford's 'friendship in the arts' as one of
the events that had contributed more to his professional happiness
than anything else that had happened to him since he came to
England from his native America, second only to the patronage of
the King,[2] recorded his impressions of the Abbey in a letter to
Nicholas Williams written on New Year's day 1801: 'When I reflect on the progress which the combination of arts have made
directed by true taste since I first rode over the ground on which
the Abbey stands, I am lost in admiration and feel that I have seen
a place raised more by magick, or inspiration, than by the labours
of the human hand. This is the sensation which the examination
of that elegant edifice produces on my feelings; and when the part
that remains to be finished is accomplished must raise a climax
of excellence without an example in the European world—and to

give an immortality to the man whose elegant mind has conceived so vast a combination of all that is refined in Painting, Sculpture and Architecture.'³

Not everyone shared West's point of view. Thomas Hope of Deepdene, the great apostle of neo-classicism, considered that Beckford was mistaken in adopting the gothic style. 'I have often regretted,' he wrote in 1804, 'that in the new building at Fonthill, where had the Grecian orders been employed, a mansion might have arisen, unrivalled in the most distant parts of the island, a style had on the contrary been adopted, which subjected every one of its details to disadvantageous comparisons with the Cathedral at Salisbury.'⁴ Beckford's answer to this criticism, as recorded by Farington, was not very convincing. He admitted the force of Hope's observation but declared that he had a particular motive in choosing the style used: 'The Gothic windows and compartments afford him opportunities to blazon and introduce the arms of the various great families that did and had existed in Europe from which his daughters are descended or to which they are allied.'⁵

It was inevitable also that people should compare Fonthill Abbey with Horace Walpole's much earlier and much smaller essay in the gothic style at Strawberry Hill, a comparison that Beckford found excessively irritating, for he disliked Walpole and always claimed that he owed nothing to the other's taste or example. 'Walpole hated me', he was to tell Cyrus Redding in his old age. 'I began Fonthill two or three years before his death. Mischief-making people annoyed him by saying I intended to buy up all his nic-nackery when he was dead. Some things I might have wished to possess—a good deal I would not have taken as a gift. The place was a miserable child's box—a species of gothic mousetrap—a reflection of Walpole's littleness . . . He built everything upon family honours and gossip—his writings are portraits of himself. He would have abused my heraldic emblazonments at Fonthill. He was full of spleen. He would have written and talked me and my buildings down to the ground—yet he affected the philosopher.'⁶

Beckford had good reason to be sensitive about his heraldic blazoning at Fonthill, for much of it was spurious despite the help he had received from Sir Isaac Heard. He claimed, among other things, that he was descended not from one, but from all, of the barons who signed Magna Carta and included most of the

Knights of the Garter among his ancestors. In the Oak Parlour, where the figures in the stained glass windows were supposed to represent the most distinguished of his forebears, there were to be seen no less than twelve crowned kings. He was, in fact, one of those people for whom genealogy was an art rather than a science. But in his estimate of Horace Walpole he very much under-rated his rival gothicist's genius, and his opinion of the master of Strawberry Hill had much in common with Walpole's own equally prejudiced verdict on Dr. Samuel Johnson: 'With all the pedantry he had all the gigantic littleness of a country school-master.'

In fact Walpole and Beckford had many characteristics in common, with their exceptional literary gifts, their artistic leanings and architectural enthusiasms, and also a certain feminine, not to say feline, quality which both shared. Walpole, so much older, took only a mild interest in the stories he heard of Alderman Beckford's son. They were bound either to like or detest each other, and it is unfortunate that they never really knew each other except through the medium of such 'mischief-making people' as those about whom Beckford himself complained.

In 1801 while the various rebuilding and refurbishing operations were in progress, Beckford, making use again of his extra-ordinary skill in obtaining permission to travel abroad to enemy countries in time of war, paid another visit to France. Rather surprisingly, considering the angry complaints he had made about his architect on his last return from Portugal, he took Wyatt with him, at least for some of the time. From France (Wyatt having by this time returned home) he travelled on to Switzerland where he would make his one and only inspection of the library of Edward Gibbon that he had purchased five years before.

Their chief object in going to France was to visit the Louvre where Napoleon Bonaparte, now styled First Consul, had concentrated the spoils of conquest extracted by the avaricious republic from its defeated and ravished neighbours, making the gallery, for a while, the most important single collection of works of art in the world. In being able to visit it Beckford became the envy of all less fortunate art-lovers, as was demonstrated by a letter he received from Benjamin West. 'What a gratification it must give to one who delights in works of Genius as I know you do,' the President of the Royal Academy wrote, 'to see collected in one point its efforts for the last two thousand years, which the Gallery now at Paris must contain. How do I envy you and Mr. Wyatt seeing that collection together. Tho' my person will not be there, I can assure you the spirit of my mind will be with you the whole time; and should the blessing of Peace be given to bleeding humanity in the course of the winter, and you to remain at Paris next May, you will see me in the National Gallery at that time.'[7] After the peace of Amiens when, paradoxically, Beckford was back in England, West was able to fulfil his ambition of visiting Paris and wrote again for information not only about the great masterpieces of the past but also to discover 'what the arts of the present time are producing' for these, he knew, his patron would not have neglected.[8]

It was West who, together with the artist William Hamilton, provided some of the designs for the stained glass windows that adorned the Abbey. These were on mediaeval themes, chivalric or ecclesiastical, and gave plenty of opportunity for the display of coats-of-arms. They were said altogether to have cost as much as twelve thousand pounds and were the work of Francis Eginton who had revived this ancient art and whose painted windows Beckford had first seen in Salisbury Cathedral. The colours would seem to have been somewhat vivid, more in the manner of later Victorian stained glass than the mediaeval originals they were intended to emulate, but the effect they produced, diffusing a richly hued opaque glow, was among the most remarkable features of the Abbey and did much to create the sense of sombre magnificence upon which many visitors were to comment.

West was also commissioned to provide pictures for the Abbey in addition to the designs for its windows. Among his paintings were biblical scenes from the Book of Exodus and the Revelation of St. John the Divine as well as a *Vision of St. Antony of Padua*. This latter may have been the picture which Samuel Rogers, who enjoyed the rare privilege of staying a night at the Abbey, later referred to when he described the splendid hospitality he had received there. 'I slept', he wrote, 'in a bedroom opening into a gallery where lights were kept burning the whole night. In that gallery was a picture of St. Antonio, to which it was said that Beckford would sometimes steal and pay his devotions.'[9]

Samuel Rogers seems, indeed, to have been rather carried away by his visit to Fonthill Abbey, though admittedly we only have it second-hand, as it was later related by Lady Bessborough in a letter to Lord Granville Leveson Gower. He entered by the great

west door which he describes as being sixty feet high, an impression produced perhaps by the fact that it was opened to him
by Beckford's dwarf 'covered with gold and embroidery' for in
fact the door, quite high enough, measured only thirty-five feet,
but led into a hall sixty-eight feet long and seventy-eight feet
high, a fact which might well account for his confusion. He then
passed through 'numberless apartments all fitted up most splendidly . . . till they came to a Gallery that surpass'd all the rest from
the richness and variety of its ornaments. It seem'd clos'd by a
crimson drapery held by a bronze statue, but on Mr. B's stamping
and saying "Open!" the statue flew back and the Gallery was seen
extending 350 feet long.' He recalled doors of 'violet velvet
covered over with purple and gold embroidery' and the chapel or
oratory with its altar heaped with gold candlesticks, vases and
chalices studded over with jewels. Everywhere was a sense of
opulence. The dining-room was modelled on the chapel of Henry
VII, 'only the ornaments gilt' and even the table was 'loaded with
gilt plate fill'd with every luxury invention could collect'.

Rogers's descriptions, like the measurements he quotes, are
always just a bit too much, but his account reflects the general
opinion people had of Fonthill Abbey as a place of voluptuous
self-indulgence and decadence, a picture very far removed from
the truth. Less prone to exaggeration was his account of Beckford's musical talents; he played for his guest with 'such *unearthly*
power that Mr. Rogers says he never before had any idea how
delighted one might be with him'. But perhaps the most characteristic glimpse we get of Beckford in this account is the picture of
him leading his guest into the grounds 'equally wonderful from
the beauty of the trees and shrubs, and the manner of arranging
them' where they were met by a flock of tame animals, 'tame
Hares, that Mr. Beckford feeds; then Pheasants, then partridges . . .'

The fascinated guest was prevailed upon to stay, and the next
day was shown through another suite of apartments 'fill'd with
fine medals, gems, enamell'd miniatures, drawings old and modern, curios, prints and manuscripts, and lastly a fine and well
furnish'd library, all the books richly bound and the best Editions.' It was, however, not from Beckford, who seemed immune
to cold and slept in a room without a fireplace, that Rogers
learnt one of the hazards of living in a gothic abbey, albeit an
abbey still only a few years old, but from 'an old Abbé, the
Librarian'. This cleric, whom we know to have been the Abbé

Denis Macquin, informed the visitor that sixty fires were always kept burning, except in the hottest weather. But even the problem of heating was not without its exotic solution; 'near every chimney in the sitting rooms there were large Gilt fillagree baskets fill'd with perfum'd coal that produc'd the brightest flame.'[10]

Rogers's visit to Fonthill was, of course, at a period when work was more or less completed (Lady Bessborough's letter, relating the occasion, was written in October 1817), though even then the tower, which again he exaggerated in height, is described as 'not finished, but great part is done'. Between Beckford's return from France in 1802 and Rogers's visit there had been many vicissitudes in the life of the Abbey. Until 1805 very little work appears to have been done, largely because Beckford, having considerably overspent himself, needed time to recoup. Work on the new north wing was held up and beyond the restoration of Wyatt's compo-cement there was little or no building done at all.

In 1807, at a time when he was selling a number of pictures from Splendens, Beckford gave Benjamin West a somewhat grim, and probably slightly exaggerated, account of his depleted fortune. 'Mr. Beckford represented to him the state of his affairs,' Joseph Farington noted in his Diary after a conversation with West, 'exhibiting a very great change indeed from his former situation. Four years ago the building of the Abbey at Fonthill had cost £242,000. He showed that Wyatt by his negligence and inattention had caused him an unnecessary expense of £30,000. He said that at present, such is the state of Commerce, that his Jamaica Estates are rather an expense to him than a source of Income. That he had, to answer claims upon him, been obliged to sell his estate in Bedfordshire which brought £62,000 and his estate in the neighbourhood of St. Pancras for £12,000. Nothing now remains to him but his unproductive Jamaica estates, and the Fonthill estate, which is reckoned at £10,000 a year; more might be made of it were the extensive park and grounds turned to greater advantage. Upon this income he knows it is impossible to keep up his former establishment, and he has accordingly reduced it to a very limited scale compared with what it had been.'[11]

One of the casualties of this period of financial stringency was the great mansion his father had built. In 1806 Beckford decided to demolish the greater part of it, using the stones as a quarry for the resumed work on the north wing of the Abbey. His cousin

Lord Douglas, who as Alexander Hamilton had been present at the famous Christmas party in 1781 and had known the house for most of his life, put in an unsuccessful plea for its preservation. 'Let me begin by interceeding for poor Fonthill,' he wrote on 27 November. 'I cannot forget my old and favourite abode, altho' the religious magnificence of its neighbouring sanctuary envelops it in a mortifying inferiority. No—save poor Fonthill. Consider it as the pilgrim's resting place to happier regions, as a preparation to the sublime bliss attending the faithful. You would not carry the profane immediately into the temple without previous ablution and preparation. If there are economical reasons for partially destroying it, at least let the shell remain, and we will one day together wander over it, and enjoy the pleasing gratification of reverting to the past . . .'[12]

The notion of wandering among the ruins of Splendens would at one time have appealed to Beckford's romantic inclinations, but the mood was now changed. All was concentrated upon the task of completing the Abbey. 'Most perfectly do I enter into your partiality towards Fonthill,' he answered, 'and gladly would I retain that scene of our happier, early hours if such a plan was in the least compatible with the completion of a building (I may declare) not only the most singular but the most habitable the invention of Man ever conceived. If the Sanctuary rise to anything like the Sublime pitch we could wish, it can only be at the expense of the common Mansion. I cannot afford to maintain both. The Taxes, repairs—in double Establishments are ruinous and besides without the materials this great saving would furnish, it would be madness to dash into the other work. One hour's conversation with Wyatt would convert you to our opinion.' In his new frenzy for mediaeval gloom and irregularity he had managed to convince himself that the balanced Palladian glories of the Alderman's great palace were things of no merit, and now railed at its 'false Greek and false Egyptian' which he somehow found to be 'of very ordinary taste' in comparison with false gothic.[13]

When he finally took up residence in the Abbey in the summer of 1807 he found himself living in a building that still echoed to the noise of carpenters, plasterers, bricklayers and stone masons. The north wing was little more than a shell, the east wing or transept, conceived on a much greater scale than the other wings with towering walls ninety-five feet high and octagonal turrets rising one hundred and twenty feet from the ground, existed only in Wyatt's plans and Beckford's imagination and would not even be started for another five years. Only St. Michael's Gallery and the block containing living-rooms at its south-western end were in readiness for occupation. The west wing had been completed but was now thrown into a state of confusion once more. Originally it had been built as a dining-hall with its minstrels' gallery and hammer-beam roof, but its vast proportions, and the impossibility of keeping it warm, had made it quite impractical for this purpose. It was now rebuilt as an entrance hall, the end wall pierced by the great double doors that would so impress Samuel Rogers, and a long flight of steps constructed to lead the visitor up to the first-floor level of the octagon.

So many differing reports exist about the state of the tower that it is difficult to say just how much work had been done on it. In 1802, five years before Beckford moved in, he told Sir William Hamilton in a letter that 'the tower sings a fine tune, and all the little turrets, flying buttresses, pinnacles, and gothic loopholes join in the chorus',[14] but in 1807 we know that it was still encased in scaffolding. Lady Bessborough's reference to the tower not being finished as late as 1817 adds to the confusion, but what Rogers saw then was more probably repair work than actual con-struction, for the tower was never sound. Even later, in 1821, the *Gentleman's Magazine* reported that 'the tower is acknowledged to be a weak and dangerous structure, and so tottering are the eight surmounting pinnacles that they are held on their bases by strong iron bars, to the no less disparagement of the building than of the builder.' These supports can be seen in John Martin's dramatic picture of the south front of the Abbey made in 1823.

The most spectacular room in the Abbey was the Grand Saloon, as the central octagon was called. Its dimensions were even more stupendous than those of the great Western Hall and were accentuated by the immense altitude of the roof in relation to the comparative modesty of the floor area, being only thirty-five feet in diameter by one hundred and twenty-eight feet in height. The confined area from which the eight pillars and arches rose, by making the intervening openings correspondingly narrow, created an impression of even greater height than was in fact the case. Recessed vestibules gave respectively on to the three wings or transepts and to the organ gallery (or later on the east transept) through soaring pointed arches on four sides. The alternate sides, framed in matching arches, formed shallower recesses containing

the 'Batalha' windows on three sides and the entrance to the spiral
tower staircase on the fourth. This staircase ascended to an arcade
above the points of the arches where small bedrooms known as
the Nunneries were situated. Higher yet was the lantern, modelled
again on a Batalha original but owing something as well to the
nearer and more familiar example of Ely Cathedral. As an architectural *tour de force* the octagon room must have had no rival in
any private house in England or indeed in Europe.

When Beckford moved into the Abbey virtually no work had
been done on the interior of the octagon, and financial worries
made him wonder in moments of depression whether he would
ever be able to complete so vast an undertaking. 'I am planning all
the reforms imaginable, seeing the desperate and despairing state
of Jamaica', he wrote in a note to Franchi on 11 November. 'I am
stopping all building little by little: I shall leave the Octagon half-
finished and without most of the mouldings; as to the other
buildings, I am not giving them any more thought . . .' It is not
surprising that occasionally his health and his morale were
affected. 'I suffer not a little from a hideous tedium and from the
lonely aspect of this tomb of an abbey,' he wrote a month later,
'but the worst of it is that in this tomb one does not find the rest
that other graves can give.'[15]

These fits of depression were brought on as much by the unreliability and constant absences of Wyatt as by the deplorable
state of the sugar market. At other moments Beckford was
possessed by a furious energy that drove him to achieve wonders
of organisation and achievement. The unfinished state of the
octagon was a special challenge; it was the show-piece of his
entire Abbey and he had no real intention of leaving it half-
finished. If only Wyatt could be persuaded to show a bit of interest
the matter could be attended to in no time. But the architect, true
to type, was nowhere to be found. Beckford's impatience reached
its limit: 'If things go on in this way,' he wrote at the end of June
1808, 'it won't be possible to lodge anyone in the tower or anywhere else. The workpeople sent for from Bath, Shaftesbury and
London have already arrived to complete the Octagon; the
scaffolding is almost in place; everything awaits Bagasse's magic
wand; the weather, everything, is favourable, if only the cursèd
architect does not fail.'[16] But Wyatt had disappeared to Windsor
and Beckford felt ready to go mad.

Eventually he was obliged to take the supervision of things into his own hands, relying upon such architectural knowledge as he possessed, meanwhile issuing a solemn warning that if things were not completed by 30 September he would dismiss all the workmen and cancel everything; a repetition of the threat he had made after the fall of the tower but reinforced this time by a vow made to St. Antony: 'Work will stop on the Octagon on the 30th. for certain, as I do not wish to break an oath sworn with heartfelt sincerity in the name of my glorious and merciful Protector.'[17] The threat worked, and soon he could report that everything was progressing as if by a miracle.

So the interior of the octagon gradually took shape with Beckford dodging about among the workmen or standing high up in the network of scaffolding oblivious of the drop of ninety feet that opened under his feet as he saw his dream take solid form around him. 'It's really stupendous, the spectacle here last night,' he wrote on 18 September, 'the number of people at work, lit up by lads; the innumerable torches suspended everywhere, the immense and endless spaces, the gulph below; above, the gigantic spider's web of scaffolding—especially when, standing under the finished and numberless arches of the galleries, I listen to the reverberating voices in the stillness of the night, and see immense buckets of plaster and water ascending, as if they were drawn up from the bowels of a mine, amid shouts from subterranean depths, oaths from Hell itself, and chanting from Pandemonium or the synagogue . . .'[18]

The colouring of the walls of the completed octagon, according to John Rutter's account, was chalky and cold, but everywhere else the interior of the Abbey blazed with crimson, purple and royal blue. In the gothic tracery of the ceiling the groins were often picked out in bright colours with gilt bosses and tinctured heraldic devices. The entrance hall alone boasted seventy-six emblazoned escutcheons. The effect everywhere was of richness and luxury in contrast to the rather grim aspect of the gothic exterior. In King Edward's Gallery the curtains were scarlet, the ceiling of carved wood with more heraldic emblems, the walls opposite the windows glowed with the rich bindings of books. In the frieze of the cornice were the arms of seventy-two knights of the Garter and the chief picture in the room was a portrait of the order's founder Edward III.

As Samuel Rogers had discovered, Rossi's statue of St. Antony, which had once found a temporary home in the octagon, was still the focal point and climax of the great uninterrupted vista which now stretched for three hundred and twelve feet from the oriel window at the end of St. Michael's Gallery, across the octagon, to the apsidal oratory that terminated the northern transept.[19] The transition from the feudal pomp of King Edward's Gallery to the conventual atmosphere of the shrine was skilfully contrived.

First came the Vaulted Corridor on the same level as the gallery but slightly narrower, having false walls and no direct lighting except for what filtered in through the bronze lattice of doors set in the walls to suggest the entrance to confessionals. The roof was arched in the form of a low vault and both walls and ceiling were covered with dark panelling, the ribs picked out in gold. The intention was to produce a 'solemn and gloomy effect'.[20] Beyond this dark corridor, and raised up one step, was the Sanctuary, which had a flat oak ceiling, heavily groined and with gilt pendants and bosses. Here the walls were covered with crimson damask and there were two narrow windows in each wall with moulded mullions and tracery. Another step led into the Oratory itself formed by the apse with a fan vault in burnished gold and deep crimson, the walls in the same crimson damask as the Sanctuary, and the lancet windows glowing with coloured glass. Here the statue of the saint stood on an altar ablaze with the light of many candles while a chased golden sanctuary lamp hung from the central boss of the roof. For a man claiming no religious beliefs it was a strange tribute to the memory of a thirteenth-century Franciscan.

In the other parts of the Abbey, especially in the apartments later fitted up in the east transept to provide a Great Dining Room, Grand Drawing Room and Crimson Drawing Room, the general effect, as the name of the latter room suggests, was to introduce brilliant colours into the hangings and decorations to counteract the coldness and chill caused by the sheer size of the interiors. Everywhere we read of gold and purple damask, crimson silk edged with burnished gold, scarlet and deep blue curtains bordered with 'regal tressure' as though to dispel the pall of gothic gloom that weighed oppressively over all, provoking even in its creator the occasional outburst against its tomblike embrace. For all Beckford's boast to Lord Douglas of its 'most habitable' qualities, Fonthill Abbey failed in just this respect, and John Rutter in his generally enthusiastic account of its architecture could not fail to note of its interior that the Abbey 'with all

its Towers, furnishes but about eighteen bedrooms, thirteen of
which, from their almost inaccessible height, their smallness,
their want of light and ventilation, from one or all of these causes
combined, are scarcely fit for their intended use; and of the other
five, not one has a dressing room.'[21] For the owner himself it
would also eventually become 'this poetic and almost uninhabit-
able place', in flat contradiction of his earlier claim.[22]

The artist William Hamilton found the air of oppressiveness
almost as much as he could bear, for all that he must have known
that it was to some extent consciously created by Beckford's
exotic imagination. The effect that Fonthill Abbey had upon him,
he declared, 'fills the mind with a sentiment which is almost too
much to support, certainly of too melancholy a cast to be long
dwelt upon'. A visitor from abroad reacted in much the same way,
and kept on repeating as he was shown round the building that *un
homme doit avoir le Diable au corps pour bâtir une maison comme ça.*[23]
The painter Constable also contrasted the Abbey's fairy-like quality with the melancholy nature of the encircling downs, and there
is something curiously wraith-like in Turner's pictures of the
thin frail-looking tower rising like a ghost above the bleak landscape. 'There can have been few houses more worth visiting than
Fonthill Abbey,' a modern writer has noted, 'if only for its per-
fumed coal in gilded baskets!—but how cold and haunted it must
have been!—haunted, when brand new, and when the gangs of
workmen were employed night and day upon the walls! Haunted,
when Nelson came to visit it; haunted the day the great tower fell
down!'[24] There was certainly something eerie about the place, a
feeling that has survived the almost total disappearance of its vast
structure and still strangely haunts its now deserted site.

22

Man of Taste

BECKFORD'S SOCIAL ISOLATION continued despite the fact that he had re-entered the House of Commons in 1806 as member for his own pocket borough of Hindon, a move prompted, no doubt, by the death of William Pitt earlier in the year and of Lough-borough the year before. But if society was not interested in the doings of the 'abbot' of Fonthill, it was certainly very interested in his children, two young women of charm, beauty and reputed wealth. Nobody expected the sins of the father to be visited on the daughters when the prospect of substantial dowries made them appear, as they approached marriageable age, such tempting propositions to fortune hunters and other eligible bachelors.

Their father's reputation had made it necessary for them always to live under a different roof, a fact that the rest of the family insisted upon and which should be remembered when he had to face the charge, on top of all others levelled against him, of neglecting his two children. Even his few intimate friends were excluded from the society of these closely guarded young ladies, and Elizabeth Craven, Margravine of Ansbach, complained loudly when their guardian refused to allow her to see them on the grounds that she wanted to have control of them herself. 'You must do me the justice to believe and know I never made one step to interfere with your family, tho' I should be gratified to be of use to your lovely Daughters', she wrote to Beckford in some indignation.[1]

While the Begum was still alive they spent most of their time with her, the indispensable Dr. Lettice taking charge of their education. After Mrs. Beckford's death their guardianship was entrusted to Lady Ann Hamilton, a sister of the Marquis of Douglas whose plea for the preservation of Fonthill Splendens had been rejected by their father. He would later marry the younger of the two girls, for all that he was nearly twenty years her senior in age. Before marriage, according to the diarist Joseph Farington, Beckford allowed each girl a thousand pounds a year, a very generous allowance for those days but one that was presumably intended to provide for their entire separate establishment. 'The eldest Miss Beckford', Farington declared, 'is much taller than her sister and handsomer with an acute countenance. The younger sister is low in stature, and ordinary in her face and general appearance.'[2] Samuel Rogers also considered the elder sister 'both in appearance and disposition a perfect angel', adding that her delight was not to be admired herself but to witness the admiration which her younger sister never failed to excite.[3]

Susan always seems to have been Beckford's favourite even before her elder sister Margaret ('the stupid egoist' as he called her) had given him just cause, as he imagined, for banishing her from his presence. It was certainly Susan whom he first attempted to marry off, hoping to give her hand to a friend of his own in the summer of 1804. The man he had chosen for her, Count Fuentes y Egmont, a member of the Spanish branch of the Pignatelli family, could hardly have been more unsuitable. Though wealthy and of impeccable lineage he was generally thought to share Beckford's homosexual interests and was very soon regarded by his intended bride as 'the author of all her miseries'. Usually docile and pliant, and genuinely devoted to her father, she flatly refused to accept the count's proposal, and both Lady Ann and her maternal uncle Lord Aboyne rallied to her support.

Beckford was extremely angry. He was not used to being crossed, least of all by his own daughter, and in answer to a long letter from Lady Ann that touchingly portrayed Susan as 'a pale dejected Victim dragg'd to the Altar' he let fly a salvo of biting invective against the young girl who had dared to question his decision. For her to refer to Egmont as the author of all her misery was, he asserted, 'a species of frantic blasphemy so odious to my ears that it works up my already wounded indignant feelings to a pitch of Frenzy. If any fewel had been wanting to perpetuate the flame of Anger and resentment long since kindled in my bosom it has now been supplied.' As to her being *dragged* to the altar, he could only say that such language was more likely to result in himself being *dragged* to the tomb from the effects of sorrow ('rage' might have been a better word), and if such a

thing happened 'want, dependance and remorse will be her
portion'.[4]

Susan, for all her tractability, was not without her share of the
family stubborness. She held her ground, even against the thun-
derbolts of her father's fury, and the count was forced to retreat
from the field. A few years later he died, still a bachelor but
consoled, as a hint in Beckford's later jottings suggests, by the
presence of certain rosy-faced 'acolytes',[5] and it may be assumed
that Susan Beckford had a lucky escape. Her father forgave her
soon enough when negotiations began for her marriage to Lord
Douglas (about which there was much financial bickering over
settlements), for not only was he heir to a dukedom, a close friend
and relative of her father and a fellow connoisseur in matters of
taste, but there could be no fear of opposition on the part of
Lady Ann, for as the prospective bridegroom's sister she strongly
supported the match. Indeed some people even went so far as to
say that she had deliberately kept other suitors at a distance in
order to preserve so rich a prize for her brother.

Douglas's terms were twenty thousand pounds, 'a sum required by the Marquis to settle some affairs',[6] but Beckford at first
demurred at so huge a sum at a time when his own finances were
depleted by falling revenues, expensive litigation and building
extravagances. Then in 1806 Lord Douglas was sent as ambassador to St. Petersburg and everything was in suspense until
he was recalled, after barely a year, having impressed the Russian
Court more by his gallantry to the fair sex than by any great skill
in diplomacy. It was not until 1810 that everything was settled
and the couple were married at a private ceremony on 26 April.
Despite considerable differences in age and temperament the
marriage was a happy one.

The prospect of seeing his daughter a duchess (to which dignity
she succeeded upon the death of her father-in-law in 1819) was for
Beckford a matter of supreme satisfaction, and the alliance of his
family with the Hamiltons in the ducal branch, connected as it was
with the Scots and English royal families and claiming the dukedom of Châtelherault in France, in some measure compensated
him for his continued ostracism by the rest of society. Most of the
upper storey of King Edward's Gallery was now made over as a
ducal suite, with a State Bedchamber hung in the inevitable
crimson, the Duke's Bedchamber, the Duchess's anteroom hung
in scarlet, her dressing-room wainscoted throughout, and bed-

chamber described as 'a large handsome room, the prevailing colour of which is crimson'.[7] If Beckford was unable to wear a coronet himself he was content to rest in the shadow of his daughter's strawberry leaves.

There can be little doubt that he contemplated some equally grand marriage for his elder daughter who still lived under the protection of Lady Ann Hamilton, but Margaret Beckford showed small enthusiasm for the people suggested to her as suitable by their wealth or position in society to claim her hand. She preferred a candidate of her own choice, a Colonel James Orde, a man some ten years her senior and hardly likely to impress her father as a son-in-law as he was without any fortune, a younger son, and his grandfather had been a clergyman, a calling for which Beckford always expressed the profoundest dislike and contempt. That he was distinguished in his profession and rose to the rank of General cut no ice at all; every pressure was brought to bear upon the unfortunate Margaret to make her give him up. Her refusal to do this produced all the anger and cutting remarks that her sister, in reverse circumstances, had been made to suffer in the past, but to no avail. She decided to act on her own in defiance of her father's wishes and without consulting any of her family.

Whatever plans Beckford may have had for her received a shattering blow on a May morning in 1811 just about a year after Susan's marriage. A hastily scribbled note from Lady Ann was delivered to him enclosing another from his daughter. The first note read: 'Margaret went out this morning to take her usual walk in the Park as I thought with Mlle. and she has just sent me the enclosed instead of returning. I dread to think—She must be gone off with Orde.' The second note read: 'No longer able to bear the very unpleasant situation in which I am placed I have *at length* resolved upon a step which I feel assured will ensure my Happiness and have now adopted this mode of communication in preference to speaking to you upon the subject and when you receive this I shall *no longer* have the name of Beckford.'[8] The first furious reaction of the father can be seen on the blank side of the letter across which is dashed in his hand the repeated word 'Off! Off! Off!'

Margaret was not forgiven this act of independence and defiance. He announced that he would never see her again and with his deadly gift for slighting nicknames referred to her insultingly as 'Mrs. Ordure.' All supplies of money were cut off at once, appeals for help or forgiveness left unanswered. Only at the very end of her brief life (she died in 1818 at the age of thirty-three) was there some sort of reconciliation, and he was able to write a note of condolence to her widower.

The violence of his anger and his refusal to forgive until the very last moment do him little credit, but in acting against his wishes and in disobeying his authority he had classed his elder daughter with the rest of his enemies, with the world that had rejected him and always refused to acknowledge his existence. This, surely, is the only interpretation that can be put on the remark he made to Samuel Rogers in the autumn of 1817, about a year before Margaret Orde's death and before his belated decision to receive her again as his daughter, with which Lady Bessborough concluded her account of Rogers's visit to Fonthill Abbey: 'Mr. Rogers happen'd to mention his Eldest Daughter to him. He answer'd: "Poor Margaret—what a fool she was!" On this opening Mr. Rogers began saying something for her. Mr. Beckford said: "She us'd me very ill; but that was her own business—why should I care? What can my daughters be to me? Or why should I trouble myself more about them than about any other two young women I might happen to meet with?" Mr. Rogers says that when a man can ask such why? it is unanswerable.' But Samuel Rogers had not the sensitiveness of a man who had known thirty years of persecution. Even his devoted daughter Susan and her husband the duke, though they came often enough to see him at Fonthill, never once invited him to visit them at Hamilton Palace.

An example of the sort of treatment Beckford had to endure from his neighbours was given by the ever curious Joseph Farington in an entry in his diary for 16 October 1806. 'Not long since,' he wrote, 'Sir Richard Hoare of Stourhead applied to Mr. Beckford to see the Abbey which Mr. B. granted and attended Sir Richard when he came for that purpose. These civilities which passed between them were reported to the neighbouring gentlemen who took such umbrage at it, as conceiving that Sir Richard was giving countenance to Mr. Beckford, that a gentleman wrote to Sir Richard in his own name and that of others to demand of him an explanation of that proceeding as they meant to regulate *themselves towards him accordingly*. Sir Richard applied to his friend the Marquis of Bath upon it, and represented that he had no further desire but to see the Abbey and the meeting with Mr.

Beckford was accidental and to him unexpected. Such is the determination of the Wiltshire gentlemen with respect to excluding Mr. B. from all gentlemanly intercourse.'⁹

It is hardly surprising that Beckford's manner, even occasionally with members of his own family, was sometimes surly and morose, that the painter Henry Fuseli considered him to be 'jealous of everybody who excells . . . an actor but no gentleman', and declared that 'you can see his character is irregular by looking in his countenance, there is a twist in his look'.¹⁰ Stories like that about Sir Richard Hoare gave rise to other rumours and legends; that the Prince Regent had wished to visit Fonthill but had been turned away; that a man had managed to climb the wall and enter the inner domain where Beckford, discovering him, had courteously shown him round the Abbey and then, turning him loose in the grounds again, had bidden him to leave by the same way he had come in, adding that he hoped he would take care to avoid the bloodhounds that roamed in the grounds every night.¹¹ Beckford's treatment of strangers was, in fact, almost invariably polite, but he had curious ways of showing his displeasure, like his use of black sealing wax as a sign of mourning after his elder daughter's elopement, his cruel powers of mimicry, and the delight he took in hurtful and uncomplimentary nicknames. His temper, too, could still be terrifying when he lost control of it. 'Such anger, such violence, *never* but once did I see before . . .' his daughter Margaret wrote after her last stormy interview with him, 'he, in language TOO *horrible* for me to repeat, left me *for ever*.'¹²

Financial worries did not improve his temper; they haunted him the whole time he lived at Fonthill Abbey and were eventually to be the reason for his having to sell it. It was shortage of cash that made him decide in 1807, within a few months of moving into the Abbey, to sell the two Claudes he had bought from Prince Altieri barely seven years before. 'If the cursed Claudes aren't sold,' he told Franchi in that November, 'I shan't know which way to turn . . .'¹³ He had admired them well enough at the time of their purchase but now affected to find the vogue for this school of art 'incredible and inexplicable'.¹⁴ Perhaps he thought the serene classicism of Claude Lorraine ill fitted for the mellow light that filtered through stained-glass windows and now preferred the more sombre scenes of mediaeval prelates or Salvator Rosa battles. He was determined, however, to get as high a price for them as he could. It was not until June the following year that the dealer Harris of Bond Street offered him ten thousand guineas for them, a profit of well over three thousand pounds. He accepted somewhat grudgingly; it was a 'sacrifice', he informed Gregorio Franchi, 'a wretched, unworthy price'.[15] Perhaps he was right, for in less than three weeks Harris had sold them for twelve thousand.

The loss of the Altieri Claudes did not exactly denude the walls of Fonthill Abbey. There remained, among other pictures, three works by Giovanni Bellini, a *St. Catherine*, an *Agony in the Garden* and the celebrated portrait of the Doge Leonardo Loredan. Other religious subjects included the *Exhumation of St. Hubert* attributed to Roger van der Weyden, Perugino's *Virgin and Child with St. John*, Paolo Veronese's *St. Jerome at Prayer*, Adam Elsheimer's small but exquisite *Tobias and the Angel* and Salvator Rosa's *Job and His Companions*. On a more secular note were Gerard Dou's *Poulterer's Shop*, which Beckford had once much admired but later dismissed as 'the first Flemish painting in the world according to the gospel of sots, fools and false connoisseurs',[16] Watteau's *The Four Ages* and two small pictures representing the elements of air and water by Jan Breughel the elder. At the sale of part of Sir William Hamilton's collection in 1801 Beckford had bought a picture which had a special appeal for him, the *Boy with a Puzzle* then thought to be by Leonardo da Vinci but now attributed to Luini. Among contemporary works, as well as the commissions executed by West, Hamilton and Tresham, was Turner's *Fifth Plague of Egypt*. Beckford had bought this in 1800 when the artist was only twenty-five years old because he considered that the picture was painted in the true spirit of his Caliph Vathek. He later employed Turner to make watercolour sketches and drawings of the construction work on the Abbey.

In various rooms, as noted by John Rutter in his *Delineations of Fonthill*, could be seen, among many works of lesser genius, Rembrandt's *Portrait of a Rabbi* and two Rubenses, a *Visit of the Magi* and a *Jardin d'Amour* with a self-portrait of the artist together with his wife, van Dyck and the model of the *Chapeau de Paille*. He also mentions a portrait of a young nobleman by van Dyck, Bronzino's *St. Louis Gonzaga*, Jan van Eyck's *Virgin and Child with Figures* and two paintings by Ludovico Carracci, a *St. Francis* and the *Libyan Sibyl*.[17] There were also works by Gaspar Poussin, Teniers, Cuyp, Wouvermans, Mieris, van Huysum and Ruisdael. In 1814, on the advice of Benjamin West, he had bought a portrait of Pope Innocent X by Velazquez. Many of these works were later sold, but nothing could stop Beckford from collecting, and the pictures he later assembled in his house at Bath (which included some of the gems from Fonthill) probably out-rivalled in merit those that had adorned the Abbey at the height of its splendour.[18]

Beckford's comments on art and on the work of various artists were always forthright and incisive and generally showed an original point of view. 'There must be a feeling for art,' he once observed, 'mere admiration won't do—people admire, and affect to be struck with works of art, because others affect the same thing. Just as an opera audience cries "Wonderful!" at a perform-ance of which it does not comprehend a syllable. The beauty of art must be inwardly felt—the mind in it must be read, interpreted. Picture shows will not do that. There is Raffaelle—he is at the head of painting, everybody says—his pictures it is safe to admire and applaud. Ask why Raffaelle is the prince of painters—they cannot tell you. Now an Italian amateur of the lowest order will explain that and more. A just taste for art is a cultivated taste; there is no royal road to it, as too many think there is.'[19]

His preference was always for the great Italian painters, though he collected other schools as well. This preference sprang from his deep love for Italy and for Mediterranean culture and from his distaste, amounting almost to repulsion, for the cold Protestantism of the north. 'One must become half-Catholic to enter fully into the glories of Italian art', he told Cyrus Redding. 'Religion with us is a cold, reluctant duty. We acknowledge God, but fear to love him. We are afraid of anything that fits our minds for devotion—we make religion a duty, not an affection—when the formality of worship is over we have done. The true spirit, superstition, de-votion, whatever you will—was in the heart of the Italian artist—it oozed out at the end of his pencil, bathing his work in the beauty of holiness.'[20] This point of view, surprisingly original for an Englishman to hold before the Tractarian Movement had changed men's attitude to both religion and art and made the cult of 'superstition' a fashionable pose, shows the extent to which Beckford's passion for the art of the Italian renaissance was a reaction from his Calvinistic upbringing with its insistence upon guilt and sin. But neither art nor 'half-Catholicism' could release him from the burden his youthful experiences had laid upon him; as old age reached him he was heard to say: 'I am almost ashamed

of being so old. Death seems to have overlooked me. The longer
we live the more we have to answer for—the more we sin.'²¹

Raphael was the artist he most admired. When Redding suggested that this painter was just as partial to fleshiness and *em-
bonpoint* in women as Rubens, Beckford answered: 'No, the women
of Raphael are Italian in grace—they look round, but firm and well
formed. Those of Rubens are Flemish and Dutch, flaccid and
oysterish, as if they had been fattened in their own quags and salt
marshes.'²² He was later to own Raphael's *St. Catherine*, now in the
National Gallery, but according to Redding he considered the
Madonna del Spasimo, which he had seen at Madrid, as the artist's
masterpiece. He first saw this picture on Christmas eve 1787 in the
Royal Palace but made no note about it in his contemporary diary.
When he came to write up his journal for publication in 1834 he
was able to give his mature judgement on the work. 'Raphael
never attained in any other of his works such solemn depth of
colour,' he wrote then, 'such majesty of character, as in this
triumph of art. "Never was sorrow like unto the sorrow" he
depicted in the Virgin's countenance and attitude; never was the
expression of a sublime and God-like calm in the midst of acute
suffering conveyed more closely home to the human heart than in
the face of Christ.'²³

His love for the Italian masters did not blind him to the glories
of other schools and other artists. Speaking of Rembrandt he
said: 'What a glorious fellow the Dutchman was, without grace or
beauty. He threw about his light like another sun. What an expressive colourist—what strength he had—the very Samson of art
—his native dykes and dams stagnating all. How unfortunate that
the nature he copied partook of his mental constitution—he
revelled in Dutch grossness, but even that he made the most
astonishing thing in painting. He was a miracle in his day, he is so
still—he will be so for ever.'²⁴ On another occasion, in Bath, he
drew the attention of a visitor to a Holy Family by Polemberg.
'Do take notice of the St. Joseph in this charming picture', he
said. 'The painters too often portray him as little better than a
vagabond Jew or an old beggar. Polemberg had too much good
taste for such caricaturing, and you see he has made him here look
like a decayed gentleman.'²⁵

The collection at Fonthill Abbey contained many priceless objects in addition to the pictures. The bureau du Roi Stanislaus
stood in a window embrasure of the Grand Drawing Room and

in King Edward's Gallery was a large table, the elaborately inlaid top of which was formed by a slab of *pietre dure* or *pietre com-messe* with a central oval of onyx, said to be the largest in the world. The table, once owned by the Borghese family, stood on a heavy oak pedestal designed by Beckford himself. He had two ebony coffers also decorated with panels of *pietre dure* or Floren-tine mosaic, mounted in ormolu with swags of fruit and flowers in coloured marble. The larger of these had come from the Palazzo Pitti.

Beckford liked to attach names to various objects in his collec-tion to suggest, sometimes truthfully and at other times more doubtfully, a previous ownership by some royal or famous personage. In this category came the 'Holbein' Cabinet, which stood at one period in the Yellow Drawing Room, and which he liked to claim had been designed by Hans Holbein for King Henry VIII and had stood in Whitehall Palace. The cabinet was in fact of mid-sixteenth century origin and probably came from Augsburg, but to encourage belief in its once august ownership he had a stand constructed for it displaying various royal symbols and devices. Similarly the bed in the Lancaster State Bedchamber, an ebony four-poster dating from the seventeenth century, was described as having belonged to Henry VII, while a set of ebony chairs of the same period and of Indo-Portuguese manufacture were boldly assigned to the former ownership of Cardinal Wolsey. To what extent Beckford himself believed in these attributions is difficult to say, but sometimes he deliberately misled the gullible. In the sanctuary were two fine carved and gilded sandalwood coffers or robe chests which he pronounced as being of the period of James I, while in fact they were of contemporary workmanship and possibly made from his own design.

Other objects had a more reliable provenance. The splendid Van Diemen box, the pride of his fine collection of Japanese lacquer, had indeed once belonged to Louis XV's mistress the Marquise de Pompadour and had come to him from the collection of the Duc de Bouillon, and another lacquer chest had very likely been owned by Napoleon I. There was also the Rubens Vase, cut from a single agate, which he bought in 1818 and which was said to have been the chief item in Rubens's own collection. 'It is truly beautiful,' Franchi wrote to inform Lord Douglas, 'and I re-peat it is the finest object in the Abbey.'[26] But Rutter is presumably writing on Beckford's authority only when he refers to two crystal cabinets formerly belonging to Pope Paul V, to a pair of carved ivory vases from the collection of the Earl of Arundel, to two gold Japanese lacquer caskets once owned by the Duc de Mazarin, and to an amber jewel cabinet made for a Princess of Bavaria in 1665. If some of these claims lacked documentation or sprang from a too enthusiastic imagination it may be said in Beckford's defence that he was by no means the first collector, or indeed scholar, whose hopeful attributions have been queried or dismissed by a more prudent posterity.

A name that occurs more than once in Rutter's list of furniture and *objets d'art* is that of Benvenuto Cellini, of whose authenticated works very few are known to exist. He speaks of a pair of candlesticks in Beckford's cell-like bedroom as 'modelled after Cellini' and another pair in the Chintz Boudoir from designs of the same artist; in the Grand Drawing Room are four more candlesticks of similar attribution and in King Edward's Gallery 'a mounted nautilus upon an ivory plinth, carved by Benvenuto Cellini'. Beckford was well aware of the unreliability of many of these claims, and when the Margravine of Ansbach was selling an ivory tankard supposedly by the artist, which he bought in 1818, he did not take the attribution very seriously. On the other hand he was convinced of the authenticity (as were most of his contemporaries) of the sixteenth-century Florentine vase of carved topaz which Rutter saw in the Yellow Drawing Room and described as 'a vase of a single Hungarian topaz, intended as a marriage present to Catherine Cornaro, executed by Benvenuto Cellini'. It was one of Beckford's most prized possessions, having, in addition to being a beautiful work of art, the double attraction of the name of a great master and a distinguished, even royal, provenance, for Catherine Cornaro's marriage was to the King of Cyprus. 'If anything could enchant a timid and religious soul,' he wrote after the vase arrived at Fonthill, 'it would be the incredibly rich and sublime effect produced by Cellini's stupendous dragon alongside the conch in the Bouchardon cabinet: diamonds, topaz and enamel—everything glitters in a magical way.'[27]

When it came to furniture Beckford's taste had little in common with the gothic style of architecture that formed the setting for a collection that was chiefly of seventeenth- or eighteenth-century origin. He himself designed, or inspired, four matching 'gothic' tables that stood in the windows of King Edward's Gallery as well as two tall cupboards with stout elaborately turned 'tudor' legs and bulbous pillars supporting a richly carved canopy that stood on either side of the fireplace, but in the other rooms he showed a preference for ebony, buhl and marquetry. This contrast with the 'mediaeval' surroundings, like the brilliant scarlets and crimsons of the hangings, was deliberately contrived, and was intended to produce a startling effect. And so, in place of ponderous refectory tables and other pieces that might be considered to evoke a monastic atmosphere, we find instead commodes of lacquer and verd-antique, ebony armoires inlaid with Florentine mosaic, a buhl and tortoise-shell cabinet made for Louis XV, a suite of chairs in gold and purple damask, three Persian cabinets and stands of ebony and ivory, and a table of oriental alabaster. So it was that a stranger, visiting the Abbey for the first time, found himself suddenly transported as he crossed the groined threshold from the grey gothic of the exterior into a veritable treasure house that glowed with bright colours and arrested the eye with rare and curious works of art. No wonder that some of them, like Samuel Rogers, were carried away by what they saw.

Beckford's collection, which spread into almost every room of the Abbey, was on a scale that makes it impossible to give the reader more than a general impression of its quality and extent. There was, for example, the small ebony cabinet of Indo-Portuguese work on a stand with spirally turned legs, the cabinet containing two blue-lined drawers. Was this where he had once hoarded the letters he had received in Switzerland from Alexander Cozens, to whom he had written, a romantic youth of seventeen, that all his letters were deposited in a drawer 'lined with blue, the colour of the Aether'? There is no record as to where or when he acquired it, but it would stand beside the bed in which he died.

Then there was the Limoges enamelled reliquary which re-sembled the one to be seen on the altar in the picture of the *Exhumation of St. Hubert*, and the curious agate cup and cover of chalice-like shape with the two bosses of chalcedony forming the stem and a silver-gilt base with chaste arabesque decorations. It was made for Beckford about 1816 and the oriental, Vathek-like nature of the cup suggests that he had some hand in its design.[28] If so it was not the only object other than furniture in the Abbey to claim this distinction, as Rutter mentions a pair of silver candlesticks and a jewel casket as being 'designed by Mr. Beckford' as well as the organ screen in the Octagon or Grand Saloon.

The two long galleries as well as various other rooms were also

K

lined with shelves to house the vast and ever-growing collection
of books. These ranged from studies on the fine arts and architecture which were placed together in the Oak Library, or 'board of
works' as Beckford called it, where they were available for reference by the craftsmen and artists whom he employed on the
construction of the Abbey, to splendid and rare editions intended
to delight the scholar and connoisseur. It was, however, not just a
collection for collecting's sake; it reflected the varied tastes and
interests of the owner who was familiar with every volume and
could place his hand on any book he required despite the somewhat haphazard method, or lack of method, in their arrangement.

Beckford had been a serious book collector since the age of
twenty-two, and one of his first purchases had been a sixteenth-
century account of the Holy Land, an indication of his abiding
interest in works of topography and travel. He was to build up the
finest collection in England of works in this field. During the
early revolutionary period in Paris, when he was closely associated
with the bookseller Auguste Chardin, he was just as busy acquiring books as pictures and other works of art. In England his chief
agent was William Clarke of Bond Street who acted for him until
his death in 1830, when his son George took on the task. Beckford
nicknamed the elder man Boletus, the Mushroom, because he had
a large and rather ugly head on a short neck and body, and made
his requirements clear in the simple statement: '*Reading*, not
vanity-books for *me*'.[29]

When he moved from Splendens into the Abbey Beckford's
library already contained about three thousand volumes (a number that would be doubled before the Abbey was sold) and in
1808, at the time he parted with the Altieri Claudes, he also sold a
number of books. As he disliked getting rid of books more than
almost anything else we may assume that these were mainly
duplicates. 'Mr. Clarke didn't make a bad sale of my verminous
cabinet of books,' he wrote to Franchi, 'certain infamous Italian
trash fetched several times their original cost, but not a soul
wanted Macklin's Bible with all its engravings.'[30] As with his
other collections he liked to possess works that had been owned
by royalty and other great personalities and could boast of having
upon his shelves books bearing the armorial devices of Francis I
and Henry II of France, of Diane de Poitiers, Marguerite de
Navarre, Cardinal de Retz, Madame de Pompadour, the Duchesse
de Berri and many others. For other books he had a special

'Fonthill' binding which was distinguished by two charges from his coat-of-arms, usually stamped in gold on the spine: the cross flory and the cinquefoil, the former deriving from his supposed Latimer ancestors and the latter from his Hamilton descent through his mother.

Apart from travel, the subjects he most favoured were history, memoirs, biography and what might come under the heading of the 'curious', works on magic, demonology and other dark sciences. His linguistic abilities were demonstrated by the presence of books in French, German, Spanish, Portuguese and Italian as well as Latin and Greek, but there was little in Arabic or Persian. There was, less surprisingly than some might think, a considerable section devoted to theology which included various lives of St. Antony of Padua. Among his own contemporaries he collected William Blake, but upon the whole modern works did not interest him very much. He showed his opinion of Sir Walter Scott's *Field of Waterloo* by inscribing his copy with the lines:

> *The corpse of many a Hero slain,*
> *Press'd Waterloo's ensanguined plain;*
> *But none, by sabre, or by shot,*
> *Fell half so flat as Walter Scott.*

When Beckford left Fonthill in 1822 he took only a third of his books and manuscripts to Bath; the rest were included in the Abbey sale, a decision he was later to regret having made. He soon began adding to this diminished stock which, as he was to have the first choice of what he took with him, we may conclude contained the cream of the Fonthill library. Once settled in Bath the urge to buy books returned soon enough and an even greater and more valuable collection was assembled. At the time of his death he had amassed over ten thousand printed books and more than eighty manuscripts.

Beckford's range as a collector covered a very wide field. In the course of his long life he patronised and encouraged many contemporary artists from J. R. Cozens, Loutherbourg, Hubert Robert, Girtin, Richard Wilson and Turner to Bonington, Copley Fielding, Etty and Landseer. William Hazlitt's famous denunciation of Beckford as the *petit-maître* of art who 'uniformly and deliberately neglects every great work, and every great name in art, to make room for idle varieties and curiosities or mechanical skill', and who 'seems not to be susceptible of the poetry of painting, or else to set his face against it', has long ago been dismissed as non-sense; Hazlitt visited Fonthill at a time when many of Beckford's best pictures had been removed and a lot of rubbish added by the auctioneer Phillips. That Hazlitt should have been taken in by this gave his intended victim a good deal of amusement: 'You pay a very ill compliment to my taste to suppose I would furnish my house with such trash,' was his comment, 'it comes from the Phillipine islands.'[31]

In spite of Beckford's aloof attitude Hazlitt's venomous journalistic attack damaged his reputation as a collector, and got more publicity than was accorded to the opinion of a genuine expert. This came from Gustav Friedrich Waagen, one of the great art critics of his time and professor of art history in the University of Berlin. Waagen never saw the Fonthill collection, but he visited Beckford's later collection at Bath which still contained many of the masterpieces that had once hung in the Abbey, pictures that were in Beckford's possession at the time Hazlitt, on false or incomplete evidence, was accusing him of having polished the surface but suppressed the soul of art. After seeing Beckford's collection Waagen wrote: 'On the whole, I came away with the conviction that Mr. Beckford unites, in a very rare degree, an immense fortune with a general and refined love of art and a highly cultivated taste. Such a man alone could have produced a creation like Fonthill Abbey, which, from the picture that I am now able to form of it, must have realised the impression of a fairy tale. The extensive Gothic building, with a lofty, very elegant tower, from the views which I have seen of it, must have had, in the highest degree, the grandly fantastic character by which this style of architecture exercises so wonderful a charm. Conceive the interior adorned with ... most important works of art, with the most elegant and costly furniture; conceive it surrounded by all that the art of gardening in England can effect by the aid of a picturesquely varied ground, luxuriant vegetation, and a great mass of natural running water; and you will have a general idea of this magic spot, which so far maintained this character that for a long time no strange foot was permitted to intrude ... Unhappily, Fonthill Abbey has resembled also in its transitory existence the frail creations of the world of enchantment.'[32] It was rare indeed for Beckford to have such words written about him during his own life-time when most scholars remained silent and few journal could resist the temptation to sneer.

23
Within the Barrier Wall

BECKFORD WAS NEARING FIFTY when the Abbey finally became his home. He was now a very different person from the whimsical, capricious being who had once lived in the great Palladian mansion that had been the pride of his ambitious father and of which no trace now remained save for one of the two pavilions that had flanked the main structure of the building. The fashionable melancholy, the wayward fantasies, the extravagant dreams that had marked his character in those days had disappeared under the abrasive impact of continual persecution and contumely. The strength of will that had always existed beneath these various poses was now revealed without any romantic trimmings, and his character took on a harder, more sardonic glint. His temper could still be violent and his tongue sharp, and his view of humanity, formed by experience, was cynical and clean-swept of illusions. Pride and arrogance, moderated by a grim sense of humour and illuminated still by a clear intelligence, alone survived to link the bitter and solitary inhabitant of Fonthill Abbey with the wistful but no less solitary child who had once wandered through the halls of Fonthill Splendens, peopling it with the creatures of his vivid imagination.

There were other changes in Beckford's life as well; there were no more grand passions, no more Louisas, no more Courtenays. As is the case sometimes with people who emerge from adolescence with distinct bisexual tendencies Beckford had gradually, with the passage of time, veered to a totally homosexual position. Since his return from Spain in 1787 women seem to have played no part in his emotional life. For a while he had found a lover in Gregorio Franchi, but the one-time choirboy was now a man in his mid-thirties and long past the age to stimulate Beckford sexually, though a strong bond of affection still existed between them. But their relationship had never achieved the ecstatic over-tones that had characterised the earlier affairs; in his relations with Franchi there was always an element of patron and dependant if not actually of master and servant. Franchi had acquired a wife during one of his visits to Portugal and was the father of a young daughter; but married life had no more appeal for him than it would now have had for Beckford, and when he returned to England his wife remained behind in Lisbon. By 1807, when Beckford had settled into the Abbey, Franchi had become a sort of Leporello to the elder man's Don Giovanni, but a Don Giovanni somewhat lacking in sexual virility and the whole scene transposed to a world of homosexual fantasy.

Franchi spent a good deal of time away from Fonthill, either in London or travelling about the country on Beckford's business. From London he would regularly regale his patron with titillating morsels of gossip about the latest doings of the homosexual underworld, a correspondence which, for reasons of discretion, was conducted in Italian. Beckford's existence was a lonely one; he had virtually no intellectual companionship except among the little court of pensioners and hangers-on that surrounded him, and for much of the time he was oppressed by boredom. It was to dispel this all-pervading ennui as much as anything else that he urged on his friend in London to provide him with more details of his erotic escapades, and followed with a sort of feverish excite-ment Franchi's hints of possible future assignations with the ephebe or 'patapouf' of the moment. For this purpose Beckford assumed the character of 'Barzaba' in the letters, the voluptuary hungry for gratification and eager to know what delights awaited him should he quit the chaste protection of the Abbey for the dangerous pleasures to be discovered and enjoyed in the shadier quarters of the capital.

In this character he followed with a mixture of fascination and desire the career of a certain young tightrope-walker, 'an angel called Saunders'[1] who performed at the Royal Circus and was variously referred to as 'the Leg' or 'the leggy Divinity'. Let Franchi seek him out, Beckford begged almost in earnest: 'I don't like the idea of your leaving London without having judged whether or not poor wretched Barzaba is justified in being so slobbering . . .'[2] The Leg's muscular but illusive charms soon gave way to others, Franchi providing the stimulation and Beck-ford following it up with plaintive cries or pressing demands for further information. At one moment it was a performer at the comic opera for whom he could do no more than gasp, 'Ah, Cooper! . . .', at other times 'Barzaba's' requirements would be less personally specific: 'the best intrigue for me would be to take into my arms some object worthy of a little tenderness; it's cruel to hear talk of fair boys and dark Jade vases and not to buy them . . .'³

The footmen and valets at Fonthill Abbey would also, in the pages of this correspondence, have comic or effeminate nicknames conferred upon them suggested by their personalities as seen through the eyes of 'Barzaba'. Thus we meet the valet Richardson as 'Mme. Bion', the dwarf as 'Nanibus', and other menservants under such names as 'the Ghoul', 'Countess Pox', 'the Turk', and 'Bijoux', whom Beckford dismisses somewhat curtly as 'not much of a jewel, I can assure you'.⁴

The desire for physical gratification would now seem to have given place, in Beckford's case, to the need for mental stimulation only. He had no real wish to encounter the Leg or embrace the actual form of the youthful Cooper. He complains to Franchi of 'Mme. Bion's' coldness without really suggesting that he would have welcomed more warmth. After the experience he had already suffered of society's hostility to men of his type he was far too prudent and too proud to place himself at the mercy of black-mailers, and he had an almost morbid interest in the occasional cases when the frightful penalties of the law were inflicted in their full force against convicted homosexuals. 'Tomorrow (according to the papers) they are going to hang a poor honest sodomite', he wrote to Franchi in September 1816. 'I should like to know what kind of deity they fancy they are placating with these shocking human sacrifices. In a numerous list of thieves, assassins, house-breakers, violators ("a man for a rape") etc. he was the only one to be sent to the gallows; all the others were "respited during pleasure." The danger must be great indeed and everyone in the country must be running the risk of having his arse exposed to fire and slaughter.'⁵

There are other indications that Beckford fought shy of physical involvement from his middle years onwards, quite apart from any prudence that might derive from a fear of blackmail or the penal-ties of the law. He preferred the mental image produced by titillating talk and salacious innuendo to any contact with crude actuality, preferring, as he had so often done in the past, the dream to the reality. Thus, when setting out for Paris after the first abdication of Napoleon in 1814, he wrote to Franchi (who had been sent on in advance) for advice as to where he should stay, at the same time stating his requirements as he saw them in his mind's eye before leaving England. 'I want', he wrote, 'some agreeable and not too large hole where one can Chardinise in the morning and have boys in the evening . . .'[6] It was a typical Beckfordian dream of a life divided between the pleasures of boys and bookshops, of art and amorous adventures.

His letters from Paris, however, suggest that it all remained a dream. No sooner is he arrived there than he complains to Franchi of his frustration. 'Angels large and small abound here,' he writes, 'but I see them from afar, as it were in the clouds. A certain object seemed to pass like summer lightning at the Marquis's. What a pity! What a pity! Such expense, so much money gone and nothing to console me (in the supreme way, I mean).' And a month later he moans: 'Poor me, without a doctor, without an object of the kind I prefer above all others. I have no spirit for anything. I am a wretched impotent old man, with all the benignity that distinguished Barzaba—sighing, looking round, slobbering etc, but sighing, looking round and slobbering in vain.'[7]

There can be no doubt that Beckford, in his rôle of 'Barzaba', with the money still at his command and, at fifty-four, all the vigour of a man who had thirty years of life still ahead of him, could have had anything he wanted in the Paris of 1814. The plain fact was, when it came to the point, that he no longer really wanted what was offered. It was the thought of it all, not the thing itself, that stimulated him; the reality, it would seem, now turned him cold. Something of his own awareness of this is manifest from an earlier admission made to Franchi on an occasion when the Portuguese secretary's jealousy had been momentarily provoked. 'Dearest Gregory,' Beckford had then written, 'Your "little bird" is wrong. I am not doing anything more than I did when you were here, I assure you. I love "the Countess" as you know. I talk like the Duke of Lafoes used to (*toujour galant*, *toujour aimable*), and do infinitely less than he; "words, words, words", that's all, I swear to you.'[8]

If Beckford chose to deny himself the physical gratification of his desires (though there is a hint of some sort of a relationship, which would seem to have been transitory and far from satisfactory, with the valet Richardson, or 'Mme. Bion' as he is called in the Italian correspondence), it was certainly not from any motives of religion. His interest in religion had not declined, and his familiarity with the Roman Missal is clear from the many quotations from the liturgy, usually ironical in their application, which occur in his letters to Franchi. St. Antony of Padua was still his symbol of childish purity, of the lost paradise of pre-adolescent innocence. 'As for me,' he would write in August 1817, 'I have a great longing for devotions, I breathe only the wish to wallow on the threshold of the Saint's chapel at Padua',⁹ but his attitude to religion was now much the same as that which he had once himself attributed to the Queen of Portugal who, fancying herself damned to all eternity, indulged in 'conversation of a rather unchaste tendency'. So with his own 'unchaste' inclinations, his undying Calvinistic conscience assured him that he was damned and beyond redemption, so why not eat, drink and be merry? 'How difficult is salvation!' he wrote on another occasion. 'Nothing now is open or offers easy progress but the broad way which leads to the abode of the Devil.'¹⁰ If, therefore, his homosexual tendencies were now more or less confined to a private world of fantasy, it arose from an inner fastidiousness of his own and not from outside pressures, whether social or religious in origin. He was content to remain at Fonthill weaving his erotic fantasies around the unsuspecting members of his staff of menservants and enjoying, vicariously and at a safe distance, the delights that Franchi dangled before him in his letters from London or Paris.

The routine of life at the Abbey was simple and orderly. Beckford was an early riser, his day rarely began later than six o'clock in the morning. He would take some chicken broth and then go out for an hour's ride before inspecting the building work or attending to other out-door business in the grounds or on the estate. Breakfast would be at ten o'clock but he wasted no time over it; half an hour at table was considered long enough. Following a custom which was already becoming a little out of date by the time he was installed in the Abbey he dined at four o'clock in the afternoon in the winter and an hour later in summer, a time which provided him with a long interval between breakfast and dinner to attend to his affairs, whether with his agent, with Wyatt, or in matters to do with his collection, his library, or the sad business of tree-felling forced upon him as a means of replenishing the vast sums of money required for the never ending building operations.

He would also find time for a long ride in the afternoon, sometimes of twenty miles or more, following the circuitous route he had devised through the woods on the Fonthill estate. Dinner was served in state, often solitary state, with a train of servants in full livery attending him. He neither ate nor drank more than sparingly but expected the highest standards to be observed by his cook. After dinner he would read (he was familiar, it was said, with five modern European tongues as well as the classics) or play the harpsichord or piano which he did, as we know from the reports of Rogers and others, with the greatest skill. 'When he touches the harpsichord,' Henri Meistre had declared, 'you fancy you hear Piccini, Gluck, or Orpheus himself playing on it.'[11] Among his favourite composers, other than Mozart, were Jomelli and Cimarosa; Beethoven was a little too modern for his ears, he found him 'crude, harsh and presumptuous'.[12] These evening relaxations would occupy him until ten o'clock when he would have supper, and immediately afterwards retire to his spartan bedroom with its simple uncurtained bed.

It will be seen that a great deal of Beckford's time was spent out of doors, and that he lived a physically vigorous, healthy life for all that he complained a great deal of biliousness, indigestion, constipation and piles. His old friend and trusted physician Dr. Ehrhart had died shortly after the move into the Abbey, leaving a sad gap in Beckford's life. Always something of a valetudinarian, despite a robust constitution, he missed the presence of a doctor in whose pills and powders he could place his confidence, and after Ehrhart's death never really trusted any other medical adviser. Though he cosseted himself to some extent, hating draughts and refusing to go out when the east wind blew, he always took plenty of exercise, riding at all times of the year and swimming in the lake when the weather permitted. He was, indeed, very much of an open-air person, and the beautiful lay-out of park and landscape garden he created within the barrier wall was as much an expression of his personality as the Abbey itself.

Beckford's planting and landscaping of the Fonthill estate predated the building of the Abbey by a number of years; some of the ideas he carried out can, in fact, be traced back to the imaginative fragment *The Dome of the Setting Sun* written while he was still a youth. He was planting saplings and trees even before the wall was built or his experiments in landscape gardening were started at Monserrate in the summer of 1794. That was the year in which Uvedale Price's *Essay on the Picturesque* was published, but Beckford's ideas on gardening were already well established by that time, and if they owe anything to outside influence it is not to Price but to William Kent and to Horace Walpole's *On Modern Gardening*. Here, ten years before the publication of Price's essay, Walpole was expressing many of the ideas that Beckford would put into practice at Fonthill: 'Adieu to canals, circular basons, and cascades tumbling down marble steps, that last absurd magnificence of Italian and French villas. The forced elevation of cataracts was no more. The gentle stream was taught to serpentize seemingly at its pleasure, and where discontinued by different levels, its course appeared to be concealed by thickets properly interspersed, and glittered again at a distance where it might be supposed naturally to arrive . . . The living landscape was chastened or polished, not transformed. Freedom was given to the forms of trees; they extended their branches unrestricted; and where any eminent oak, or master beech had escaped maiming and survived the forest, bush and bramble were removed, and all its honours were restored to distinguish and shade the plain.'[13]

In this way Beckford created the Bitham Lake by damming a stream and allowing the water to find its own irregular margin, planting an American garden on its eastern side where were to be found rhododendrons, magnolias, and azaleas with the Carolina rose and Portugal laurel growing as though naturally among the trees.[14] There were no formal gardens at all, but patches of flowers would be hidden near the Abbey buildings to be discovered in some break in the trees or clearing in the shrubberies, or, like the Alpine garden, formed from an old quarry beyond the lake. The herb garden, as suitable for a monastic community, was not far from the building but shaded and concealed by trees as was the special garden set aside for the use of the dwarf. There were no gravel paths or surfaced drives within the enclosure; even the great Western Avenue, stretching for nearly a mile from the main door of the Abbey, was covered with closely mown grass, while the trees and shrubs that bordered it were again made to follow an irregular line as though the avenue had been cleared from the primitive woods. It was a foible of Beckford's that the grass should always be cut at night so that his eye would never be disturbed by the sight of the gardeners at work.

Once the site for the Abbey had been chosen the whole landscape was designed as a setting for the building, so that its tower and turrets would appear to grow from a natural background.

Round the house itself the ground was cleared of trees, nor were any flower gardens visible; all was bare grass except for a fig tree and an apricot as might have been planted by some mendicant friar returning to his mother house from distant lands. Carefully planned vistas were contrived to give 'pictureque' views from the windows of the Abbey and also, for the benefit of a wanderer in the park, to provide no less romantic glimpses of a great building either reflected in the waters of the lake or rearing up its many pinnacles against a background of rich and varied foliage. Here, in creating these set pieces, Beckford took as his guide the works of the great landscape painters, in particular Salvator Rosa, Nicolas Poussin and Claude Lorraine.

Care was also given to the colour effect of the foliage of trees, contrasting one species with another, and allowing for the variations produced at different times of the year. His guiding principles were naturalness and simplicity. Certain exotic foreign trees were introduced, but placed in such a manner as to blend as unpretentiously as possible with the native varieties. The purpose everywhere was to produce a scene of natural beauty, to banish all notions of a formal plan or parterre or even a conventional park with its avenues of trees drawn up in lines like regiments on parade. Beckford's idea was to approach nature as a painter did his pigments and produce a scene in the manner of an old master, and he considered his success in this as no less important than his efforts in any other of his artistic activities. His mastery of the art may be judged from a contemporary opinion. 'The grounds of Fonthill', wrote John Rutter, 'exhibit the true spirit of English gardening, carried to its utmost extent of a bold and varied simplicity. Every tree, every shrub, and every flower, has contributed to the production of one unequalled effect of wild profusion. The woodbine and the jasmine not only interlace the thickets with their green and fragrant tendrils, but the rose and rhododendron bloom beneath the larch and the hawthorn, and the furze and the lily blossom in equal companionship. These appearances are occasionally presented in the secluded spots, which the rambling feet of the stranger light upon; but they are not confined to particularly favourable situations. The union of the garden and the grove is almost universal; and it is impossible to imagine a more charming feature of the place, or one which more clearly indicates the care with which its scenery has been created, and almost matured, by one tasteful possessor.'[15]

Beckford was essentially a countryman and would only occasionally be lured up to London, when he would install himself in the house he had leased in Upper Harley Street. An auction or picture sale might tempt him to leave Fonthill, but for the most part he relied upon Franchi to keep him informed about the activities of the art market. He also now occasionally attended to his duties as a Member of Parliament, something he had not dared to do so long as Pitt or Loughborough were still alive. He was present at the opening ceremony at the end of November 1812 when the Prince Regent, far from popular with the public, had been received without acclamation as he drove to the House of Lords. 'Yesterday I heard the Royal bird singing', Beckford informed his son-in-law Douglas the following day. 'He warbles wonderfully and with infinite grace.'[16]

But Beckford never remained for long in London, if only to escape the snubs and annoyances he still had to contend with. His relations with Franchi, real or imagined, gave opportunities for malicious sneers from his enemies and even the dwarf's role in his life at Fonthill became a subject for popular speculation. 'I am sick of hearing nonsense about Mr. Franchi, and if possible sicker of the egregious absurdity about the poor helpless Dwarf . . .' he broke out in indignation at the report of these innuendoes.[17] He declared that he cared nothing for the buzz and gossip of the world and that paragraphs in the newspapers amused rather than alarmed him, but the fact that they still occurred from time to time, even after the turn of the century, shows how well Loughborough's work had been done.

More wounding perhaps than these predictable reactions from mud-raking journalists was the attitude of the official world of art. Beckford's patronage of contemporary artists was considerable and was accepted with every apparent sign of gratitude and respect. Artists were among the few who accepted invitations to Fonthill where they were entertained with lavish hospitality, could enjoy at leisure their host's collection of pictures or avail themselves of those volumes devoted to art history which he always placed at their disposal. Their own efforts would be appreciated and encouraged and their works often purchased. Yet never once was Beckford himself invited to the annual dinner of the Royal Academy, for all that two successive presidents, Benjamin West and James Wyatt, were his friends and had enjoyed his patronage to a considerable degree. Wyatt, who had additional reason for being grateful to Beckford in that he had once bailed him out from a spunging house,[18] did at least put forward his name on one occasion but the proposal was received with embarrassment. 'A dead silence', according to Joseph Farington, was the result, until West ingeniously suggested that if an invitation was sent it would be taken as a compliment but not accepted. More timid or prudish academicians feared that Beckford might turn up after all and 'if he were to come, would it not be improper?' At the very thought of such a situation arising the proposal was quickly dropped.[19]

News, therefore, of any sort of praise or approbation must have come as a welcome, almost overwhelming experience to anyone so solitary, so scorned by his fellow men, and so sensitive to insult as was Beckford during the years of his lonely occupation of Fonthill Abbey. It was thus that he had welcomed Samuel Rogers's visit in 1817 for all that he privately considered his guest as 'a castrated *bore*' and with his gift for the telling sobriquet referred to his cadaverous, parchment-faced visitor as 'the Yellow One' or 'the Yellow Poet'. But so rare a thing was a visit from a social equal and a fellow author that Rogers was admitted to the privilege enjoyed by very few of having the 'Episodes' of *Vathek* read aloud to him, a privilege the poet himself enjoyed with mixed feelings as he found them 'extremely fine, but very objectionable on account of their subject', and considered that they showed the author's mind to be 'to a certain degree diseased'.[20] Beckford admitted the authorship of his pseudonymous novels and hinted that he was toying with the idea of having his travel diaries edited for publication. One of the few remaining copies of *Dreams, Waking Thoughts and Incidents* was produced and presented to the fortunate guest. To Franchi, Beckford was able to write with a note of triumph as well as humour: 'He said the finest and most poetic things in the world to me on his own behalf and on that of Byron, to whom he is going to scribble down in verse everything he has just swallowed.'[21]

The reference to Lord Byron, then at the very zenith of his fame and notoriety, must have been especially pleasing to Beckford. The poet's interest in him and his work dated from his reading of *Vathek*, probably about 1809, when a new edition of the book had been issued. Byron was at once captivated by the strange oriental story, confessing later to Beckford's daughter Susan that he considered it his 'gospel' and carried a copy of it about with him in his pocket.[22] It was perhaps this very copy which Caroline Lamb had found in his rooms in Albany and written 'Remember me' on the first page, an action which had resulted in the poet dashing off, upon the same blank page, the lines beginning:

> *Remember thee! remember thee!*
> *Till Lethe quench life's burning stream*
> *Remorse and Shame shall cling to thee,*
> *And haunt thee like a feverish dream!*[23]

He had praised the book publicly in the notes to *The Giaour*, published in 1813, when he had written that 'for correctness of costume, beauty of description, and power of imagination, it far surpasses all European imitations: and bears such marks of originality, that those who have visited the East will find some difficulty in believing it to be more than a translation.' But there were other less openly admissible reasons why he should show an interest in the author of *Vathek*, the man of whom he had spoken as 'the great Apostle of Paederasty'. Byron's own nature was strongly bisexual and the life history of the Caliph of Fonthill was no less interesting to him than that of the Caliph Vathek. For a long time he had hoped to meet so fascinating a person, and the chance had almost presented itself in June 1809 when he found himself staying in the same inn as Beckford on the road to Falmouth. 'We tried in vain to see the Martyr to prejudice, but could not', he wrote to tell his friend Francis Hodgson, adding the curious piece of information: 'what we thought singular, though perhaps you will not, was that Ld. Courtenay travelled the same night on the *same road* only one stage *behind* him'.[24]

Byron's hopes of a meeting had little chance of fulfilment. His life, like Beckford's own early life, was spent so much in foreign travel, in a voluntary exile from a country that failed to appreciate his style of living and frowned upon his reputation for moral laxity, that the chances of an encounter in England were remote. The parallels between the two men's mode of existence were almost too close for comfort, but Byron, by twenty-eight years the younger, had always just managed to escape the fate of public condemnation. Much was forgiven a poet and a peer, but Beckford can hardly have been unaware of the rumours that circulated in society about the younger man's strange tastes, and he showed a strong reluctance to acquiesce in the suggestions for a meeting that reached him through Rogers and others, and possibly directly from Byron himself.[25] Perhaps he was afraid of what might have transpired in conversation, or what new torments might have been devised by his enemies and their allies of the gutter press, enemies equally to Byron as to himself, if word of their having met were ever to become public property.

When asked in old age why he had never agreed to meet Byron he always replied that it would have led to nothing. 'We should have met in full drill,' he declared to Cyrus Redding, 'both talked at the same time—both endeavoured to have been delighted—a correspondence would have been established, the most insufferable and laborious that can be imagined, because the most artificial. Oh, gracious goodness, I have had the opportunity of enjoying the best qualities of his mind in his works; what more do I require?'

These remarks show only the considered opinion of old age. At the time when he could have met Byron, in his mid-fifties and at the height of his period of cynicism and isolation, there were more immediate reasons for his refusal. There was too much in the life of this brilliant and famous young man to remind Beckford of how his own life might have developed had circumstances been only slightly different; had his infatuation for William Courtenay been less intense, his disregard for convention less provocative, if his control of his own mercurial temperament had been exercised with more maturity and discretion. These were melancholy and depressing reflections. To meet Byron would be like coming face to face with an image of his former self, yet one endowed with greater genius and destined for less misfortune. It was more than he could bear to risk.

No such meeting ever took place, though on one occasion Byron was to encounter another close relative of Beckford's, apart from his daughter the Duchess of Hamilton. In 1816 the poet called on Madame de Staël at Coppet and was more amused than surprised when one of the other guests, a lady no longer in her first youth, swooned away as he entered and had to be carried out of the room. It was Mrs. Hervey, the romantic novelist. Her dramatic fainting fit had little effect beyond causing Madame de Staël's daughter, the Duchesse de Broglie, to remark rather unkindly that it was a bit too much to expect from someone of sixty-five years of age, and Byron himself seemed unaware that the lady in question was sister to the author of *Vathek* whose work he so much admired.[26]

Byron wrote to Rogers in the hope, at least, that he would be able to persuade Beckford to allow him to see the unpublished 'Episodes' which the lucky Rogers had had read aloud to him. 'Your account of your visit to Fonthill is very striking;' the letter began, 'could you beg of *him* for *me* a copy of the MS. of the remaining *Tales*? I think I deserve them, as a strenuous and public admirer of the first one. I will return it when read, and make no ill use of the copy, if granted . . . If ever I return to England, I should very much like to see the author, with his permission. In the meantime you could not oblige me more than by obtaining me the perusal I request, in French or English—all's one for that, though I prefer Italian to either . . .' Rogers passed on the request. Beckford was tempted, no doubt a little flattered by the interest of so celebrated an admirer, about the only contemporary poet for whom he had himself a good word to say; he 'hesitated, half consented', according to Rogers's reply, but finally decided that the stories could not leave Fonthill, 'the place of their birth, from which they had never wandered'.[27]

Beckford's hesitation over the question of sending the 'Episodes' to Byron is typical of his whole attitude to the friendly overtures he received from the poet. His trust in the good faith of others had been so undermined by the treatment he had come to expect from them that he found it increasingly difficult to reach out his hand to grasp another's even when offered in obvious friendship and homage. Furthermore his experience of writers, from Henley onwards, had not encouraged his belief in their good intentions, and his fear of losing sight of the precious manuscript of the 'Episodes' was genuine. He was soon to have a fresh example of the usual sort of treatment meted out to him by the world in general. When discussing the possibility of having his travel diaries edited for publication Rogers had suggested that Tom Moore might undertake the task, and wrote to the Irish poet hinting that Beckford would pay him well, perhaps as much as a thousand pounds. Moore, however, reacted with horror at the thought of a contract that might compromise his social reputation. 'If he were to give me a hundred times the sum I would not have my name coupled with his,' he answered. 'To be Beckford's *sub*. not very desirable.'[28] This was the sort of conduct that Beckford had come to expect. Though he affected a proud indifference to it his life in fact became ever more solitary and embittered.

It was, therefore, a simple and comparatively frugal life that was lived behind the protection of the twelve-foot-high wall that kept the world at bay; frugal, that is, when there were no guests to be impressed with a sudden burst of luxury and magnificence. It was an existence very far removed from that entertained by public imagination or encouraged by gossips and paragraph-writers who continued to couple Beckford's name with scenes of debauchery and vice.

His little court was composed for the most part of scholars or artists, and age was overtaking all of them. Ehrhart, the free-thinking, free-speaking physician was already dead; the Abbé Macquin, if hardly a pillar of religious orthodoxy, spent his days in supervising the library or pursuing heraldic research; Gregorio Franchi, prematurely middle-aged, was already beginning to suffer the pangs of rheumatism and gout. Clarke the bookseller, with his great mushroom head on a stocky trunk, would appear from time to time, and there would be prolonged visits from the artist John 'Warwick' Smith whom Beckford called 'Father Bestorum' as his age (he was eleven years Beckford's senior) made him the father of all the beasts or 'animals' of Fonthill. Even Lord Roden, a brother-in-law of General Orde, one of the Abbey's few visitors from the great world outside, whose acquaintanceship with Beckford has remained something of a mystery, can hardly have figured in their society as a gay young dog when it is remembered that his nickname was 'the Professor' and that he was nearly five years older than his host.

If Beckford can be said to have built his Abbey in some sense as an act of defiance against the world, and in particular against those who continued to scorn him, then it was an act he had to pay for in terms of loneliness and, for all his protests to the contrary, of boredom, as well as by the ever-growing threat of financial ruin.

24
Fonthill Sold

❧

BECKFORD, as we have seen, was able to go to Paris once again in 1814. The fall of Napoleon, which had made this visit possible, had been greeted at Fonthill Abbey with a fine display of flags on the top of the tower and by many sighs of relief within its walls not only from Beckford himself but from the Abbé Macquin, a confirmed royalist who had come to England in 1792 from his professorship of rhetoric at Meaux as a refugee from revolutionary terror. Beckford, unlike his son-in-law Lord Douglas, had always despised the French emperor and his regime, referring to him contemptuously as 'our great Cuckoo-Philosopher'[1] and had foreseen the beginnings of his decline as early as 1808.

The end of the war had seen a momentary rise in the price of sugar which had given Beckford the misleading notion that prosperity was returning to his Jamaican estates and that the coffers at Fonthill, emptied by law suits, building extravagance, general mismanagement and the decline of trade during the war years, would soon be overflowing once more. The temptation to visit Paris was more than he could resist; it was the same temptation that had lured him there in the early years of the revolution when art treasures and pictures were to be snapped up for bargain prices, and he felt all his old enthusiasm returning. 'There is nobody like myself at looking out for the grandest and most beautiful things, nobody so disposed to throw from the arena all other athletes—the infamous Edwards, the terrific Spencer, the idiotic Devonshire . . .'[2] he told Franchi, who had been sent on in advance to spy out the land and to reserve for his master whatever he thought the latter might wish to purchase. It was a wise precaution as competition was clearly going to be strong.

Beckford did not reach Paris until October and was to remain there for most of the rest of the year; he was not back in England until just before Christmas. There had been many changes in the city, which he had not seen since before the proclamation of the empire, and much of it he disliked. 'Everywhere one discovers a sham style—' he wrote to Lord Douglas, 'false Roman of the false Empire which I no longer respect and which I like no better than Birmingham gold or Pinchbeck's masterpieces', an opinion which may have been intended as a snub to his son-in-law's Bonapartist sympathies. He thought the singing at the opera no more than 'piercing and often discordant shrieks' though he admired and praised the scenery and costumes and considered the ballet 'ravishing and perfect'.[3] The Louvre he found in confusion (they were preparing for a special exhibition) and deplored the way some of the pictures had been cleaned. He was particularly disappointed by those of the period before Raphael, a period in painting that had always interested him. These he found all repainted and regilded and considered them unauthentic and without value.

Some of his old friends were still to be seen, having survived all the vicissitudes of the revolution, terror, republic, empire and royal restoration. Chardin, the bookseller who had helped to hide him from the attentions of the Committee of Public Safety twenty years before, was still in business and in enjoyment of the annuity Beckford had settled on him. At the Portuguese embassy he found another old friend, one who recalled a less turbulent era in his past history. This was Dom Pedro, now forty years of age and, since the death of his father in 1803, the sixth Marquis of Marialva and his country's ambassador to the court of Louis XVIII. It was a meeting that recalled many nostalgic and sentimental memories, and sad ones, too, for not only was the Marquis Diogo no longer living but Dom Pedro's sister, the placid and beautiful Donna Henriqueta to whom Beckford had so nearly been betrothed, had also been for four years in her grave. 'I did not find him so changed in appearance as I had expected,' Beckford informed Franchi, 'and certainly he is not changed in his feelings towards me. On seeing me he seemed to see his Fatherland, his father, his sister and all the happy serene days of his youth—irrevocable and for ever departed . . .'[4]

Despite some frustrations in relation to certain 'objects', those 'angels large and small' that seemed to flutter in particular in the vicinity of the Portuguese embassy, Beckford's spirits were soon bubbling over in the stimulating atmosphere of restoration Paris, not least as a welcome contrast to the pall of boredom that always threatened to descend on him in the solitary seclusion of his Abbey. But, alas, he was no longer so rich as he had once been, and there were many hesitations, retreats, self-communings and doubts before he could commit himself to a purchase. It was not any longer a case of plunging in and carrying off the prize under the very nose of royal agents; only after much heart-searching did he pluck up the courage to buy *The Poulterer's Shop* of Gerard Dou. It was now considered 'a great fling' what would once have been a matter of course; so too with Gasper Poussin's *Calling of Abraham*—'a great bargain! A great bargain!' he wrote as much in justification as in triumph.

Paris had worked its old spell on him. He had been able to throw off the worries that surrounded him so increasingly at Fonthill, the anxiety that sprang from rising building costs and diminishing income, from the snubs, slights and sneers of society, from the consciousness that life was passing him by. Once again he was reminded that only in England was he treated as a pariah, and, safe from the hypocritical censure of his fellow-countrymen, felt again something of the delirium he had known as a young man. In such an euphoric moment he dashed off a revealing self-portrait of himself to Franchi: 'Every hour I improve in knowledge and taste. The Abbé will tell you, when you see him, what I am and to what pitch of Frenchiness and flowery Parisian manner of speaking I have attained. In spite of my face and dress they take me for a Frenchman; if you had heard me this morning discoursing in various quarters on politics, military and naval matters, Greek, the court, cooking, botany, astronomy and bigotry, you would have thought yourself in the Senate, the University, the theatre, the chapel and the brothel. How strange my make-up is! The working of my brain is enough to perplex anyone wanting to know about the composition of the human spirit! The weather itself is not more variable than my disposition —one minute sunshine, the next darkness . . .'[5] The words might well have been written by the precocious young man who had alternately shocked and charmed the Paris of thirty years ago rather than by a disillusioned man in his mid-fifties.

Beckford went to Paris again in 1819 but very little is known of this last visit to the city that had witnessed so many of his curious adventures and usually had so bracing an effect upon his spirits. On this occasion, however, everything seemed to go wrong and some undisclosed misunderstanding resulted in a dispute with Dom Pedro and the friendship between them came to an abrupt end. Dom Pedro had only a few more years to live; he died four years later in his fiftieth year and no reconciliation took place between them. The cause of the quarrel is not known, but Beckford left Paris in a hurry, probably in a temper, and never went abroad again. His spirits did not revive until he reached London from where he wrote, with typical Beckfordian bombast: 'I came like a thunderbolt, having electrified by shere weight of money the passporteers, Customs-ites, inn and post-house keepers, in short *everybody* along the *whole* route—of me alone do they talk and think, to me only do they drink . . .'[6]

It was not just to impress others, but to keep his own spirits up, that Beckford wrote in this way, for in fact his affairs had reached such a low ebb that his whole future, and that of the Abbey which devoured so much of his income and capital, was in the balance. He had three law suits still unsettled, his debts continued to mount, and the price of sugar, which had risen so encouragingly in 1814 had now slumped to the lowest price ever. The outlook was grim indeed.

Beckford was now paying for the lack of interest he had always shown for his business affairs, though he might have taken warning in the past from the fact that as he grew poorer the Wildman family, his legal advisers for many years, grew richer. Thomas Wildman had died in 1796 but his two remaining brothers continued to plunder their client, demanding the vast sum of £86,000 from him in 1802. Further neglect, neglect of a very costly nature to Beckford, was revealed when it was discovered that they had failed to secure his title to certain of his properties in Jamaica, nor was his confidence in them increased when they appropriated another West Indian estate for themselves. Beckford dismissed them in a fury of impotent rage while the Court of Chancery reaped a rich harvest from the resulting confusion and costly litigation.

His new solicitor, Richard Samuel White (known at Fonthill as *Rottier*—the Belcher), tried to instil some notions of economy in his client, but by this time Beckford had become a hopeless case as far as his extravagances were concerned, and when he decided, in the face of much legal opposition and continual pleas for prudence, to start work on the east transept of the Abbey in 1812, he did his best to conceal the fact from his solicitor, safely out of the way in London, until the work was too far advanced for it to be countermanded. Indeed Beckford was for ever devising ways to deceive the long-suffering White in order that he could continue to spend money on pictures, books, manuscripts, *objets d'art* and the ever-expanding gothic galleries of his house.

In the years prior to 1819 various schemes for raising money had been initiated and carried out, but these did little more than pay the interest on Beckford's debts. All available timber on his estates, except for the immediate neighbourhood of Fonthill and the area within the barrier wall, was felled and sold, and though a programme of replanting was undertaken at the same time, the sight of so many fine trees sacrificed on the altar of extravagance must have been a sad one. Next his estates in Bedfordshire and property at St. Pancras were sold as well as Witham Priory, the former monastic site that had once seemed to link him in a sentimental association with the monks of the Grande Chartreuse. Finally in 1817 he had given up the lease of his London house and put all its contents on the market. The sale caused something of a stir, for various pictures from Fonthill Abbey were included, among them one of Benjamin West's biblical studies, a Salvator Rosa, and others attributed to Holbein, Rubens, Brueghel and Giorgione. The Prince Regent came to see what was offered for sale, as did Queen Charlotte and some of the princesses. Under such circumstances Beckford was not flattered by this mark of royal condescension: 'I have said nothing about these royal visits, about the Queen and the Princesses', he wrote from the Abbey (where he remained) to Franchi, who was in charge of the proceedings in London. 'As a matter of fact, they matter no more to me than I to them. The occasion of these visits is melancholy, not happy—mortifying, not honourable . . .'[7] All the same, Gerard Dou's *Poulterer's Shop*, bought only five years before in Paris, was sent up to London in the hope that the royal connoisseur of Carlton House might decide to add it to his collection.

By the beginning of 1821 Beckford's affairs had reached a state of crisis. He was overdrawn on his account with his sugar merchants in London for more than £70,000 and Fonthill itself was mortgaged for almost the same amount. Even after the sale of the various properties in England and Jamaica his debts still amounted to the vast sum of £150,000, and though he had assets to set against this there was no solution to his financial problems that would allow for his remaining in possession of Fonthill Abbey. If

all his realisable assets were sold he would be left with a balance of
about £87,000, still a considerable fortune in those days, but this
could only be raised by the sale of his entire landed property,
which would include the Abbey, most of its contents and its
domain.

In a last desperate attempt to save the building upon which he
had lavished so much of his genius as well as his fortune he wrote,
in February 1821, through the medium of Franchi, to his son-in-
law (now Duke of Hamilton) proposing a scheme which he hoped
would keep his creditors at bay and at the same time secure the
Abbey for himself during his lifetime and for his descendants after
his death; this was that in exchange for an immediate advance of
£80,000 he would bequeath his entire inheritance to Hamilton
and his heirs. For some time the duke considered the plan and the
various modifications of it put forward by the lawyers, for he
wished to save the Fonthill estate if he could and had a genuine
desire to assist his father-in-law and friend, but in the end it became impossible. Too much was vague, too much left to chance,
such as the possibility of a purchaser appearing who would buy an
unprofitable Jamaican plantation at a time when sugar was being
sold in England at a sum below its cost price. The scheme was
canvassed throughout 1821 and the early months of the following
year, but by August 1822 the duke tactfully withdrew from the
negotiations. 'I wish to assist Mr. Beckford,' he wrote to the
solicitor, 'but I must say that the present proposition appears to
me to create insurmountable difficulties . . . My affection for Mr.
Beckford would lead me to make any specified and limited sacrifice that was within my power. But to engage in obligations
without knowing their extent, as a man of business you must feel
would be exposing myself and family, in transactions of so extensive a nature, to difficulties that no man can or ought to
encounter.'[8]

The Duke of Hamilton's inability, despite much good will, to
step forward like some *deus ex machina* and resolve all difficulties,
made the sale of Fonthill inevitable. Once the decision was taken
Beckford set about the task in a business-like manner and arranged
with the auctioneer Christie for the Abbey and its contents, together with the five thousand acres that surrounded it, to be
offered for sale by public auction. The announcement immediately
aroused immense interest. A catalogue was issued and in a short
space of time seventy-two thousand copies of it were sold at the

price of one guinea each.⁹ The chance to see the interior of the famous Abbey, that for so long had been forbidden to all but the most favoured few, gave rise to a positive invasion, from four to seven hundred people a day crossing its threshold, inquisitive to see with their own eyes the legendary setting in which the mysterious 'Caliph' had lived in luxurious seclusion. They were led by the Duke of Gloucester who was both nephew and son-in-law to George III, recently dead, and brother-in-law of the reigning monarch, but not notable in any other respect, as well as three more dukes, various lesser nobles, and vast numbers of the general public. Beckford fled to Bath to avoid seeing this profanation of his sanctuary, having first uttered a prayer that his patron saint, who had inspired him to build the Abbey, would arm him with supernatural courage to do without it and also, possibly, to erect yet another such monument to his glory.¹⁰

In spite of his distaste at the thought of so many curious people passing through the rooms of the Abbey and gazing open-mouthed at his treasures, he was well pleased with the interest and notoriety caused by so unusual an event. Rarely had a sale been so much publicised or attracted such widespread attention in the press. For the first weeks of September it was the great topic of conversation as more and more people applied for tickets of admission and read the list of rare and valuable items that were to come under the auctioneer's hammer. This sort of publicity was precisely what Beckford had hoped would occur, for his ambition was to attract someone with the means to purchase the entire estate intact and so prevent it from coming to auction at all. It was a bold speculation, all the more so when the price he was asking was three hundred thousand pounds, and neither his lawyer, nor Franchi, nor the Duke of Hamilton thought that he had the remotest chance of getting such a sum. The duke's agent, indeed, had considered it impossible to put a price on the Abbey at all, as stripped of its contents it might fetch no more than what the materials it was composed of would fetch in the market.¹¹

The public auction was announced for 17 September, but suddenly it was postponed until 8 October. Negotiations had been going on behind the scenes in just such a way as Beckford had hoped, and when the postponement was arranged Christie must have felt a little uneasy as to whether he would make any profit out of Fonthill above the considerable one he had already made on the sale of the catalogues. His suspicions were well grounded.

Through the agency of Phillips, the rival auctioneer, Beckford had been put in touch with a quaint and decidedly eccentric individual whom Phillips believed might buy the whole property outright. The publicity surrounding the proposed sale had resulted, it would seem, in the very effect Beckford had calculated and he had caught the fish he had been angling for. All the same, he can hardly have been much impressed when he was first introduced to John Farquhar, for despite a reputation for great wealth the prospective purchaser lived in unbelievable squalor and presented such a dirty and unkempt appearance that Beckford promptly nicknamed him as 'Old Filthyman' in his correspondence with Franchi.

Farquhar's appearance was so unprepossessing that when he first came down to view the property Franchi (as he confessed in a letter to the Duke of Hamilton) took him for a member of the lower orders. But in spite of his grubby aspect and the dirty state of his rooms in Baker Street, he was quite able to produce the sum of money that Beckford was asking. As a young man he had gone out to India and had set himself up as a merchant in Bengal after a brief service in the army of the East India Company. His fortune, which was said to have amounted to half a million pounds when he came home, was made by selling gunpowder to his former military employers, and since returning to England he had augmented it considerably by speculating in the Funds. He had never married, lived a miserly existence, and was over seventy years of age when some curious whim decided him to become master of Fonthill Abbey.

The business was quickly transacted. Farquhar saw the Abbey and its grounds on 27 September and the agreement to purchase it was reached on 5 October, the day Christie's 'view' of the premises came to an end. Three days later the agreement was signed and Farquhar handed over a deposit of ten thousand pounds; the very day upon which the unfortunate Christie had hoped to preside over the opening of a highly profitable auction. Farquhar paid £275,000 for the Abbey and a further £25,000 for the contents save for those, including a third of all books, manuscripts, prints and drawings, that Beckford had reserved for himself, and some pictures which had already been removed to Bath, making the total of three hundred thousand pounds which Beckford had all along decided was his price. Neither Franchi nor the Duke of Hamilton had been aware of what was going on in these secret negotiations until the deal was more or less completed. Their surprise was mutual. 'If I ever see M. de Beckford on a path that is *not tortuous*,' the former wrote to the duke, 'I shall be astonished; and still more so if I ever see him on what could be called a straight one.'[12]

Farquhar must have looked upon his purchase of Fonthill as something of a speculation, like so many of his financial undertakings and frequent, but often reckless, excursions into the art market, for a year later he himself put most of the contents of the Abbey up for sale. This was the occasion when Hazlitt saw some of the inferior pictures and bric-à-brac introduced by the auctioneer Phillips under the impression that it was all part of the Beckford collection, and penned his bitter and biased attack. Beckford's own opinion of this sale (at which he is said to have bought back some items at less than Farquhar had paid him for them) was summed up in a remark he later made to Cyrus Redding: 'Do not suppose that more than half of what was sold at Fonthill was mine. I disposed of my superfluous furniture, for which I had no use, and also of some costly things, not of much utility—suitable there only. I would not disgrace my house with Chinese furniture—that was not mine—it was put in by the auctioneer. Horace Walpole would not have suffered it in his toyshop at Strawberry Hill.'[13] The reference to Walpole was enough to indicate Beckford's contempt.

When all the business of selling Fonthill was settled and over Beckford wrote in the course of a letter to his old friend Dr. Schöll in Geneva: 'Let me announce a great piece of news: Fonthill is sold very advantageously. I am rid of the Holy Sepulchre, which no longer interested me since its profanation; I am delivered of a burden and of a long string of insupportable expenses. At present I have only to distribute my funds prudently and await the outcome of events. For twenty years I have not found myself so rich, so independent or so tranquil.'[14] This was now to be his official attitude to the sale of Fonthill Abbey, coupled sometimes with certain disparaging remarks about the architecture. Did he design the building himself? he was once asked long after he had ceased to possess it. 'No,' he answered, 'I have sins enough to answer for, without having that laid to my charge. Wyatt had an opportunity of raising a splendid monument to his fame, but he missed it.'[15]

Beckford was, in fact, probably glad enough to leave Fonthill

Abbey by the time he was compelled to sell it, and the fact that he was able to secure such a satisfactory price enabled him to do so without the loss of face that would have been inevitable had it gone for less. His disenchantment probably began after Wyatt's tragic death as the result of a carriage accident in 1813, for despite all the frustrations he had had to endure from his architect's neglect, he had obviously found their relationship a stimulating one, and for all the unkind remarks made later at Wyatt's expense Fonthill Abbey represented a genuine partnership between the two of them. The architect's sons Philip and Benjamin had carried on their father's work, but it was not the same. Without 'Bagasse' to harry and coax Beckford's enthusiasm began to dwindle and all the faults, bunglings and inconveniences of the vast building seemed to assume a more menacing and irritating aspect.

Of these imperfections there were many; more than enough to exasperate a less patient man than Beckford. Repair-work and re-building was constantly necessary. In 1814 Franchi reported to the Duke of Hamilton that the walls of the Fountain Court were having to be rebuilt in stone, the chimney flues changed, and 'a thousand other errors' attended to, and that the work had been going on for two years;[16] five years later Beckford complained that the tower which housed his bedroom suite was in a state of collapse.[17] Dampness in the Lancaster Gallery was so bad that the cabinets and showcases it contained were found 'all covered with lichen and stalactites like Fingal's cave' and the lacquer festooned with a white beard, while the tower swayed so ominously in a storm that the dwarf ran out of the house in terror and Beckford himself declared that the place made his flesh creep.[18] In winter, what with the cold, the damp and the exposure to wind the place became almost impossible for anyone to live in. 'Really,' Beckford exclaimed after a stormy night in November 1815, 'this habitation is deathly in the stormy season—this morning I'm more yellow, rent and wretched than a dry leaf.'[19]

Such were some of the vicissitudes of life at Fonthill. A younger man could take it all in his stride, no doubt, but though Beckford had boasted in 1821 that his strength was undiminished, declaring boldly, 'I preserve the same vigour, the same terrible energy and the same *detestations*—I despise fools and faineants of whatever nationality, titled or untitled, as I have always despised them—and perhaps even with redoubled vigour!',[20] the fact remained that he had now passed his sixtieth birthday, and though his health was in general good the list of minor ailments he suffered from grew longer with the years. But the chief complaint that afflicted him at Fonthill attacked not his body but his mind, and that was boredom. The very vastness of the Abbey seemed to emphasise the solitariness of the individual who inhabited it, and it was only in London or in Paris that his old vivaciousness seemed to return to him.

He once told Cyrus Redding that he had never felt a moment's ennui in his life, but that was after he had left Fonthill for the more gregarious atmosphere of Bath, when he had a house in London again and felt himself once more in the swim of life. As long as the walls of the Abbey were rising, new wings being built or additional turrets variegating the roof line, his mind was occupied and his energy employed and he could afford to despise life beyond the barrier wall and cry, 'Blessed Abbey, save and defend me from such riff-raff and such riff-raffery as this.'[21] But with Wyatt gone and the Abbey finished (or as finished as he cared to make it) the threat of boredom grew and the consciousness of his loneliness deepened. The Abbey, which had once symbolised his defiance of the world, was becoming more and more of a monument to the world's rejection of him. Only occasionally did his pride allow him to admit the true state of his feelings when fits of depression descended on him, and it was then that the desire to flee from the Abbey took possession of him. On one such occasion he wrote to Franchi: 'No one who does not understand my strange composition can guess what is passing within me at this time. It isn't living, but languishing suspended between life and death with bowed head . . .'[22] It was from states of mind such as this that he fled with a sigh of relief when the ownership of Fonthill Abbey passed out of his hands.

Beckford's manner of leaving Fonthill was characteristically eccentric. He had moved back into the Abbey after the hullabaloo of the public 'view' and the sale was over and resumed his habitual routine there. On the morning when he was due to leave he rose at his usual hour and after breakfasting ordered the pony to be saddled for his ride. He then sent for his gardener and rode with him round the estate, ordering an improvement here, an alteration there, just as though it was a day like all the others that had gone before it. He then returned to the house, entered his carriage, and drove away without a word in the direction of Bath.

25
Bath

As BECKFORD'S CARRIAGE trundled him towards Bath after the sale of the Fonthill estate in the autumn of 1822 he could once more think of himself as a rich man. No longer a millionaire, of course, but now clear of debts and with a substantial sum of money left over to invest in a new home from where he could continue his agreeable existence as collector, dilettante and (as he had now almost become) professional eccentric. The building of Fonthill Abbey, as he once told Redding, had cost him, spread over sixteen or eighteen years, the sum of two hundred and seventy-three thousand pounds and 'some odd hundreds'.[1] He had just sold it for three hundred thousand; that in itself was a comfortable thought. As he had confided to Schöll, he had not for a very long time felt *'si riche, si indépendant ni si tranquille'*.

It is not immediately clear why he should have chosen Bath as his place of residence. An earlier impression of the town, written only six years previously, had been decidedly unfavourable. 'But Bath does not please me', he had then written. 'After the great spectacle of the Abbey it seems to me incredibly dingy and wretched; and the infamous old men and youths carried in chairs and mechanical carriages round the smoking baths horrify me—a horror not softened by the tender glances of certain old women clad in flounces supremely *à la mode*, who come and go eternally in this paradise of idlers and corpses.'[2] He had, however, known it all his life and it had the advantage of familiarity. Furthermore, in the past year he had spent a good deal of time there while Fonthill Abbey had been thrown open to the public, and this closer contact may have helped to change his opinion of the town. He was certainly tired of the solitude and isolation of Fonthill. Salisbury, another possible choice, was too dominated by the bishop and the cathedral chapter, who had always treated him coldly and would

only have exacerbated his profound dislike of the clergy; nor had
he much admiration for the cathedral itself where Wyatt's restoration work was 'infamous' and the building recalled to him 'the
disgust and stink of Protestantism' which, in his estimation, did
not deserve 'the sonorous name of Heresy'.[3] In Bath he would be
surrounded by squares and crescents of classical elegance and
would have easy access to a sylvan and undulating countryside.

Beckford set himself up temporarily in Pultney Street while he
looked about for more permanent quarters. At first he had hoped
to buy Prior Park, the great Palladian mansion built by Ralph
Allen on the outskirts of the town, but the price asked was too
high. 'I should have liked it very much,' he commented regret-
fully, 'it possesses such great capability of being made a very
beautiful spot.'[4] His choice was a curious one for Prior Park was
in many ways similar in style to Fonthill Splendens, the house he
had pulled down in order to build his gothic Abbey. He considered another house in the same neighbourhood before finally
deciding to settle in Bath itself, buying first number twenty-one
Lansdown Crescent (then numbered as 1, West Wing, Lansdown
Crescent) and some time afterwards the next house, number
twenty. Though forming part of the gracious curve of the crescent
the two houses were separated by a roadway that led to the
mews and gardens behind, so Beckford threw an elegant bridge
across the opening to join them together. Later on, when he sold
number twenty-one, he retained the bridge but covered the far
end with looking-glass so as to retain the illusion of space. From
the windows of his drawing-room on the first floor he could look
right across the town of Bath to where Prior Park stood on the
wooded hill opposite, a view, one may suppose, that reminded
him more of the Splendens of his youth than of the purchase he
had so recently failed to achieve.

The advent of so interesting a personage as William Beckford
in Bath caused something of a flutter in a town where the fashionable invalids, assembled in the Pump Room, had little more to do
between their unpalatable therapeutic potations than indulge in
the enjoyable and refreshing pastime of disseminating gossip.
Despite his sixty-two years Beckford was still credited with all his
old unproven vices and a good many more besides. His servants,
it was averred, went in fear of him and trembled at his fits of
passion which were said to be like tempests of madness; nor were
they allowed to look at him but must hide or turn away when he

passed them by. But what could one expect, when all was said and done, of a man whose house was full of dwarfs and who had constructed a bridge between his two houses for their occupation? The legend of his wealth, too, survived all the rumours of financial difficulties at Fonthill; his income, it was solemnly declared, amounted to no less than a guinea a minute, and his fastidiousness was such that he would handle no coins until they had first been washed. Faint echoes of distant scandals, augmented by the newcomer's known authorship of *Vathek* and growing self-identification with the character of the Caliph, revived old stories of oriental orgies and exotic Eastern rites. These and other tales were exchanged over the cooling glasses of spa water with an excited thrill of horror not unmixed with a certain pride that so singular an individual had selected Bath as the scene of his declining years.[5]

Beckford was by now quite indifferent to such onslaughts upon his reputation, if anything he sought to encourage the sense of mystery that surrounded him, and though his household only accommodated a single dwarf his master made the most of the situation. 'He is a Giaour,' he told one inquisitive visitor, 'and feeds upon toadstools.' The dwarf had, by now, become something of a privileged servant and his duties appear to have been light. When Sir Jerom Murch, who had the distinction of being seven times Mayor of Bath, called at Lansdown Crescent he found the odd creature grandly installed in a chair in the hall. 'The visitors were admitted by the hall porter and passed on to a servant in the interior,' he recalled, 'while this wretched looking object sat in his armchair grinning.'[6]

Beckford was, as it happens, a good and humane employer by the standards of his day, a fact that is verified by the testimony of Cyrus Redding. 'He did not like to part with his domestics,' Redding affirmed, 'he boasted of his trust in them; they had been with him many years. Some had been born from domestics of his father, and he had had three generations of one or two in his establishment.'[7] There were occasions when he vented his rage on them, but even this had its advantages, for afterwards he would be overcome with remorse and reward the victims of his uncontrollable temper with a surreptitious guinea. They were said, indeed, sometimes to provoke his anger solely for the sake of the subsequent recompense. His years in Bath were, in fact, to see him gain a belated mastery over this unpleasant fault. 'Mr. Beckford's character underwent a great change after he came to reside in Bath', his architect Goodridge recorded. 'His paroxysms of passion, when first I knew him, were most fearful; but in his latter years he had obtained a wonderful mastery over himself, and which was seldom broken through. He used to say that he could not now afford it.'[8]

If his temper improved, his impatience did not. He still expected to see his wishes fulfilled with a minimum of delay and became strident and unreasonable when frustrated. 'Upon my word, I can bear the state of suspense no longer', he would fulminate at his agent in London when waiting to hear of the purchase of some work of art, or again: 'Suspense of any kind I detest.' The unfortunate agent would be subjected to peremptory attack at the slightest hint of delay. 'I beg a decisive answer immediately', he would be told. 'Keeping me under a cloud of uncertainty is, as you are well aware, high treason to all my habits and feelings; nothing can be more repugnant to my wishes.'[9] The passage of time made no difference to this incurable foible. 'What! not a line! not a word about the Edinburgh sale?' he wrote at the age of eighty-two. 'Where are the Flamens? the Grimaldis, the etc., etc., etceteras? All the echoes of Lansdown are repeating, Where? Where?'[10]

After some years in his two houses in Lansdown Crescent Beckford bought a third, the house adjoining number twenty. The reason he gave for purchasing a third house was characteristic of his large ideas and of his desire for independence and seclusion. 'Had I not bought this house,' he declared, 'I should have been perpetually annoyed by the ticking of some cursed jack, the jingling of some beastly piano, horrid-toned bells tinkling, and so on. The only way to avoid this was by buying the house; and so I bought it, to the infinite annoyance of the Bath aristocracy, an odd breed I believe.'[11] For a while he occupied all three houses, and was able to create there the effect of a long vista which he had always admired, and which was seen by Sir Jerom Murch when he paid one of his visits. 'He made openings in the walls of the drawing-room storey,' Sir Jerom recorded, 'which showed a fine vista extending the entire length of the three houses and the arch. The grandeur of these rooms, quiet as it was, contrasted with the simplicity of the others for his private use, especially his bedroom, with its little narrow uncurtained bed, reminding one of the Duke of Wellington's answer at Apsley House with regard to his own;

L

on hearing the remark that there was no room to turn, he said,
"Turn, turn, when one wants to turn, it is time to turn out." '12
It was when he sold the end house, about the year 1832, that he
preserved the vista effect by covering the end wall with mirror
glass.

Beckford's true reason for purchasing number nineteen was
probably because he had already decided to sell number twenty-
one, the house on the far side of the dividing lane. The newly
acquired house was not for long left empty as a somewhat expensive sound-barrier, but was soon fitted out in the grand style he
preferred, with a charming library on the ground floor and the
staircase leading up to the first floor roofed over with a barrel-
vaulted ceiling. This, he maintained, was to protect him from the
draught, but it was also no doubt this quaint but architecturally
effective idea that gave rise to the rumour that his servants were
not permitted to look at him, and that he liked to pass up and
down stairs unobserved. The houses were furnished in the boldly
colourful style he had previously used at Splendens and Fonthill
Abbey, with scarlet and purple draperies predominating. The
sight of the dining-room, when first seen by the German art
critic Gustav Friedrich Waagen, produced in that otherwise sober
scholar a positive explosion of enthusiasm. 'I shall never forget
the dining-room,' he wrote, 'which, taken all in all, is perhaps one
of the most beautiful in the world. Conceive a moderate apartment of agreeable proportions, whose walls are adorned with
cabinet pictures, the noblest productions of Italian art of the time
of Raphael, from the windows of which you overlook the whole
paradisaical valley of the Avon, with the city of Bath, which was
now steeped in sunshine. Conceive in it a company of men of
genius and talent, between the number of the Graces and Muses,
whose spirits are duly raised by the choicest viands, in the preparation of which the refined culinary art of our days has displayed its
utmost skill, by a selection of wines, such as nature and human
care produce only on the most favoured spots of the earth, in the
most favourable years, and you will agree with me that many
things here meet in a culminating point, which, even singly, are
calculated to rejoice the heart of man.'13

Beckford lacked two things in Bath that he had long been
accustomed to, a tower and an extensive garden, but he was not
destined to be long without either of them. Lansdown Crescent
was then on the perimeter of the town with fields and farm land

reaching almost to the garden walls. Within a year of settling there he began to purchase tracts of land extending from the back of his house to the top of Lansdown Hill, about a mile's distance away and rising eight hundred feet above sea level. On this vantage point, commanding splendid views of the surrounding countryside and of the Bristol channel, he planned to raise to St. Antony that other monument to his glory that he had promised himself when he had asked the saint to inspire him with supernatural courage to bear the pain of parting from Fonthill. A tower of some sort or other was, it would seem, as much a necessity to him at the age of sixty-two as it had been in his adolescent fantasies and in the soaring reality of the Abbey spire. He still must have it in his power to ascend, like the Caliph Vathek, to a place from where his mind could 'extend beyond the reach of his sight, and extort from the stars the decrees of his destiny'.

He chose as his architect Henry Edmund Goodridge, a young Bath man still in his twenties, the son of a successful builder, who had already done a certain amount of work in Bathwick and in the town of Bath itself but who was otherwise largely unknown. After the battles with James Wyatt, Beckford probably wanted a young man who would show less independence and whose local connection would make him more readily available to fulfil his patron's demands. As with the original conception of the convent on Stop's Beacon the new tower was not intended as a residence, but was to be a retreat for study or pleasure with sufficient room to accommodate a portion of his library and to house a selection of his works of art. There was to be a small Italianate pavilion on two floors, built in the local stone, with a tower rising to the height of 154 feet which owed more to the style of the Greek revival, being crowned by a lantern of cast-iron and wood modelled on the Choragic monument of Lysicrates in Athens. Below the lantern was a belvedere with three plate glass windows in each of the four walls from where Beckford could enjoy what he considered, with some justification, to be 'the finest prospect in Europe', a fact that he claimed reconciled him to the loss of his other tower and its surroundings of 'almost Oriental beauty'.[14]

Beckford had turned his back completely on the gothic style. To construct anything in gothic after Fonthill Abbey would, to say the least, have been something of an anticlimax, and to create a sort of miniature Abbey after parting from the splendours of the original was obviously out of the question. He had, in fact, never considered himself as a special champion of the gothic revival; his reasons for employing it at Fonthill had been peculiar to the requirements of the building itself, as he had himself made clear when answering certain criticisms brought against his choice of architecture by Thomas Hope. For much the same reason he felt no need to justify the use of classical models on this occasion, nor did he ever do so. All he had to say upon the subject of building a new tower was that he wished to have something more than a study on the top of Lansdown Hill where the view was so extensive, and so: 'I erected the tower, or else, as you know, I should see nothing.'

The Lansdown Tower was completed within five years of Beckford's arrival in Bath and is one of the very few of his architectural creations to have survived, at least in its external form, to the present day. The central body of the building, which is of two storeys, is flanked by the tower on one side and by a single-storey wing or annex on the other, so that despite the classical treatment of the elevation the building has an irregular 'romantic' sky-line. The roof is concealed by a stone parapet pierced at intervals by balustrading, and the windows, with their gilt lattice, contrive to introduce a slightly bizarre oriental note. Despite this typically Beckfordian touch the general impression made by the Lansdown Tower is one of classical order and proportion in contrast to the wild profligacy of Fonthill Abbey. It is the perfect setting for the scholarly pursuits of a serene old age.

The tower and single-storey wing project slightly from the front elevation and are joined on the ground floor by an open loggia through which the building is entered. Inside, the visitor found himself in a vaulted corridor with an opening to the tower staircase on the right and to the wing, which contained a bedroom and kitchen, on the left. Directly opposite the front entrance was a door leading to the Scarlet Drawing Room, the largest room in the tower but modest in comparison with the rooms in Lansdown Crescent or with the vast spaces of Fonthill, the end wall of which opened into an apse pierced by three of the gold latticed windows. This room could also be approached by another door from the vaulted corridor which opened into a narrow vestibule or ante-room. The first floor was reached by the same spiral staircase that ascended to the belvedere at the top of the tower. Here was to be found the Crimson Drawing Room and two rooms devoted to

Beckford's collection of books, the Small Library and the Etruscan Library, which were directly over the loggia and the vaulted
corridor. Next to the Crimson Drawing Room, and entered from
a door at the head of the staircase or from the drawing-room itself, was the Sanctuary, a narrow passage-like room with no
windows but lighted from above by glass-covered openings in the
saucer domes at each end of the barrel-vaulted ceiling. At the far
end, illuminated by the shafts of light that filtered down from the
shallow dome, stood the statue of St. Antony of Padua which had
once caught the eye at the far northern extremity of the great
vista of galleries at Fonthill Abbey.

The reader will have noticed that once again Beckford's preference for brilliant reds and crimsons predominated. The general
effect produced by surviving pictures of the interior of Lansdown
Tower almost suggest the somewhat heavy, over-furnished style
of the Victorians, an epoch still almost twenty years ahead, rather
than the delicate elegance of the reign of George IV, though this
was due partly to the smaller rooms and lower ceilings which
made the furniture look proportionally larger and heavier. Many
of Beckford's greatest treasures found their home in the tower. It
was here that Waagen saw works by Claude Lorrain, Paul Brill
(appropriately a Tower of Babel), Johann Breughel, Perugino (a
Madonna and Child with St. John), Polemburg (a Repose in
Egypt) and Giovanni Bellini's two portraits of the Doges Ven-
dramin and Loredan as well as many other works of art;[15] while
H. V. Lansdown recorded seeing others by Francesco Mola,
Parmigiano, Murillo and Canaletto. Of his first impression of the
building this young artist wrote: 'Who but a man of extraordinary genius would have thought of rearing in the desert such
a structure as this, or creating such an oasis ? The colouring of the
building reminded me of Malta or Sicily, a rich mellow hue prevails; the ornaments of the Tower are so clean, so distinct, such
terseness. The windows, small and few compared with modern
buildings, give it the appearance of those early Florentine edifices
reared when security and defence were as much an object as
beauty.'[16]

While work was still in progress on the building of the Lansdown Tower alarming news was brought to Beckford's notice
about the dangerous state of his former great tower at Fonthill.
He received an urgent summons to visit Wyatt's old clerk of
works who was seriously ill and not considered likely to recover.

Beckford hurried to see the stricken man, and in a death-bed confession was told that the tower rested only upon the flimsy
foundations laid for the earlier structure of wood and compo-
cement. It had been intended to build a relieving arch into the
foundations to carry the weight of the new stone tower, so much
higher and heavier than its predecessor, but this essential work,
as the dying man now admitted, had never been done, and the
tower might collapse at any moment. Beckford was horrified at
the news and hurried to inform Mr. Farquhar, but the old man received it with a surprising calmness, declaring that the tower
would at least outlast him.

Farquhar, alas, was soon to be proved mistaken in his sanguine
estimate. On 21 December 1825, he was sitting on the lawn in
front of the Abbey when ominous cracks were observed in the
tower walls. Being himself in fragile health he was quickly carried
inside in his chair, protesting still that there was no danger,
when the three-hundred-foot tower suddenly collapsed in upon
itself. 'It first sank perpendicularly and slowly,' declared an eye
witness, 'and then burst and spread over the roofs of the adjoining
wings on every side, but rather more on the south-west than on
the others. The cloud of dust which arose was enormous, and
such as completely to darken the air for a considerable distance
around for several minutes. Such was the concussion in the interior of the building, that one man was forced along a passage,
as if he had been in an air-gun, to the distance of 30ft., among
dust so thick as to be felt. Another, on the outside, was in the like
manner carried to some distance. Fortunately no one was
seriously injured.' Strangely enough Farquhar, who was in a remote corner of the building, heard nothing and only realised
what had happened when he saw the villagers running up to see
the ruins. Both new and old owner reacted to the disaster in a
manner more characteristic of the eighteenth century in which
they had been born than of the nineteenth into which they had
survived. Farquhar's comment was: 'Now the house is not too
big for me to live in', while Beckford simply remarked that the
tower had made an obeisance to Mr. Farquhar which it had never
made to him.[17]

The falling masonry did considerable damage, destroying the
octagon, bringing down the roof and southern wall of the Great
Western Hall, levelling a section of St. Michael's Gallery and
filling the Fountain Court with debris and rubble. In the ruined

shell of the Western Hall the Alderman's statue remained in its
niche in the northern wall, surveying, as was inevitably said, the
ruins of his son's ambitions. Farquhar moved out and Fonthill
was again offered for sale, though no one had the courage or
enterprise to restore the ruined building which gradually fell into
a state of decay. Its second owner succumbed himself soon afterwards, dying from an attack of apoplexy, but before his death a
curious rumour circulated that he intended to bequeath the remains of the Abbey to its original owner with whom he had
re-established friendly relations after the fall of the tower had
brought them into contact with each other again. When asked
later whether he would have welcomed such a legacy Beckford
replied: 'Good heavens, yes. I should have been in ecstasy at it,
for it would have falsified the old proverb "You can't eat your
cake and have it too." '18

A legend claims that Beckford was able to see the tower of
Fonthill Abbey from his new tower on Lansdown Hill, and that he
was the first person in Bath to know of the disaster because, looking as was his custom in the direction of Fonthill, he saw that the
tower was no longer there. In fact in December 1825 the Lansdown Tower was still incomplete, and though Beckford was quite
likely to have scaled the scaffolding as he used to do when the
octagon of Fonthill was being built, there is no corroboration of
this romantic tale. Indeed, it is impossible to know whether the
tower had reached a sufficient height at that time for the feat to
have been possible. Beckford never made any such claim himself,
and it seems unlikely, had such an extraordinary event actually
occurred, that he would not have boasted of it.

With the land he had purchased connecting his new tower with
the houses in Lansdown Crescent Beckford was able to pass between the two places entirely on his own property, and with his
genius for landscape gardening he had soon transformed this rural
walk into a realm of surprising beauty and charm. The ascent to
the tower by this private route began just behind the crescent,
beyond the kitchen garden, which itself extended for seven or
eight acres. A massive embattled gateway, a reminder of the lost
glories of Fonthill Abbey and Beckford's last essay in the gothic
taste, guarded the southern entrance to the mile-long walk. At
places the turf-covered way narrowed to little more than a path
bordered by fruit trees or flowering shrubs, at others it opened
out into quite extensive plantations. Where shade was needed his

ingenious gardener Vincent transplanted trees that had already reached a height of twelve feet or so and established them so well that, in Beckford's words, the Bristol folk travelling along the lower road saw trees upon Lansdown Hill where none had appeared a few weeks before: 'they rub their eyes—they cannot believe their own sight—how can it be!'[19] Such feats delighted him and helped to confirm him in his self-identification with the Caliph to whom such miracles were commonplace. Thus, when the walk up to the tower had to cross a public footpath he tunnelled under it and made the subterranean passage into a grotto, while an old quarry was so transformed as to remind one impressionable visitor of the Roman campagna or the ruins of the baths of Caracalla.

With his love of the exotic Beckford introduced many rare specimens of tree and shrub into this secluded domain. 'How on this happy spot specimens of the productions of every country in the world unite!' wrote the enthusiastic Howard Lansdown. 'Shrubs and trees, whose natural climates are as opposite as the Antipodes, here flourish in the most astonishing manner. We were shown a rose tree brought from Pekin and a fir tree brought from the highest part of the Himalaya Mountains . . . Here are prime trees of every species and variety—a tree that once vegetated at Larissa, in Greece, Italian pines, Siberian pines, Scotch firs, a lovely specimen of Irish yew, and other trees which it is impossible to describe.'[20] The extraordinary effect produced in so short a time reflects not only Beckford's skill and enthusiasm, but the understanding relationship that existed between him and his head gardener Vincent, a man almost his own age who had been in his employment for the greater part of his life.

Yet even Vincent, who was accustomed to talk with his master as man to man, was occasionally the victim of his ungovernable temper, and an astonished visitor once saw him rushing for shelter among some young trees to escape from the blows of his enraged master's cane. 'It was a curious thing to see two persons both beyond seventy pursued and pursuing', the witness recalled. 'It came to nothing more than a short race, Vincent dodged among the trees and his master, recollecting himself, ceased the pursuit. The next morning he sent five pounds to Vincent, who said he should like to race every day upon the same terms.'[21] Despite such unseemly outbursts it was a relationship of mutual respect and trust, and when Beckford died it was observed that no one was more moved by emotion at his funeral than this old retainer.

In 1826, after the fall of the Abbey tower and before the new tower on Lansdown Hill was ready for occupation, the urge to travel suddenly returned and Beckford decided that he would like to see Rome again. His habitual impatience with all building work may have contributed to this decision. They could get on with the job in his absence and he would return from his travels to find the new tower all ready and waiting for him. Tremendous preparations were made for the journey, travelling carriages ordered, every conceivable necessity packed, the servants equipped with new liveries. As in the old days before the Revolution and Napoleonic wars had changed the face of Europe, he intended to travel *en prince*.

In August the procession set out with Beckford, very much the Caliph, riding at its head. August, however, is not the best time of the year for travelling, even in England. It was an unusually sultry day, the sun shone relentlessly, the heat became intolerable. By the time they had reached Marlborough, where they intended to put up for the night, Beckford's nerves were on edge, his temper flared up, and he retired to bed in a rage. Next day he had a fever, but insisted upon continuing his journey to London. Once arrived there Franchi came round from his house in Harley Street to find his patron in bed, the servants trembling and everything in confusion. What was to be done? The following day, however, showed some improvement; Beckford got up and went round to Franchi's house where he imprudently demonstrated his returned vitality by leaping about the place like a young man, but to such effect that a sleepless night followed and he rose the next morning feeling every day of his sixty-five years. The whole expedition was called off and he returned to Bath by easy stages. It was his first concession to the inexorable encroachment of old age.

26

The Aging Egotist

AFTER THE SAD COLLAPSE of his plans to visit Italy Beckford settled down once again to his accustomed routine and made no further attempts to travel abroad. Though his declining years never quite achieved that serenity for which he had created so ideal a setting, he did manage, during his years at Bath, to appear a little less of a recluse, though still retaining a cold aloofness in the face of his critics. 'No one was so inaccessible to strangers or so difficult to become acquainted with, unless they were connected with literature or art', Redding declared,[1] which was another way of saying that 'society' had not lifted its ban against him, but to a younger generation of writers and artists he was becoming a figure of legendary fascination and curiosity.

He was a familiar figure in the streets and particularly in the bookshops of Bath. Small of stature, slim, with the trim figure of a young man and bright steel-grey eyes, only his features showed any sign of age where the hair was now white and loss of teeth had made the mouth sink a little so that the aggressive chin and sharp pointed nose looked more prominent than ever. He still dressed in the manner of a country squire and in the fashion of the regency: white neckcloth, green tail coat, buff-coloured waistcoat, knee-breeches and brown top boots. When he went out riding he was attended by a small retinue; first rode the steward of his household, then two mounted grooms carrying long whips and after them, followed by two or three favourite dogs, came Beckford himself mounted on a grey Arab. Two more grooms closed the little procession.

In the summer of 1828 Beckford received a letter from Robert Hume, who acted as his agent in many of the art purchases he undertook in London. The letter was dated the first of August and contained alarming news about Franchi. Hume had not seen the now ailing Portuguese for a fortnight or so, but calling that morning had, to his great concern, found Beckford's old friend 'on the verge of dissolution', having not slept for fifteen days. 'I remained with him nearly two hours endeavouring to sooth and cheer him', Hume wrote. 'He thinks he shall never get up again and from the whole circumstances and appearances I think so too. I waited to see the Physician . . . who told me he could do nothing more for him but that it was possible that he might rally for a time but that was more than could be expected. The Doctor thinks something in particular is on his mind as the Medicins do not take effect. He is occasionally deaf, lost and sinking, and seems almost gone off. He then revives a little and will converse for some minutes when he again sinks and has not power to give utterance to his thoughts. I told him as he was so incapable of writing that I would write to let you know his present state which is most pain-fully affecting and momentous. He thanked me and begged I would do so . . . He is reduced astonishingly and his case seems hopeless.'[2]

Another letter arrived the following day with further distressing details of the sick man's plight: 'I was again with poor Franchi last night . . . *His mind* is most seriously oppressed. I have no doubt he is without money from some phrensied ejaculations that escaped him such as "Money for my Doctor. O dear, it will kill me" and other somewhat similar, and upon enquiring of his man he told me he thought he had only a few pounds left and that several bills had been sent to him that he could not pay . . . The incapability of meeting claims seems to be hastening him to his grave . . . I shall be most happy in case he holds out to have your acquiescence in proposing him some little aid in this most grievously anxious moment as the Dr. says medicins are useless where the mind is disordered.'[3]

Was it only the need for money that gave rise to these piteous cries in the dying man's few lucid moments? What else lay on the conscience of this former chorister whose life had been spent for so many years in the service of Beckford's bizarre and aberrant tastes? Did memories of his Catholic upbringing stir somewhere in his troubled mind or did he dwell on those carefree days in Portugal when he had first encountered this exotic friend who represented liberation and freedom from the trammels of family, convention and faith, days long past and for ever lost? All we can say is that Beckford, and Beckford only could have brought him comfort and help at this moment, if only in the form of a discharge from his financial worries or a few words spoken in his native language of affection and courage. But Beckford did nothing. His reply to Hume's letter was such as a man might write upon hearing of the illness of an acquaintance or of a servant deserving of some slight show of respect. 'Your communications respecting Franchi have filled me with the deepest sorrow,' he answered, 'all I can do is write to express what I feel ... God send he may be still preserved to us. Assure him of my warmest and best regards—it is in vain to hope from bodily medicines, but the mind—that extraordinary and susceptible mind he is gifted with—may still work miracles. I have just heard from the Duchess who not having received any intelligence of Franchi since the 20th. ult. is in a state of the most painful anxiety concerning him—the Duke the same. Franchi may rest assured of the intense affectionate interest we take in him.'[4]

There was so much more that Beckford could have done than merely write to express what he felt that one instinctively recoils from his apparent lack of concern. In 1817 he had written to Franchi: 'My dear Gregory, be persuaded that you have in me a friend who interests himself with all his heart in every step of yours in this sad life. Nothing that you suffer or enjoy is a matter of indifference to me.'[5] Now, as his friend lay dying in great mental and physical agony, he did not bother to stir from the comfort of Lansdown Crescent or even address a line personally to the man whom he had once held in the closest affection and who had given him a lifetime of loyal friendship. Franchi died on 29 August without seeing Beckford or receiving any message from him except for what Hume may have passed on to him at second hand. Neither Beckford nor any of his family attended the funeral; it was left to the Duchess of Hamilton to pay for the tombstone. Beckford's chief concern, indeed, as a later note from Hume shows, was to make sure that all his letters to Franchi were secured and returned to him before they could fall into other hands.

Like many people who have never suffered from real ill health, Beckford had an impatience and lack of sympathy with the sufferings of others. For some years now Franchi, a victim to rheumatism, arthritis and gout, had been living on his own in London, but there had been no break in their affectionate relations. Beckford's discreditable behaviour at the time of his friend's death emphasises perhaps more than any other event in his life his complete selfishness and his lack of any genuinely deep feelings for other people. Though now upon the threshold of old age he was still as emotionally immature as he had been when a young man; if he could manage to avoid facing up to the cruel and unpleasant realities of life he would do so, at whatever cost to others.

For Beckford, as we have seen in so many instances at all periods of his life, the world of fantasy and imagination, like the world of art, had always possessed as great a reality and certitude as the world of everyday existence. His creative impulse, which sprang from this secret world of fancy, had, during the later Fonthill years, been for the most part absorbed by the problems of the building itself, its design, construction and constant modifications, though he had managed to do a certain amount of literary work as well. A translation from the Arabic called *Al Raoui*, attributed to Beckford but thought by some, like the English translation of *Vathek*, to be the work of Henley, had appeared in 1799; and in 1815 he was working on a further 'Episode' to *Vathek* centred on the Caliph's father Motassem, but as no trace of this tale survives beyond the references to it in his letters it may be presumed that it was the story he confessed to having destroyed as being too wild and improper for publication. He had also revised both the French and English texts of *Vathek* for editions which appeared in 1815 and 1816 respectively. The English text was still Henley's, for Beckford had never objected to this rendering of his original version (in the preparation of which, in fact, he had himself collaborated to a considerable extent) but only in the unauthorised manner in which it had been offered to the public in defiance of his instructions.

After moving to Bath he began once again to sort through his papers and diaries, transcribing and editing his correspondence, and showing a renewed interest in his published works. The bookseller William Clarke, 'Boletus' of Fonthill Abbey days, issued a new English edition of *Vathek* in 1823 which had considerable success with both critics and public, even William Hazlitt, making some amends for his previous misinformed strictures on the author's taste, praising its 'masterly performance' and 'extraordinary power of thought and facility of execution'. In December of the same year *Vathek* was presented as a play. 'More laurels', his agent Hume wrote from London, 'The Caliph Vathek has been received by the public with unbounded applause at the Coburg Theatre.'[6] Encouraged by these successes Beckford turned to his early *jeu d'esprit* and a second edition of the *Biographical Memoirs of Extraordinary Painters* appeared the following year. It was pleasant to enjoy a little public acclaim, and he began to reconsider again the idea he had first toyed with at Fonthill of revising the long suppressed *Dreams, Waking Thoughts and Incidents* of which now only about six copies survived after his wholesale destruction of the original edition in 1801.

His first plan had been to entrust the editing to some professional hand, but he now wisely decided to undertake the task himself. It was more a question of pruning than rewriting, of expurgating from the text those 'wayward' passages which even before public scandal had marked him down had been thought by his friends to encourage the rumours of decadence that surrounded his name. Beckford now wished to play down the image of the romantic, sensation-seeking youth guided more by emotion than reason and replace it with the picture of a young man of position and culture at home and at ease in the cosmopolitan world of the *ancien régime*. The opening paragraph beginning, 'Shall I tell you my dreams?' disappeared and, taking his reader directly to Ostend, he began his new version with the more prosaic statement: 'We had a rough passage and arrived at this imperial haven in a piteous condition', a change characteristic of his treatment of the original text throughout this revision.

The incidents remain, many of the dreams and waking thoughts were banished. Thus, when he found himself in Padua at the shrine of his patron saint, after the emotional storms surrounding his stay in Venice, the reader is spared the knowledge that he 'fell down on the steps before the shrine' in the company of other melancholy sinners, nor is he told that while at Mantua the sensitive young author 'gathered a tuberose that sprung from a shell of white marble . . . and carrying it home, shut myself up for the rest of the night, inhaled its perfume, and fell a dreaming'. The effect of this winnowing, which was applied drastically from beginning to end, is to tell us less about the secret life and character of the author, but the result is a better organised, more 'classical' book, with all Beckford's keen observation and vivid evocation of life and landscape as clear-cut and captivating as ever.

So much purging, however, diminished in size what was originally not a very long book, and in order to extend the work to fill the standard two volumes then required by publishers Beckford decided to include his travels in Portugal and Spain with those in Italy. The diaries he had kept in the years following his wife's death were transcribed and, once again, a careful process of editing went with it. All references to his feud with Walpole were cut and the reader, unaware of Beckford's delicate social position at the time, would have no idea that the author was not upon the most cordial footing at the Portuguese and Spanish courts. So too with his relations with Dom Pedro and Franchi and the involved emotional entanglements of Madrid; of these there is no mention. While *Dreams, Waking Thoughts and Incidents* is, if anything, improved by the cuts made for the 1834 edition, the Portuguese and Spanish diaries are infinitely reduced in interest and value. It was only after the publication of the unexpurgated *Journal of William Beckford in Portugal and Spain*[7] in 1954 that it was realised that this was one of his best and most revealing works.

The task of editing and transcribing his travel diaries occupied Beckford during the early 1830s when he had passed his seventieth birthday. When the work was completed he entrusted the business of finding a publisher to his bookseller William Clarke. The name of Richard Bentley was suggested, a leading publisher who was soon to launch *Bentley's Miscellany* upon the world and who, from his premises in New Burlington Street, could issue books bearing the impressive legend, 'Publisher in Ordinary to His Majesty'. Bentley was at once interested in the work while Beckford adopted his usual attitude of lofty detachment: 'Upon the subject of publication I am as cool as the very freshest cucumber that ever issued from Kew.' It was Bentley who suggested that the text should be expanded, as a result of which the Portuguese and Spanish passages were added as well as the account of the visit to Aranjuez in 1795. The delicate question of payment was next raised. After some negotiations with Clarke, Bentley offered five hundred pounds. The proud author was prepared to haggle but the desire to see his book in print got the better of him; besides, as he pointed out to Clarke, 'we all run the chance of removal from this wicked world when we least expect it ... *now* is the propitious time—*now* shines the favouring star.'[8] Bentley's 'paltry' offer was accepted.

Italy, with Sketches of Spain and Portugal was published in two volumes in 1834. On the title page it was described as being 'by the author of Vathek' from which some have inferred that it was still considered imprudent to give the author's name, though in fact Bentley was only following the usual practice of the day. The work was an instant success at home, in America and on the

continent, and before the year was out a second edition was
called for. Gratifying letters of appreciation reached the author in
his retreat at Lansdown. Talleyrand, in his last year as King
Louis-Philippe's ambassador in London, had declared that the
proper title for it was simply 'The Book', while an unidentified
countess compared it, more strangely, with *Robinson Crusoe*. When
Beckford was told of the comparison he was delighted 'beyond
expression, beyond idea'. 'What!' he wrote to Clarke, 'is Defoe to
be thrown down too, as well as Walpole, Gray, Byron, etc.? O
glorious me! O fortunate Beloved!'[9] More solemn and sobering
than these flowery tributes were the words of John Gibson
Lockhart whose flattering notice appeared in the *Quarterly Review*
for June that year. 'We risk nothing in predicting', he wrote,
'that Mr. Beckford's Travels will henceforth be classed among the
most elegant productions of modern literature . . . and will keep
his name alive, centuries after all the brass and marble he ever
piled together have ceased to vibrate with the echoes of *Modenhas*.'

Not surprisingly Beckford basked in this late-flowering success
and was eager for more. What other manuscripts, what other
accounts of travels or adventure had he locked away in the recesses of 'Lansdown Baghdad' as he called his house in Bath?
Searching through his papers he came across the brief notes he had
jotted down of the visit to the monasteries of Alcobaça and
Batalha that he had made forty years before in the June of 1794.
As he turned over the closely-written pages with their erasures
and interpolations a flood of memories surged up in his mind recalling, even in detail, the happenings of that distant summer. 'I
invoked the powers of memory,' he was to write, 'and behold, up
rose the whole series of recollections . . .' Though the account he
began to commit to paper was based, and often closely based,
upon the notes he had made at the time of his visit to the monasteries, it was very much an original work that he now produced
in which imagination and memory are woven in and out of the
contemporary fragment, now stating facts, now allowing fancy to
play its part; here adding a character or an incident, there introducing reflections drawn from the experience of old age. The
result was a complete work of art, the most unflawed and brilliant
product of his pen.

We have already followed Beckford on this excursion to the
Portuguese monasteries and noted some of the discrepancies between the events recorded in his contemporary diary and the

account he published so long afterwards, not least the addition of the wholly fictional twelfth day recording his audience with the Regent. To these must be added the sombre tale of the 'tall, majestic, deadly-pale old man' who wandered through the moonlit gardens of Batalha calling down judgement and woe upon Portugal, and the altogether different, light-hearted and amusing encounter with the Bird-Queen on the return journey, when the scarcely maintained decorum in the presence of this strange old lady and her ancient attendants was shattered by Franchi's sudden imitation of the cuckoo. Though neither event is recorded in Beckford's diary the former, at least, may well have occurred during his stay at Batalha. An experience that made his hair stand on end and feel as though a spirit was about to pass before him would not easily be forgotten, and it has been pointed out that a person similar to the 'spectre-like form' he claimed to have seen and heard could well have been sheltered in the monastery at the time.[10] As for the Bird-Queen, living surrounded by her richly gilded cages containing birds of 'every variety of size, song, and plumage' with her 'conclave of araras and cockatoos' and her three nephews 'as like one to the other as if they had been not only twins but triplets; all sleek and smooth, and sallow', perhaps Beckford had encountered her upon some other occasion in Portugal and had included her in his present narrative to add a note of fantasy to the story, or perhaps, like the 'gothic' tale he had introduced into his earlier travel book, this was just another of his exercises in romance, a figment of his vivid imagination.

The prevailing note struck by the *Recollections of an Excursion to the Monasteries of Alcobaça and Batalha*, which was published in the summer of 1835, is one of youthful exuberance; the eager curiosity and delight in new surroundings and sights experienced by the traveller, still in his early thirties, is quickly conveyed to the reader and remains with him to the end of the narrative. The delight and wonder at the landscape and architecture, the amusement at the behaviour of the worldly prelates and well-fed monks, 'no wretched cadets of the mortification family, but true elder sons of fat mother church', are all described with the sharp irony of a fresh young mind. Though certain darker meditations cast a fleeting shadow from time to time the general feeling is one of strong sunlight, of bright colours and of tropical luxuriance; all the more extraordinary when it is remembered that the author produced it in a matter of a few months only and at the age of seventy-four.

Some later critics have complained that the first of Beckford's travel books is too weighed down with romanticism, though this, in the opinion of Charles Whibley, was not without its compensations. 'It imparts to his travels a note of lyric jubilation hitherto unknown in English literature', he wrote in 1900. 'If his book is not good prose, it might have been admirable verse, and he who contained so many prophesies in his brain was thus an inventor of the prose poem.'[11] A similar view was expressed by Rose Macaulay writing nearly fifty years later: 'A poet, he fortunately wrote little verse: what he did write was bad . . . Beckford was not a poet in verse at all; his poetry lit his imagination and soaked his prose. He wrote of Portugal and life among the Portuguese elegantly, wittily, ironically, beautifully.'[12] Beckford's poetry, other than the satirical lines he included in his pseudonymous novels, was mostly religious and of a somewhat lugubrious character; it is indeed far from good. But in prose he always found a means of expression suitable to his theme, whether in the self-conscious romanticism of his adolescent efforts like *The Vision*; the crisp, epigrammatic style of *Vathek*; or the clear, lucid prose of his last book with its undercurrent of irony and melancholy. He always displayed the facility of a born writer, and in his last work, by adding discipline to this natural dexterity, he succeeded in producing a minor masterpiece.

While Beckford was working on these volumes which brought a refreshing and welcome addition of fame to his latter years, he was also busy on another book which showed that the old Adam was not dead. Only day when Cyrus Redding was visiting him in Lansdown Crescent he noticed a manuscript on the library table. 'That', said Beckford, 'is my *Liber Veritatis* which I thought of changing to *The Book of Folly*. I pull the peerage about sadly.'[13] What Redding saw was Beckford's revenge on the House of Lords for not being a member of it himself. It began in 1829 when he read the *Annual Peerage of the British Empire* edited by Edmund Lodge, the Norroy King of Arms, assisted by the Misses A. E. and Maria Innes. The very thought of these intrepid spinsters ('the Misses Innes of——, I recollect not of what ilk . . .') venturing into the world of heraldry and genealogy was a challenge to Beckford, and he set about the demolition of their researches with relish.

What he read confirmed his worse fears about the contemporary aristocracy. 'Our female nobility', he wrote in comment, 'have shewn themselves in repeated instances most condescendingly ready to marry any person of tolerable substance and decent or even indecent manners who might fancy they acquired a sort of éclat by marrying them. Some of these Ladies have bestowed their hands upon commoners with very uncommon names. Lady Grace Stratford, daughter of the first Earl of Aldborough of a most stupendously ancient family . . . married the Rev. Hayes Quead . . . Lady Mary Julian Maitland became the spouse of Mr. Thomas Hogg.' The sentence admirably sets the tone of all that follows. In the *Liber Veritatis*, his detailed commentary on the Misses Innes' work, all his snobbery, envy and malice are enrolled in a vituperative attack upon the lineages, real or pretended, of the recently ennobled families, especially those springing from the professional or manufacturing classes (families, in fact, very little different from his Beckford forebears) and, worst of all in his eyes, from medical practitioners, or *apothecaries* as he always calls them, finding in that word more scope for his contemptuous abuse.

No one escaped his biting jibe or sneering comment. Of his one-time friend 'Kitty' Courtenay's mother he wrote: 'The newly acknowledged Earl of Devon's Mother, Fanny Clack, owed her birth to a publican at Wallingford whose sign at least displayed the symbol of innocence, for it was the sign of the Lamb.' His former legal adviser Wildman, whom he certainly had no reason to love, was served no better: 'The daughter of the Earl of Wemyss and March chose to marry a little mean looking Mister Wildman, the son of a far meaner acting Solicitor of Lincoln's Inn, the abuser of his best client's confidence, as I know to my heavy cost.' But it was for Emma Hamilton, by this time more than ten years in her grave, the usurper of the position of his own beloved Catherine Hamilton, that he reserved his most barbed and deadly shaft: 'Happy would it be, were it possible to banish from all recollection the too seductive Enchantress Sir William Hamilton so far forgot himself as to marry, the termagant cast off mistress of his own nephew, the boon promotress of tipsy revels, the Circe, who transformed into *tame* Boars so many gallant, *wild* young officers, the prime manager of the capitulation so shamefully violated at Naples, the ready instrument of a ruthless Queen's atrocities, the Cleopatra who proved the bane of our most triumphant admiral and fixed a foul and sanguine spot upon his glorious memory.'[14]

It would be tedious to go into further details or to follow the elaborate abuse he heaped upon the family of Sir Hugh Smithson,

who was fortunate enough, by marrying the heiress of the last
Earl of Northumberland, to be himself created a duke, a crime
Beckford found unforgivable, for was not 'Duke Smithson' descended from a positive line of apothecaries? The book, which
even Beckford did not dare to publish,[15] shows him at his very
worst, arrogant, snobbish and petty-minded, and is made all the
more ridiculous by the fact that he was himself still vainly and
foolishly angling for a peerage whenever he thought the opportunity presented itself, hoping to enlist the help of the Duke of
Beaufort upon one occasion, and making his final unsuccessful
bid at the coronation of Queen Victoria. Beckford attempted to
pass off the *Liber Veritatis* as a sort of joke, but it was a joke with
a very sour taste.

In fact, for all the extraordinary creative energy he could still
show in his building operations on Lansdown Hill, in his continued collecting of works of art, and in the preparation of his last
published works, Beckford's character had not shown much development with the passing years. For all the sophistication, the
erudition, and the impressive style of life he had achieved, his
personality was still in many essentials superficial as well as immature. He remained an enigma, even to his daughter and to the
son-in-law who was also now his oldest surviving friend. The
death of Franchi, upon whom he had once lavished so many
caresses, cost him no more than a few conventional phrases of
grief. In 1836 he faced another bereavement; he lost his favourite
terrier 'Tout'. The eyes that had remained dry when Franchi died
now overflowed with tears. He buried the dog in the garden of
the Lansdown Tower, raised a stone over its grave, and announced that he would himself be buried by its side when death
claimed him. His heart and soul, he told his daughter almost a year
later, were still penetrated by the excess of sadness brought on by
the loss of this animal; he missed its delicate proportions, its
coquetry, its gentleness, the grace of all its movements which he
could no longer enjoy. Dogs, after all, make few demands and
offer unconditional devotion. That he should have been so
stricken by the death of an animal and so unmoved by the passing
of someone whom we must assume had at one time been his lover
as well as his life-long friend is a sad comment on the extent of his
selfishness and the shallowness of his human affections.

27

The Last Initiation

ONE OF THE CONSEQUENCES of the sale of Fonthill and of Beckford's move to Bath was that he was able to afford a London house again and usually contrived to visit the capital at least once a year, generally for the season. For some years he lived in Park Street, off Park Lane, a house that left something to be desired in its plumbing arrangements, or lack of them, for he usually referred to the place as 'Cesspool House' and seemed to have very little to say in its favour, for all that he continued to make use of it until 1841, when he moved to Gloucester Place, which was his London home for the last three years of his life.

It was no longer the call of duty that brought up him to London; he had resigned his seat in the House of Commons in 1820, not that he had ever been conspicuously diligent in fulfilling his parliamentary obligations, and now that he no longer owned a borough of his own there was little chance, even if he had wished it, of his being adopted as a candidate anywhere else. His time in London was now spent in more agreeable pursuits; hunting round the book and print shops, visiting picture dealers, attending the auctions of works of art, or frequenting the opera where he would follow the performance from the score and show evident signs of distress if singer or orchestra made a slip. He preferred the works of his elders or contemporaries, Sacchini, Cimarosa, Mozart; for the moderns, Weber, Meyerbeer, even the melodious Donizetti, he had little time. For exercise he would ride in the park, an elegant figure on his white Persian mare, and on his expeditions to shops and dealers it was usually his custom to walk, with his carriage following at a discreet distance. He would only make use of it if it rained or when he was so loaded down with spoils that it would be impossible to carry them all himself. When purchasing a picture he would never haggle. He knew the value of most things well enough, and would simply name his price. The dealer could take it or leave it. Usually Beckford got what he wanted.

In art shops and at private views, indeed, his reputation as a connoisseur was such that other purchasers, eager for a bargain, would attempt to eavesdrop on his conversation in the hope of obtaining a useful tip. Beckford was well aware of this and would sometimes intentionally lead them astray if he thought they needed a lesson in good manners or if the eavesdropper happened to be someone he particularly disliked. A friend, upon one such occasion, was amazed to hear him very loudly praising some worthless specimen of modern art, and could not resist asking him why he had done it when they were outside the shop. 'Didn't you see that old fool B—— standing close behind me?' Beckford replied, 'I'll take you anything he buys that trumpery, and thinks he will make a good speculation of it.'[1] Surely enough his gullible victim fell for the trick and carried off his dud picture in triumph.

Beckford could be equally, though more truthfully, outspoken at exhibitions when he questioned the attribution of some work of art displayed as being from the hand of an old master. The young artist W. P. Frith once saw him in such a mood. He had gone to Phillips's auction room in Bond Street to see a *Holy Family* reputed to be by Raphael when he observed an old gentleman briskly mounting the stairs. 'He was a short man,' Frith recalled, 'dressed in a green coat with brass buttons, leather breeches, and top-boots, and his hair was powdered.' On being told that the man was Beckford, Frith, who had just read *Vathek*, followed him into the gallery and stood nearby. 'I stood close to the picture,' his account continues, 'and studied Mr. Beckford who proceeded to criticise the work in language of which my respectable pen can give my readers but a faint idea. It must not be thought that the remarks were addressed to me or to anybody but the speaker himself. "That d——d thing a Raphael! Great heavens! think of that now! Can there be such d——d fools as to believe that a Raphael! What a d——fool I was to come here!" and without a glance at other pictures, the critic departed.'[2]

His visits to London also helped him to keep in touch with his family. Both his town houses were conveniently near to Portman Square where the Duchess of Hamilton lived, and he would call there in the afternoon as he returned from his walk. Here he might also see his two grandchildren, by this time themselves grown up and launched on the world. In 1832 his grand-daughter, named

Susan like her mother, married the Earl of Lincoln, son and heir of the fifth Duke of Newcastle, and he just lived long enough to see his grandson allied, in 1843, to Princess Mary of Baden, a cousin of Prince Louis-Napoleon. He could hardly have chosen better marriages for them had he planned it all himself. As for his Orde grandchildren, he hardly ever saw them, contenting himself with making them a small financial allowance. Fortunately, he did not survive to see Lady Lincoln's marriage founder in scandal and divorce only six years after his death, a disaster which many, no doubt, attributed to her unfortunate Beckford blood.

Visits to London, however, were comparatively infrequent, and Bath remained his principal home for the remainder of his life. Here, in the graceful rooms of the houses in Lansdown Crescent or in the tower on top of the hill, he continued to surround himself with beautiful objects of every sort, often adding to his collection, eagerly reading the catalogues of sales, and only occasionally selling a picture when he wished to raise money for some special purpose.

In 1839 when Sir Thomas Lawrence's great collection of old master drawings, perhaps the best ever assembled, was offered to the nation under the terms of his will, Beckford was dismayed when the offer was refused. Attempts to buy the collection by public subscription failed for want of support and Parliament declined to vote any money for their purchase. Beckford attempted to remedy the matter himself: 'I shall keep them in the country if I do no more,' he declared, 'they will else be dispersed . . . It is shameful the country does not buy them.' He visited his banker to see if he could raise the money, but alas, it could not be done. The collection fell into the hands of a dealer who disposed of it at immense profit and Beckford was left to reflect dismally on the state of official patronage in England. 'Except for a few gentlemen there is no sound taste for the arts in England', he observed. 'Collections are made from ostentation by people of wealth, who do not know a good from a bad picture. The government is not sensible, in the true point of view, of the value of art to the nation. A minister picks a committee of taste out of the House of Commons as he would a committee for any other purpose, and this committee does nothing but blunder.'[3]

Since Franchi's death Robert Hume, who had started in life as an upholsterer, continued to act as Beckford's agent in London for the purchase of works of art. He also introduced the work of contemporary artists to his patron's notice. 'Etty has recently read some of your works,' he informed Beckford in December 1835, 'and is more than delighted with the glowing Pictures which you have so decidedly sketched to the task of Artists. I feel that he will try his talents to produce something that may invite your critical glance. He is anxious to be worthy of placing his work in your collection.' The reference to Etty's having read Beckford's work was no doubt intended to flatter, but the reply showed no more than a polite interest in the artist's work: 'I am under no apprehension of not being satisfied with Etty's works and am proud of having to hear that he is pleased with mine.'[4] William Etty's reputation as a master of the nude was already established, but his voluptuous naked females, usually standing knee-deep in water, were not exactly Beckford's taste. He did, however, purchase an Adam and Eve from the artist, but before it was delivered Etty asked Hume 'in his whispering tone' whether he might not first exhibit it at York. Beckford's draft reply, which contained a certain note of asperity, suggests that he did not set a very high value on the work: 'Oh by all means let the good people of York be made as happy as an Adam and Eve of Etty's creation can make them.'[5]

Being Beckford's agent was not always an easy task, for as a patron he was often hard to please. It must have been with the feeling of having secured something of a *coup* that Hume wrote to him in July 1836: 'Mr. Buchanan has called to ask if you would like to see a *Monstrous* fine Hobbema, whether it is the Deluge or the Day of Judgement I don't know but I will go and see.' The reply he received from Bath, however, was little short of a snub. 'Pray assure Mr. Buchanan', Beckford answered, 'with many thanks for the offer, that I have not the smallest spark of curiosity to see the monstrous fine Hobbema he talks of—not I—I am not partial to this black green Master.'[6]

Beckford's interest in adding to his collection never flagged; advancing age did not dim his enthusiasm. In 1842, almost at the end of his life, an event occurred which kindled this passion once more, the Strawberry Hill sale, something for which he had been waiting ever since Horace Walpole's death forty-five years before. For all his dislike for Walpole and his contempt for his interpretation of gothic there was much at Strawberry Hill that he coveted. When the sale was announced he wrote to his agent (no longer Hume, but the bookseller Henry Bohn), 'You will find me all agog, *all ardour, all intrepidity*.' Various prints and books were knocked down to him including Walpole's own copy of his *Historic Doubts on the Life and Reign of Richard III* with manuscript notes in the author's hand. 'A folio of prints, etc., from the antique, in the Cabinet de Girardon, *I must have*', Bohn was told. 'The impressions are good, particularly the portrait,—it is scarce —MISS IT NOT.' It was not missed, and became Beckford's for the modest sum of two pounds and fifteen shillings. But books were his chief interest at this sale, more choice or rare editions to add to his own library. When all was over he wrote to Bohn from Bath on 3 May: 'We have paid quite dear enough for *every* article. The Banquet being over—now comes the reckoning. Have the goodness, therefore, to send the books and the account that I may settle it immediately.' And then, as a final dig at Walpole and his gimcrackery: 'I wish to forget the egregious follies committed at this high-puff sale.'[7]

There were many pictures hanging in his Bath home to remind Beckford of his earlier days, recalling a past that grew ever more remote. West's portrait of the Begum (a copy, probably from Casali) hung in the crimson, scarlet and purple 'Duchess' drawing-room—'a truly royal room' in the estimation of H. V. Lansdown, and so named from the full-length picture of the Duchess of Hamilton by Thomas Phillips that hung in the place of honour. Here too was Reynold's portrait of Beckford himself at the age of twenty-one and the dramatic picture of Louisa by the same artist. What memories did this canvas recall? Certainly no feelings of remorse, to judge by the matter-of-fact description of it he gave to the young Lansdown. 'Sir Joshua took the greatest pleasure and delight in painting that picture, as it was left entirely to his own refined taste', he was told. 'The lady was in ill-health at the time it was done, and Sir Joshua most charmingly conceived the idea of a sacrifice to the Goddess of Health. Vain hope! Her disorder was fatal.'[8] Thus was Louisa brusquely dismissed nearly forty years after her death for all that her former lover, endlessly engaged in copying out and carefully editing his correspondence, was still transcribing, and often embellishing, long letters and paragraphs addressed to 'My dear Louisa'.

Portraits of Beckford's formidable father and of that choleric individual his great-grandfather, the Governor of Jamaica, were displayed on the north staircase together with Romney's charming study of Margaret and Susan Beckford as little girls. In the dining-room could be seen one of Turner's drawings of Fonthill Abbey (Beckford had sold another as being 'rather too poetical, too ideal, even for Fonthill').[9] But the visitor would look in vain for Romney's portrait of William Courtenay which Beckford had once commissioned with such eager enthusiasm. The reasons for this are obvious enough, but the picture was neither sold nor destroyed. It was hidden away in some loft or attic to gather dust for many years until the details surrounding its creation were long forgotten. It then emerged to hang on the walls of Hamilton Palace under the false impression that it represented Beckford himself as a boy, an ironical case of mistaken identity that was not corrected until the present century.[10]

It was to 'Lansdown Baghdad' that young artists and writers, men born long after the scandals of his youth had caused such outcry in society, now came to pay their court to the Caliph, to 'the Old Man of the Mountain' as he called himself. To the journalist and editor Cyrus Redding he would talk of politics, recalling memories of the great Chatham and his son, always contrasting the latter unfavourably with the former, unable still to conceal his dislike for '*sober, honest* Mister Pitt'. He would relate once again his encounter with Voltaire half a century before, referring to the patriarch from memory as a 'very dark-complexioned, shrivelled, thin old man, stooping much from age'.[11]

He continued to see himself as a Whig, a champion of liberty. 'As to the people,' he told Redding, 'I should have been as happy to serve them as my father was, had it ever been in my power. I belong, as my father did, to the popular side.'[12] In spite of this libertarian boast he was unable to reconcile himself to the idea of the abolition of slavery. The prejudice inherited from his West Indian slave-owning ancestors was too strong, and for once his imagination failed to envisage the iniquity and inhumanity of the system and rebel against it. Perhaps if he had ever visited his Jamaican properties and seen the institution in operation he might have joined his voice with the emancipationists, but he preferred to shut his eyes to the evil. It is an unfortunate stain on his reputation, the more so as he did not suffer from racial prejudice, as is clear from his published writings and as was shown when he once met a clergyman who claimed descent from the Indian princess Pocahontas. 'That is a descent from a real sovereign of nature,' Beckford declared, 'not one of our modern mushrooms. If the reverend gentleman could give it me, I would willingly give him any three of my ancestors he liked to pick out in exchange.'[13]

In spite, however, of belonging to 'the popular side', Beckford had little or no sympathy with the cry for reform that came from the newly created labouring classes produced by the Industrial Revolution. In 1834, the year that saw the formation of Robert Owen's National Consolidated Trades Union and the transportation of the Tolpuddle martyrs, Beckford was full of despondency when he surveyed the political scene that May. 'We are on the eve of terrific explosions,' he wrote in alarm to Hume, 'for the moment the masses move in right or wrong causes, that moment the troops will be let loose upon them . . . and then, no species of life or property will be worth insuring.' Everything seemed wrong with the world just then. 'Heaven above is as much out of joint as Earth beneath', the letter continues. 'My fair flowers are withering in pale, sickly sunshine after a bitter night of frost and snow.'[14]

He felt nothing but antipathy for the industrialisation that was covering the land with its scars and blemishes and creating, with new wealth, a new sort of poverty to go with it. 'Nowhere is there any Country left,' he wrote sadly to the son of his old friend Schöll, 'the forests are being felled, the mountains violated. One sees only canals, the rivers are neglected; everywhere gas and steam, the same smell, the same puffs of disgusting smoke, thick and foetid; the same common and mercantile view wherever one turns. An oppressive monotony and an unholy artifice spits every minute in the face of Mother Nature, who will soon find her children changed into Automata and Machines.'[15] This last sentence contains the essence of his fear for the future as he watched the advance of the Industrial Revolution, a fear he expressed in vivid terms to Redding: 'A universalism rules. Soon no single voice will be listened to, there will be no solitary advocates of new truths in anything. What the many do and dream will be the law. All important truths have been the result of solitary efforts. None have been discovered by masses of people; it is fair to suppose they never will.'[16]

In his concern for the state of the country he trembled when he thought of the fate that awaited its artistic heritage should the 'terrific explosion' he dreaded ever occur. 'Well, well, depend upon it we shall have a tremendous outbreak before long', he told the impressionable young Lansdown in 1838. 'The ground we stand on is trembling, and gives signs of an approaching earthquake. Then will come a volcanic eruption; you will have fire, stones, and lava enough. Afterwards, when the lava has cooled, there will be an enquiry for works of art. I assure you I expect everything to be swept away.'[17] The accession of the young Queen Victoria the previous year had hardly calmed his nervous apprehension. 'God send the ingenuous and candid young Queen may establish herself in the affections of the people by keeping Joseph Surface and all his ravenous dirty adherents at an eternal distance,' he had written, 'more precisely as I despise and abominate the whole squad.'[18]

From these gloomy political visions it was a pleasure to turn to more cheerful subjects, to talk about art, about the people he had once known, about the strange adventures of his life. He was never happier than when discussing the merits of artists or comparing their work, often with sly touches of humour. 'How different is that lovely creature from Mr. Etty's beauties', he said when showing off Raphael's *St. Catherine*. 'They are for the most part of a meretricious character, would do well enough for a mistress; but there,' and he pointed to St. Catherine, 'there are personified the modesty and purity a man would wish to have in a wife . . .'[19] So, too, with the people he had known; he would discuss the empress Josephine whom he had met in the days when she was Madame de Beauharnais, or tell stories of Madame de Staël. 'A woman in her inclinations,' he pronounced, yet 'she thought like a man, wrote like a man . . . She would have exchanged her fame for beauty—how womanish!'[20] Nor could he ever resist a dig at the reputation of Emma Hamilton, that notorious wife and mistress and beauty all in one. 'She affected sensibility, but felt none,' he would tell his listeners, 'was artful; and no wonder, she had been trained in the court of Naples—a fine school for an Englishwoman of any stamp. It was a hell of corruption. Nelson was infatuated. She would make him believe anything—that the profligate Queen was a Madonna. He was her dupe . . .'[21]

Soon he would be carried away and the exaggerations would begin, the stories of his music lessons from Mozart and his composition of 'Non piu andrai', or the occasion when he claimed to have looked on the features of the Emperor Charles V. He had been asked by King Charles III of Spain, so he assured his guests, what favour he would care to receive at the king's hands as a parting civility upon leaving Madrid. 'To see the face of Charles V,' was Beckford's answer as the account has come down to us, 'that he might judge of the fidelity of the portraits by Titian.' The obliging king gave his consent and off went the fortunate recipient of royal favour to the Escorial where 'the marble sarcophagus being moved from its niche and the lid raised, the lights of the Pantheon once more gleamed on the features of the dead emperor.'[22] It was one of the finer flights of Beckford's fancy for, as we know, he never met the King of Spain at all nor was he ever presented at the Spanish court. No wonder that people were fascinated by his sparkling conversation and by the extraordinary stories he read or related to them. 'I cannot trust myself', wrote Harrison Ainsworth after a visit in April 1841, 'to tell you how infinitely delighted I have been with your enchanting productions —with your manner of reading them—and with your brilliant and unequalled powers of conversation—unequalled by any person I have ever heard—because what I should say might appear like flattery. But I assure you, in perfect sincerity, I have never received such high gratification.'[23]

It was pleasant to be sought out by these young admirers and to receive their homage; to feel, even, that he had disciples among the younger generation of writers. This certainly must have been his experience when, in 1832, he received through the post a copy of Benjamin Disraeli's *Contarini Fleming*. He read it with great enthusiasm and when he had finished wrote the author a brief letter. 'His answer is short, but very courteous', a gratified Disraeli informed his sister. 'It commences with four exclamations. "How wildly original! How full of intense thought! How awakening! How delightful!" This really consoles one for Mr. Patmore's criticism in the *Court Journal*.'[24] So began the friendship between the thirty-year-old Disraeli and the seventy-two-year-old Beckford; it was confirmed when the former sent a copy of his eastern romance *Alroy*. The Caliph's curiosity was now seriously aroused. 'There are innumerable passages in Alroy of the most exquisite beauty, which fully justified my predilection for the most original author . . .', he confided to his bookseller George Clarke. 'Had I remained in town I would have seen him, but I would not advise an excursion to Bath for that purpose. I should remain inaccessible. We are probably destined to meet, but when and where is doubtful.' Clarke, meanwhile, was instructed to discover more information about the young author.

Clarke's reply was not too encouraging. To begin with,

Disraeli *smoked*. The bookseller discovered the author, his brother and father, scarcely visible through the fumes of tobacco they exhaled. Furthermore, though clearly an 'oriental voluptuary' he doubted whether the other had sufficient French to comprehend *Vathek* in the original. Beckford was a little alarmed. 'It is a great pity', he answered, 'that the fire of such genius should evaporate in smoke.' He also preferred the way the author's distinguished father spelt their name: 'for my part I think D'Israeli in better taste.' What worried him most was that a man of such obvious literary talent should want to stand for parliament or engage in politics at all: 'What can possess so bright a genius to dabble again and again in such a muddy horsepond?' But when Clarke dared to say that he considered Disraeli the most conceited person he had ever met in the whole of his life, he received a sharp rebuke. What appeared as conceit, Beckford informed him, was only the irrepressible consciousness of superior power.[25]

It was not only books that Beckford received from his new admirer. 'I send you some tribute in the shape of a piece of marble which I myself brought from the Parthenon', Disraeli wrote in an undated letter before their one and only meeting. 'It may be sculptured into a classical press for the episodes of Vathek, which otherwise may fly away without the world reading them. I think it very unfair that I should hear of Mr. Beckford only through my friends and that I am not permitted personally to express to him how very much he has obliged B. Disraeli.'[26] Some time after this a meeting took place in London. 'I made Beckford's acquaintance at the Opera on Thursday', Disraeli noted in his diary for 16 June 1834. 'Conversation of three hours; very bitter and *malin*, but full of warm feelings for the worthy.' No more is known of those three hours of talk than this brief reference. The friendship continued in exchange of letters; Disraeli hoped to be able to review *Italy, with Sketches of Spain and Portugal* in the *Edinburgh Review* but other arrangements had been made; Beckford continued to receive copies of his novels. But after Disraeli's election as a Member of Parliament in 1837 the correspondence ceased, and when *Coningsby* made its appearance in 1844 Beckford was already dead. Disraeli left little evidence to show his real opinion of Beckford except to say that he considered him a remarkable man, and one possessing the greatest taste.

These encounters with the younger generation relieved some of the solitude of Beckford's latter years. He remained, all the same, an isolated figure, still shunned by his contemporaries except for his immediate family, a small enough circle, and for one or two acquaintances such as Samuel Rogers who visited him occasionally during his last years in Bath. He retained his zest for life, even in old age. 'I enjoy too good health, feel too happy, and am much too pleased with life, to have any inclination to throw it away for want of attention', he once said. 'When I am summoned I must go, though I should not much mind living another hundred years . . .'[27] His eightieth birthday passed and he remained active in mind and body, declaring that he was almost ashamed of being so old, it was as though death had forgotten him or unintentionally passed him by. In 1842 he calmly ordered his tomb, as he wished to lie at rest in the garden by his tower, close to the graves of his two dogs Tout and Tiny. 'The Tomb . . . is quite delightful,' he wrote laconically, 'admirably well proportioned, and of a beautiful, quiet colour in perfect harmony with the surrounding vegetation. Hewn out of a solid block of granite—it would require a tremendous apparatus and the labour of many men to remove the slab which covers it.'[28]

In his adolescent story *The Vision*, the hero, so closely modelled upon Beckford himself, is warned by the sage Moisasour when he begs for further enlightenment into mysteries as yet unexplored to repress so daring a curiosity, for 'this last initiation is Death'. As Beckford drew near the door that would admit him to this final initiation he approached it with an admirable composure. 'For my part I am perfectly resigned,' he wrote in the concluding part of the letter just quoted, 'perfectly ready to quit the moment proper notice in the shape of acute disease is given. Between the horrors in many shapes of the present times and the just apprehension of those in the womb of futurity which are already casting their baleful shadows before them—the dead are infinitely more to be envied than the living. I can hardly conceive a pleasanter spot to lie quiet in than the summit of Lansdown.'

He was eighty-two years old when he wrote these words; life still had two more years to give him. Twinges of rheumatism would attack him from time to time, and he complained of pains in the eyelids, but otherwise his health was tolerably good. He could ride up the hill to his tower and had no difficulty in climbing the spiral staircase to the belvedere one hundred and thirty feet above the ground level from where he could enjoy the distant view or the nearer prospect of the gardens he had created at its foot. His interest in all aspects of life remained; one of the last books he read was the future Cardinal Wiseman's *Lectures on Science and Revealed Religion* which Sir Jerom Murch had seen open on a table with marginal notes in Beckford's hand on almost every page.[29]

The winter of 1843–4 was severe and the old man looked forward eagerly to the return of spring. But the season seemed slow in coming and he grew restless and depressed as he waited for some indication that winter was past. A few rays of sunshine at the end of March raised his hopes and almost banished the spirit of melancholy that had settled upon him. He took a sheet of paper and wrote some lines, first in French and then in English: '*Enfin— il plaît au ciel de nous accorder quelques indices de printemps* . . . At length it has pleased Heaven to grant us a few indications of Spring—a light greenish gauze begins to extend itself over my miniature forests upon Lansdown—the grass awakes—the breath of violets is no longer repressed—the lambs have found their delicately thin nourishment—I hear on all sides upon the sod the almost imperceptible sound of their nibblings.

Gia riede primavera
Now spring returns, but not to me return
Those thrilling joys my vernal years have known.

In the midst of this sweet revival, and of this pastoral charm I remain—alas—sad and sickly—I am not tired of life, but life is tired of me.'[30]

In April he went out for a walk, for once ignoring the east wind whose cold blast had usually been a warning to him to remain indoors. He caught a chill which soon developed into fever and influenza. He struggled against his growing weakness but the illness increased its hold. By the twenty-first of the month he realised that the end was near and wrote to his daughter begging her to come to his bedside. The doctor had assured him that he was getting better, but Beckford, who had little faith in doctors or their remedies, knew that he was wrong. A horrible shivering made him tremble from head to foot: '*O abregez la distance!—je ne puis plus la supporter*', he wrote in desperation to his daughter, 'O shorten the distance!—I can bear it no longer.'

The Duchess hurried to Bath, bringing with her Dr. Bowie, a distinguished London physician. By this time, however, Beckford was beyond the help of medical aid; neither Bowie nor his own physician Dr. Liston could do more than make the dying man's last hours as comfortable as possible. The Duchess, determined that the death-bed should be as decorous as circumstances would permit and anxious, no doubt, for her father's spiritual welfare, asked if he would see the rector of the parish. When this offer was declined she suggested sending for a Roman Catholic priest, having good reason to believe that his presence might be welcome, but this too was refused.

A hastily convened conclave was then held with Bowie and the architect Henry Goodridge, who was also present, and at the latter's suggestion the doctor approached the sick man's bed with some conventional religious observations on the common depravity of man and the need for atonement. Beckford, as the doctor informed Goodridge, 'listened with much calmness and attention, clasping his hands with evident approval and acquiescence'.[31] What else could he do? But he remained silent, only at the very end muttering some almost incomprehensible words expressing a wish that he had not written some particular thing 'but it was impossible to ascertain what he intended'.[32] He left the world without committing himself to any religious creed, expressing neither hope nor fear. He died on 2 May 1844, in his eighty-fourth year, expiring so quietly and peacefully that the exact moment of death could not be ascertained. His body was embalmed the same evening.

Beckford, whom society had rejected for so many years, was buried with the utmost pomp. The hearse was drawn by six horses and a carriage-and-six followed containing the Duke and Duchess of Hamilton, the Marquis of Douglas and Lady Lincoln. A carriage-and-four came next in which sat the dead man's brother-in-law, the Marquis of Huntley, who had once slapped his face in the hope of provoking him to a duel. Many other carriages followed. Thousands of spectators lined the route and it was noticed that numbers of the poor were present as though mourning a benefactor, one who, if such was the case, had exercised his charity in secret. His wish to be buried in the shadow of Lansdown Tower was not immediately fulfilled as the Bishop of Bath and Wells declined to allow interment in unconsecrated ground, but soon afterwards the Duchess presented the tower and grounds to the Parish of Walcot as a public cemetery, and Beckford's remains were removed to the spot he had chosen. His granite tomb can still be seen there. It carries, after his name and the date of his

M

death, a slightly amended quotation from *Vathek*: 'Enjoying humbly the most precious gift of Heaven—Hope.' Upon the other side are engraved some lines that had concluded one of his religious poems:

> *Eternal power!*
> *Grant me through obvious clouds one transient gleam*
> *Of Thy bright essence in my dying hour.*

By some curious chance the remains of Fonthill Abbey that had stood for nearly twenty years undisturbed, a roofless and crumbling ruin rising desolately from the rubble and debris of the fallen tower, were finally demolished and cleared away in the year of Beckford's death.[33] No new house was built on the old site and a smooth green lawn covers the ground where the vast building had formerly dominated the scene. Only a small fragment still remains standing. It consists of the northern end of King Edward's Gallery; the Oratory, Sanctuary, and Vaulted Corridor crowned by the Lancaster Tower; so that the visitor surveying the site where the great Abbey once rose so proudly finds now only the shrine of St. Antony of Padua, the 'Glorious Protector' whose hand, as Beckford always believed, was not stretched over him in vain.

Notes and References

Abbreviations

Alexander, *EWS*	*England's Wealthiest Son*, by Boyd Alexander
Alexander, *Journal*	*Journal of William Beckford in Portugal and Spain*, edited by Boyd Alexander
Alexander, *Fonthill*	*Life at Fonthill 1807–22*, edited by Boyd Alexander
Chapman	*Beckford*, by Guy Chapman
Melville	*The Life and Letters of William Beckford*, by Lewis Melville
Oliver	*The Life of William Beckford*, by J. W. Oliver
Redding	*Memoirs of William Beckford of Fonthill*, by Cyrus Redding
Dreams	*Dreams, Waking Thoughts and Incidents* in *Travel Diaries of William Beckford*, edited by Guy Chapman
Italy	*Italy, with Sketches of Spain and Portugal*, second edition, revised, of 1834
Morrison Papers	*Collection of Autograph Letters and Historical Documents formed by Alfred Morrison* (Second Series, 1882–93)
Morrison: *Hamilton Papers*	*Collection of Autograph Letters and Historical Documents formed by Alfred Morrison; The Hamilton and Nelson Papers*

Chapter 1

1 Pitt did not attend the ceremony in person but the Alderman's brother-in-law Lord Effingham stood proxy for him.
2 See Alexander, *EWS*, pp. 200 et seq.
3 Walpole to Mann, 26 May 1762. For Beckford as Pitt's 'Zany' see Walpole to Montague, 24 Nov. 1760.
4 Walpole to Mann, 26 July 1770.

5 See *Elizabeth Lady Holland to her Son* (London, 1946), p. 210, also Walpole, *Memoirs and Portraits* (ed. Hodgart), p. 226 and J. Britton, *Autobiography*, Vol. II, p. 22.

6 Walpole to Bentley, 23 Feb. 1755.

7 J. Britton, *Graphical and Literary Illustrations of Fonthill Abbey*, p. 25.

8 For details of the interior of Splendens see Phillips's catalogue of the sale of the contents, 1801.

9 The most likely candidate would seem to be a Mr. Hoare, either James or George Hoare, both obscure London builders. (See J. Harris, 'Fonthill, Wiltshire' in *Country Life*, 24 Nov. 1966.) Prof. Chapman's claim that the house was built 'under the direction of Sir John Soane' (*Beckford*, p. 31) may be dismissed on the grounds that in 1755 Soane was under two years old. The house has also been attributed to Flitcroft and James Paine.

10 Alexander, *Fonthill*, pp. 38–9.

11 It has also been suggested that Beckford was born in London. For the arguments in favour of Fonthill see Oliver, pp. 3–4. For the Alderman's letter to Chatham see Taylor and Pringle, *Correspondence of William Pitt, Earl of Chatham*, Vol. II, p. 11 and Melville, p. 13.

12 See Oliver, p. 6. Letter of Robert Drysdale to Robert Nairne, 1768.

Chapter 2

1 Redding, Vol. II, p. 299.

2 See Alexander, *EWS*, pp. 160–1. Also *The Beckford Family* (ed. W. Gregory, Bath, 1898), p. 139, for a 'Contemporary Tribute' at the time of Beckford's death which quotes the opinion of an architect: 'I should have thought him a regular architect! When he saw the ground plans he told me in a moment the intended size of all the apartments.' Also quoted in *The Times*, 23 May 1844.

3 Oliver, p. 11.

4 Lansdown, *Recollections of the late William Beckford*, pp. 33–4.

5 For a discussion of this interesting topic see C. B. Oldman, 'Beckford and Mozart', *Music and Letters*, April 1966.

6 See Oliver, p. 5, Drysdale to Nairne, 1768.

7 *Ibid.* p. 6, Drysdale to Nairne, 19 Dec. 1769.

8 Letter by Drysdale from Fonthill, undated; see Chapman, p. 35.

9 Beckford to Chatham, Soho Square, 25 May 1770 (*Correspondence of Lord Chatham*, Vol. III, p. 463).

10 *Political Register of 1770*, Thurs. 21 June. See also W. Gregory (ed.), *The Beckford Family*, p. 11.

11 Walpole, *Memoirs and Portraits*, p. 229.

12 Macaulay, *Historical Essays* (Oxford, 1913), pp. 781–2.
13 Blunt, *Mrs. Montague, 'Queen of the Blues'*, Vol. i, p. 234.

Chapter 3

1 Alexander, *EWS*, pp. 51–2 et seq.
2 See S. Ayling, *The Elder Pitt* (London, 1972), p. 25.
3 *Farington Diaries*, Vol. iv, 14 Dec. 1807.
4 Unpublished MS of Redding in Beckford Papers. See Alexander, *EWS*, p. 41.
5 Pitt the Elder to his nephew Thomas (Lord Camelford). See S. Ayling, *op. cit.* p. 108.
6 Taylor and Pringle, *Correspondence of Chatham*, Vol. iv, p. 290. For Thucydides' speech see Redding, Vol. i, pp. 88–9.
7 Taylor and Pringle, *op. cit.* Vol. iv, p. 313.
8 'L'Esplendente', p. 13. See Alexander, *EWS*, p. 42.
9 Alexander Cozens is first mentioned by Beckford in a letter of April 1775, but by that time he appears as an established figure in his life.
10 Beckford to Mrs. (later Countess) Harcourt, 15 Aug. 1781. See also A. P. Oppé: *Alexander and John Robert Cozens*, pp. 34 and 36, also Melville, p. 165.
11 Morrison Papers, Vol. i, pp. 198–9.
12 Melville, p. 87.
13 Beckford Papers, viii, 5d.
14 *Ibid.* Neither fragment is dated. A similar fragment about Pan written on paper with the same watermark as the two above is dated in pencil 'Fonthill, 1779'.

Chapter 4

1 In dating the composition of *Biographical Memoirs* in 1777 when Beckford was sixteen I am following Mr. Boyd Alexander. See Alexander, *EWS*, pp. 47–8, and p. 273 (note 20).
2 *Biographical Memoirs* (1824 edition), pp. 13–15, 47–8, and 134.
3 Melville, p. 68.
4 Lansdown, *Recollections of the late William Beckford*, p. 35.
5 Beckford to Mrs. Hervey, April 1778. Oliver, p. 23.
6 Melville, pp. 49–51.
7 See Alexander, *EWS*, p. 112.
8 Melville, p. 27; Oliver, pp. 25–6. Both based on Beckford's own account to Cyrus Redding in old age.
9 Oliver, p. 25.
10 Melville, pp. 35–6.

11 Melville, p. 31; Oliver, p. 21. For 'Delivered up to a Sword', etc., see Melville, p. 40.

12 Oliver, p. 18.

13 Melville, p. 41. The 'Long Story' was published in 1930, edited by Guy Chapman under the title of *The Vision*.

14 *The Vision*, p. 67.

15 *Ibid.* pp. 5–6.

16 *Ibid.* p. 7.

17 *Ibid.* p. 11.

18 The fragment was discovered among the Beckford Papers by Mr. Boyd Alexander, and is quoted in part in *Beckford, Auteur de Vathek* by André Parreaux, pp. 102 et seq.

19 Beckford's impressions of the Grande Chartreuse were published in *Dreams* and later, slightly modified, in *Italy*. This and the following quotations are from the latter (second edition, revised, 1834), Vol. I, pp. 309 et seq.

20 *Ibid.* Vol. I, pp. 330–4.

Chapter 5

1 In 1774 Elizabeth March had married Colonel Thomas Hervey, a nephew of Dr. Johnson's friend Henry Hervey.

2 Alexander, *EWS*, p. 67.

3 Oliver, pp. 28–9.

4 See Oliver, pp. 15–17.

5 Letter dated '9 o-clock, Sept. 13th. 1777', Melville, p. 30.

6 See Chapman, pp. 59–60; Oliver, p. 32.

7 Letter dated 24 Nov. 1777, Melville, p. 37.

8 The lines were printed in *Dreams*, but excluded by the more mature judgement of Beckford when he published *Italy* in 1834. See also Melville, pp. 27–8, where the whole poem of fifty lines is printed.

9 Chapman, p. 50. The complete letter from which the passages that follow are taken is found in Melville, pp. 60–6.

10 See Oliver, p. 34; Alexander, *EWS*, pp. 71–3.

11 16 Nov. 1780; Melville, p. 96.

12 See Chapman, pp. 55–8. I have slightly simplified the punctuation.

13 Melville, p. 76. *Werther* had been published five years before in 1774.

14 Melville, pp. 77, 78. The Hon. Louisa Pitt, daughter of George, 1st Lord Rivers. Born 1754, married Peter Beckford in 1773.

15 Melville, p. 78.

16 See Alexander, *EWS*, p. 68.

17 Melville, p. 80. Letter dated 6 Feb. 1780.

Chapter 6

1 Ferenguis or Farangi, oriental word for a foreigner (literally a Frank) possibly first introduced to European readers in Niccolao Manucci's *Storia do Mogor* in the late seventeenth century.
2 Melville, pp. 83–4. Oliver, p. 36.
3 See Alexander, *EWS*, pp. 74–5.
4 Redding, Vol. II, pp. 220–1.
5 See Oliver, pp. 39–40. Redding, Vol. II, p. 296.
6 *Dreams*, Vol. I, pp. 2–3. (Chapman's edition of 1928, *The Travel Diaries of William Beckford of Fonthill*.)
7 *Italy*, Vol. I, p. 9. Unless otherwise stated all references to Beckford's Grand Tour are taken from *Italy*, second edition, revised, of 1834.
8 *Dreams*, Vol. I, p. 10. The last sentence was omitted in *Italy*.
9 Alexander, *EWS*, p. 263.
10 For an account of this extraordinary affair see Chapman, pp. 68–9.
11 Noted by Beckford in 1838. See Chapman, p. 69.
12 See Chapman, p. 70 and Alexander, *EWS*, pp. 76–7.
13 *Dreams*, Vol. I, pp. 113–14. The last half of the last sentence was omitted from *Italy*.
14 *Ibid.* Vol. I, p. 125. Passage completely changed in 1834 and all references to his religious feelings omitted, but a thunder storm added. See *Italy*, Vol. I, pp. 158–9.
15 Oliver, p. 47; Melville, p. 93.
16 Oliver, p. 46. Melville (p. 92) indicates that the letter was to Miss Burney, through whose introduction Beckford first met Pacchierotti in London. On his return journey, 17 Dec. 1780, Beckford met Farinelli, then seventy-five, in Bologna and reported that 'his modulation is still delightful and some of those thrilling tones which raised such raptures in the year '35 have not yet entirely deserted him.' See Oliver, pp. 53–4.

Chapter 7

1 Melville, p. 98. Written in Rome, 6 Dec. 1780.
2 Beckford to Lady Hamilton, 29 Dec. 1780. Oliver, p. 54.
3 Oliver, p. 55.
4 Beckford to A. Cozens, Naples, 7 Nov. 1780. Melville, pp. 95–6.
5 Letter from Strassburg dated 28 Jan. 1781. See Oliver, p. 59.
6 A suggestion which has been made in a recent work of fiction based on Beckford's life.
7 Letter dated Naples, 16 Nov. 1780. Melville, p. 96.

8 Oliver, pp. 49–50.
9 *Ibid.* p. 56.
10 *Ibid.* pp. 59–60, Melville, pp. 100–1. Letter dated Strassburg, 28 Jan. 1781.
11 See Melville, pp. 101–2.
12 See Chapman, pp. 81–4, from a draft in the Beckford Papers dated 22 Feb. 1781.
13 Melville, p. 105.
14 Oliver, p. 64. Letter dated Naples, 19 March 1781.
15 *Ibid.* p. 65. Melville, p. 105.

Chapter 8

1 Letter dated Portici, 8 May 1781. Oliver, p. 68. For Beckford's reply see Melville, p. 114 and Oliver, p. 69.
2 Letter dated 6 July 1781. Oliver, p. 71.
3 Oliver, p. 72. When Beckford transcribed this letter (*c.* 1830) he added to his description of Burton's playing: 'His compositions have a cast of that wildness and energy I used to admire so much in those of that moonstruck, wayward boy Mozart.' This phrase was not in the original letter of 1781.
4 Letter dated 30 Aug. 1781. Melville, p. 119.
5 See Alexander, *EWS*, p. 14.
6 Chapman, p. 94.
7 *Ibid.* pp. 94–5.
8 Melville, pp. 117–18.
9 Oliver, p. 79.
10 The text 'from the original Italian of Sig. Venanzio Rauzzini' was published in Salisbury by 'Collins and Johnson, on the Canal' in 1781. See Oliver, pp. 82–4.
11 Letter dated 14 Oct. 1781. Melville, p. 121; Oliver, p. 85.
12 See Melville, p. 123.
13 Chapman, pp. 100–1.
14 Letters dated 2 June and 20 July 1782, Melville, pp. 151 and 161. For the letter in May (dated Tunbridge, 6 May 1783) see Chapman, pp. 154–5.
15 For Beckford's full description, written in 1838, see Oliver, pp. 89–91.

Chapter 9

1 See *The Works of Jeremy Bentham*, Vol. x, p. 285.
2 George Selwyn to the Earl of Carlisle, 8 Feb. 1782. (E. S. Roscoe and H. Clergue, *George Selwyn, his Life and Letters*, p. 187.)

3 See A. M. Broadley and L. Melville, *The Beautiful Lady Craven*, Vol. II, pp. 110–11.

4 Letters dated 21 and 29 Jan. 1782. Morrison Papers, Vol. I, Letter 1, pp. 182–3, and Letter 2, p. 183.

5 See *Italy*, Vol. I, pp. 263–79.

6 Letters of 11 and 22 March 1782. See Oliver, pp. 104–5 and 108.

7 Alexander, *Journal*, p. 289.

8 See Chapman, p. 116, who sees in this a reference to Courtenay. The letter is dated 4 Feb. 1782.

9 Letter dated 6 Feb. 1782. Chapman, p. 117. 'My William' was her son William, later second Lord Rivers.

10 Letter of 8 March 1782. Chapman, p. 119.

11 Copy of 1838–9 of a letter dated 11 March 1782. Chapman, pp. 121–2.

12 Born Elizabeth Berkeley (1750–1818). She married William, 6th Lord Craven on 30 May 1767. On his death in 1791 she married secondly Christian Frederick, Margrave of Brandenburg-Ansbach-Bayreuth with whom she had been living for some years in the character of 'adopted sister'.

13 Walpole to Mann, 30 Oct. 1785.

14 *Memoirs of the Margravine of Anspach* written by herself, Vol. I, pp. 238–9.

15 Quoted from *The Jockey Club* in Broadley and Melville, *op. cit.* Vol. I, Introduction, p. xxv.

16 See Oliver, p. 110.

17 This and the quotation that follows relating to Lady Craven's operetta are from Beckford's account given in Oliver, pp. 109–16.

18 Or the former Duke of Queensberry's house in Burlington Gardens, as newspaper reports suggest. (See Alexander, *EWS*, pp. 15 and 268.)

19 Morrison Papers, Vol. I, Letter 3, p. 183.

20 Letter dated 29 May 1782, quoted by Oliver, p. 100.

21 Morrison Papers, Vol. I, p. 185.

22 *Ibid.* Letter 14, p. 185.

Chapter 10

1 Letter to Henley dated 18 Nov. 1783. Morrison Papers, Vol. I, Letter 28, p. 189.

2 Chapman, p. 108.

3 Oliver, p. 100.

4 Melville, p. 143.

5 Oliver, p. 100.

6 The oriental and pseudo-oriental origins of *Vathek* are explored

in detail by André Parreaux in *William Beckford, Auteur de Vathek,* ch. VI, 'Vathek et le conte oriental au XVIIIe siecle', pp. 301 et seq. See also Alexander, *EWS,* ch. VI, 'The Origins of Vathek 1780–81', pp. 79–90.

7 But not to Orientals. See F. Moussa Mahmoud: 'Beckford, Vathek and the Oriental Tale' in *William Beckford of Fonthill, Bicentenary Essays* (Cairo, 1960).

8 C. Redding, 'Recollections of the Author of Vathek', *New Monthly Magazine,* June 1844. Quoted by L. Melville in the Introduction to *The Episodes of Vathek* translated by Sir Frank T. Marzials, p. ix.

9 F. Moussa Mahmoud, *op. cit.* p. 74. See also Alexander, *EWS,* p. 91.

10 Quotations from the text of *Vathek* are taken from Henley's translation (original edition, 1786), the fourth revised edition of 1823. The punctuation has been simplified.

11 Beckford to Lady Craven, Jan. 1790. See Alexander, *EWS,* p. 157.

12 Beckford's idea of the flaming heart was probably derived from Gueullette's *Mongul Tales* (1736). See M. P. Conant, *The Oriental Tale in England in the Eighteenth Century,* p. 37: 'One special interest in the *Mongul Tales* must not be omitted, the incident of the sinners with flaming hearts, since this was probably the source of the parallel passage in Beckford's *Vathek.* It is worth remark as external evidence that *Mongul Tales* is in the catalogue of Beckford's library.'

13 From Redding's unpublished manuscript, quoted by Alexander, *EWS,* p. 92.

14 Beckford to Cozens, 2 June 1782, Melville, p. 151. To Lady Hamilton, same date, Melville, p. 152.

15 *Italy,* Vol. I, p. 291.

16 Letter dated Rome, 30 June 1782. Melville, p. 158.

17 Chapman, pp. 135–6.

18 Letter dated 29 June 1782. Oliver, p. 121; Melville, p. 156.

19 *Memoirs of Thomas Jones* (Walpole Society, Vol. XXXII), pp. 112–13.

20 Melville, pp. 159–60. Letters dated 9 and 20 July 1782.

21 *Ibid.* pp. 161–2. The letter is dated 27 Aug. but as Lady Hamilton is referred to in it as being still alive, when in fact she died on that day, it must have been written earlier.

22 Thomas Jones, *op cit.* p. 114.

23 *Ibid.* p. 114.

24 See Melville, pp. 162–3. Letter dated Geneva, 12 October 1782.

25 Melville, p. 165. Oliver, pp. 131–2. Dr. Oliver thinks this letter is addressed to Louisa but Chapman (p. 141) disagrees. The phrase 'My dear Friend' would imply Cozens rather than Louisa or Courtenay, both of whom he would address more fulsomely.

Chapter 11

1 Written from her father's house at Stratfieldsay. Oliver, p. 130.
2 These included the MS of the *Thousand and One Nights* brought to England by Edward Wortley Montague (now in the Bodleian Library). Beckford appears to have borrowed them from the Duke of Bedford.
3 See Morrison Papers, Vol. 1, p. 187, Letter 20.
4 See Alexander, *EWS*, p. 91.
5 *The Episodes of Vathek* (trans. Sir F. T. Marzials), p. 46.
6 *Ibid.* p. 161.
7 *Ibid.* p. 184.
8 Morrison Papers, Vol. 1, p. 189, Letter 25, dated Tues., 13 Feb. 1783.
9 Oliver, p. 133.
10 *Ibid.* pp. 135–6. Letter dated Nice, 11 Jan. 1783.
11 Morrison Papers, Vol. 1, p. 189, Letter 26. See also Oliver, p. 129. Thomas Wildman was Beckford's lawyer and man of business.
12 See Oliver, pp. 137–8. Letter dated 29 March 1783.
13 *Ibid.* p. 139.
14 See Melville, p. 166, and Chapman, pp. 154–5.

Chapter 12

1 See Chapman, p. 157.
2 Letters from Secheron (8 June), Geneva (28 July) and Evian (26 Aug.), 1783. Melville, pp. 166–8.
3 See Alexander *EWS*, p. 106.
4 See Chapman, p. 165.
5 For this correspondence, from which the extracts here are taken, see Oliver, pp. 134–59 and Chapman, pp. 155–69.
6 Morrison Papers, Vol. 1, p. 189, Letter 28 dated Geneva, 18 Nov. 1783. It was some time before the spelling of the Caliph's name was settled. 'Vathec' and 'Vatteck' appear as well as 'Vathek'.
7 Letter dated Paris 13 Jan. 1784. Beckford Papers, 1. 8.
8 For Beckford's account of this visit to Paris see Oliver, pp. 161–93. The quotations, unless otherwise stated, are from this source.
9 See Chapman, p. 174. The full account is given in Oliver, pp. 172–81. Of this story and the episode of the lioness Professor Chapman comments: 'Without further evidence I refuse to believe either tale.'
10 Morrison Papers, Vol. 1, p. 191, Letter 31.
11 Chapman, p. 177.

Chapter 13

1 Melville, p. 229. Letter dated 14 April 1784.
2 Chapman, p. 178.
3 Morrison Papers, Vol. I, p. 192, Letter 33.
4 *Ibid.* Letter 32, dated 6 May 1784.
5 Melville, p. 171.
6 Chapman, p. 180. Letter dated 17 June 1784.
7 *Farington Diary*, Vol. IV, p. 243.
8 Morrison Papers, Vol. I, p. 192, Letter 35, dated 13 Oct. 1784.
9 The Act (25 Henry VIII, c. 6) of 1533 was repealed in 1547 but re-enacted under Elizabeth I in 1562 (5 Elizabeth I, c. 17). It was finally repealed in the nineteenth century by Sir Robert Peel.
10 Later told by Mrs. Beckford to Josiah Boydell. See *Farington Diary*, Vol. I, p. 237.
11 *Ibid.* Vol. IV, pp. 242–3.
12 Dated Fonthill, 22 Nov. 1784. See Alexander, *EWS*, pp. 108–9.
13 For a selection of these press attacks see Chapman, pp. 185–6.
14 Mrs. Elizabeth Carter to the 'blue-stocking' Mrs. Montague. Quoted by Alexander, *EWS*, pp. 110–11.
15 See *Pembroke Papers 1780–1794* (edited by Lord Herbert), pp. 369 and 274.
16 Morrison: *Hamilton Papers*, Vol. I, p. 95. Letter 133, undated.
17 See *Thraliana, the Diary of Mrs. Hester Lynche Thrale 1776–1809* (edited by K. C. Balderston), Vol. II, p. 799. It should be pointed out that Mrs. Thrale tended to discover this 'odious propensity' in both men and women almost wherever she looked.
18 See L. A. Marchand, *Byron's Letters and Journals*, Vol. I, p. 210.
19 See H. A. N. Brockman, *The Caliph of Fonthill*, p. 188.
20 Morrison: *Hamilton Papers*, Vol. II, p. 193. Letter 673.

Chapter 14

1 *Farington Diary*, Vol. I, p. 51. 4 June 1794.
2 For a detailed discussion of Beckford's fortune see Alexander, *EWS*, ch. XVI.
3 See Lord Clark's 'Foreword' to the catalogue of the Beckford Exhibition, Salisbury and Bath, 1976.
4 See Melville, p. 132.
5 Chapman, pp. 191–2 quoting Morrison Papers, Letter 42, undated.
6 Alexander, *Journal*, p. 61. Entry for 4 June 1787.
7 See *Farington Diary*, Vol. VI, p. 273.

8 See Melville, pp. 128–9 and Chapman, pp. 192–3.
9 See Melville, pp. 130–1.
10 Chapman, pp. 195–6. Draft dated 18 May 1785.
11 *Ibid.* p. 196, 31 May 1785.
12 Alexander, *EWS*, p. 112.
13 Beckford to Robert Pigott, 26 Feb. 1786. Melville, pp. 171–2.
14 Morrison Papers, Vol. I, p. 196. Letter 45.
15 See Alexander, *EWS*, p. 120.
16 See Oliver, p. 198.
17 Oliver, p. 258; Chapman, p. 235.
18 Alexander, *Journal*, p. 165. (Monday 20 Aug. 1787.)
19 Oliver, p. 202.
20 See Melville, pp. 137–9.
21 André Parreaux in *William Beckford, Auteur de Vathek* (pp. 224–35)
    casts many doubts on the theory that the Lausanne edition is a
    retranslation of Henley, and suggests that Beckford did in fact have
    a second French version of the text in his possession, though
    Beckford denied this in 1783 and no MS of *Vathek* in French has
    survived. The exact origin of the Lausanne edition cannot finally be
    established beyond doubt. A complete version of the French text
    of *Vathek*, based on the Paris edition of 1787, with the Episodes
    placed within the body of the story as Beckford intended was
    published in 1929, edited by Guy Chapman. No English translation
    in this form has yet appeared.

Chapter 15

1 Drysdale to R. Nairne, 13 Nov. 1786. See Oliver, p. 204.
2 *Italy*, Vol. II, p. 16.
3 *Ibid.* Vol. II, p. 19.
4 Undated letter to Wildman, quoted by Alexander, *EWS*, p. 127.
5 See Alexander, *Fonthill*, p. 83.
6 Sacheverell Sitwell, *Beckford and Beckfordism*, p. 14.
7 See Alexander, *Journal*, pp. 117–18.
8 *Ibid.* p. 48.
9 *Ibid.* p. 104.
10 *Ibid.* pp. 42, 44 and 125.
11 *Ibid.* p. 89.
12 *Ibid.* pp. 62–3. Entry for 4 June 1787.
13 *Ibid.* p. 201.
14 *Ibid.* p. 224.
15 *Ibid.* p. 41. Entry for 27 May 1787.
16 *Ibid.* p. 86.
17 *Ibid.* pp. 242 and 243–4.

18 *Ibid.* p. 44.
19 *Ibid.* p. 115.
20 *Ibid.* p. 97. In Letter XXXI, pp. 222 et seq. of *Italy*, Vol. II, Beckford describes an interview he had with the Prince of Brazil. This
account was written long after the event when he edited the
Journal for publication in 1834. There is no mention of this meeting
in the contemporary diary. As Beckford was anxious to show his
acceptance in royal circles it seems unlikely that he would have
omitted to record so important an event had it actually taken place.
Lacking further evidence this encounter with the Prince must be
considered as historically non-proven.
21 *Ibid.* p. 281.
22 *Ibid.* p. 238.

Chapter 16

1 Alexander, *Journal*, p. 313.
2 *Ibid.* pp. 311, 313 and 317, entries for 6, 12 and 19 Jan. 1788.
3 *Ibid.* p. 300.
4 *Ibid.* p. 308.
5 *Ibid.* p. 309.
6 *Ibid.* pp. 318–19.
7 See Chapman, p. 226. The name of this chorister has not survived.
He is referred to simply as '*ce maudit petit Ki-Ki*'.
8 Quoted by Alexander, *Fonthill*, Introduction, p. 29.
9 Melville, pp. 176–7. Letter dated Madrid, 30 May 1788.
10 See Alexander, *Journal*, pp. 87 and 132–3. Entries for 18 June and
14 July.
11 Redding, Vol. II, p. 42.
12 Melville, p. 178.
13 Oliver, pp. 207–8. Letter dated 1 Jan. 1790.
14 Chapman, p. 233.
15 J. Britton, *Illustrations of Fonthill*, p. 27.
16 Redding, Vol. II, pp. 94–5.
17 See Oliver, pp. 257–8. It is difficult to say exactly when work on
the wall began. This draft letter to Lady Craven is undated but the
evidence, as Chapman states (p. 235) strongly suggests 1790. By
1793, when work on the wall was well under way, Lady Craven had
already become the Margravine of Ansbach (she married on 30
Oct. 1791), so the plans for the wall at least must date from the
period when this letter was written, even if work was not started
until later.

Chapter 17

1 Oliver, p. 209. Letter dated 29 Nov. 1790.
2 See Alexander, *EWS*, p. 141, quoting Redding manuscript.
3 Morrison: *Hamilton Papers*, Vol. I, p. 153, Letter 191.
4 See Chapman, p. 236.
5 Beckford Papers, II, 19a.
6 Walpole to Lady Ossory, 23 Nov. 1791.
7 Redding, Vol. II, p. 326.
8 Morrison: *Hamilton Papers*, Vol. I, p. 156, Letter 196.
9 Quoted by Alexander, *EWS*, p. 23.
10 Melville, p. 179; Chapman, p. 238.
11 Morrison: *Hamilton Papers*, Vol. I, p. 165, Letter 205.
12 *Ibid.* Vol. I, pp. 157–8, Letter 198.
13 *Ibid.* Vol. I, p. 165, Letter 205 and p. 169, Letter 211.
14 *Ibid.* Vol. I, p. 169, Letter 212.
15 *Buck Whaley's Memoirs*, pp. 304–5.
16 *Ibid.* p. 298.
17 *Recollections of Valentine, Lord Cloncurry*, p. 11.
18 See Melville, p. 179.
19 See Oliver, p. 215.
20 See Oliver, p. 216, Alexander, *EWS*, pp. 140–1.
21 See Boyd Alexander, in The British Historical Society of Portugal's *Second Annual Report and Review*, p. 17. Letter of July or Aug. 1789.

Chapter 18

1 Beckford Papers, VIII, 5. Fair copy and draft with letter to Lord Thurlow, dated Geneva, 22 May 1778.
2 See Alexander, *EWS*, p. 153.
3 *Ibid.* p. 157, Letter written in Jan. 1790.
4 Morrison: *Hamilton Papers*, Vol. I, p. 183, Letter 230 dated 24 Dec. 1793.
5 *Ibid.* Vol. I, p. 188, Letter 235.
6 Melville, p. 277.
7 This interesting connection between Beckford's architectural sketch of 1793 and the later Fonthill Abbey plan was first pointed out by Mr. Boyd Alexander. See his *EWS*, pp. 160–1.
8 The contemporary diary of 1794 was discovered in the Beckford Papers by Mr. Boyd Alexander and published as an appendix to the 1972 reprint of the *Recollections*, pp. xxxvii–xlix.
9 *Recollections of an Excursion to the Monasteries of Alcobaça and Batalha* (1972 edition), Appendix, p. xlv.

10 *Ibid.* pp. xl and 15.
11 *Ibid.* pp. xliv–xlv (fourth day).
12 Marchand, *Byron's Letters and Journals*, Vol. II, p. 107.
13 Morrison: *Hamilton Papers*, Vol. I, p. 213, Letter 269 dated Lisbon, 26 Sept. 1795.
14 For this and the quotation below see Morrison: *Hamilton Papers*, Vol. I, pp. 215–16, Letter 271.
15 See draft letter to Sir William Hamilton, dated 21 Nov. 1795. Oliver, p. 224.
16 *Italy*, Vol. II, p. 372.
17 *Ibid.* Vol. II, p. 371.

Chapter 19

1 Morrison: *Hamilton Papers*, Vol. I, pp. 227–8, Letter 292, dated Fonthill, 2 Feb. 1797.
2 Melville, p. 241.
3 Quoted by Boyd Alexander, 'The Marquis of Marialva's Friendship with Beckford' in the British Historical Society of Portugal's *Second Annual Report and Review*, pp. 17–18.
4 Beckford Papers, II, 17.
5 See *Farington Diary*, Vol. I, p. 217.
6 Melville, p. 201.
7 *Farington Diary*, Vol. I, pp. 219–20.
8 Melville, p. 211.
9 Beckford Papers, II, 17, Letter dated 27 Dec. 1797.
10 See Thomas Moore's *Memoirs*, Vol. II, p. 197. A précis of Beckford's two pseudonymous novels can be found in Redding, Vol. II, ch. V.
11 For the details of this episode see Boyd Alexander's 'The Marquis of Marialva's Friendship with Beckford', *op. cit.* pp. 18–19.
12 Melville, p. 222.
13 See Chapman, p. 259.

Chapter 20

1 See Alexander, *Fonthill*, p. 128.
2 *Ibid.* pp. 74, 76 and 97.
3 *Ibid.* pp. 73 and 93.
4 Melville, pp. 221–2.
5 See Alexander, *EWS*, p. 159. Knoyle lay to the west of the Fonthill estate.
6 Morrison: *Hamilton Papers*, Vol. I, p. 227, Letter 292.

7 Now in the possession of the Society of Antiquaries of London, MS 260.

8 See J. Wilton-Ely, 'A Model for Fonthill Abbey, Wiltshire' in *The Country Seat*, p. 203.

9 Redding, Vol. II, p. 332.

10 Beckford Papers, IV, 4.

11 See G. Reitlinger, *The Economics of Taste*, p. 40 and W. T. Whitley, *Artists and their Friends in England*, Vol. II, pp. 357–8. Farington, on the other hand, says 'Beckford wrote from Portugal to have them purchased without mentioning any sum' (Vol. I, p. 369). According to Whitley Beckford had made an offer for the pictures to Prince Altieri when he first saw them, but was refused.

12 Morrison: *Hamilton Papers*, Vol. II, p. 78, Letter 438 dated 23 Dec. 1799.

13 See Farington MS Diary, pp. 1,361 and 1,400.

14 The watercolour by Wild (1791–1835) painted *c*. 1799, now in the Victoria and Albert Museum, shows various features other than the spire that were never built.

15 J. Rutter, *Delineations of Fonthill Abbey*, p. 110. Another tradition states that the tower caught fire and Beckford 'enjoyed from his garden the magnificent spectacle of its conflagration'. See C. L. Eastlake, *A History of the Gothic Revival*, p. 63. Redding (Vol. II, p. 156) also mentions a fire 'near the Summit'.

16 Melville, p. 225, Letter dated 21 May 1800.

17 Oliver, p. 238.

18 See T. J. Pelligrew, *Memoirs of Lord Nelson*, Vol. I, pp. 402–3.

19 Melville, pp. 232–3.

20 For a contemporary account of the fête see J. Britton, *Illustrations of Fonthill Abbey*, pp. 28–31. The quotations are from this account.

Chapter 21

1 See K. Clark, *The Gothic Revival*, p. 87 and J. Britton, *Illustrations of Fonthill Abbey*, p. 13. Heights varying from 240 to 300 ft. have been given for the tower of which no exact measurement seems to have been recorded, but give or take a few feet it may be said to have been about the same height as the campanile of Westminster Cathedral.

2 See letter dated 12 May 1801, Beckford Papers, III, 12.

3 Beckford Papers, III, 11.

4 See D. Watkin, *Thomas Hope and the Neo-Classical Ideal*, p. 141.

5 *Farington Diary*, Vol. II, p. 217.

6 Quoted by Melville, p. 299.

7 Beckford Papers, III, 12.

8 *Ibid.* Letter dated 7 Aug. 1802.
9 S. Rogers, *Table-Talk*, p. 217.
10 See Countess Granville, *Lord Granville Leveson Gower, Private Correspondence 1781 to 1821*, Vol. II, pp. 544–5.
11 *Farington Diary*, Vol. IV, p. 242.
12 Oliver, p. 246; Beckford's reply, p. 247.
13 See Alexander, *Fonthill*, pp. 41–2.
14 Morrison: *Hamilton Papers*, Vol. II, p. 193, Letter 674.
15 Alexander, *Fonthill*, pp. 57 and 58.
16 *Ibid.* p. 74.
17 *Ibid.* p. 79.
18 *Ibid.* p. 81.
19 John Charles Felix Rossi, R.A. (1762–1839), the English-born son of an Italian from Siena, was sculptor to George IV. In 1797 he was responsible for a bust of James Wyatt now in the National Portrait Gallery.
20 J. Britton, *op. cit.* p. 45.
21 J. Rutter, *Delineations of Fonthill*, p. 63.
22 Alexander, *Fonthill*, p. 303. A comment of 1819.
23 For these two quotations see Alexander, *EWS*, p. 167. The latter remark was made by a Genoese visitor named Durazzo to the poet Tom Moore.
24 Sacheverell Sitwell, *British Artists and Craftsmen*, p. 239.

Chapter 22

1 Beckford Papers, II, 19b, Letter dated 20 July 1809.
2 See *Farington Diary*, Vol. III, pp. 95 and 248.
3 S. Rogers, *Table-Talk*, pp. 218–19.
4 See Oliver, pp. 263–5.
5 See Alexander, *Fonthill*, p. 270.
6 See *Farington Diary*, Vol. III, p. 95.
7 Rutter, *Delineations of Fonthill*, p. 44.
8 Oliver, p. 267. Margaret Beckford's note was dated 16 May 1811.
9 *Farington Diary*, Vol. IV, p. 33.
10 *Ibid.* Vol. I, pp. 187–8.
11 See Melville, pp. 217–18. When taxed with this story by Redding Beckford strongly denied its truth. See Redding, Vol. II, pp. 224–5. Another version of the story was related by Prince von Pückler-Muskau in his *Briefe eines Verstorbenen*, Vol. I, pt. 2, pp. 292–5.
12 Alexander, *EWS*, p. 187.
13 Alexander, *Fonthill*, p. 55.

14 Alexander, *EWS*, p. 253.

15 Alexander, *Fonthill*, p. 69.

16 Alexander, *EWS*, p. 253.

17 Rutter mentions the latter as being at Fonthill in 1822 though according to G. Reitlinger (*The Economics of Taste*, pp. 243–501) Beckford sold it in 1806 for £787. The Rembrandt *Rabbi* was bought in 1807 for £882.

18 Twenty pictures at one time in Beckford's possession are now in the National Gallery, London. Others hang in the London Museum, the Berlin Museum, the Metropolitan Museum and Frick Collection in New York, the National Gallery of Art in Washington and the Thyssen Collection.

19 Redding, Vol. II, pp. 347–8.

20 *Ibid.* Vol. II, pp. 351–2.

21 *Ibid.* Vol. II, p. 285.

22 *Ibid.* Vol. II, p. 313.

23 *Italy*, Vol. II, p. 343.

24 Redding, Vol. II, p. 335.

25 H. V. Lansdown, *Recollections of the late William Beckford*, p. 19.

26 Alexander, *Fonthill*, p. 255. The Rubens Vase is now in the Walters Art Gallery, Baltimore.

27 *Ibid.* pp. 323–4.

28 See C. Wainwright, 'Some Objects from William Beckford's Collection now in the Victoria and Albert Museum', *Burlington Magazine*, Vol. CXIII, Jan.–June 1971, p. 264.

29 See A. Hobson, 'William Beckford's Library', *Connoisseur*, Vol. 191, No. 770, p. 302.

30 Alexander, *Fonthill*, p. 70. Macklin's Bible was a contemporary work (published 1800) in six illustrated volumes.

31 See Melville, pp. 319–20, For Hazlitt'e attack on Beckford see the *London Magazine* for Nov. 1822 and Oct. 1823, reprinted in *Works* (1934), Vol. X, pp. 55–60 and Vol. XVIII, pp. 173–80.

32 G. F. Waagen, *Works of Art and Artists in England*, Vol. III, pp. 129–30.

Chapter 23

1 Alexander, *Fonthill*, p. 43.

2 *Ibid.* p. 58.

3 *Ibid.* pp. 72 and 121.

4 *Ibid.* p. 70.

5 *Ibid.* p. 194.

6 *Ibid.* p. 155. The bookseller Chardin, who had helped him during the Revolution, was still living in Paris.

7 *Ibid.* pp. 160 and 166.

8 See Alexander, *EWS*, p. 116, Letter of August 1809.
9 Alexander, *Fonthill*, p. 218.
10 *Ibid.* p. 133.
11 See *The Beckford Family* (ed. W. Gregory), pp. 30–1. Meistre visited Beckford in 1792. His opinion of his playing coincides with that of Lady Craven and Samuel Rogers who both praised his skill.
12 See Alexander, *Fonthill*, p. 237.
13 H. Walpole, *Anecdotes of Painting in England* (edition of 1828), Vol. IV, pp. 265–6. The essay was written in the 1770s and published by the Strawberry Hill press in 1785. Beckford bought Walpole's own copy with MS notes at the Strawberry Hill sale in 1842.
14 See J. Rutter, *Delineations of Fonthill*, p. 90.
15 *Ibid.* p. 84.
16 Alexander, *Fonthill*, p. 134.
17 See Alexander, *EWS*, p. 183.
18 *Farington Diary*, Vol. II, p. 204.
19 Farington MS Diary for 18 April 1797. See also Alexander, *EWS*, p. 184.
20 S. Rogers, *Table-Talk*, p. 217.
21 Alexander, *Fonthill*, pp. 224–5.
22 See H. V. Lansdown, *Recollections of the Late William Beckford*, p. 32.
23 See L. Marchand, *Byron, A Portrait*, p. 170.
24 L. Marchand (ed.), *Byron's Letters and Journals*, Vol. I, p. 210.
25 Beckford told Redding that Byron had written to him suggesting a meeting, but no letter from the poet survives in the Beckford Papers.
26 See L. Marchand, *Byron, A Portrait*, p. 245.
27 See Oliver, pp. 286–7.
28 See P. W. Clayden, *Rogers and His Contemporaries*, Vol. I, p. 274.

Chapter 24

1 Alexander, *Fonthill*, p. 70.
2 *Ibid.* p. 152. James Edwards was a bookseller and collector, Lord Spencer and the Duke of Devonshire were both leading collectors and connoisseurs. They were all his sale room rivals.
3 *Ibid.* pp. 161–2.
4 *Ibid.* p. 159.
5 *Ibid.* p. 167.
6 *Ibid.* pp. 309–10.
7 *Ibid.* p. 205.
8 Alexander, *EWS*, p. 191. For Beckford's debts see also *ibid.* pp. 189–90 and Chapman, pp. 286–9.
9 See Melville, p. 314.

10 See Alexander, *Fonthill*, p. 338.
11 See Alexander, *EWS*, pp. 189–90.
12 *Ibid.* p. 195.
13 Quoted by Melville, p. 320.
14 Alexander, *Fonthill*, p. 240.
15 Quoted by Melville, p. 224.
16 Alexander, *Fonthill*, p. 150.
17 *Ibid.* p. 306.
18 *Ibid.* p. 173.
19 *Ibid.* p. 189.
20 *Ibid.* pp. 332–3, Letter to Dr. Schöll.
21 *Ibid.* p. 109.
22 *Ibid.* p. 313.

Chapter 25

1 Redding, Vol. II, p. 314.
2 Alexander, *Fonthill*, p. 222.
3 *Ibid.* p. 66.
4 Melville, p. 322.
5 See B.M. Add. MSS 32, 567 ff. 315–17 for reports of rages, washing money, etc.; W. Gregory, *The Beckford Family*, p. 145 for income; Chapman, p. 290 for dwarfs.
6 W. Gregory, *op. cit.* p. 102.
7 Redding, Vol. II, p. 154.
8 Quoted by Oliver, p. 319.
9 From letters to Robert Hume, Beckford Papers.
10 Redding, Vol. II, p. 386.
11 *Ibid.* Vol. II, pp. 363–4.
12 See W. Gregory, *op. cit.* pp. 101–2.
13 G. F. Waagen, *Works of Art and Artists in England*, Vol. III, pp. 121–2.
14 See J. M. Crook, *The Greek Revivals*, p. 103.
15 See G. F. Waagen, *op. cit.* Vol. III, pp. 114 et seq.
16 H. V. Lansdown, *Recollections of the Late William Beckford*, p. 29.
17 See H. A. N. Brockman, *The Caliph of Fonthill*, pp. 180–1, quoting from *The Gardener's Magazine* for Sept. 1835. For Farquhar's comment see also Melville, p. 227.
18 See Brockman, *op. cit.* p. 182.
19 See Redding, Vol. II, pp. 348–9.
20 H. V. Lansdown, *op. cit.* p. 26.
21 See W. Gregory, *op. cit.* pp. 70–1.

Chapter 26

1 Redding, Vol. II, p. 291.
2 Beckford Papers, VI, 13.
3 *Ibid.*
4 *Ibid.*
5 Alexander, *Fonthill*, p. 219.
6 Beckford Papers, VI, 13. For Hazlitt's criticism of *Vathek* see *Works*, Vol. XIX, p. 98.
7 *Journal of William Beckford in Portugal and Spain 1787-1788*, edited with an Introduction and Notes by Boyd Alexander.
8 See Chapman, p. 307 and Melville, pp. 331-2.
9 Melville, p. 333.
10 See Boyd Alexander's Introduction to the Centaur Press edition of *Recollections* (1972), pp. xxiii-xxiv.
11 C. Whibley, *The Pageantry of Life*, p. 202.
12 R. Macaulay, *They Went to Portugal*, p. 109.
13 Redding, Vol. II, p. 341.
14 See G. Chapman (ed.), *The Vision: Liber Veritatis*, pp. 112, 137 and 111.
15 It was first published with *The Vision*, edited by Guy Chapman, in 1930.

Chapter 27

1 See Redding, Vol. II, pp. 389-90.
2 See W. P. Frith, *My Autobiography and Reminiscences*, Vol. II, pp. 131-2.
3 See Redding, Vol. II, p. 347. Lawrence was said to have spent over £60,000 on his collection but offered it to the nation for only £18,000.
4 Beckford Papers, VI, 13.
5 *Ibid.* Hume's letter containing Etty's request is dated 15 July 1836.
6 *Ibid.* Beckford's reply is dated 21 July.
7 See Melville, pp. 301-3.
8 H. V. Lansdown, *Recollections of the Late William Beckford*, p. 9.
9 *Ibid.* p. 15.
10 This confusion lasted for many years and the picture, described as 'William Beckford', appeared as the frontispiece to Lewis Melville's biography in 1910.
11 Redding, Vol. I, p. 142.
12 *Ibid.* Vol. II, p. 316.

13 Melville, p. 280.

14 Beckford Papers, VI, 13, Letter dated 15 May 1834.

15 See Oliver, p. 313, Letter dated 8 July 1833.

16 Redding, Vol. II, p. 316.

17 Lansdown, *op. cit.* p. 36.

18 Beckford Papers, VI, 13. Beckford to Hume, 17 May 1839.

19 Lansdown, *op. cit.* p. 11.

20 Redding, Vol. II, p. 353.

21 *Ibid.* Vol. II, pp. 326–7.

22 This fantastic story was firmly believed by Beckford's daughter Susan who related it to the equally credulous historian William Stirling. See his *The Cloister Life of Charles the Fifth* (London, 1852), pp. 234–5.

23 Quoted by Oliver, p. 320 (note).

24 For this and the following quotation see Melville, pp. 335–9 and Oliver, pp. 229–301.

25 See W. F. Monypenny and G. E. Buckle, *Life of Benjamin Disraeli*, Vol. I, pp. 191–2.

26 Beckford Papers, VII, 2d.

27 Melville, p. 344.

28 Oliver, pp. 321–3. The tomb cost him £511 18s.

29 See W. Gregory, *The Beckford Family*, p. 100.

30 See Oliver, p. 325.

31 *Ibid.* p. 329.

32 Redding Manuscript II, p. 116. Quoted by Alexander, *EWS*, p. 239.

33 See H. A. N. Brockman, *The Caliph of Fonthill*, p. 182.

General Sources

Manuscript sources

The Beckford Papers
  References to this primary source in the notes follow the system of cataloguing in use when the papers were in the possession of the Duke of Hamilton. The Beckford Papers are now owned by Messrs. B. H. Blackwell of Oxford.
The British Library, London
  Add. MS 32,566. J. Mitford's Note Books, Vol. VIII, report of Samuel Rogers's visit to Fonthill.
  Add. MS 32,567. J. Mitford's Note Books, Vol. IX, account of Beckford at Bath.
Society of Antiquaries of London
  MS 260. Sketches of Batalha Abbey, Portugal, by James Murphy, c. 1788.

Books

Alexander, Boyd, *England's Wealthiest Son: A Study of William Beckford*. London, 1962.
  (ed.), *The Journal of William Beckford in Portugal and Spain 1787–1788*. London, 1954.
  (ed.), *Life at Fonthill 1807–1822, with Interludes in Paris and London from the Correspondence of William Beckford*. London, 1957.
  (ed.), *Recollections of an Excursion to the Monasteries of Alcobaça and Batalha* by William Beckford, with his original Journal of 1794 and Introduction and Notes. Fontwell, 1972.
Annual Register for the Year 1844.
Anspach, Margravine of, *Memoirs*. 2 vols., London, 1826.
Balderston, K. C. (ed.), *Thraliana, The Diary of Mrs. Hester Lynch Thrale, 1776–1809*, Vol. II. Oxford, 1942.
Bentham, J., *The Works of Jeremy Bentham*, Vol. X. Edinburgh, 1843.
Blunt, R., *Mrs. Montague, 'Queen of the Blues', Her Letters and Friendships from 1762 to 1800*, Vol. I. London, 1923.

Britton, J., *Autobiography*, Part Two. London, 1849.

Graphical and Literary Illustrations of Fonthill Abbey, Wiltshire, with Heraldical and Genealogical Notes of the Beckford Family. London, 1823.

Broadley, A. M. and Melville, L., *The Beautiful Lady Craven*. London, 1914.

Brockman, H. A. N., *The Caliph of Fonthill*. London, 1956.

Chapman, Guy, *Beckford*. London, 1937/52.

(ed.), *The Travel Diaries of William Beckford of Fonthill*, 2 vols. London, 1928.

(ed.), *Vathek, with the Episodes of Vathek* by William Beckford, with a Historical Introduction and Notes. Cambridge, 1929.

(ed.), *The Vision: Liber Veritatis* by William Beckford of Fonthill, with an Introduction and Notes. London, 1930.

Chapman, Guy and Hodgkin, J., *A Bibliography of William Beckford of Fonthill*. London, 1930.

Clark, Kenneth, *The Gothic Revival*. London, 1962.

Clayden, P. W., *Rogers and His Contemporaries*, Vol. 1. London, 1889.

Cloncurry, Lord, *Personal Recollections*. Dublin, 1849.

Conant, M. P., *The Oriental Tale in England in the Eighteenth Century*. New York, 1908.

Crook, J. Mordaunt, *The Greek Revival*. London, 1972.

Dale, A., *James Wyatt*. Oxford, 1956.

Davis, T., *The Gothic Taste*. Newton Abbot, 1975.

Eastlake, C. L., *A History of the Gothic Revival*. London, 1872.

Farington, Joseph, *The Farington Diaries*, Vols. I–VII. London, 1921–7.

Frith, W. P., *My Autobiography and Reminiscences*, Vol. II. London, 1888.

Gemmett, R. J., *William Beckford*. Twayne's English Authors Series, 204. Boston, 1977.

(ed.), *Biographical Memoirs of Extraordinary Painters* by William Beckford, with an Introduction and Notes. Cranbury, New Jersey, 1969.

(ed.), *Dreams, Waking Thoughts and Incidents* by William Beckford, with an Introduction and Notes. Cranbury, New Jersey, 1971.

Gore-Browne, R., *Chancellor Thurlow*. London, 1953.

Granville, Countess, *Lord Granville Leveson Gower, Private Correspondence, 1781 to 1821*, Vol. II. London, 1916.

Gregory, W. (ed.), *The Beckford Family, Reminiscences of Fonthill Abbey and Lansdown Tower*. Bath, 1898.

Herbert, Lord, *Pembroke Papers (1780–1794)*, Letters and Diaries of Henry, 10th Earl of Pembroke and his Circle. London, 1950.

Herrmann, Frank, *The English as Collectors, A Documentary Chrestomathy*. London, 1972.

Hibbert, Christopher, *The Grand Tour*. London, 1969.

Higginson, A. H., *Peter Beckford, Esquire. Sportsman, Traveller, Man of Letters.* London, 1937.

Howarth, R. G., *Letters of George Gordon, 6th Lord Byron.* London, 1933.

Hussey, Christopher, *The Picturesque.* London, 1967.

Irwin, D., *English Neo-Classical Taste.* London, 1966.

Jones, Thomas, *Memoirs of Thomas Jones, 1803.* Walpole Society, Vol. XXXII, London, 1951.

Lambert, R. S. (ed.), *Grand Tour: A Journey in the Tracks of the Age of Aristocracy.* London, 1935.

Lansdown, H. V., *Recollections of the late William Beckford of Fonthill, Wilts., and Lansdown, Bath.* Bath, 1893.

Lees-Milne, James, *William Beckford.* Tisbury, 1976.

Lowe, Alfonso, *La Serenissima.* London, 1974.

Macaulay, Rose, *They went to Portugal.* London, 1946.

Maddox, Willes, *Views of Lansdown Tower, Bath, the Favourite Edifice of William Beckford, Esq.* Bath, 1844.

Mahmoud, F. Moussa (ed.), *William Beckford of Fonthill 1760–1844,* Bicentenary Essays. Cairo, 1960.

Marchand, L. A., *Byron's Letters and Journals,* Vols. I and II. London, 1973.

Byron, A Portrait. London, 1971.

Marzials, Sir Frank T., *The Episodes of Vathek,* with a translation by Sir Frank T. Marzials and an Introduction by Lewis Melville. London, 1912.

Melville, Lewis, *The Life and Letters of William Beckford of Fonthill.* London, 1910.

Monypenny, W. F. and Buckle, G. E., *The Life of Benjamin Disraeli, Earl of Beaconsfield,* Vol. I. London, 1910.

Moore, T., *The Works of Lord Byron with his Letters and Journals,* Vol. IV. London, 1834.

More, P. E., *The Drift of Romanticism.* Shelburne Essays, Eighth Series. Boston, 1913.

Morrison, A., *Collection of Autograph Letters and Historical Documents* (Second Series), Vol. I. Printed for Private Circulation, 1893.

The Hamilton and Nelson Papers, 2 vols. Printed for Private Circulation, 1893–4.

Murphy, J. and de Sousa, L., *Plans, Elevations, Sections & Views of the Church of Batalha in the Province of Estremadura in Portugal.* London, 1795.

Oliver, J. W., *The Life of William Beckford.* Oxford, 1933.

Oppé, A. P., *Alexander and John Robert Cozens.* London, 1952.

Parreaux, André, *William Beckford, Auteur de Vathek.* Étude deal Création Littéraire. Paris, 1960.

Praz, Mario, *The Romantic Agony*. Oxford, 1933.

Redding, Cyrus, *Memoirs of William Beckford of Fonthill*, 2 vols. London, 1859.

Reitlinger, G., *The Economics of Taste*. London, 1961.

Rogers, S., *Recollections of the Table-Talk of Samuel Rogers*. London, 1856.

Roscoe, E. S. and Clergue, H., *George Selwyn, His Letters and Life*. London, 1899.

Rowdon, M., *The Fall of Venice*. London, 1970.

Rutter, J., *Delineations of Fonthill and Its Abbey*. London, 1823.

Sitwell, Sacheverell, *Beckford and Beckfordism, An Essay*. London, 1930.

Steegman, J., *The Rule of Taste from George I to George IV*. London, 1936.

Storer, J., *A Description of Fonthill Abbey, Wiltshire*. London, 1812.

Summers, M., *The Gothic Quest, A History of the Gothic Novel*. London, 1938.

Summerson, J., *Architecture in Britain, 1530–1830*. London, 1953.

Taylor, W. S. and Pringle, J. H., *Correspondence of William Pitt, Earl of Chatham*, Vols. II and III. London, 1838–9.

Waagen, G. F., *Works of Art and Artists in England*, Vol. III. London, 1838.

Walpole, H., *The Letters of Horace Walpole*, ed. P. Cunningham, Vols. II–VIII. London, 1857–9.

Memoirs and Portraits, ed. M. Hodgart. London, 1963.

Watkin, D., *Thomas Hope and the Neo-Classical Idea*. London, 1963.

Whaley, Thomas, *Buck Whaley's Memoirs*, ed. by Sir Edward Sullivan. London, 1906.

Whibley, Charles, *The Pageantry of Life*. London, 1900.

Whitley, W. T., *Artists and their Friends in England*, Vol. II. London, 1930.

Articles and monographs

Alexander, Boyd, 'Fonthill, Wiltshire, The Abbey and its Creator', *Country Life*, Vol. CXL, nos. 3,639 and 3,640, 1 and 8 Dec. 1966.

'The Marquis of Marialva's Friendship with Beckford', British Historical Society of Portugal's *Report and Review for 1975*. Lisbon, 1975.

'William Beckford, Man of Taste', *History Today*, Vol. X, No. 10, October 1960.

'William Beckford as Patron', *Apollo*, Vol. LXXVII, No. 5, July 1962.

Beckford Exhibition Catalogue (Salisbury and Bath, 1976). Essays by J. Lees-Milne, J. Millington, W. Wilton-Ely, C. Thacker and C. Wainwright.

Gottlieb, H. B., *William Beckford of Fonthill, 1760–1844*. A brief Narrative and Catalogue of an Exhibition to mark the Two Hundredth Anniversary of Beckford's Birth. Yale, 1960.

Graham, K. W., 'Vathek in French and English', *Studies in Biography*, Vol. 28, pp. 154–67. Charlottesville, University of Virginia.

Hamilton Palace Sale Catalogue. 'Catalogue of the Collection of Pictures, Works of Art, and Decorative Objects the property of His Grace the Duke of Hamilton which will be sold by Messrs. Christie, Manson & Woods . . . June, 1882.'

Harris, J., 'Fonthill, Wiltshire: Alderman Beckford's House', *Country Life*, Vol. CXL, No. 3,638, November 1966.

Hobson, A., 'William Beckford's Library', *The Connoisseur*, Vol. 191, No. 770, April 1976.

Lees-Milne, J., 'Beckford in Bath', *Country Life*, Vol. CLIX, No. 4,113, April 1976.

Millington, J., *William Beckford and His Tower*. Bath, 1975.

Oldman, C. B., 'Beckford and Mozart', *Music and Letters*, Vol. XLVII, No. 2, April 1966.

Praz, Mario, Introductory Essay to *Three Gothic Novels*. Penguin Books, London, 1968.

Summers, P., *William Beckford, Some Notes on his Life in Bath 1822–1844*. Privately Printed, 1966.

Thacker, C., *Masters of the Grotto, Joseph and Josiah Lane*. Tisbury, 1976.

Wainwright, C., 'Some Objects from William Beckford's Collection now in the Victoria and Albert Museum', *Burlington Magazine*, Vol. CXIII, No. 818, May 1971.

   'William Beckford's Furniture', *The Connoisseur*, Vol. 191, No. 770, April 1976.

Wilton-Ely, J., 'A Model for Fonthill Abbey, Wiltshire', Essay in *The Country Seat* (London, 1970), pp. 199–204.

Index

DATE DUE			

Fothergill 170205